Appalachia/America

Copyright © 1981
by
The Appalachian Consortium Press, East Tennessee State University
and the
Appalachian Studies Conference.

Appalachian Studies Conference (3rd: 1980: East Tennessee State University)
Appalachia/America.

  1. Appalachian region--Congresses. I. Somerville, Wilson, 1949 -
II. Title.
F106.A6 1980   974   81-713
                                              AACR2

This publication was made possible through a grant from the Appalachian Regional Commission.

TABLE OF CONTENTS

	Introduction, Wilson Somerville	1
I	Appalachia: Labor and the Economy	
	The Wheeling Convention of the Miners for Democracy: A case Study of Union Reform Politics in Appalachia, George W. Hopkins	6
	The Roles of Transnational Corporations and the Migration of Industries in Latin America and Appalachia, Helen M. Lewis and Myles Horton	22
	Appalachia and the Third World: Eco-Development as an Alternative in the New Economic Order, Gene Wilhelm, Jr.	34
	The Economy of West Virginia and the Oppression/Liberation of Women, Rick Simon and Betty Justice	44
II.	Land in Appalachia	
	Where American History Began: Appalachia and the Small Independent Family Farm, John Opie	58
	Losing a Bit of Ourselves: The Decline of the Small Farmer, Stephen L. Fisher and Mary Harnish	68
	Comparative Regional Issues: Land Use and Environmental Planning in the Adirondacks and the Appalachians, Peter G. Marden et al.	89
	Community Development Perspectives of Ohio Appalachians: A Regional Study, Ted L. Napier and Elizabeth G. Bryant	99
III	The Experience of Urban Appalachians	
	Appalachian Youth in Cultural Transition, Clyde B. McCoy and Virginia McCoy Watkins	114
	The Impact of Urban Housing Programs in Appalachian Neighborhoods, gary L. Fowler	126
	Elderly Appalachians in Cities: A Case Study of Cincinnati, David P. Varady	139
IV	Education in Appalachia	
	Innovative Approaches to Vocational-Technical Education in North Central Pennsylvania, Robert A. Rusiewski	158
	Cora Wilson Stewart and the "Moonlight School" Movement, James M. Gifford	169
	Untying Some Knots in Knott County: Two Educational Experiments in eastern Kentucky, William Terrell Cornett	179
V	Values and Culture in Appalachia	
	Poetry at the Periphery: The Possibility of People's Culture in Appalachia, P.J. Laska	190
	Alther and Dillard: The Appalachian Universe, Frederick O. Waage	200
	Women Folk Healers of Appalachia, Karen Shelley and Raymond Evans	209
	Religious Language and Collective Action: A Study of Voluntarism in a Rural Appalachian Church, Michael V. Carter	218
	Goals for the Collection and Use of Appalachian Oral Materials in the 1980s, James Robert Reese	230

VI   Abstracts

      Mary Breckenridge and the Frontier Nursing Service: The Appalachian Rural Experience, Carol Crowe-Carraco ... 238

      The Blue Ridge Parkway: A Unique Part of Rural America, Granville B. Liles ... 239

      A Heritage of Regional Landscapes: Appalachian Baptistry Paintings, Jack Welch ... 240

      Bringing Sister Home: The Fight For Job Equity in Appalachia, Leslie Lilly ... 241

      Multiculturalism in Southern Appalachian Schools: A Diagnosis and Attempted Prescription, David N. Mielke ... 241

      Appalachian Youths in the Juvenile Justice System: Clues in the Search for a Distinct Culture, Phillip Obermiller and Dan McKee ... 242

      Problems of Urban Appalachian Youth in Cincinnati, Larry J. Redden ... 243

      Struggling to Stay Together: Black and White Miners in West Virginia and Alabama, 1880-1910, Richard Straw ... 243

      The Assimilation of Appalachian Migrants, Frank J. Traina ... 244

      The Cultural Context of Philosophic Criticism, Frans van der Bogert; Some Special Problems of Teaching Introductory Philosophy and the Occasional Essential Relevance of Appalachian Studies for Teaching Philosophy, H. Phillips Hamlin; Academic Philosophy and Appalachian Culture, Richard A. Humphrey; Teaching Philosophy in Appalachia: An Existentialsist Approach, Gary Acquaviva. ... 245

      Film Reviews: "They Shall Take Up Serpents," "Gandy Dancers," and "Buna and Bertha" ... 247

Introduction

The third annual Appalachian Studies Conference was held March 21-23, 1980, on the grounds of East Tennessee State University in Johnson City, Tennessee. Sponsors, along with the host institution, were the Appalachian Consortium, Inc., and the Appalachian Studies Conference. Scholars, teachers, and regional activists began the Appalachian Studies Conference in 1977 in the belief that "shared community has been and will continue to be important for those writing, researching, and teaching about things Appalachian." To this end, the organization held its first meeting at Berea College in Berea, Kentucky, in 1978 and its second at Jackson's Mill, West Virginia, in 1979, under the sponsorship of Davis and Elkins College. The ongoing efforts of conference planners have made this annual event an important opportunity for interested citizens of varying occupations and disciplines to exchange information and ideas on regional issues.

As a beginning to the 1980 conference, the Appalachian Consortium Press held an open house in the Down Home Pickin' Parlor in Johnson City to honor Jim Wayne Miller and the publication of his new book of poetry, *The Mountains Have Come Closer*. Miller read selections from his book which deals with a mountain man, the Brier, who comes to the realization that he is thoroughly disoriented by contemporary culture. The poems describe how the Brier, by taking a fresh look at his heritage, works past the vapid, throwaway clutter of mainstream America to a new affirmation of himself.

This reading fittingly evoked the aim of the conference, which was to encourage a new look at the region in a national and international context. The conference title, "Appalachia/America," raised the question of the uniqueness of the "Appalachian experience." To what extent could Appalachia be viewed as a microcosm of America and the world, mirroring the problems and potential of a global community?

Behind this purpose and the line of questioning which evolved from it, lay the continuing concern in Appalachia over regional autonomy. Self-determination for communities and individuals was the bedrock issue in the reading of papers and in the special events of the conference. Alternative methods of achieving such self-determination were evaluated in the light of national and global events.

While this publication exists to record the contribution of authors to this dialogue, some mention should be made of conference events, other than the presentation of papers, that, likewise, drew attention to major issues in Appalachia. The following brief overview of these special events indicates the diverse ways in which this meeting promoted the examination of regional concerns in a larger context.

Darrell V. McGraw, Jr., Justice of the West Virginia Supreme Court of Appeals, spoke on the topic of "Appalachia: Resources and People." He depicted the influence that non-indigenous people have upon West Virginia government and observed that many top level officials in the state are trained outside the area to serve national economic interests with no commitment to the needs of the region. McGraw felt that the West Virginia picture was not entirely dismal, but that Appalachians need to decide whether they prefer "distant, absentee corporate ownership and direction or fundamental economic change that gives people a right to participate in decisions which affect regional development and lifestyles."

In another speech, Robert J. Higgs, professor of English at East Tennessee State University, lamented the state of contemporary American humor, which he found to be mostly insipid and sentimental. He maintained that a culture that is alive and well is always in tension -- a tension which exists at the archetypal level between the Hero and the Natural. However, Higgs sees no one capable of playing the natural today: "We are afraid to speak out on anything. We need fools in Congress again," fools whose wit has traditionally been a curb to the powerful. Higgs's antidote to the current crisis was the example of Appalachia's own "last of the naturals," Sut Lovingood, the creation of Tennessee humorist George Washington Harris.

Drama, presented by the Road Company of Johnson City, raised questions about Western man's ability to come to grips with his own inventions. The play by Jo Carson, entitled "Horsepower: An Electric Fable," chronicles the changes brought about in an Appalachian family by technological advances. The action takes on mythic overtones when the son, Isaac, tears through the fabric boundary of this dream world in pursuit of a symbolic horse. This act designates his personal culpability in a society where the pursuit of power and its benefits separates man from his own internal resources.

This show came together after months of public workshops and private conversations in which hundreds of people shared their perceptions of the current energy situation. The Appalachian Regional Commission and the Tennessee Arts Commission subsidized the conference performance.

In another event, the Six State Land Ownership Task Force, which also received funding from the Appalachian Regional Commission, gave a preliminary report on its survey of ownership and taxation patterns in more than eighty counties of Alabama, Kentucky, Tennessee, Virginia, North Carolina, and West Virginia. The researchers, trained at the Highlander Center in New Market, Tennessee, with help from Appalachian State University's Center for Appalachian Studies, have been compiling data on those land and tax patterns that apply, in particular, to large corporate and absentee landowners. In twenty counties, case studies will correlate these patterns with the migration of industry, the availability of land for housing, the ability of the tax base to support needed schools and services, and the viability of small farms to remain in operation. Hence, this survey will provide essential facts to community groups that are struggling to assert themselves in determining the allocation and use of resources within the region. In short, these findings will give extra underpinning to the argument for local initiative, as put forward by Judge McGraw in his speech. Beyond its application within Appalachia, the final report will offer other regional groups a basis for conducting similar studies. In their conference remarks, task force members expressed concern about the problem of poorly kept records in some Appalachian counties and emphasized the need to make land ownership information more accessible and to maintain it more accurately.

Other special features at this conference included two new film documentaries by Appalshop, Inc., a regional educational media center located in Whitesburg, Kentucky. The first, called "Oaksie," portrayed basketmaker, fiddler, and harp player Oaksie Caudill from Cowan Creek, Letcher County, Kentucky. The other film, "Strip Mining: Energy, Environment, and Economics," measured the social, environmental, and economic costs of a highly visible and controversial type of mining, which accounts for over 50 percent of the coal produced in Appalachia. In addition, the Roadside Theater, a touring group and part of Appalshop, Inc., entertained conference participants with their skillful and uproarious renditions of jack tales. The Institute for Appalachian Affairs at East Tennessee State University, in conjunction with Appalachian Community Arts, held a workshop on "Art as Community Expression," with music, storytelling, a slide presentation, a photographic display, and general discussion on the importance of art as a community development tool. Rounding out this exploration of Appalachian culture were a display of books and magazines from regional presses and educational groups, a quilting demonstration by members of the Clinchfield Senior Adult Center of Erwin, Tennessee, an exhibition of Appalachian quilts and crafts, and a photographic portrayal of "The Appalachian Farm at the Turn of the Century," assembled by the Archives of Appalachia and the B. Carroll Reece Museum of East Tennessee University.

As for the proceedings which constitute this volume, thirty-two authors read their papers in sessions that touched on virtually every aspect of the Appalachian experience. For the purposes of publication, their articles have been grouped into broader categories than those used in the conference format, with an abstract serving as an introduction to each one. The section headings highlight five major issues in Appalachia: labor, land, urban life, education, and culture (from folk to literary). A final section of this volume includes abstracts of papers which were not published, along with a review of a three-part film session.

An editorial decision was made not to publish papers that had appeared previously. Three articles were not published for this reason, and abstracts for them appear in the final section, as well. They are as follows: Carol Crowe-Carraco, "Mary Breckenridge and the Frontier Nursing Service: The Appalachian Rural Experience," published in slightly different form in *The Register of the Kentucky Historical Society* 76 (July 1978): 179-91; Granville B. Liles, "The Blue Ridge Parkway: A Unique Part of Rural America," printed as a booklet by the Appalachian Consortium Press, Boone, North Carolina, 1980; and Jack Welch, "A Heritage of Regional Landscapes: Appalachian Baptistry Paintings," *Goldenseal* 6 (April - June 1980): 40-46. P. J. Laska's article was accepted for publication prior to its appearance in another journal, and, therefore, is included in this volume with acknowledgment to the *West Virginia Art News* and *Hyperion* for permission to reprint it here.

Thanks are due to many people for work on the conference and the publication of the conference proceedings, but they are first and most gladly given to Martha McKinney, program coordinator, and Richard Kesner, head of local arrangements and member of the program committee. Both were instrumental in organizing the conference and were encouraging and helpful at every stage in the production of this volume. Others who played an essential role in planning the conference were officers Joan Moser, chairperson; Anne Campbell, secretary/newsletter editor Polly Cheek, treasurer/membership secretary; and program committee members Jane Horton, Gordon McKinney, Milton Ready, Carl Ross, Linda Scott, and Rose Mary Tennant.

The publication of these proceedings was made possible through the financial assistance of the Appalachian Regional Commission. Dennis Pelletier created the graphic design for the cover, Gail Powell and Pat Fitzpatrick worked swiftly to turn out clean, typed copy, and Rosemary Barson gave special care to the layout and printing of this volume. The various authors deserve major acknowledgment for their contributions and cooperation during the editing process. Finally, some recognition, however inadequately it may be noted here, belongs to all those who attended the conference and who contributed to this inquiry by their interest.

Wilson Somerville

Editor

I. Appalachia:
Labor and the Economy

THE WHEELING CONVENTION OF THE MINERS FOR DEMOCRACY: A CASE STUDY OF UNION REFORM POLITICS IN APPALACHIA

George W. Hopkins

Abstract

After the murder of insurgent leader Joseph "Jock" Yablonski in late 1969, the reform movement within the United Mine Workers of America continued its struggle to oust the administration of Tony Boyle. When federal courts finally cleared the way for a new election in May 1972, the dissidents quickly organized a convention in Wheeling, W. Va. This paper will focus on the efforts of union reformers at the convention to reconcile enthnic tensions and divergent policy interests within the rebel movement. Not until the Wheeling convention did the various reform groups in the union unite under the banner of Miners For Democracy and merge their strength. Because of the pragmatic politicking at the convention, the insurgent coalition was able to present a united front against Boyle and the loyalist faction. After a bitter campaign, the MFD slate won the Labor Department-supervised election in December 1972.

The legacy of John L. Lewis dominated the United Mine Workers of America (UMWA)--and much of Appalachia--after the union chief's retirement in 1960. While Lewis had helped build the CIO in the 1930s, and had won a Welfare and Retirement Fund for the miners in the late 1940s, he had stabilized the coal industry in the 1950s by sacrificing the jobs of three fourths of his soft-coal miners to automation. This decision allowed the industry to meet the threat posed by alternative fuels; however, it also forced many miners in southern Appalachia to work in small, unsafe, non-union mines or remain unemployed. While Lewis may have hoped that other industries in Appalachia would absorb his discarded miners, the union patriarch did little to help them through job retraining or relocation programs. During the 1950s, as his sensitivity to rank-and-file concerns further dimmed, Lewis endorsed the tightening of Welfare and Retirement Fund eligibility rules, thus denying benefit and pension payments to many miners and their dependents. Lewis was able to make these decisions and enforce them without significant internal opposition because of his dictatorial control over the union.[1]

When Lewis's chief administrative assistant, W. A. "Tony" Boyle assumed the UMWA presidency in 1963, he ran the union even more autocratically. Boyle tried to stifle and then, failing that, to co-opt the "black lung" rebellion of miners in the southern coalfields in 1968. Meanwhile, dissatisfaction grew in the northern coalfields. Retired anthracite miners in eastern Pennsylvania despaired over their thirty-dollar-a-month pensions, little more than a quarter of what bituminous pensioners received. Many working miners in the northern fields resented their district officials, most of whom were appointed by Boyle instead of being elected by the men in the pits. By 1969, the UMWA leadership had become so bureaucratized and unresponsive to its members that the Boyle administration met the electoral challenge of insurgent leader Joseph "Jock" Yablonski with blatant intimidation of his supporters and vote fraud on election day. While Boyle claimed victory, Yablonski refused to concede, declaring that the contest had been "the most dishonest election in the history of the American labor movement." He pledged to file suit in federal court under the Landrum-Griffin Act to have the election over turned because of the numerous irregularities at the polls. Three weeks later, hired assassins murdered Jock Yablonski, his wife, and daughter. But the rebels vowed to continue the struggle to oust Boyle and clean up the union.[2]

However, the reformers faced several problems, the foremost being their own internal divisions. Yablonski's campaign had temporarily brought together northern and southern miners opposed to Boyle and various policies of the union and its Fund. With the fiery, charismatic Yablonski dead and his running mate, Elmer Brown, unable to fill the void, the two wings of the reform movement drifted apart. Rebel miners in the northern coalfields--western Pennsylvania, southern Ohio, and northern West Virginia--were mainly of eastern European extraction and were primarily concerned with moralistic/abstract goals such as union democracy and an end to corruption in union affairs. Dissident miners in the southern coalfields--southern West Virginia, southern Virginia, Kentucky, Tennessee, and Alabama--were generally of Anglo-Saxon and Afro-American origin and were primarily interested in practical benefits such as compensation for "black lung" and pensions for disabled miners and their widows. A majority of miners lived in the southern coalfields.

Several organizations emerged in the coalfields which reflected these diverse interests and constituencies. In the northern coalfields, Miners For Democracy (MFD) began as a loosely organized internal union reform group in April, 1970, after a series of meetings which had begun at Yablonski's funeral. Mike Trbovich, Yablonski's national campaign manager in 1969 and long-time personal friend, became chairman of the group. During the next two years, MFD would run a slate of candidates in the District 5 (Pittsburgh area) election, keep alive the issues of the 1969 campaign, and work with attorneys Joseph Rauh and Chip Yalbonski (Jock's son) in filing suit to overturn the election. MFD leaders also testified before Congressional committees about fraud and intimidation during the 1969 election and the 1970 District 5 election as well as commenting on various health and safety bills before Congress.[3]

In the southern coalfields, three different organizations fought for rank-and-file interests. The Association of Disabled Miners and Widows, Inc., had filed a class action suit against the UMW Welfare and Retirement Fund in 1969 on behalf of all union miners and their dependents who had been unjustly denied hospital and disability benefits as well as pensions. While this group waited for its legalistic strategy to work, a more militant organization, the Disabled Miners and Widows of southern West Virginia, led by black miner Robert Payne, used direct action tactics against the union. In the summer of 1970, Payne and his group led a strike against the union, shutting down mines in the southern fields by picketing, in an unsuccessful effort to win benefits and pensions from the UMWA Fund. Meanwhile, the Black Lung Association (BLA) became the dominant insurgent group in the southern coalfields. Arnold Miller became the chief spokesman for the group. The BLA built a grassroots network of independent chapters throughout southern Appalachia. Working with sympathetic lawyers and social workers, BLA organizers trained miners and their wives and widows about the regulations and procedures involved in the federal black lung, workmen's compensation, social security disability and union pension programs. These people then assisted others in filing claims. BLA members helped guide their constituency through the maze of union, state, and federal bureaucracies.[4]

All of these groups considered themselves part of the UMWA reform movement, but they found it hard to work together in practical terms. Northern rebels (except in the eastern Pennsylvania anthracite region) tended to be active, working miners while southern dissidents tended to be retired and/or disabled miners and their wives/widows. Leadership and personality problems complicated the internal politics of the reform movement as well. After two years of education and agitation, the reformers still had no realistic chance of overthrowing Boyle from within. But in May, 1972, a federal judge finally voided the results of the fraudulent 1969 election and ordered a new election. That same month, another federal judge ruled illegal the district trusteeships through which the UMWA hierarchy maintained its tight grip on most of the union. Suddenly the insurgents had the opportunity to remove Boyle and his appointed district officials from office.[5]

The obvious key to a winning ticket would be a slate that represented the strength of Miners For Democracy in the northern coalfields and the strength of the Black Lung Association and the disabled miners and widows groups in the southern coalfields. Only by reconciling the ethnic tensions and divergent policy interests between the two regions could the insurgents present a united front against Boyle. A convention of rebel miners would have to select a balanced ticket and draft a platform fusing the concerns of the various dissident reform groups.

The formerly defunct MFD Steering Committee reactivated itself in the wake of the court rulings. At a meeting held in Charleston, W. VA., on May 6, the Steering Committee decided on Wheeling, West Virginia, in District 6, as the site of the rebel convention. Wheeling was roughly equidistant from the various areas of reform movement strength--southern West Virginia, northern West Virginia, Pennsylvania, and southern Ohio. The miners had also considered a proposal offered by attorneys Chip Yablonski and Clarice Feldman to adopt a weighted delegate vote system based on the number of dues-paying members, and an approximation of the amount of election fraud in 1969. The weighted vote system competed with several alternatives. To base voting solely on the number of union members in a district would inflate the strength of the reform movement in some districts. Conversely, giving each district an equal number of votes would underrate rebel strength in some districts. A majority vote of those attending the convention would give the home district undeserved influence. There also existed a slim possibility that Boyle supporters might try to pack the convention and nominate Boyle and embarrass or discredit the reformers. Though some delegates quibbled about the allocation of votes, the steering committee gave tentative approval to the weighed vote system. The delegates at Wheeling, chosen at district meetings, would have to give the system final approval.[6]

Although the steering committee had decided that no individual should announce his candidacy for international office, that an open convention should democratically choose the insurgent slate, Harry Patrick recalled that "there was a lot of jockeying for position, a lot of campaigning before the convention started." The stakes were high--the future of the reform movement, the presidency of the union, power, and status. The very nature of an open convention meant that there would be pre-convention politicking and maneuvering, a testing of the possibilities by some and attempts by others to influence the final outcome. The role black miners would play was unclear. Another major imponderable was the role the Yablonski brothers would play. Sons of the martyred leader, they were both lawyers, not miners, and thus were prohibited by the UMWA Constitution from running for office. But especially to MFD supporters in the north, their opinions and feelings would count.

In the northern coalfields, Mike Trbovich, MFD chairman, seemed to be the heir apparent. He had spoken at innumerable rallies and demonstrations. His name headed the lawsuit that finally overturned the 1969 election. Trbovich believed he had earned the presidential nomination of the rebel group because of his work within the reform movement. However, Trbovich also knew that several key dissidents in various northern districts disliked him personally. To guarantee his nomination at the top of the insurgent ticket, Trbovich reached a private understanding with BAL President Arnold Miller--in return for Miller's support for his presidential bid, Trbovich pledged to support Miller for the vice-presidential slot. When Miller accepted the offer on the eve of the convention, Trbovich seemed certain of his reward for his service to the rebel cause.[8]

However, Trbovich lacked the support of the Yablonski family. Chip and Ken Yablonski, the lawyer-sons of the slain leader, had worked with Trbovich during the preceding two years. They had distributed press releases and brought litigation in Trbovich's name, "things of that nature which were entirely proper and Mike deserved a lot of credit for sticking his neck out." On the other hand, Chip Yablonski noted that, "We had been partially responsible for Mike Trbovich's identity within the reform movement and his viability as a candidate." The Yablonskis decided not to endorse Trbovich because they doubted his abilities; he was from a small district in western Pennsylvania, and they were convinced that the ethnic prejudice his name would incur in the southern coalfields would seriously jeopardize any chance of the insurgent slate beating Boyle.[9]

Instead, the Yablonskis supported Tom Pysell from District 6, the host district for the MFD convention. Pysell was president of the seven-hundred-man UMWA local at Consolidation Coal's Ireland Mine near Moundsville, West Virginia--one of the largest locals in the union. The average age of miners in his local was twenty-five and almost one third of them were Vietnam veterans. The local showed its militance and aggressiveness by its frequent wildcat strikes over safety grievances--and they were backed up by their local president. This had earned Pysell favorable publicity in the reform movement. The Yablonskis were concerned that none of the insurgents held offices at the district level or higher. With Pysell's solid base of support, the Yablonskis believed he could be a winner. They had confidence in his abilities; moreover, his name was easily pronounceable and would not be a liability for ethnic reasons. With Yablonski backing, Pysell was definitely a contender. Northern reformers would not come to Wheeling united behind one candidate.[10]

In the southern coalfields, Arnold Miller had emerged as the leading spokesman for the reform movement. A retired miner with black lung, Miller was president of the Black Lung Association, current Chairman of the MFD Steering Committee, Chairman of his home district 17 MFD and was actively involved in both disabled miners and widows groups. He knew that a divided reform movement in the southern fields would seriously weaken the reform movement as a whole. By working with all of the reform groups Miller not only bridged the gap between the two wings of the movement but he also personified what they had in common--opposition to a union leadership unresponsive to the felt needs of both working and disabled miners and their widows.[11]

Miller had of course sought--and--received--a fair amount of publicity for his activities. He also knew the political implications of his actions. Miller seemed to be on friendly terms with black miner Levi Daniel, who headed reform efforts in nearby District 29. However, Miller faced opposition within his own District 17 from reformers in Logan County who thought Miller's relocation of BLA headquarters to Charleston was too remote from the coalfields. They also felt that Miller spent too much time courting the media and prominent

West Virginia politician John D. "Jay" Rockefeller IV. John Mendez, one of the few active miners in the southern coalfields who identified with Miners For Democracy as well as the Black Lung Association and disabled miners and widows groups, emerged as Miller's chief critic and rival. However, a majority of southern reformers reluctantly concluded that Mendez's Mexican heritage limited his potential voter appeal in the region as much as a Slovakian background would have. Miller would go to Wheeling with his home base relatively secure and a covert deal with Trbovich guaranteeing him the second spot on the rebel slate.[12]

In northern West Virginia, an area allied more with the northern coalfields than with the southern but with contacts in both, Harry Patrick had been a National Co-Chairman of Miners For Yablonski in 1969 as well as Yablonski's campaign manager in District 31's Morgantown--Fairmont area. Patrick had emerged as a spokesman for rank-and-filers dissatisfied with the 1971 contract. He was now Chairman of District 31 MFD and a National Co-Chairman of Miners For Democracy. He also knew Arnold Miller, Robert Payne, and other southern reformers. While he had not considered running for national office, he received encouragement from a number of miners within and outside of his district. Patrick headed for Wheeling with a new perspective on his possible role at the convention.[13]

Other MFD supporters in various districts were also politically ambitious. However, none of the insurgent leaders held a major union office. This meant that the slate selected at Wheeling to oppose Boyle would be an all rank-and-file ticket. Journalist Tom Bethell found that, "some reporters are having trouble taking such a slate seriously--thinking, apparently, that unless a high-ranking official like Yablonski makes the race, it isn't for real." He tried to counter this attitude with Arnold Miller's statement that, "You could pick the next three men at random to come up out of any mine, and they'd be an improvement over Boyle, Titler, and Owens." Don Stillman, editor of *The Miner's Voice*, expressed the same attitude in even stronger terms:

> The media and some liberals parrot the same mistaken line back and forth that the reform movement doesn't have any real leaders. They appear to be searching for the same type of flashy, well-dressed labor bureaucrat with a rose in his lapel [Boyle] that the rank-and-file is so dissatisfied with. Arnold Miller, Mike Trbovich, Karl Kafton, Harry Patrick, Lou Antal, Ed Monborne, Tom Pysell, and a host of others are names familiar in the coalfields--they are coal miners who traveled and campaigned with Yablonski. The rank-and-file in the UMW wants leaders who understand what working in the pits means. Because it is a legitimate reform movement composed of working miners, the money and the time to travel have hurt MFD some. But there is no lack of leadership at the top of the movement.

These MFD leaders and their supporters gathered at the field house of Wheeling College in Wheeling, West Virginia, to select the rank-and-file slate that would oppose the "labor bureaucrats" whom they had fought for so long.[14]

On Saturday, May 27, 1972, the insurgent convention began its deliberations. Three hundred and eighty-seven delegates from the sixteen largest and most important of the union's twenty-three districts assembled in the field house; by Sunday, over 450 miners would take part in selecting the insurgent slate. The delegates were either working miners or pensioners who had come to the convention at their own expense. No salaried staff officers or appointed officials were present. The hardships the insurgents had endured were reflected in their serious, purposeful behavior. With one leader murdered, the possibility of a bomb at the convention, and the knowledge that whoever was nominated to oppose Boyle might be exposed to violence, miners well understood the importance of this gathering.[15]

Karl Kafton, from the host District 6, served as Permanent Chairman of the convention. He introduced Pittsburgh's famed "labor priest," Monsignor Charles Owen Rice, who delivered the invocation. Chip Yablonski spoke next, telling the miners that, "If my dad could have had his way in 1969, he would have wanted a convention like this to nominate him." Yablonski commented on the trial that overturned the 1969 election: "We went through 6,700 pages of transcript and 10,000 pages of exhibits, and I can tell you that that was the crookedest election that was ever held." After brief speeches by Ken Yablonski, Representative Ken Hechler (D.-W.Va.), the only Congressman to support the insurgents, and Robert Payne, MFD attorney Joseph Rauh delivered the keynote address: "I recall, in a lifetime in the labor movement, of no precedent for this meeting." Rauh declared that, "Not in our lifetime has there been a rank-and-file convention of union members to choose the candidates who will run against an entrenched union bureaucracy and to write the platform upon which those candidates will run." Rauh refused to endorse any individual but pledged to "work like hell for whoever [sic] you choose."[16]

After receiving praise from the mainly non-miner speakers who had helped them in many ways, the insurgents settled down to hear the Platform Committee report. This committee had been authorized at the May 6 MFD Steering Committee meeting to draft a platform that would include the interests and concerns of all the major groups in the reform movement. Subtitled "The Miners' Bill of Rights," the MFD platform began with the issue of primary importance to underground workers: safety, "the first and most basic right of all coal miners." Declaring that "Safety must never be arbitrated," the platform demanded strict enforcement of safety laws backed up by union officials. Dust levels in the mines must be strictly controlled. Moreover, welfare and retirement benefits should be raised. Pensions should be increased. Eligibility rules should be liberalized so that all victims of the mines could receive necessary health care. Meanwhile, the platform compromised on strip-mining, stressing that "BOTH jobs and land" should be protected; non-union strip-miners should be unionized while reclamation laws should be sternly enforced.[17]

The insurgents indicted Boyle and the UMWA hierarchy, declaring that the reign of "union leaders who refuse to leave their mahogany-paneled offices in Washington, D.C." was over. The rebels announced an end to "sweet heart contracts and sell-out unionism . . ." To make the union leadership responsive to the membership, MFD called for the relocation of UMWA headquarters to the coalfields, an end to nepotism in hiring, the restoration of district autonomy, and rank-and-file ratification of all contracts.[18]

The MFD platform disappointed some observers. Compared to Yablonski's 1969 platform, the rebels said little or nothing about reviving UMWA support for regional and national social reform efforts. Nor did the MFD platform say much about increasing taxes on coal companies to redistribute wealth or pressuring government agencies to do more to reduce unemployment in Appalachia. Yet the situation in 1972 differed from three years earlier. Yablonski had run for the UMWA presidency without any serious individual or organizational rivals to his postition as Boyle's chief opponent. Moreover, Yablonski hoped for financial contributions from non-miner liberal supporters and drafted his platform in part with that group in mind. While Miners For Democracy also hoped for outside liberal financial support, the primary problem facing the reformers revolved around finding the best way to coordinate or merge the strength of the various dissident groups into a united movement against Boyle. More than one insurgent candidacy would split the reform vote and guarantee Boyle's re-election. Individual and organizational jealousies as well as genuine differing interests and priorities among the rebels had to be resolved without alienating or angering important individuals or groups in the insurgent camp. Therefore, reconciling these differences amicably led to the almost exclusive focus on internal union problems in the MFD platform.[19]

The MFD platform was unanimously approved. While some observers found this dismaying, wondering why so little debate occurred, others noted that "there was nothing much to argue about." Because the platform had been carefully worked out in committee, the concerns of all the various reform groups had been voiced, as well as the interests of the constituencies to whom the rebels must appeal. Union democracy, district autonomy, and an end to corruption in the UMW reflected issues in western Pennsylvania, northern West Virginia, and southern Ohio. Assistance to black lung victims and pension relief for disabled miners and widows expressed demands in southern West Virginia, southern Virginia, and eastern Kentucky. Both regions supported strong health and safety law enforcement. The platform demonstrated understanding and sympathy for the problems of pensioners and made special mention of the plight of pensioners in the anthracite district. The need to organize non-union miners to gain royalties for the welfare and retirement fund was discussed. The compromise on strip-mining was not so controversial since few delegates were abolitionists. Moreover, the reformers hoped to unionize strip-miners in Appalachia and the West in order to bring their production under union contract--not eliminate their jobs. If any group had felt its concerns had been omitted or threatened and had staged a floor fight, the platform could have been a divisive force fragmenting the reformers. That may also have been the reason that the platform was silent on ethnic and racial tensions within the union. MFD played it safe by omitting any mention of the subject--perhaps a victory of pragmatism over principle. However, because all the reform groups had their interests acknowledged and no group felt its interest was threatened, the platform served as a strong cohesive force uniting the insurgent movement.[20]

Beneath the orderly facade of the convention proceedings ran an undercurrent of tension and excitement. Politicking was the name of the game. Miners discussed the various reform leaders and speculated about possible slates. Rumors of deals and offers swept through these gatherings. While more experienced participants and observers found nothing unusual in the political maneuvering going one, some miners, especially those attending their first convention, were upset at the politicking they saw and heard. Some had naively expected a "clean," open, apolitical contest for political positions. Moreover, the political skills of most of the miners at the convention were not especially subtle. But while the politicking of the Miners For Democracy may have been a bit crude at times, it was proof positive that this was truly a rank-and-file convention, a rough-hewn example of grass-roots union democracy in action.[21]

The MFD chairman became the main issue frankly discussed in various caucuses and meetings. And Trbovich was vulnerable. Ethnicity was a key factor -- his name alone caused concern among his friends as well as his critics. "Trbovich" was hard to pronounce; when Mike was introduced at rallies in the northern coalfields, his last name had often been garbled. "Yablonski" had been easier to pronounce. Moreover, many Slovak miners in the northern fields did not believe a "hunky" could win southern votes for his presidential bid. In addition, to some miners Trbovich represented an ethic stereotype: "a man with a rough and chiseled countenance and thick silver hair, who favored loud shirts and boldly patterned suits . . . perhaps too much of a dandy." The clash of regional and cultural styles between northern and southern Appalachia would clearly be a factor in selecting a candidate.[22]

Trbovich's record as MFD chairman could also be viewed critically. As the visible symbol of the reform movement for the past two years and the acknowledged front-runner for the presidential nomination, Trbovich had to accept responsibitity for MFD's failures as well as successes. Miners For Democracy as an organizational entity was still very weak throughout the coalfields. Some miners thought that Trbovich lacked the intelligence and charisma necessary for the leader of a movement. Others thought Trbovich too often reacted to events instead of creating them. One observer summed up much of this criticism: "he had angered many with his interim management of MFD by alledgedly speaking too much and organizing too little."[23]

To complicate matters further for Trbovich, personality conflicts and feuds with other reformers eroded his support. Trbovich's small home District 4 in western Pennsylvania backed the MFD chairman without hesitation. But next door in the larger and more important District 5, Trbovich faced stiff opposition from Lou Antal, the key MFD leader in the area. Antal was not challenging Trbovich for the MFD presidential nomination; Antal coveted the District 5 presidency. But Antal disagreed with Trbovich on the role and scope of a district officer's authority vis-a-vis the national leadership. Moreover, Antal simply did not believe that Trbovich had the necessary qualities to win the election and lead the union. Antal spent much of his time at the convention criticizing Trbovich's performance as MFD chairman. While District 5 delegates would support Trbovich, Antal's words would influence delegates in other districts.[24]

Added to Trbovich's troubles was his loss of support by the Yablonskis. This had an unfortunate whipsaw effect on Trbovich's candidacy. Some delegates, especially in the northern coalfields, looked to Chip and Ken Yablonski to indicate their choice for president. Because they were the sons of the martyred leader, their wishes would receive special consideration. For these delegates, the Yablonskis' rejection of Trbovich and support for Pysell caused them to reconsider the chairman's candidacy. On the other hand, many miners, especially in the southern coalfields, had always been suspicious of the Yablonski brothers and all the non-miners aiding the reform effort. To these delegates, Trbovich had been associated in their minds with the Yablonskis, Rauh, Hechler, and others for so long that they were already quite alienated from him. The whipsaw effect of this put Trbovich in a classic damned-if-you-do and damned-if-you-don't situation: spurned by some miners for his close ties to the Yablonskis, he also lost support when they shifted their support to Pysell.[25]

Northern miners disenchanted with Trbovich considered Tom Pysell. The youthful, militant president of a large local, Pysell was an attractive candidate. But he too had deficiencies: Pysell was an outside employee at his mine; he was not a deep miner; he did not go underground to confront coal dust, methane gas, cave-ins, and explosions. That might easily work against him in a campaign. He was also seen by some miners as the pawn of the Yablonski brothers. His candidacy seemed too sudden. These miners respected the Yablonskis, but they felt that the brothers were attempting to manipulate the convention to "put their own men in office." Moreover, Pysell came from District 6, which was also the home of well-known rebel Karl Kafton, the permanent chairman of the convention. Again it might look manipulative to some if Kafton worked hard for Pysell while chairing the convention. A final obstacle for Pysell was that, despite the publicity he had garnered in the last few months, he was still not widely known throughout the coalfields.[26]

Those northern delegates who would not vote for Trbovich and who believed that Pysell did not have enough support to get the nomination then considered a man many southern delegates had been talking about--Arnold Miller. The southern reformer possessed a number of attractive qualities. In contrast to Trbovich, his name posed no problem. As one participant stated: "'Arnold Miller' is a good Anglo-Saxon name and would have heavy support in the heaviest voting areas." Another observer put it more bluntly: "You don't have to be a genius to remember that one." Moreover, Miller had not antagonized any of the key people in Miners For Democracy, mainly because his work had been confined to the southern coalfields. His personal feuds also seemed to be under control; after John Mendez failed to get majority support from his and Miller's home District 17 delegation, Mendez left the convention-- and the mantle of southern reform leadership -- to Miller.[27]

And many northern delegates were impressed by Miller's record as a reform leader. Miller had been one of the original founders of the Black Lung Association. He had helped expand the BLA into a service organization functioning in seven states. His work with Designs for Rural Action, a federally funded antipoverty program for which he had worked part-time, had helped link Appalachian activists and miners together. His skill in trying to unite an effective coalition of dissident active miners, black lung victims, disabled miners and their wives and widows, anti-poverty workers and other non-union reform supporters in the southern fields had been reflected in part in the publicity he had received. And that publicity was important -- while some southern reformers might carp that Miller had received an excessive amount of credit for work done by others, that people like Bill Worthington, Hobert Grills, Charles Brooks, John Mendez, and others deserved as much recognition as Miller, that Miller had cultivated the media and arrogated too much authority or power to himself, northern reformers tended to dismiss such talk as "sour grapes." All that most northern reformers knew was that Miller headed the reform movement in the southern coalfields. Moreover, Miller's restrained conduct at the convention had made a favorable impression on those put off by Trbovich's style of leadership.[28]

And, finally, from a geopolitical point of view, Miller came from the area with the heaviest concentration of votes. Of all the caucuses and factions meeting that Saturday night, no group was more impressed with this fact than the one composed of Chip and Ken Yablonski, Tom Pysell, Ed Monborne, Ken Dawes, Bill Savitsky, and others who were the core of the anti-Trbovich movement among the northern delegates. Their districts included the bulk of northern votes and population, having twice as many convention votes as pro-Trbovich northern districts, 49 to 24, and representing twice as many miners as their opponents in the northern fields, 62,000 to 30,000. That statistic alone was strong criticism of Trbovich's leadership and activity as chairman aside from any geo- and ethnopolitical calculations. By Saturday night, it became apparent that Tom Pysell could not win the nomination. This gathering of district leaders, who could influence or control of the votes in their delegations, was looking for someone to support.[29]

The group appraised the situation. The convention had approved the weighted vote system tentatively agreed to at the May 6 MFD Steering Committee meeting in Charleston. Thus there were 130 votes to be cast Sunday morning. The candidate with more than 65 votes would carry the Miners For

Democracy banner against Boyle. If the northern forces at the convention had been united, they could have easily nominated their candidate: Districts 2 (central Pennsylvania),4 (southwest Pennsylvania), and 5 (northwest Pennsylvania), 6 (southern Ohio and the western panhandle of West Virginia), 8 and 11 (Indiana), 12 (Illinois), 25 (eastern Pennsylvania), and 26 (Nova Scotia) together had 73 votes, 8 more than the minimum needed. If they picked up swing District 31's (northern West Virginia) 11 votes, they would have a landslide. Conversely, if the southern forces at the convention were united, they still could not win. Districts 17 (southwest West Virginia), 19 (eastern Kentucky), 23 (western Kentucky), 28 (southwest Virginia), 29 (southeast West Virginia), and 30 (northeast Kentucky) only totaled 46 votes. Even if they picked up District's 31's 11 votes, they were still short of the mark. However, while southern delegates seemed united behind Miller, northern delegates were clearly divided.[30]

The anti-Trbovich group decided that a successful insurgent presidential candidate had to meet at least two basic requirements: he had to be from a big district and he had to be Anglo-Saxon. Fearful of prejudice within the union, the group concluded that neither miners of Afro-American or eastern European origins should head the rebel slate. While the caucus agreed rather quickly that a black presidential candidate might limit support for the dissidents, extended debate took place over the other prohibition. The Yablonskis were convinced that a "hunky" could not win the southern coalfields and thus the reform ticket would lose. They had experienced ethnic prejudice in their hometown of Clarksville, Pennsylvania, where there was a strict dividing line between the Anglo-Saxon population and those of eastern European descent. If ethnic bias was still quite evident in an area containing many ethnic residents, what would it be like in southern West Virginia, eastern Kentucky, Alabama? Their father had known that his ethnicity was a problem in the southern fields in 1969. One retired Kentucky miner but put it bluntly: "I ain't going to vote for no hunkie." The Yablonskis did not think the situation had really changed since then.[31]

Edgar James, a non-miner graduate student serving as assistant editor of *The Miner's Voice,* totally disagreed with that ethno- and geopolitical view. James thought the Yablonskis overemphasized anti-ethnic sentiment in the southern coalfields. He noted that a significant number of people of eastern European heritage lived in the area, although they were a minority. James believed that such an ethnic candidate for union president could win majority support in the south. But the bottom line for the Yablonskis, as they expressed it in a moment of frustration during the deliberations, was their conviction that, "Those fucking hillbillies won't vote for a hunkie." The tenacity of the ethnic and cultural stereotypes by which many miners in each region viewed the other -- or at least the perception of such rigid stereotypes by these northern delegates -- settled the issue. The ethno- and geopolitical argument remained convincing to the group.[32]

Given the prerequisites of a big district and an Anglo-Saxon, how well did Arnold Miller fill the bill? His ethnic background was correct, and he came from the second largest district in the union--it contained more miners than any of the districts represented in the anti-Trbovich group. Moreover, as a retired miner, Miller would appeal to many pensioneers--and Yablonski had only been credited with 7 percent of that group's vote. Arnold Miller's District 17 had 16 votes at the convention. Those plus the anti-Trbovich coalition's 49 votes made a total of 65. The minimum needed to win the presidential nomination was any fraction over 65. Surely Miller would get other southern votes to offset any slippage that might occur in the anti-Trbovich coalition. The ethno- and geopoliticians had found their man.[33]

Once the group had decided on Miller for president, the rest of the slate had to be balanced. With Miller's strength in the southern fields heading the ticket, support from Pennsylvania was the next consideration. Trbovich seemed the likely choice for vice president. Not only would his selection assuage his hurt feelings but having the MFD chairman on the slate would symbolically unite the two wings of the reform movement. District 31 in northern West Virginia was a crucial swing district and its mix of cultural and ethnic backgrounds also made it problematic. But young Harry Patrick had emerged as a militant rank-and-file spokesman during the 1971 contract strike. The group would support Patrick, a member of the MFD Finance Committee, for secretary-treasurer.[34]

Chip Yablonski later recalled: "I got far more involved in it than I wanted to be." But with the vindication of their father's sacrifice seeming to hang in the balance, the Yablonskis discussed the candidates with rebel leaders and reached a consensus that "the winning combination would be with Arnold, Mike, and Harry." Hillbilly, Hunky, and Hybrid -- the stereotypical slate was an ethno- and geopolitician's dream ticket for Appalachia.[35]

The Yablonskis had not controlled the Saturday night meeting. They were not delegates and could cast no votes on the convention floor. Their original choice for president had fizzled out. They were respected, they had influence -- but they could not dominate. Monborne, Pysell, Dawes, Savitsky and the others had come to the meeting because they were opposed to Trbovich. They had chafed under his leadership and believed that if he carried the MFD banner, the reform movement would lose and perhaps suffer irreparable damage. Convinced that none of them could win, they looked elsewhere. Their decision was not so much pro-Miller as anti-Trbovich. They did what they thought was best for the reform movement. They were not particularly happy at the end of the meeting. They did not really know Miller, nor did they believe that they could control him--they just knew that he fit the criteria which they had agreed was a prerequisite for victory against Boyle. Arnold Miller had merely been the beneficiary of some cold, hard, pragmatic calculations. Northern men were going to support a southern candidate.

Meanwhile, Miller, who had reached an understanding with Trbovich before the convention about the vice presidency, learned that many northern delegates now preferred him for the top spot on the slate instead of Trbovich.[36]

Sunday morning came too early for many of the miners who had spent much of the night discussing the candidates. Tension began to build as the miners filed into the Wheeling College field house to select a slate to represent Miners For Democracy against Boyle and the hierarchy. Six men were nominated for the presidential slot on the MFD ticket: Levi Daniel, Arnold Miller, Harry Patrick, Tom Pysell, Bill Savitsky, and Mike Trbovich. Patrick declined in favor of Trbovich, as did Daniel. But Miller accepted the nomination. As he did, murmurs spread throughout the convention. The deal with Trbovich was off. A few delegates shouted, "Doublecross!" Pysell and Savitsky then declined in favor of Miller. Trbovich, who had expected everyone else to decline, which would have brought him the nomination by acclamation, had a surprised look on his face as he accepted the challenge from Miller.[37]

Each district caucused, discussed the candidates, and voted. The results were double-checked and finally announced: Miller, 70 and 9/10; Trbovich, 57 and 1/10 (2 votes were not cast). Northern men had nominated a southern man as their presidential candidate. The northern votes split dramatically: 46 and 9/10 for Miller (Districts 2, 6, 12, and 25) and only 26 and 1/10 for Trbovich (Districts 4, 5, 8 & 11, 26). Southern votes had also shattered: 24 for Miller (Districts 17, 19, 28, and 30), 18 for Trbovich (Districts 23 and 29). District

31's border area 11 votes had swung to Trbovich. Only Pysell (District 6) and Miller's (District 17) delegations had split their votes--both overwhelmingly for Miller.[38]

Neither region had voted as a bloc. Insurgents in both areas seemed less impressed by the men they knew and hoped the other region's leader would be an improvement. The major southern defection from Miller was Levi Daniel's District 29 in Southeastern West Virginia. Perhaps Daniel hoped that Trbovich would reward him with the second spot on the ticket--or perhaps he had privately faulted Miller's leadership until now. But the southern split could not prevent Miller from winning. With over half the southern votes and almost two thirds of the northern votes, Arnold Miller won the presidential nomination of the Miners For Democracy. While Miller had skillfully maneuvered himself through the convention, the anti-Trbovich coalition in the northern coalfields had also succeeded in their aim--and Trbovich knew who had engineered his defeat.

A chagrined Trbovich then won the vice-presidential spot, despite competition for that nomination as well. Harry Patrick defeated two other candidates to garner the secretary-treasurer position. That left six minor offices to fill: three international auditors and three international tellers. But in the celebration that followed the major nominations, little strategic thought was given to selecting the nominees for minor offices. Harry Patrick recalled: "When the top three was filled, everything just kind of went haywire after that. No one sat down and gave any real thought . . . I think we should have recessed for like two hours and got our heads screwed back on right and took this into consideration." Instead of a recess, nominees were hastily picked--three from Pennsylvania, two from Ohio, and one from Virginia. With hindsight, the major nominees wished that a broader geographical and racial balance had been reflected among the minor office nominees. An auditor or teller from Alabama, Colorado, eastern or western Kentucky, or other areas would have increased chances for victory. The selection of a black miner would also have strengthened the slate.[39]

Almost three years to the day after Jock Yablonski had announced his candidacy challenging Boyle, a grass-roots convention of rebel miners chose a full rank-and-file reform ticket to oppose Boyle again. The process of fusing together an effective, coherent reform organization from dissident groups sharing the same interests but have quite different cultural and political attitudes and styles was no easy matter. Although there had been some communication and cooperation between the northern and southern wings of the reform movement during the previous two years, no merger of their respective strengths occurred until the Wheeling convention. Then a platform fused the northern concern for union democracy with the southern concern for black lung and pension reform. That fusion was then personified in a slate which represented southern Appalachia in Arnold Miller, western Pennsylvania in Mike Trbovich, and the border area of northern West Virginia in Harry Patrick. Continuity with Yablonski's effort was also evident in that all three major nominees had played active roles in the 1969 campaign. While the convention left some scars--Trbovich, who felt betrayed by his own organization and by Arnold Miller, who internalized his anger and bitterness until after the election; some black miners wondered about the reformers' commitment to racial equality when they looked MFD's "lily-white" ticket--no serious damage had been done to the rebel movement. Harry Patrick spoke for the insurgents after the convention when he declared: "We came out unified and strong and we're ready to go."[40]

Miners For Democracy was now a reality. The pragmatic, strategic decisions reached at the Wheeling convention resulted in an ethnically and geographically balanced slate and an inclusive reform platform that allowed the insurgents to focus all their energies against Boyle and the heirarchy. After an intensive six-month campaign, the MFD slate won the Labor Department-supervised election in December 1972 -- and democracy was finally re-established within the United Mine Workers of America.

NOTES

The author gratefully acknowledges the financial assistance provided by the American Council of Learned Societies and the College of Charleston for this study.

1. This essay is a substantially condensed version of the paper presented at the Appalachian Studies Conference. The most recent scholarly study of Lewis is Melvyn Dubofsky and Warren Van Tine, *John L. Lewis: A Biography* (New York: Quadrangle/The New York Times Book Co., 1977), especially pp. 469-517 for background on Lewis's post-war policies. A partial list of significant secondary works on Lewis would include Saul Alinsky, *John L. Lewis: An Unauthorized Biography* (New York: Vintage Books, 1970); Morton Baratz, *The Union and the Coal Industry* (New Haven: Yale University Press, 1955); Harry Caudill, *Night Comes to the Cumberlands: A Biography of a Depressed Area* (Boston: Little Brown and Co., 1963); Joseph E. Finely, *The Corrupt Kingdom: The Rise and Fall of the United Mine Workers* (New York: Simon and Schuster, 1972); Brit Hume, *Death and the Mines: Rebellion and Murder in the United Mine Workers* (New York: Grossman Publishers, 1971); Bill Peterson, *Coaltown Revisited: An Appalachian Notebook* (Chicago: Henry Regnery Company, 1972); J. B. S. Hardman, "John L. Lewis, Labor Leader and Man: An Interpretation," *Labor History* 2 (Winter 1961): 3-29; Nat Caldwell and Gene S. Graham, "The Strange Romance between John L. Lewis and Cyrus Eaton," *Harper's Magazine* 223 (December 1961): 25-32; A. H. Raskin, "John L. Lewis and the Mine Workers," *Atlantic* 211 (May 1963): 52-57; T. N. Bethell, "Conspiracy in Coal," *The Washington Monthly* 1 (March 1969): 16-23, 63-72.

2. Hume, *Death and the Mines.*

3. See George W. Hopkins, "The Miners For Democracy: Insurgency in the United Mine Workers of America, 1970-1972," Ph. D. dissertation, University of North Carolina, Chapel Hill, N.C., 1976, pp. 66-201.

4. George W. Hopkins, "Southern Coal Miners and Union Insurgency, 1968-1972," in Gary M. Fink, Leslie A. Hough, and Merl Reed, eds., *Essays in Southern Labor History,* Volume 2 (Westport, Conn.: Greenwood Press, 1980), forthcoming. On April 28, 1971, Federal Judge Gerhard Gesell found the UMWA and its Welfare and Retirement Fund guilty of willful mismanagement and misuse of Fund assets. Boyle was cited for violating his fiduciary trust to UMWA members. Boyle, the union's trustee for the Fund, and the allegedly "neutral" trustee, Josephine Roche, an old Lewis crony, were ordered to resign their postions. After careful study, Judge Gesell awarded $11.5 million in damages to disabled and retired UMWA miners and their widows, to be paid by the union and its bank, the National Bank of Washington, in which UMWA and Fund monies had been kept. *New York Times,* April 29, 1971, p. 1; *Coal Patrol* (independent newsletter), April 16-30, 1971, pp. 1-2; *New York Times,* January 8, 1972, pp. 1, 37.

5. The federal court decision overturning the 1969 UMWA election is available in the Miners For Democracy Collection at the Wayne State University Archives of Labor History and Urban Affairs, Box 18, File 2; for a brief summary, see the *New York Times,* May 2, 1972, pp. 1, 28; the demise of district trusteeships appeared in the *Wall Street Journal,* May 12, 1972, p. 6, and the *New York Times,* May 25, 1972, p. 29, as well as the rank-and-file newspaper of the Miners For Democracy, *The Miner's Voice,* May 1972, p. 12, and ibid., June, 1972, p. 11.

6. Ibid., May, 1972, p. 3.

7. Interview with Patrick. There is no official record of the proceedings of the Wheeling conventon; nor is there a detailed account of the internal politics of the convention. Press coverage, with a few exceptions, tended to be superficial. Thus, source material for much of this paper is composed of interviews, substantiated where possible in the written record, and compared to the recollections of other participants and observers to determine as clearly as possible the internal dynamics of the rebel convention.

8. Interview with Trbovich; interview with Edgar James, former associate editor of *The Miner's Voice;* Edgar James, "UMW Still Subject to Lewis Legacy," signed article in the weekly newspaper *In These Times,* March 1-7, 1978, Vol. 2, No. 15, p. 11, includes details on the Trbovich-Miller deal.

9. Interview with Joseph A. "Chip" Yablonski

10. *The Miner's Voice,* February-March, 1972, p. 1; Don Stillman, "Murder and the Mines," *New Politics,* May 1972, p. 28.

11. Interview with Miller.

12. These criticisms of Miller were aired in an interview conducted by sociologist Paul Nyden with Charles Brooks, a black miner who was the first president of the Black Lung Association and who had to resign the post because of poor health. See Paul Nyden, "Miners For Democracy: Struggle in the Coal Fields," Ph. D. dissertation, Columbia University, 1974, pp. 700-701, 705-706. My own interview with Richard Bank, a former VISTA, attorney in West Virginia, and an aide to Miller, also touched on those issues.

13. Interview with Patrick.

14. Other possible MFD rank-and-file candidates included Bill Savitsky, Chairman of District 25 MFD, a long-time reformer in the anthracite fields who had been a strong Yablonski backer; Ed Monborne, Chairman of southwest Pennsylvania's District 2 MFD, an early Yablonski supporter; Lou Antal, a veteran rebel and the MFD candidate for the District 5 presidency in 1970 who had been counted out in a mini-version of the 1969 election; Karl Kafton, another long-time rebel and a friend of Yablonski; and Levi Daniel, Chairman of southern West Virginia's District 29 MFD, a black miner who helped lead the struggle for black lung compensation and had built support of Yablonski in the southern fields, Wheeling College was a liberal Catholic school, many of whose students had worked in the 1969 campaign of Catholic insurgent Jock Yablonski. Quotations from *Coal Patrol,* May 20, 1972, p. 7; Stillman, "Murder and the Mines," p. 28.

15. The presence of federal bomb detection experts from the Treasury Department's Alcohol, Firearms, and Tax Division as well as Wheeling City Police underscored the threat the convention posed to Boyle. After Yablonski's murder, the safety of rebel miners had to be taken seriously. However, no bombs were discovered at the convention. Observers, press, and staff would bring total attendance to approximately 750. New York Times, May 28, 1972, p. 45; *Coal Patrol,* June 1, 1972, p. 1; H. W. Benson, "Miners For Democracy: A Report from West Virginia," *Dissent* 19 (Fall 1972): 632.

16. *Coal Patrol,* June 1, 1972, p. 2; Phil Primack, "Miners For Democracy:

Closing In On Tony Boyle," *The Nation,* June 19, 1972, p. 787; Benson, "Miners For Democracy," 637-638; a copy of Rauh's keynote address is available in the Miners For Democracy Collection, Box 66, File 37.

17. *The Miner's Voice,* May 1972, p. 3, 7-10.
18. Ibid., 9-10.
19. Nyden, "Miners For Democracy," 547-548.
20. *Coal Patrol,* June 1, 1972, p. 1; Benson, "Miners For Democracy," p. 634.
21. *Wall Street Journal,* May 30, 1972, p. 5; Coal Patrol, June 1, 1972, p. 1; interview with Patrick; Joseph Rauh, "Internal Union Problems: A Study of the United Mine Workers Union," in Emanuel Stein and S. Theodore Reiner, eds., *Proceedings of New York University Twenty-Sixth Annual Conference on Labor* (New York: Matthew Bender, 1974), p. 299; interview with Stillman; interview with Patrick; interview with Yablonski.
22. Don Stillman definitely thought Trbovich's name could be a liability for the rebel ticket. Because he and Ed James would have major responsibilities in coordinating campaign advertising and images for whomever won the nomination, Stillman recalled: "We decided if it was Trbovich, all our stuff would have to say 'Vote Mike' and build it around 'Mike' rather than his last name because it was going to be a tough one to deal with." Interview with Stillman; interview with James; interview with Bank; *Coal Patrol,* June 1, 1972, p. 2; James Humphreys, "Miller Vs Boyle: Revolt in the Coal Fields," *New south* 28 (Winter 1973): 41.
23. Interview with Tom Bethell, editor of *Coal Patrol;* interview with Stillman; interview with Lou Antal of District 5; Humphreys, "Miller Vs Boyle," 41.
24. Interview with Antal; interview with Trbovich; interview with Yablonski; interview with Bethell; interview with Patrick.
25. Interview with Trbovich; interview with Yablonski; interview with James.
26. Interview with James; interview with Trbovich; Coal Patrol, June 1, 1972, p. 1.
27. Interview with Bank; interview with Stillman.
28. Interview with Miller; interview with Bank; Nyden, "Miners For Democracy," pp. 547-48.
29. Interview with Yablonski; interview with Antal. Table 1 represents the anti-Trbovich northern districts, their convention votes, and district population. Table 2 represents the pro-Trbovich northern districts.

Table 1

Chairman	District	Convention Votes	Population
Ed Monborne	2	11	15,730
Tom Pysell	6	11	13,202
Ken Dawes	12	10	15,210
Bill Savitsky	25	17	17,832
		49	61,974

Table 2

Chairman	District	Convention Votes	Population
Mike Trbovich	4	7	8,047
Lou Antal	5	12	13,096
unknown	8&11	2	4,946
Jake Campbell	26	3	4,331
		24	30,420

30. The *Miner's Voice,* June, 1972, p. 3, shows the weighted votes allotted to each district at the MFD Steering Committee meeting in Charleston on May 7.

31. Interview with Yablonski; interview with James; interview with Bank; Peterson, *Coaltown Revisited,* p. 105.

32. Interview with James.

33. Ibid.; interview with Yablonski. There was another reason for supporting Miller. A three-way race between Trbovich, Miller, and Pysell might produce a deadlocked convention. Several observers saw that as a potentially dangerous situation because these "people hadn't had that much experience working with each other. You didn't have a very natural cement." Given the tensions already evident at the convention, a deadlock might result in "the very bad spectacle of the reform wing of the mine workers engaged in barroom brawl" at the convention. Selecting a winning ticket would also eliminate the threat of a deadlock. Interview with Bethell.

34. Interview with Yablonski

35. Ibid.

36. Confidential statements of MFD participants; Primack, "Miners For Democracy," p. 787.

37. Confidential statement of an MFD participant; *The Miner's Voice,* June 1972, p. 3.

38. Ibid.

39. Ibid.; interview with Trbovich; interview with Patrick.

40. Ibid.; interview with Trbovich; interview with Miller; interview with James; interview with Stillman; Paul Nyden, "Black Coal Miners in the United States," Occasional Paper No. 15, American Institute for Marxist Studies (AIMS) (New York: AIMS, 1974), p. 57. After the election, Miller appointed Daniel the provisional president of District 29 until an election could be held. However, Daniel lost the election.

TRANSNATIONAL CORPORATIONS AND THE MIGRATION OF INDUSTRIES IN LATIN AMERICA AND APPALACHIA

Helen M. Lewis and Myles Horton

Abstract

The growing role of transnational corporations in the world is the subject of this study. Special comparisons are made between their activities in Latin America, particularly Brazil and Peru, and Appalachia and the rural South. The analysis concludes with suggestions of community and worker response to the changing shape of industry.

The pace and extent of multinational activity is increasing. Corporations are changing the nature of their activity or entering a new stage and, thereby, reshaping the competitive context which portends enormous consequences for communities and workers in America/Appalachia. Our paper is designed to stimulate discussion and will deal with aspects of multinational activity under the following headings:
I. The nature of transnationals and the direction of change in their activities.
II. Understanding the process: dependency and colonialism models.
III. Development in Latin America (Brazil and Peru).
IV. Similarities and differences of development in Appalachia and Latin America (Brazil and Peru).
V. What difference does this perspective make in Appalachia, and how can communities and workers most effectively organize in response to the changing shape of industry?
I. The nature of transnationals and the direction of change.

> I have long dreamed of buying an island owned by no nation and of establishing the world Headquarters of the Dow Company on truly neutral ground of such an island, beholden to no nation or society.
> --Carl A. Gerstacker, chairman of Dow Chemical Company[1]

The growth of multinational corporations or transnationals represents a new stage in capitalist development and poses new problems for third world and exploited regions, internal peripheries or colonies, such as Appalachia. Transnationals can also turn whole countries into "Appalachias" or "Latin Americanize" the United States.

The international corporation has interests separate and distinct from the interests of every government including its own government of origin. The dependence of the leading United States based corporations on foreign profits has been growing greatly since 1964. United States corporations have been shifting more and more of their assets abroad: about one third of the chemical industry, one third of the pharmaceuticals, three fourths of the electrical industry, and two fifths of the consumer-goods industry.[2]

Although the United States is still the dominant transnational, Germany, Japan, France, Holland, and Great Britain are actively involved. Some of these are investing in the United States at the rate of 15 percent a year.[3]

What is happening is not just the old pattern of runaway industries looking for new raw materials or cheap labor, although that is part of the total process. The industrial system is changing from national or regional operations to a globally integrated production system. The large corporations are developing a global grid of producing subsidiaries which utilize labor, raw materials, markets, and political systems throughout the world.

It is estimated that by 1985, three hundred giant multinationals will produce more than one half of the world's goods and services.[4]

This triumph of multinationals is made possible by jet aircraft, international telecommunications, and computers.

Some of the characteristics of transnationals are:

1. The corporations are large, capital intensive, technologically oriented and managerially intense. They are looking for greater growth and profitability through world markets.
2. They seek growth centers -- countries which are developing and willing to cooperate politically and economically and follow the capitalist path.
3. Global corporations have destroyed the concept of market. They conduct most transactions with themselves.
4. Profit maximization is the major guiding principle. Decisions are based on hard, cold business facts.
5. They develop global standardization of business procedures and measures, and a uniformity in work habits, products, and services.
6. Corporations transform production techniques to make for manufacturing flexibility: shifting tooling, interchangeable parts, and multiple sources of goods.
7. The internationalization of the division of labor allows the rational placement of plants according to type of labor available. The experience of the Ford Motor Company in Europe demonstrates the advent of this sort of manufacturing flexibility.

    Ford developed a uniform European car with standardized interchangeable parts, thereby making manufacturing flexibility possible. They placed the labor intensive assembly in countries with the lowest labor costs, and the engines and more complicated parts where a skilled labor force existed. In addition, multiple sources existed for each component; so that if there was labor trouble in one source, overtime at the other source could keep assembly lines going.

    Assembly was placed in Saarlous, Germany, which had high unemployment and a concentration of migrant workers dependent on the employer to stay in the country. Wildcat strikes were illegal as well. The Ford plant could rely on the needs and fears of the workers to ensure docility, and on the involuntary scab labor of migrant workers.

    In addition to manufacturing flexibility and internationalization of the division of labor, there has been a revolution in production technique. A transformation of the production process has occurred, encouraged by the development of smaller cars. It has resulted in new machines, new plants and new routines, more robots (Unimate Welders), highly automated machines, and the use of shifting tooling (including computer tapes) which can be transferred to a job site to replace labor or avoid labor disputes.[5]
8. They have shaken off traditional sources of countervailing power: outgrown trade unions, consumer groups, and local and national governments.
9. Nations now compete for corporations and use their legal and financial resources, raw materials, and labor to attract foreign capital for development.
10. The free flow of goods, investments, and technology may eventually

equalize standards of living and wage scales. In each country where a corporation concentrates wealth, the gap between rich and poor widens.

11. Transnationals use foreign countries to avoid ideological barriers to sales--i.e., weapons sales by Brazil.

Carl A. Gerstocker, chairman of Dow Chemical, told a White House Conference on Industrial Worlds Ahead:

> We appear to be moving in the direction of what will not really be multinational or international companies as we know them today but what we might call "Anational" companies--companies without any nationality, belonging to all nationalities.[6]

12. Migration of industries or "going transnational" is encouraged when big changes in production are needed. These give an industry the impetus to move to a more congenial environment to recoup capital investment sooner.

Changes which facilitate or encourage companies to go international are:

   a. Modernization of existing facilities such as oil refineries or steel mills.
   b. Installing environmental safeguards or changing to pollution-free procedures.
   c. Requirements for new safety devices.
   d. New or different products being introduced.
   e. Major changes in design (large cars to small cars).
   f. The saturation of a market, as with the ratio of one car per two persons in the United States, prompting the development of markets elsewhere.
   g. Decline or depletion of a resource such as gasoline for cars -- and the subsequent move to a locale with the resources or substitute (i.e., land for gasahol).

An example of such a business exodus is U.S. Steel in Youngstown, Ohio, which is closing down and investing in more profitable areas such as oil, chemicals, and banking. In 1974-79, the company spent only half the $7.6 billion needed to maintain plant and equipment. They refused to modernize and closed. It was "too old to save." No major expenditures to modernize were made after World War II. In order for the plant to be rebuilt, the government would now have to subsidize the industry, grant tax concessions, restrict imports, and ease pollution controls. While the government puts money in to rebuild the industry, the company can still use its own money to diversify and buy into other industries, a policy aimed at taking nothing less than the largest possible profit margin.

II. Understanding the process: dependency, underdevelopment, colonialism.

Latin American scholars have developed several models to explain the role of transnationals in Latin America and the development of underdevelopment in peripheral societies. Some of these theories have influenced Appalachian scholars.[7]

Andre Gunder Frank's essays on the development of underdevelopment emphasize the relationship between transnationals and patterns of development in Latin America. He concludes that transnational development has resulted in a dependency relationship (subjection and economic dependencies) and a transformation of the class structure and culture. Transnationals support the class interests of the local dominant bourgeoisie who make and change policy to support dependence. Local capitalists produce an unbalanced, disarticulated economy, as well as repressive and economically active central governments. F. H. Cordosa also points to the ways the dominant class tries to impose upon the whole society that form of domination which serves their own interest, and Samir Amin in *Accumulation and World Scale* further points to the asymmetrical relationships resulting in the dependent country where there is a distortion toward exports and unequal specialization to the advantage of the dominant country.

Dos Santos also comments on the structure of dependence.[8] Most often dependent countries use harsh repression to keep labor working and to cut down on peasant revolt or worker uprisings. The state becomes very involved in the economy and uses its power to serve the interests of the capitalists and to insure a favorable investment climate. Foreign investors make alliances with conservative agrarian and military elites and help reactionary groups control the state.

This state of dependence is natural to the economic system of transnationals: monopolistic control of large-scale capital and complex technology which leads to unequal development. It benefits few and results in misery and social marginalization for many.

Andre Gunder Frank points to the difference between earlier colonialism and exploitation by transnational capitalism.[9] The earlier form of exploitation was colonialism with outside countries controlling and exploiting raw materials. The industries were largely agricultural or extractive: minerals, timber, coffee, bananas, and sugar cane. Earlier colonialism was not interested in using the area as a market for goods. It sought only to control and exploit the mineral and agricultural products without seeking to industrialize the area. The transnational, however, wants to industrialize the country, internationalize the market, and orient the production toward high income consumption to develop and support a middle class market.

III. Development in Latin America: Brazil and Peru.

The "Brazilian Model" of development has been praised by development economists. Also called the "Brazilian Miracle," it has been characterized by a rapid rise in gross national product and a heavy emphasis on foreign investment through multinationals. The greatest growth was between 1968 and 1974. By 1978, Brazil was the ninth largest automobile producer in the world. It exports both parts and finished vehicles, having increased export from $7.9 million in 1969 to $514 million in 1976.

Brazil began encouraging automobile development in 1956, hoping to promote a local industry. However, it created no obstacles or restrictions on operation for foreign capital and provided tax incentives and subsidies.

There was cooperation between the transnationals, the Brazilian bourgeoisie, and state capital. However, there was little development until 1964 when the military regime "stabilized" the work force by destroying the working class radical movement, neutralizing unions, and mandating sacrifice on the part of the workers. The new labor climate, with a quiescent labor force, attracted industrialists, and both Brazilian and foreign capital investments increased to produce a big boom with spectacular profits. United States investments increased five hundred percent between 1964 and 1977. Labor costs were kept very low, but income of the middle class technical staff increased to provide a local consumer market for cars and other goods.

In the process there was a concentration of production and many local entrepreneurs were forced out as too small or inefficient to compete. The state joined with foreign investors in joint ventures.

In addition to automobiles there has been a big increase in chemical manufacturers and weapons. Brazil exports $500 million a year in weapons--missiles, tanks, tank destroyers, amphibious landing vehicles. The government does not restrict resales, there are no ideological strings, and the equipment is low cost and designed for less well trained soldiers.[10]

In petrochemicals Brazilians have received new Inter American Bank loans to increase production. They are producing ethylene, propylene, benzene, and butadiene to further produce thermoplastics and synthetic rubber. They also produce PVC (polyvinyl chloride), styrene, and polystyrene. Union Carbide, Dow, Solvay, Phillips, and Koppers are involved. Benzene, PVC, and butadiene are cancer-causing. Many other companies produce health hazards for workers and the community. As environmental and health protection legislation limits production in the United States and other western countries, the industries are moved to less-developed and less regulated countries. Third world nations are being used as dumping grounds for hazardous products and polluting industries.[11] Aldrin, dieldrin, ehptochlor, and chlordane are banned in the United States but are made for export and come back to the country on imported foods. Of United States pesticide manufacture, 40 percent is for export.

To avoid regulations, much asbestos manufacture has moved to Mexico, India, and Brazil. As a beneficiary country, Brazil has a preferential tariff on United States imports, and some of the asbestos textiles enter the United States free or at very low tariffs. Brazil also provides a hazard-pay increment for workers in hazardous industries. If the hazard is controlled or eliminated, the pay increases are discontinued. By making hazardous work economically attractive and by making workers suffer pay cuts in exchange for improved working conditions, the law undermines all efforts to improve working conditions in hazardous industries.

Brazil like many other Latin American countries has new coalitions of young military officers, young businessmen, and technicians--all middle-class, foreign educated, dedicated to modernization, development, and efficiency. This cadre has given rise to authoritarian governments with technocratic and development aspirations.[12] In Brazil the military has embraced industrialization and developed an authoritarian regime to promote the development process and work for full integration of the Brazilian economy in the structure of international capitalism.

In addition to the increase in manufacturing in Brazil, multinational corporations are carving out "homesteads" from hundreds of square miles in the Amazon, dispossessing and destroying native populations.[13] One example of multinational entrepreneurship supported and encouraged by the government may be seen in Daniel K. Ludwig, an American businessman, who owns three million acres of the Amazon. He is investing one half billion dollars in planting rice and Cmelina trees for pulp paper. He moved a power plant and paper mill from Japan, and the Brazilian techno-military bureaucracy works with Ludwig to bring growth to the unexplored areas, to increase reserves of foreign currency, and to attract foreign investors. He has been allowed to move out Indian populations, which has resulted in their death. Approximately eight thousand Yanomamo Indians have been displaced by road construction crews, lumbering and mining companies, and prospectors who have brought environmental destruction and disease. A huge network of roads has now opened up the Amazon. Ludwig has created an agro-industrial enclave disregarding the ecology of the region or the needs of the people. The lumber project may disrupt the native forest and the costly rice project may bring about a food shortage.

The Amazon area also contains the world's largest reserves of iron ore and enormous amounts of manganese, as well as oil, timber, gemstones, and hydroelectric potential. A recent bank loan is financing a floating sawmill to move up and down the river exploiting the timber.

Agricultural production has been diminishing for the past thirteen years as Brazilians have concentrated on producing commercial crops for export. Both urban and rural workers are malnourished. Emphasis has also been placed on airports and roads, so transnationals may export their products. Poor farmers, semi-proletarians, and peasants have a hard time surviving. Even the middle farmers and rich land owners are losing power to transnational and Brazilian corporations. Five percent of the rural population owns 69 percent of all cultivated land.

Large sugar and coffee growers are allies of transnationals. In expansion and modernization of exports, industries, agriculture, land, and capital is concentrated in fewer and fewer hands and more and more small producers have gone under.

Concentration and modernization have resulted in a large number of landless, dispossessed peasants who work as day laborers. They are now the mass of unemployed who live in slums of towns and cities. They were expelled from plantations by owners to avoid minimum wage for agricultural laborers. They are highly exploited and receive fifty cents to one dollar per day. Agriculture is developing in Latin America capitalist style, and millions are being impoverished in the process. Brazil is the world's second largest exporter of food while 40 percent of its population suffers from malnutrition.[14]

Northeastern farm workers in large sugar cane operations suffer from malnutrition, and 66 percent of the children die before age five. The worker must work twice as long as in 1964 to earn enough for food. There has been recent labor activity, and the plantation owners, for the first time, have signed a labor agreement with 250,000 laborers who have been virtual slaves to the owners.

These are some of the negative effects of the large agribusiness development in Brazil:
1. Marginalizes the national investor.
2. Introduces foreign technology and know-how (capital intensive).
3. Creates unemployment for rural workers.
4. Displaces rural people.
5. Increases urban unemployment through regional migration of landless peasants.
6. Destroys small and middle farmers.
7. Proletarianizes the Brazilian rural labor.

The "Brazilian miracle" has also produced great tensions and hardships for industrial workers. Brazilian industrial workers made sixty-six dollars a month in 1977. As Brazil concentrated income in the upper classes and controlled labor, the disparity between rich and poor increased, and repression became a necessary part of the development. Industry grew at the expense of the majority of the people. Even with strong control there was considerable unrest and numerous strikes broke out in 1978-79.

The state has intervened in many ways to promote exports and enlarge or decrease local buying power depending on the import/export balance. Inflation was 75 percent in 1979, and Brazilian money was devalued by 30 percent to further increase exports and investments. Inflation has further resulted in a decline of real salary of the workers.

In Peru one can see the ways in which international corporations must change local patterns of health care, farming, and diet in order to develop a consumer market for pharmaceuticals, medicines, hospital-clinic-medical care equipment and supplies, fertilizers, pesticides, and processed foods. Peru has one of the oldest and most sophisticated non-Western "folk medicines" which serves a large proportion of the population, not only rural, but urban as well. The medicine relies heavily on local herbal prescriptions, and to change the population into consumers of Western goods, the local healers and herbalists must be discredited or retrained and credentialized. The first International Congress on Folk Medicines gave lip service to the great folk tradition but clearly came out for the superiority of scientific medicine. In many cases this official line is destroying the only available medicine and health care for the very poor. Retrained midwives now charge more and use sterile practices in non-sterile situations which are less safe than the traditional methods. The displacement of traditional healers by Western trained scientific practitioners, which happened in the United States over one hundred years ago, is now happening in Peru. There are some who are fighting against the invasion of petrochemical fertilizers and herbicides and are seeking to maintain traditional farming and nutrition practices, but the powerful advertising and popular appeal of processed foods, such as Pepsi, Coke and fast foods, is hard to counter without full support of the state. The many exhibits and demonstrations at agricultural fairs for fertilizers and pesticides compound the problem.

IV. Similarities and differences of development in Appalachia and Latin America.

Among the twenty-five largest United States' based transnationals are companies familiar to Appalachia: Exxon, Gulf, Continental Oil, Eastman Kodak, Occidental, Union Carbide, Ford, DuPont, all of which own and operate mines and factories in the region.

Appalachia and the rural South have been the traditional sources of cheap labor for runaway industries. Early, there was a great migration of New England textiles. When the industries needed modernizing, the old plants were closed and new plants built in the South, and the cheap southern labor paid for the remodeling. One of the first "foreign" transnationals, Bemberg, came to Tennessee for cheap labor, and others such as Enka followed to Tennessee and North Carolina. Appalachia has also been the source of raw materials, and the timber and coal were "developed" in the traditional colonial-exploitation pattern by American and British companies, more recently joined by German and Japanese firms. Most of the coal companies have now been replaced by large transnational oil companies: Exxon, Gulf, Standard Oil, Continental; and the area is now being more thoroughly integrated into the international economy. In particular, we are seeing the coal industry integrated into the worldwide energy industry as large oil (energy) companies have bought out the coal companies. We see what looks like contradictory behavior: new mines being developed, mines closing, new growth expected, large numbers of miners unemployed, coal production increased in the West, a big push for synfuels investment by the Federal government. In terms of international energy corporation needs and goals, it makes sense. The Appalachian coal fields are being integrated into the international economy, and decisions are made in those terms: profit is being maximized, labor is being stabilized, the government is pushed to invest in expensive ventures, local elites are mobilized, and areas and communities and workers are traded off against each other.

Beginning in the sixties, the area, which fit the colonial pattern of exploitation (export of raw materials and cheap labor), was geared up for more industrialization with the building of roads and infrastructure services by the Appalachian Regional Commission. The area was also developed as a market for consumer goods, and all the major retail stores and fast-food outlets came to Appalachia. There was an increase in local entrepreneurs, especially in strip mining, which cut in local capitalists, and there has been the development of technocrats and managers with the help of local colleges. An increase in income in the middle class has come about, but the poor have lost ground, and there are wider divisions between the rich and poor.

Actually, the integration of the United States into the international economy is making the whole country into Appalachia, an underdeveloped society. Former industrialized communities of New England and the Midwest are now Appalachianized: exploited but not developed. Michael McKale sees the United States being "Latin Americanized" through the effects of wage leveling, a decreased standard of living, and growing lack of democratic participation.[15]

Manual labor operations are being exported to low-labor-cost countries, and the income distribution and trading patterns of the United States are beginning to resemble underdeveloped countries. The United States' major exports are agricultural products, timber, and coal--raw materials rather than finished products.

There have been dramatic layoffs and plant closures in Detroit, Youngstown, and Pittsburgh. This is all part of the integration of the United States' industrial system into a modular global economy. As industries need to modernize, change style or product, or install pollution devices, it becomes profitable to move and make the changes (or avoid controls) in another country.

Although Appalachia and the rural South may still be the recipients of some runaway industries which come for lower wages and docile (right-to-work, non-union) labor, other labor intensive industries are also leaving Appalachia and the South for cheaper labor in Taiwan, Hong Kong, Mexico, and Brazil. Chemicals and oil refineries are looking for clean, uncluttered land with less health or environmental controls in Mexico, Brazil, or other Latin American countries.

As production workers are being displaced in the United States, there is some growth in managerial, research, and service jobs. Research and development planning still takes place in the home base of the transnationals.

As transnationals, especially banking institutions, helped engineer a devaluation of the United States dollar, european transnationals began to invest more in the United States now own Borax, Bic, Ovaltine and Good Humor. Industrial wages in the United States are now lower than many European countries, and labor is forced to accept lower wages or no-strike, no-wage-increase deals to attract foreign industries such as VW to Pennsylvania and West Virginia. States and regions now compete against each other to attract industries and advertise their low labor costs and tax incentives.

Although there are some specific similarities between Appalachia and third world countries-such as, (1) absentee ownership of industry and land, (2) receivers of runaway plants, (3) low local tax base because of tax incentives, (4) development of native managers to control for the owners, (5) development of a consumer market, (6) growing control of labor by legislation, injunction, court orders and state police to provide a stable labor force-it is best to see Appalachia/America in the context of global capitalism. Appalachia remains as a part of the United States, home base of many transnationals, and shares with others some of the surplus value derived from the exploitation of lower-paid workers in other parts of the world in terms of cheaper consumer goods and exported raw materials.

We are part of the home base of transnationals and are called on to assist with their operations in foreign countries. In Latin America the United States has been involved militarily and economically since the Monroe Doctrine in

1823. All military interventions are accompanied by the establishment of financial institutions, including, the Export-Import Bank, 1934; the World Bank and International Monetary Fund, 1944; the Alliance for Progress, 1961 -- all developed to assist corporate ventures of the United States in Latin America. The government sometimes ends up underwriting loans or investments both at home and abroad (i.e., Lockheed, Chrysler). The World Bank, UNESCO, and other international organizations also become agents, perhaps inadvertently, for the multinational developers, and work to pave the way or facilitate their entry into third world countries. The United Nations Economic Commission on Latin America has pushed for development of roads, power, and basics for heavy industrialization to foster economic independence and national development, but the penetration and control by multinationals makes economic independence impossible.

The consolidation of capitalism on an international basis requires armies, diplomatic corps, state bureaucracies, the World Bank, the International Monetary Fund, and international planning and coordination which is the role of the Trilateral Commission. Carter may be considered the first multinational president, since he was a member of the Trilateral Commission and is considered by many as "their candidate."

The Trilateral Commission was formed in 1973 by a group of bankers, corporate leaders, and intellectuals from the United States, Japan and Western Europe. Zbigniew Brzezinski was named director and David Rockefeller was financial backer. They are equipped to take over bankrupt cities, as they did New York City, as well as nations. When they do so, they organize the government efficiently and gear it to serve the business community. Social services are cut to a minimum.

Corporations are now in a position to have cities, states and countries compete for their "jobs." The local government is asked to foot the bill on roads, water systems, airport modernization, and transit systems, in order to make development possible. The government may also be asked to provide tax relief, subsidies, buildings, and training for the labor force. The corporations pit countries against countries, and within countries, states or counties or regions against each other, to provide cheaper labor, better tax relief, and more subsidies than the next locale. Corporations also want the state to use welfare policies to resolve social conflicts and protect the corporate system.

> V. What difference does this perspective make in Appalachia, and how can communitites and workers most effectively organize in response to the changing shape of industry?

In Appalachia we have just begun to understand the nature of corporate control, outside ownership, and the effects of exploitation. Now we must try to understand what it means to be integrated into the international capitalist system. This seems far more complex; yet we must try to understand how this reality changes the nature of the problems and the ways of dealing with them. We will continue to have large numbers of absentee owners of land and minerals and industries. A recent newspaper article reported that large timber owners are returning to the area to do again what they did before, as mountains have been reforested and can provide a new crop. Oil, gas, and uranium will be developed along with the coal, since the energy conglomerates own it all.

We are now the site of runaway or expanding industries from other countries such as the VW plant in Charleston. As our wages decline, unions weaken, and state and local governments and unions "sell" their workers. This trend can be expected to continue. As a region, Appalachia will compete with other regions and the thirteen Appalachian states will compete with each other for runaway industries and new industries. Workers may be able to take over some discarded plants, but will be left with outmoded, unsafe, and unprofitable operations and the burden of competing with the newer operations from other parts of the world.

We can expect government services to become fewer and weaker as the state takes on a role of caretaker and opts for a free market economy. The government will use welfare, social services, and education to serve the needs of business, and will be encouraged to invest in expensive developments such as synfuels or other energy development.

We can expect growing attempts to control the labor force through "union busting" or more sophisticated legal maneuvers and psychological strategies. The large oil companies seek to employ more technically oriented, skilled middle-class miners to avoid militant trade unionists. The destruction of coal camps and homogeneous communitites is designed to produce less militant workers. The "line" is that one is not a coal miner but a skilled technician, and class consciousness is destroyed or avoided.

The use of Appalachia as a market and the development of a local bourgeoisie to operate banks, fast-food franchises, markets, and regional offices has led to a growing role for local colleges in the training of managers for industry. The developing middle class must be trained, and colleges and universities have received funds and encouragement to meet the needs. As a result, the business education programs are the largest programs in almost every school, replacing teacher training. Business and economics are being merged in some places as skills and "right thinking" economics are taught together. Again, Appalachian colleges are serving the needs of the economic system in educating the local bourgeoisie who serve the needs of the multinationals which employ them. Today they are not "teachers" but "managers."

Their adaptation to this role makes progressive social change more difficult. The rising middle-class managers are trained to serve the needs of their employers, with allegiances to the multinationals. It becomes much harder to identify the "outside exploiter." The semblance of prosperity keeps the middle class loyal, and it is more difficult to educate about global issues and problems. The Appalachia/American middle class receives dividends as they profit from the cheaper labor of third world countries and purchase low cost luxuries.

Appalachian studies in Appalachian colleges have a responsibility to research and educate around these changes and the impliations of the integration of the region into the international economy. Cross-cultural studies are important and necessary. Workers in Appalachian industries need to understand their connections and kinship with workers in other parts of the world.

The possibility of an international labor organization seems remote. Some argue that the internationalization of industry and labor forces makes possible linkages between workers all employed by the same company. While capital can defend itself against isolated, national laborers through multiple sourcing, an organized global work force could stop production worldwide.[16] An international workers' organization could support workers' struggles against repressive regimes and fight against second-class status immigrant workers, no-strike legislation, and government mandated "sacrifice" on the part of the working class.

There are some signs of change in Brazil. In 1978-79 workers at Brazilian autoworks struck for wage increases, trade union rights, job security, and democratization of the political system. The union bypassed the state bureaucracy and forced the firms to negotiate directly. The State control of labor was broken.

The organization of an international work force would be difficult. Cultural and language differences are hard to overcome, but understanding the interrelationships and interdependencies is a first step. The development of coalitions of workers within Appalachia, especially in the energy field, would add great strength to the battles of coal miners, oil workers, and nuclear workers who are often employed by the same corporations. Such would be a first step for the region.

Communication between communities and workers trying to deal with environmental and occupational health hazards would begin to develop international networks to fight such hazards. There is an urgent need for systematic monitoring and reporting of the national and worldwide movements of hazardous industries and hazardous wastes.

In Appalachian studies, we must not limit our programs to the exotic, romantic Appalachian cultural history. It is important to develop pride in the region's rich heritage, but it is also important to see Appalachia as part of a worldwide process of development and change. We must deal with economic and political questions and build an understanding of what is happening in the region and how it is related to the global economic system.

We also must try to influence our regional educational institutions to develop broader courses in political economy. They must not concentrate only in training managers and technicians to keep the system running, but must provide a broader education so the managers and technicians can understand what they are doing, why and to and for whom.

NOTES

This paper grows out of a variety of contacts the authors have had with individuals in Latin America and Appalachia. Horton has been in communication with a number of non-formal educators in Latin America over the years and has been interested in the workers' and peoples' movements throughout the area. Various delegations of workers, educators, and religious workers have visited the Highlander Research and Education Center in New Market, Tennessee, a resource for community groups founded and directed by Horton, and through which Lewis has conducted programs in health care. In 1979 Horton visited Brazil, Argentina, and Peru, attending a conference called by the Catholic Bishops in Brazil, and in his visit met and talked with people concerned with the problems of domination and exploitation by multinational corporations. Together, Horton and Lewis attended an International Congress of Folk Medicine in Peru in October 1979, at which they met people from throughout South America and took the opportunity for travel in Peru. --Ed.

1. Carl A. Gerstacker quoted in Richard J. Barnet and Ronald E. Muller, Global Reach, *The Power of the Multinational Corporations* (New York: Simon and Schuster, 1974), p. 16.

2. Ibid., p. 56.

3. James Cook, "A Game Any Number Can Play," *Forbes,* June 25, 1979, pp. 49-55.

4. Harvey D. Shapiro, "Giants Beyond Flag and Country." *New York Times Magazine,* March 18, 1973, pp. 20-35,

5. Merg Hainer and Joanne Koslofsky, Introduction to "Car Wars", *NACLA's* Latin America and Empire Report,* July-August 1979, pp. 3-10; and Rick Knonish and Ken Mericle, "Mapping Out Auto: Latin America--Wheels, Deals, and Class Struggle," Ibid., pp. 10-22. (*North American Congress on Latin America)

6. Shapiro, "Giants Beyond Flag and Country."

7. See Ph. D. dissertations by David Walls, Doug Arnett, and John Wells, and an Office of Technology Assessment report by Lee Balliet, "A Pleasing Tho' Dreadful Sight': Social and Economic Impacts of Coal Production in the Eastern Coalfields," Appalachian Center, University of Kentucky, 1978. For a review of theorists see Steven Jackson, Bruce Russett, Duncal Snidal and David Sylvan, "An Assessment of Empirical Research on Dependencia," *Latin American Research Review* 14 (1979): 7-28.

8. Theotonio Dos Santos, "The Structure of Dependency," *American Economic Review,* May 1970, pp. 231-36.

9. Frank, Andre Gunder. *Latin America: Underdevelopment or Revolution,* (New York: Modern Reader, 1969).

10. News articles in *The Times of the Americas,* December 1979, and January 1980.

11. Barry I. Castleman, "The Export of Hazardous Factories to Developing Nations," *International Journal of Health Services 9* (1979): 569-606.

12. Victor Alba, "Technocrats and Militarists, "A new 'Conquest' of Latin America," *Secolas* 1, March 1970.

13. Marcos Arruda, H. de Sousa, and C Afonso, *The Multinational Corporations and Brazil* (Toronto: Brazilian Studies, L.A. Research Unit, 1975).

14. Roger Burbock and Patricia Flynn, "Seeds of Hunger--Roots of Rebellion," *NACLA's Latin America and Empire Report,* January-February, 1978, pp. 2-10.

15. "For a Society Overcoming Domination," Project Secretariat, International Study Days, 101, Paris, January 1980, p. 11.

16. Merg Hainer and Joanne Koslofsky, "The World Car--Shifting into Overdrive," *NACLA's Latin America and Empire Report,* July-August, 1979, pp. 22-37.

APPALACHIA AND THE THIRD WORLD: ECO-DEVELOPMENT AS AN ALTERNATIVE IN THE NEW ECONOMIC ORDER

by Gene Wilhelm, Jr.

Abstract

This essay proposed that it is only reasonable and just that everyone on the planet earth is entitled to a basic minimum share of the earth's air, water, land, and mineral resources. This eco-share, or minimum level of living for everyone, is best expressed in social rather than economic terms. The concepts of eco-development and eco-growth are positive approaches to solving the basic needs of Appalachia and and the Third World. They concentrate upon the positive viable assets of particular environments and local resources, both human and natural, for meeting the basic needs of the people without altering or destroying the environment.

INTRODUCTION

The twentieth century has been a period of unprecedented economic growth and technological progress which, while bringing benefits to many people, also have caused severe social and environmental consequences.[1] Inequality between the poor and the rich among and within nations is still growing and there is ample evidence of increasing deterioration of the biophysical environment on a world-wide scale.[2] Such conditions affect all of humanity and the entire ecosphere but are epitomized by Appalachia and the Third World.[3]

When discussing the relationship between Appalachia and the Third World, it is evident that there are important differences between regions and countries, and between poor countries and poor regions in wealthy countries.[4] The simple truth is that the world is not environmentally homogeneous. Countries differ in their renewable and non-renewable resources. Some nations always will be struggling against poor soils, unpredictable climates, and extremes of heat and cold. Others never will be self-sufficient in food, energy, or raw materials.[5]

The environmental inequalities in the world are paralleled by socioeconomic and political ones, which are a major obstacle to the satisfaction of basic human needs, especially in Appalachia and the Third World, and a barrier to the harmonious development of mankind.[6] As Schumacher observed:

> One of the unhealthy and disruptive tendencies in virtually all the developing countries is the emergence, in an ever more accentuated fashion, of the "dual economy," in which there are two different patterns of living as widely separated from each other as two different worlds. It is not a matter of some people being rich and others being poor, both being united by a common way of life: it is a matter of two ways of life existing side by side in such a manner that even the humblest member of the one disposes of a daily income which is a high multiple of the income accruing to even the hardest working member of the other.[7]

The relief of the poverty affecting so large a part of humanity is hampered by the present concentration of the world's economic strength in the developed nations and by the considerable waste of natural resources there. The western nations, Japan, and Russia, for example, account for only one fourth of the world's population but use 90 percent of the entire world's natural resources. The United States of America, with 6 percent of the world's population, uses over one third of the world's resources and produces half of the world's pollution.[8] As a result, the typical American consumer has from twenty-five to fifty times as great an environmental impact on our world life-supporting sytems as a peasant in any developing country.[9]

Therefore, it is the thesis of this essay that regardless of such environmental, social, economic, and political differences, Appalachia and the Third World are members in the "commonwealth of poverty, dependency, maldevelopment, and ecology."[10] Further, it is only reasonable and just that everyone on the planet earth is entitled to a basic minimum share of the world's air, water, land, and mineral resources. This eco-share, or minimum level of living for everyone, is best expressed in social rather than economic terms. In this regard the concepts of eco-development and eco-growth are positive approaches to solving the basic needs of Appalachia and the Third World. They concentrate upon the positive viable assets of particular environments and local resources, both natural and human, for meeting the basic needs of the people without altering or destroying their environment.[11]

DEVELOPMENT THEORY

Debate over the nature of change in Appalachia and the Third World has been growing among scholars since the 1960's. One scholar has examined recently the contemporary explanatory models of Appalachian poverty and underdevelopment and has drawn an analogy between peripheral countries in the Third World system and peripheral regions, such as represented by Appalachia, within developed nations.[12] Many social scientists, in fact, have questioned recently the so-called "development-modernization paradigm." That particular model, developed in the 1950s and refined during the 1960s, was based, among other things, on the belief that people in an undeveloped country or region could attain a modern outlook through education and work. It stressed the development of institutions in which the modernized citizens could lead their country or region from their traditional attitudes into a "westernized" society. The role of missionaries, teachers, health personnel, engineers, and lawyers in this process has been evident both in Appalachia and the Third World.[13] The modernization theorists argues, in essence, that when certain conditions involving education, employment, and organized institutions prevailed, a society would begin the process of moving from a traditional to a modern condition.

The development-modernization approach was challenged in the late 1960s, especially by leftist social scientists who argued that it put too much emphasis on individuals and institutions in isolation and ignored the economic and historical conditions under which social change took place. They advanced, instead, the "dependency theory," which stressed the dominance of Third World countries by the capitalist economics of the West, and argued that those economics prevented developing nations from taking independent action. In its simplest form, the dependency theory maintains that developing countries are puppets incapable of controlling their own destiny.

Neither the modernization nor dependency models have adequately explained the process of socioeconomic and political change in the Third World or in Appalachia, for that matter. The modernization theory places inordinate attention on the borrowed institutions that are bought to a society rather than on the exerience of the society receiving those structures. On the other hand, the dependency model suggests that all Third World nations are locked in irrevocably as agents of a global system. However, it has been shown in Iran, as elsewhere, that such nations can and do revolt from the global system. On close examination many concepts, attitudes, and values expressed in these two paradigms are found in the subculture of poverty, regional development, and internal colonialism models often applied to Appalachia.[14]

Most recently a wide-ranging debate has materialized over different paths to development. Third World countries are talking about "self-reliant change," or "culturally rooted change," or "alternative development." In fact, there has been a growing demand, especially since 1972, for a coordinated and comprehensive world approach to the problems of poverty, food and nutrition, trade and commerce, investment, industry, and technology.[15] This, in turn, has led to developing countries demanding fundamental structural changes. The developing world does not want a new deal but a new order. It wants an organized system of new relationships based on a global recognition and acceptance of the principle of interdependence in economic influence, collective responsibility, and shared decision-making.[16] The recent "awakening" among people of Appalachia demands similar recognition of authority.

Thus the United Nations Declaration for a New International Economic Order (NIEO) was proclaimed on May 9, 1974, at the Sixth Special Session of the UN General Assembly in order to mitigate the economic difficulties of the developing nations by immedite and effective international measures. Again, the NIEO was reinforced in September 1975 at the Seventh Special Session of the UN General Assembly.[17] The NIEO demands were essentially: transfers of technology from the West; price indexing; energy development; either a debt moratorium or a minimum of an additional one billion dollars in aid for the poorest nations; and many associated programs. Viewed in detail, the NIEO appeared to be a drastic solution. A black writer who favored the changes stated candidly at the time: "The demands are so fundamental that they pose very grave problems for the future of capitalism and ultimately for the political stability of the constitutional democracies of the West."[18]

Proponents of the NIEO also called for a new international standard of conduct in law as well as in economics and politics. The very fabric of international law was seen to be biased in favor of the developed world. In the economic arena, for example, it was suggested that the terms of international trade be changed and controls of the conduct of multinational corporations made more comprehensive. Politically, greater power of decision was to be given to the poorer, newer nations through increased authority wielded by international organization.[19] Although a confrontation occured between the developed and Third World nations in 1975-1976 through a series of encounters in the United Nations, a new terrain of international relations has been gradually revealed. Both the developed and Third World nations seem to have moderated their positions somewhat in extended and difficult negotiations, but it is too early to know the final outcome. Regardless, even if the NIEO could be fully implemented, there is still an apparent lack of awareness, sensitivity, and comprehension on the part of all nations about world ecosystems and man's role in them and too much emphasis on economic determinism.

ECOLOGY VERSUS ECONOMICS

In determing the appropriate size and growth rate in development, we encounter some of the basic differences between economic and ecological viewpoints. Different ecological cycles have different optimal rates, which must not be exceeded if we are to avoid overload or breakdown. But the tendency in our present linear economic system is to maximize growth rates by using and abusing these natural cycles in our air, water, and land. As the rate of production increases, supplies of finite resources diminish and the amount of waste and heat pouring into the air, water, and land increases.[20]

To prevent ecosystem breakdown, economists would pay maintenance costs while continuing to increase production rates. Ecologists agree that this solution would work if mankind had infinite resources, infinite energy, unlimited funds, were not governed by the second law of energy (which automatically yields more environmental disorder or entropy per unit of order established by man), and had a clearer idea of the actual limits of the ecosphere.[21] To be both economical and ecological, man must stablize, not maximize, growth by deliberately operating some environmentally disruptive activities (such as strip mining in Appalachia) at a slower rate so that energy consumption is reduced. Further, optimum growth for private profit is not necessarily the optimum for the social economy and quality of life, because many external costs, such as pollution, are shifted to the consumer. The "ideal goal" is simultaneously to optimize both growth and the quality of life for all.[22]

This ideal focuses attention on two other major differences between economics and ecology: a difference in time perspective and a difference over the best means for justly distributing the world's resources and wealth. Economics is centered on the short term while ecology is focused on the long term. Economics deals with day-to-day activities and thus economists find it difficult making five-year plans. Yet ecologist insist that 25, 50, or 100-year plans be made. Many western economists think that the best way to get a reasonable distribution of the world's wealth and resources to the poor is to increase the economic growth rates of the industrialized countries (maximizing the linear system for a few), so that the spillover that trickles down from this growth will raise the absolute level of living for everyone. Ecologists challenge this view. Because resource supplies and allowable recycling rates cannot exceed certain natural limits, man must find a better, quicker, and safer way for fairly distributing the world's wealth than letting it trickle down. The closer man comes to the limits of the system, the less effective the conventional cure for poverty becomes, and the more maldistribution of wealth becomes the key environmental and political issue.

It appears that all existing economic systems (capitalism, socialism, and communism) have the same fatal flaw: the need to increase growth and pollution continually. Increasing pollution, for example, is a problem in both industrialized capitalist countries and industrialized socialist and communist countries. In truth, as Echeverria states, "the destruction of the environment is a universal tragedy."[23] The author continues:

> Much of today's problems arise from the concept that humanity's first priority is economic growth. Growth we must have...But a nation's growth is more than the abstract and complacent statistics of Gross National Product. Rather than this narrow economic growth our own objective must be an all-embracing human development....

Economic growth with its meaningless figures has come to dominate our social mentality. It has created one of the most serious problems of our century: the acceptance of natural destruction as an inevitable sacrifice to economic development....At present we are sold ecology in tiny doses, like pills from a chemist. This is a totally inadequate response. We need a truly ecological programme, one which ceases to regard our planet as just another consumer object.[24]

DEVELOPING A NEW MODEL

Present growth patterns and practices are self-destructive and cannot be sustained. On the other hand, there is no society that is likely to accept "no growth" as an option. The only real alternative then is a new approach to growth, what I call "eco-growth," both in developed and developing societies.

The eco-growth approach is based upon removal of the artificial and self-defeating conflict between ecology and economics which is now built into our system of economic decision-making. Man must make ecology and economics the allies they can and should be in evolving an approach to growth, the prime goal of which will be to produce a better quality of life for people.[25]

A promising approach towards environmentally sound eco-development and eco-growth is the application of the concept of self-help in Appalachia and the Third World. This is designed to aid the people of a developing region of a country or the world by relying as much as possible on local resources, both natural and human, to meet the basic needs of the people without harming their environment.[26] After all, development does not start with goods; it starts with people and their education, organization, and discipline. If aid is given to introduce certain new economic activities, these will be beneficial and viable only if they can be sustained by the already existing educational level of fairly broad groups of people, and they will be truly valuable only if they promote and spread advances in education, organization, and discipline.[27]

One must look outside the developed and Third World nations for an example of present-day eco-development and eco-growth. The Peoples' Republic of China has to a considerable degree been able to integrate ecological and social objectives in her economic development strategy. This has been a natural outcome of a systematic plan to mobilize large numbers of people and make them participate in the development process and influence the necessary changes.[28]

China's development strategy includes two concepts which are almost lacking in most other developing countries where the approaches to economic development have been heavily influenced by models from already industrialized countries. First, China's manpower has been efficiently mobilized in nearly all spheres of economic activity, but in particular for rural development. Second, China has systematically utilized local resources and waste materials of all kinds in order to optimize the economic results. The mobilization of large numbers of people for various development projects has its basis in a system of well-organized local planning with a considerable degree of local control. This has established an environment which can efficiently control some of the undesired effects of economic development and growth and provide long-term viability for modern technology.[29]

Underlying the Chinese concepts of local planning and control of development are at least three major factors which were nearly recognized by the central government. First, the natural environments within each locality (region, county, commune) have differences in climate, topography, soil, vegetation, and mineral resources. Naturally these have important implications for economic and social planning. Second, there is no uniformity in the level of economic and social development and identical treatment of the localities would lead to difficulties in determining the priorities. A third and possibly more important motivation for local planning lies in China's normative development strategy which stresses the improvement in the general well-being of people throughout the country. access to services, culture, educational opportunities, and a high degree of participation. The meaning of development consequently includes much more than mere economic growth. People become involved in the decision-making process and determine their own development priorities and strategies.

The present Chinese view on environment and development is apparent in the following statement:

> Economic development and environmental protection are interrelated and promote each other. The former gives rise to the environmental problem and the latter constitutes an important condition for developing the economy; economic development increases the capability to protect the environment, and environmental improvement in turn promotes economic development. This is the independent relationship between the two.[30]

This interaction is obvious in the area of irrigation and flood control, where the cumulative effect of massive farmland construction is now beginning to add a considerable degree of stability to China's agriculture. In the past five years, more than 100 million people in China have in the winter-spring seasons taken part in construction work to improve farmland and establish irrigation and drainage facilities. These rural masses, mainly organized by brigades and communes although coordinated at higher levels, have, on the average, been able to extend the irrigated area every year by more than 1.3 million hectares and achieved flood control in another 1.3 million hectares.[31] Similarly, mass mobilization has been used for the successful eradication fo schistosomiasis. Here too, large numbers of people have been mobilized and organized to drain and collect the snail-infested muds and dispose of them in other places. In this way it has been possible to achieve an almost complete eradication with little or no use of chemicals.

China's soil cover was extremely poor in many areas of the country when the new regime took over. In order to reduce the silt content in the rivers, it was necessary to plant trees or other types of vegetation so as to prevent soil erosion or sand drifting. This has been done on a very considerable scale, particularly after the introduction of the peoples' communes which made it possible to mobilize large rural manpower forces to improve conditions to their own long-term benefit. In fact, the area covered by trees and other forms of natural vegetation has almost doubled since 1949 when forests covered roughly 9 percent of the total land area. This would, of course, not have been possible if the bushes and tree saplings were collected for firewood. Consequently, the development of local coal mines and an efficient distribution of coal at low prices has been a major contributing factor.[32]

Making use of various types of waste products has parallels in almost all areas of Chinese economic planning. The use of night soil as fertilizer is well-known and has until recently provided Chinese agriculture with a major share of added nutrients. The use of local resources and waste materials has immediate economic benefits aside from their ecological considerations. In sum, the Chinese leadership has opted for retaining a majority of the country's population in rural areas for a considerable period of time. Accordingly, the countryside has been provided with the necessary infrastructure and financial resources for self-sustained development.

Eco-development and eco-growth demand that conservation become a way of life and incentives for it must be built into our economic system. In practical terms, this will mean a redesign of industrial systems in which the residues of one process become the raw materials of another. Technologies for recycling and reusing materials and abatement of pollution must be integrated into such systems, not merely added onto them.

On the local, regional, national, and international levels, the eco-growth approach will require new dimensions of cooperation between one sector of society and another. It will require a revamping of the present system of arrangements and institutions to enable them to better support and serve the interests and aspirations of the developing world, whether it be in Appalachia or the Third World. A New International Economic Order is a necessity as much for the industrialized countries which are resisting it as it is for the developing countries which are pressing for it. The healthy functioning of our interdependent technological society requires the full participation and active cooperation of the people who live in the developing world. This dictates that we heed their demands for a more just and equitable share of the benefits which this modern technological civilization makes possible.

Finally, we need an additional concept to help organize our affairs, one that would directly measure the quality to life resulting from our total activities and environment. Certainly this would require some subjective measurements. As one example of an attempt being made throughout the world to develop new means of measuring progress, the Overseas Development Council has established an index of the physical quality of life that uses infant mortality, life expectancy, and literacy as measures. The index shows, for example, that Sri Lanka, whose GNP per capita is near the bottom of the scale at $130, has a physical quality of life index of 83, well above the 67 average for the upper-middle-income countries whose average GNP per capita is many times higher.[33] Other authors have suggested a Gross National Quality Index in which we would list and put a price tag on all the "deficits" included in the GNP. The total of these undesirable effects would be subtracted from the GNP to obtain the Gross National Quality or GNQ.[34] Fortunately, a small number of scholars are working on this crucial facet of eco-development.[35]

An eco-growth society will require important changes in the attitudes, values, and expectations of the people, particularly of the industrialized world and the more privileged sectors within the developing world. As Strong indicates:

> We must rediscover our communal values and downgrade our competitive drives. We must learn to applaud and look up to those who adopt lifestyles that are modest in terms of the amount of space they monopolize or the amount of materials and energy they consume; ostentatiously wasteful and indulgent living should become socially reprehensible in all our societies. There should be an acute sensitivity to all activities which create risks of damage to our natural heritage, or impair the quality of life for others.[36]

The new thinking and doing required for aid and development in Appalachia and the Third World must be different from the old because it will take basic needs of mankind seriously. It will not go on mechanically saying: "What is good for the rich nations certainly must be good for the poor." It will care for people because people are the primary and ultimate resource of any country. Development cannot be an act of creation; it cannot be ordered, bought, or planned. Development requires a process of evolution, education, organization, and discipline. It follows from this that development is not primarily a problem for economists, least of all for economists who follow the linear economic model so common today. Economists have their usefulness at certain stages of development, but only if the general guidelines of a development policy "to involve the entire local population" are already firmly established.[37]

As Strong concluded:[38]

> Today, for the first time in history, we do have the knowledge, the resources and the technology and management capacity to assure that every person on this planet has access to the basic resources and environmental conditions required for a good and satisfying life. Our future really turns now on whether we will have the enlightened moral and political will and the sense of our own ultimate self-interest that is needed to enable us to change our ways before it is too late.

CONCLUSIONS

What is urgently needed today is a New International Development Strategy that would examine, evaluate, and eventually select appropriate development patterns and lifestyles everywhere in the world. Such development patterns and lifestyles cannot be uniform for all countries or even all regions within countries. Since prevailing conditions differ from place to place and culture to culture, alternative approaches become necessary. What is at issue is not only the need for alternative approaches but also the need for a choice between them and the bases of such choice. It is clear that rational choices must stem from a process of harmonization of social aspirations, particularly of economic policies and considerations with environmental goals and objectives. If environment is thought of as the frame of the resource base available to man, development is the process by which resources are used to give man a better quality of life, a better environment. In short, sustained development needs a sustained resource base.

There is an emerging consensus in the United Nations Environment Programme that environmental protection and economic development are not only compatible but also interdependent and mutually reinforcing in character. Conflicts, options, and trade-offs are more apparent than real and exist only if objectives of both development and environmental protection are considered within an inadequate time frame. A certain poignancy is added to the situation by the fact that, while the developed countries have the technology and the financial means to retreat from a wrong decision, the developing countries have none.

High consumption societies or sectors of societies in developed and developing countries must take stock of the world's nonrenewable resource base and the carrying capacity of the biosphere as a whole. It is becoming increasingly clear that the pressure on the resource base of the planet and the deterioration of the environment is multiplying at such a rate as to threaten an eventual collapse of life-sustaining systems. The balance of responsibility, in this situation, would appear to rest more with the developed countries which account for the lion's share of the consumption of energy, minerals, and chemcials and also for a large share of pollution.

Two of the essential steps needed for the realization of alternative, and hopefully more acceptable, development patterns and lifestyles for the next decade are being considered in 1980 by the UNEP:

1. A realistic, long-term, and truly scientific assessment of the risk and uncertainties involved in all processes of change which result from the interaction of man on life-supporting systems; and

2. Patterns of development and lifestyles, covered political, economic, and social structures, production and consumption patterns, transfer and adaptation of appropriate technology, and energy/resource use, are being identified. Through a series of seminars in various parts of the world, patterns can thus be geared to minimize or negate environmental damage and help avoid the emergence of hard options between economic and ecological considerations.

NOTES

1. "The Belgrade Charter: A Global Framework for Environmental Education," *Connect* 1 (January 1976): 1.

2. *The State of the Environment, 1976* (United Nations Environment Programme, Nairobi, Kenya); *The State of the Environment: Selected Topics, 1977* (United Nations Environment Programme, Nairobi, Kenya); *The State of the Environment: Selected Topics, 1978* (United Nations Environment Programme, Nairobi, Kenya); and *The State of the Environment: Selected Topics, 1979* (United Nations Environment Programme, Nairobi, Kenya).

3 See David S. Walls, "Central Appalachia: A Peripheral Region within an Advanced Capitalist Society," *Journal of Sociology and Social Welfare* 4 (November 1976): 232-246; and David S. Walls, "Three Models in Search of Appalachian Development: Critique and Synthesis," a paper originally presented at the joint session of the Rural Sociological Society and the Society for the Study fo Social Problems, Montreal, August 25, 1974, and revised in May 1976.

4. John Friedman, "Poor Regions and Poor Nations," *Southern Economic Journal* 32 (April 1966): 465-470.

5. Lester R. Brown, *The Twenty-Ninth Day* (New York: W. W. Norton & Co., 1978), pp. 202-205.

6. See Luis Echeverria, "The Ecological Rights of Man," *Uniterra* (October 1978): 4-5 Echeverria was the President of Mexico (1970-1976) and "father" of the New International Economic Order.

7. E. F. Schumacher, *Small Is Beautiful: Economics As If People Mattered* (New York: Perennial Library, Harper & Row, 1975), p. 164.

8. G. Tyler Miller, Jr., *Living in the Environment: Concepts, Problems, and Alternatives* (Belmost, California; Wadsworth Publishing Co., 1975), p. 13. The author recently published a second edition (late 1979) of this book in which he states on p. 1:" . . .the 220 million Americans, who make up only 5 percent of our total (world) population, used about 35 percent of all our supplies and produced over one-third of all our artifical pollution last year."

Regardless of the exact statistics, it is still obvious that the USA is singly most responsible for impairing our earth's life-supporting system.

9. Ibid., p. 13.
10. Wayne M. Clergern, "What is the Third World?" paper presented at the First National Conference on the Third World, Omaha, Nebraska, October 1977, p. 3.
11. "UNEP Paper Offers New Development Concepts," *Uniterra* (August 1977): 3.
12. Walls, "Three Models," pp. 1-74.
13. See Gene Wilhelm, Jr., "Folk Culture History of the Blue Ridge Mountains," *Appalachian Journal* 2 (Spring 1975) pp. 210-212; and Gene Wilhelm, Jr., "Appalachian Isolation: Fact or Fiction?" in *An Appalachian Symposium,* ed. J. W. Williamson (Boone, N.C.: Appalachian State University Press, 1977), pp. 77-90.
14. Walls, "Three Models," pp. 1-74.
15. "The New International Economic Order: Policy Implications for African Agriculture," *Ninth FAO Regional Conference for Africa, Item 16 of the Provisional Agenda,* Freetown, Sierra Leone, November 2-12, 1976, p. 1.
16. This plea started as early as the mid-1960s; see United Nations Conference on Trade and Development (UNCTAD), *Towards a New Trade Policy for Development* (New York: United Nations, 1964).
17. Clegern, "What is the Third World?," p. 13.
18. Preston Green, "The New World Economic Order: Capitalism's Greatest Challenge," *First World: An International Journal of Black Thought* 2 (Spring 1978): 6-10.
19. Joseph S. Nye and Robert Keohane, "Transnational Relations and World Politics: An Introduction," *International Organization,* No. 25 (1971), pp. 329-349.
20. Gene Wilhelm, Jr., "Eco-Development and the New World Order," paper presented at the First National Conference on the Third World, Omaha, Nebraska, October 27-29, 1977, p. 6.
21. Miller, *Living in the Environment,* pp. 325-326.
22. Ibid., p. 326.
23. Echeverria, "The Ecological Rights of Man," pp. 4-5.
24. Ibid., p. 5.
25. Maurice F. Strong, "New Growth Policy," *Uniterra* (August 1978): 4-5.
26. "UNEP Paper Offers New Development Concepts," p. 3.
27. Schumacher, *Small Is Beautiful,* p. 168.
28. Jon Sigurdson, "Eco-Development Chinese Style," *Uniterra* 1 (November) 4-5.
29. Ibid., p. 4.
30. Kee-ping Chu, "Environment and Development," *Peking Review,* No. 20, 1976.
31. Sigurdson, "Eco-Development Chinese Style," p. 5.
32. Ibid., p. 5.
33. Russell W. Peterson, "Impacts of Technology," *Uniterra* 4 (October 1979): 5.
34. U. S. Department of Health, Education, and Welfare, *A Report On Measurement and the Quality of Life* (Washington, D. C.: Government Printing Office, 1972).
35. Miller, *Living in the Environment,* p. 332.
36. Strong, "New Growth Policy," p. 5.
37. Wilhelm, "Eco-Development and the New World Order," p. 12.
38. Strong, "New Growth Policy," p. 5.

THE ECONOMY OF WEST VIRGINIA
AND THE OPPRESSION/LIBERATION OF WOMEN

Rick Simon
Betty Justice

Abstract

Women in West Virginia historically have participated in the paid labor force at a rate less than women in the United States as a whole and at a rate less than women in all other individual states. This fact is explained by the dominant influence of the coal industry on the state's economy. Women have been excluded from direct participation in the coal industry, but more significantly the structure of the industry industry hindered the development of a diversified economy which included work of the type traditionally performed by women.

By June 1979, 50.7 percent of women in the United States sixteen years of age or older were in the paid labor force.[1] Unlike technology which creates an infrastructure and a potential for change in social relations, the emergence of women from the family into the paid labor force and the absorption of previous family economic functions into the commodity market necessarily change the very patterns of social life-how we spend time together, raise our children, have our fun-in fact our basic values. However, a discussion of the scope of such changes is not our object. Rather we want to examine a tiny aspect of this phenomenal change-the failure of West Virginia to conform to this pattern, in fact to lag to such an extent that it has for all of this century engaged less of its female population in the paid labor force than has the United States as a whole and for the most part at a rate less than all the individual states. (See Table I)

To understand the female labor participation rate in West Virginia, we believe that it is necessary to analyze the role/oppression of women within the capitalist mode of production generally, i.e., the social organization of the economy and of social classes. Our view of the status of women within the capitalist mode of production is that:

1. The role of women in the capitalist mode of production has been in the home performing unpaid labor in the maintenance and reproduction of the society's labor power. Their role in the paid labor market has historically been that of a reserve army of labor.

2. Women, particularly since World War II, have increasingly been incorporated into the paid labor market; this increased participation is in part a response to changes in the structure and needs of capitalist production.

3. The history of women in West Virginia clearly illustrates the twofold oppression of women, as workers within the home and as wage laborers.

4. In Appalachia, particularly in the coal fields, there is also a relative oppression of women in the labor market. First, women have been excluded from employment in the largest and highest paying industry. Second and more significant in terms of women's current rate of participation in the paid labor market, the coal economy does not stimulate but actually hinders the development of a diversified economy which includes "women's work"--jobs in the clerical, service, sales, and light manufacturing occupations which account for the overwhelming proportion of women engaged in the paid labor force in the United States.

Two conclusions follow from this analysis:

1. To increase the job opportunities for women in West Virginia, it is not enough to open up the traditional male occupations to women. Rather, to correct the labor force participation deficiency for women, it is necessary to restructure the entire economy.

2. In order to eliminate sexual oppression both in West Virginia and the United States as a whole, it is necessary to change the mode of production. This does not mean that women should submerge the goals of their sex, nor the immediate struggles for women's rights are unimportant, but rather that systemic problems are corrected only by systemic change.

ROLE OF WOMEN IN THE CAPITALIST MODE OF PRODUCTION

The capitalist system of production is characterized by wage labor wherein a worker sells time to an employer. In the labor process, a good or service is produced which may satisfy some social need but more importantly must be sellable in the marketplace at a profit, the motive force of the capitalist system of production. The analysis of the role of women within the society is therefore incomplete without an examination of their position in and relation to production for profit. The economic oppression of women under capitalism is twofold: "outside the market place" through the indirect production of profit in the home *and* "inside the market place" in the direct production of profit.

Historically, under capitalism, the man has engaged in paid labor, earning an income to maintain a family of "workers." Women's labor, traditionally within the home, has been unpaid and officially considered "non-work" since it is performed outside the "market" context.[2] However, women's work within the home has been a necessary function for the maintenence and continuance of capitalism. The woman within the home has played an important role in maintaining the workers who produce profit directly and a primary role in the physical and nutritive reproduction of the future labor force. "Every individual man is forced to use his wife's expenditure of herself in the family in order to 'earn' money in the form of wages. He is dependent for his survival on her.[3] The extent of this non-work has been estimated by the Chase Manhattan Bank to take 99.6 hours per week.[4] By utilizing the unpaid services of the wife, the cost of reproducing and maintaining labor is reduced and profits correspondingly increased.

Although the primary role of women has been in the home, women have also participated in the direct production of profit, particularly serving as a reserve army of labor. Women from the poorest groups in the society, especially black women and recently immigrated women, have long experienced attachment to the paid labor market. For instance, as early as 1900, 20 percent of all women in the United States were in the paid labor force. Women, however, have found (as have men to a lesser extent) the labor market open to them only in certain places, sectors, and times. Much of women's work outside the home has been and yet is an extension of work previously performed within the home. Examples are the production of clothing, hospital work, restaurant work, and jobs required in the socialization of the young, such as teaching. "The predominance of women in the lower grades of teaching and social work is no coincidence. These are capitalism's human face in labour...Women are the soft cops..."[5] As the nature of work has changed with the impact of technology and as expanded consciousness and economic necessity have encouraged long term attachment to the labor market, the range of occupations open to women have changed.

However, the capitalist mode of production is not necessarily evenly developed throughout a society, and it is sometimes necessary to examine the particular form of the mode of production within a region to understand the role of women in its economy. The capitalist mode of production was introduced into West Virginia in the late 1800s with the advent of the coal industry. This mode of productin dominated the organization of production in the state by World War I. But in West Virginia, the development of the capitalist mode of production was limited by the class structure of the coal industry which impeded the development of internal markets and limited capitalist penetration of new spheres of production. The role/oppression of all workers in West Virginia, but particularly of women, has been and is yet affected by this new but incomplete expression of capitalism within the state.

Women in West Virginia have faced the same two fold oppression in the home and in the paid labor market. But as the development of the capitalistic mode of production in West Virginia has been limited, the rate of participation by women in the paid labor force has remained throughout the twentieth century one of the lowest of all the states in the United States. For instance in 1970, the state's women had a labor force participation rate of 29.4 percent the lowest in the nation (See Table 1). By 1976, the rate had increased to 28.1 percent but yet remained the lowest in the United States. This backwardness is demonstrated not only by the participation rate of women but by that of men as well.[6] Despite massive out-migration of workers of both sexes, a pattern resulting in a higher participation rate for the remaining population, West Virginia has for much of this century ranked near the bottom in terms of the male labor participation rate. For instance, 1976 figures indicate that West Virginia had a rate less than that of all other states other than Florida where a massive retired population pulls down the rate (See Table 1). This figure for West Virginia is especially significant since it reflects the rate during a period of boom in the coal industry.

In order to understand its impact on women, capitalist production in West Virginia is examined in its initial period of development from 1880 to 1930, in the transitional period following mechanization and the consolidation of wage labor relations, and in the period of the last two decades characterized by the penetration of capitalism into all aspects of Appalachian life, particularly the family.

LABOR PARTICIPATION IN THE COMPANY TOWN ERA

The development of the coal resources in West Virginia led to significant social and economic changes. In 1880, the state was characterized by a subsistence agricultural economy with some commercial trading. By 1930, the economy was characterized by capitalist relations, particularly the development of wage labor in the mining of coal. Industrialization increased, though not significantly, the participation of women in the paid labor market (See Table 1). This fact is attributable to the impact of the dominant industry--coal--on the West Virginia economy. First, the coal industry itself did not directly employ women, not as miners nor as clerks in company stores or offices. Second, the coal industry was located primarily in rural areas where labor participation rates generally tend to be lower. Moreover, the coal industry limited the development of an internal market and the expansion of capitalism into new spheres of production. The coal operators adopted policies which monopolized the use of the land and the labor force.[7] Access to land and labor, even if not consciously prevented by coal operators, was difficult in the environment of closed coal towns. The lack of a diversified economy, manufacturing and retailing and wholesaling, further limited the job opportunities for women since the lack of a consuming population meant that the service, clerical, and sales industries (women's work) remained at a primitive level. Requiring large numbers of workers most of whom were male and many of whom had wives and daughters, the industry created a concentration of women in communities with virtually no job opportunities for them.

The very low labor participation rates of women in West Virginia, in fact, hide the crucial role of women in the coal economy. Responsible for producing and reproducing a labor force for coal mining, women produced goods within the home. Though not unlike the role of women in working class families throughout the country, women's significance in the coal field economy was probably much greater. Profitability in the coal industry, routinely characterized by overproduction until 1930, was based on the direct reduction of wages to or below a cultural subsistence.[8] In this context, home production meant sheer survival.

Maintaining profits through the reduction of wages required tight control of the labor force and an ability to prevent unionization. One aspect of this policy was the elimination of competing demands for the labor force. Another was relocation to avoid unions. For instance, there were important shifts in production from unionized coal fields in Illinois and Pennsylvania to "wilderness" West Virginia following the first UMW national agreement in 1898 and again in the 1920's.[9] Locating in "wilderness" areas provided several advantages, particularly the opportunity to recruit a labor force[10] and the opportunity to establish company towns suited to the control of labor either through repression or paternalism, and was by design meant to limit job opportunities for miners and their families.

A study of women in coal miners' families based on the 1922 United States Coal Commission investigation states:

> Women are naturally an important fact in an industry like coal mining which of necessity is carried on in many instances in isolated localities. The presence of the family is essential to keeping the mine workers in these regions, and help of the wives in maintaining normal homes means greater efficiency on the part of the mine workers themselves.[11]

This study interprets the structure of the coal town as a geoeconomic necessity; we assert that it is a social necessity of the mode of production. Both views agree that the family was necessry for the production and reproduction of an efficient work force.[12]

Women provided to the family and to the coal economy the production of goods within the home. Though there is no data to quantify the extent of this production, it is safe to assume that activities such as gardening, food preservation, baking, and domestic textiles were considerable. Many wives also contributed directly to family income through work performed in the only place of opportunity--the home.[13] In 1922, 21.3 percent of the wives of West Virginia miners were engaged in some paid work.[14] Of these, 97 percent of them were employed in the home, most providing for boarders and lodgers and a few doing only laundering or other services.

> In the more isolated bituminous mining regions, this involves not only cooking and the care of sleeping quarters but doing the laundry for boarders and lodgers. In many camps it is customary for boarders to bring their own food, the wife of the household cooking for each boarder as well as her own family. While this system probably makes for greater satisfaction among the boarders it must entail much more cooking on the part of the housewife than if the same food were cooked to be eaten by family and boarders alike.[15]

Thus it is clear that women in coal communities worked-often without pay and when for pay, in the home performing work of the same kind. Women worked out of the economic necessity created by an industry which directly required the families of its employees to absorb some of the costs of production while at the same time, both by intention and by its inherent structure, limiting the job opportunities of family members, particularly those of women.

TRANSITION TO A "MODERN" ECONOMY

In the 1930's, the coal operators were no longer able to prevent the unionization of their labor force. Moreover, coal operators competed not only with each other but increasingly with the oil and gas industries as well as for markets. Faced with these changes, the operators initiated mechanization through the adoption of machine loading technology. A corollary development was the increase of profits through increased productivity and less reliance on the reduction of wages to create profits. Along with these changes, operators sold company houses to miners and loosened the tight control that they had formerly held on coal communities. The increasing use of the automobile also encouraged the decline of the company town.

These changes had two important implications for women in the coal fields. First, the unionization resulted in wages equal to or above the subsistence level, thereby reducing the necessity for supplementing the family income. Secondly, the quality of life in coal communities improved with the introduction of public services such as running water. Both of these changes eased the burden of women.

The changes in the coal economy were part of national changes which were reducing the role of the family within the capitalist mode of production. First, there was a decreased scope of production within the family unit. Second, the separation between home and work was expanding. Third, decreased time was required for procreation.[16] Capitalism survives by incorporating ever more spheres of production into commodity production--production for exchange in a market for a profit. As a result, the scope of production within the family declines and the separation of home and work expands. As to the first, the introduction of laborsaving devices (which are themselves often new commodities) has reduced the time required for the care of a family. For instance, innovations make the preservation an preparation of food a minor task today compared to the efforts it required a century ago. But beyond these innovations, capitalism penetrated the family further and produced, as a commodity, foods that are essentially fully prepared, leaving only the labor of heating, serving, and cleanup. But more recently, the drive for profit has penetrated even further into the family. It is estimated that today American families eat more than one third of all their meals in restaurants. Thus the heating, serving, and cleanup have now been incorporated into the profit system.

The increasing commoditization of functions previously performed within the family has meant it has become almost entirely a consuming rather than a producing unit. This pattern is as true for leisure and entertainment activities as it is for the more primary survival functions. Other than church activities, fun and fellowship are pursued almost entirely in a market context. Increased penetration of capitalism into the home has decreased the economic functions of the family and particularly those of the wife who, under capitalism, had performed a majority of domestic economic functions. With the expansion of commodity production has come an increased demand for labor, and women have thus become more integrated, albeit at the margins, into paid commodity production.

THE MODERN ERA

Women's participation in the paid labor market has expanded significantly since World War II. Nationally the increase has been from 35.8 percent in 1945 to 50.8 percent in early 1979. In West Virginia the increase has also been apparent, but as compared to the national figure, the overall labor participation of women in the labor market remains the lowest of any state. In this section we examine the sectors in which women's employment has increased and the reasons for the continued low rate of participation of West Virginia in the paid labor market.

The occupation structure for women in 1960 and 1970 in West Virginia is shown in Table 2. The concentration of women in traditional "women's work" is obvious. Service workers (including household), clerical and kindred, sales, and profession and technical make up 80.8 percent of the state's employment of women in 1970. Although participation of women in the labor force in West Virginia increased overall by 23.1 percent from 1960 to 1970, the largest gains in actual number of jobs were in those categories where women were already employed. There were some shifts reflecting trends in the national economy such as the decline in the proportion of women employed in private household work and the increase of women employed in clerical and kindred occupations.[17]

What explains the low labor participation rate of women in West Virginia in 1970? Unlike the earlier part of this century, the coal industry no longer dominated the State's economy. Employment in the coal industry was in 1970 about 10 percent of total employment. The company towns had long since been transformed into "independent" communities. Although the link between the coal industry and labor participation rates is not as clear now as it once was, the relationship still exists. Although there have been important changes in the coal economy, they have not changed the nature of the mode of production in West Virginia relative to other regions of the national economy. The lack of industrial diversification which characterized the coal fields in the pre 1930s perists today.[18]

The lack of industrial diversity in West Virginia today is a legacy of the past. Even after fifty years of expanding coal production which ended in 1927, West Virginia by the 1940s was still relatively deficient in its social infrastructure (roads, schools, health facilities) and in its small internal market. The decreased demand for coal and the huge out-migration of the population in the 1950s served to intensify the state's deficiencies.

Even the recent growth of coal employment has not changed the industrial structure nor increased the job opportunities for women. The coal industry is still characterized by a blue collar work force accounting for more than 90 percent of its employees, the highest proportion of any industry. "Women's work"--office work, clerks, sales--is virtually nonexistent in the industry, certainly within the state where extraction is done primarily by corporations based outside the state. Moreover, coal does not generate much of a demand for suppliers to the industry nor does it attract an "industrial complex" centered on coal inputs.[19] Finally, much of the value-added tax generated by coal mining leaves the region in the form of interest dividends, royalties, and rents, limiting the internal market in its size and diversity.

The structure of the coal economy is such as to limit the job opportunities for, and labor participation of, women. This point is illustrated in Table 3, wherein counties are classified as either coal or non-coal counties, the former producing at least 2.4 million tons of coal in 1970. The counties are also classified as rural or urban, the latter if at least 30 percent of the population live in urban areas.

Using the *County and City Data Book*, the labor participation rates of women were computed and averages for four different types of counties determined.[20] Table 3 illustrates that in rural counties, the labor participation of women is lower in the coal counties than it is in the non-coal counties. This shows that the extent to which a county is rural does not alone explain the non-participation of women in the labor force. Rather the nature of the coal economy itself is an important variable affecting female labor participation in coal and non-coal counties.[21]

The impact of the coal industry on industrial structure can also be seen by an examination of the industrial structure itself. The 1970 census data reveals that the central Appalachian economy is less diversified in terms of population employed in different industries.[22] Central Appalchia had less of its labor force employed in retail and wholesale, professional services, manufacturing, domestic and entertainment, finance, insurance and real estate, business and repair services and construction than did the nation as a whole. However, central Appalachia had more than thirteen times the national average in forest and mining industries and, curiously enough, educational services.

The impact of the coal economy on job opportunities for women is illustrated in the number of women employed in professional and technical (including educational) occupations. Nationally, the figure was 15.4 percent, whereas West Virginia had a higher rate of 16.6 percent. Amazingly, the statistics for rural coal counties had an even higher percentage of women workers in this occupational category. Five rural coal counties (Logan, McDowell, Mingo, Raleigh--no longer rural--and Wyoming) actually had more than 20 percent of their women workers in this occupational category. In fact, membership in this category was probably made up almost entirely of school-teachers and health professionals. Ironically, in counties where health and educational services were notoriously lacking, that occupation accounted for a higher percentage of the female work force than was true of the rest of the state and of the nation. This anomaly is explained, not by the fact that there was an exceptional number of professional and technical workers in an absolute sense or a high per population ratio, but by the fact that there were so few jobs available to women in other occupational categories that their access to participation in this particular category skewed the percentages.[23] Clearly, the dominant mining industry has not engendered a balanced economy within the region.

CONCLUSIONS

Women within the capitalist mode of production suffer a twofold oppression, in the home and in the labor market. In West Virginia, women suffer a twofold discrimination within the labor market. They have until recently been excluded from the primary source of employment in the state, the coal industry. Moreover, the coal industry has influenced the structure of the economy such as to prevent diversification and thus has reduced further the opportunities for employment available to women.

The entry of women into blue collar jobs in West Virginia in industries such as mining, basic steel, chemicals, and construction will not significantly change women's labor participation rates relative to the national average. There are a limited number of jobs in any of these industries, and the numbers are increasing in only a few of them. Moreover, since women's entry is at the bottom of seniority systems in the state's highly unionized basic industrial sector, they are subject to layoffs and will not become fully integrated (under present practices and laws) for decades. Finally, though entry into the blue collar sector will increase the labor participation rate of women, that is a national trend and does not mean an improvement in the state's rate relative to the rest of the country.

Opening of blue collar jobs to both sexes does mean an opportunity for women to engage in more remunerative employment and probably over the long run will create attitudinal changes as to the appropriateness of thinking of certain work as "women's" work. But the opening the blue collar jobs to women does not affect the basic industial structure. The unavailability of work for either six continues to be a persistent problem in the West Virginia economy. Until the structure of the economy changes, West Virginia clearly will not have jobs for all of its citizens.

This conclusion is equally applicable to rural counties, as to the industrial counties in Appalachia. In rural counties where few traditional male jobs exist, breaking down the traditional sexual occupational boundaries will not have a significant quantitative effect on women's employment. In rural counties, as in coal counties, it is necessary to change the economic structure of the local economy in order to provide job opportunities for women.

One final conclusion, only suggested in this paper, is that to eliminate sexual oppression both in West Virginia and the United States as a whole, it is necessary to change the mode of production. The history of West Virginia shows that the sexual discrimination of female labor was not simply attitudinal but served the existing mode of production. In the company town era, women's work underpinned the profits of coal employers in allowing lower paid wages to miners. In the modern era, the segregation of women's work serves the profits of their employers in that job discrimination reduces the level of remuneration necessary to attract workers. In order to remove the financial incentive in sexual discrimination, it is necessary to change the mode of production based on production for profit.

TABLE 1

Male & Female Labor Force Participation Rates*
United States and West Virginia, 1900-1977.

	Female		Male	
	United States	West Virginia	United States	West Virginia
1900	20.4%	9.3%A	87.7%	80.0%
1930	24.3	13.2B	84.1	72.4+
1950	29.0	19.6--	78.9	74.6--
1960	37.1	24.3--	82.4	67.8--
1970	42.8	29.4B	79.2	66.9--
1976	49.4	38.1B	78.5	72.0A

*Male or female labor force divided by male or female population above some age; for 1900-1930, it is population ten years old and over: for 1950, fourteen years old and over: for 1960-1977, sixteen years old and over.
A second lowest of any state
B lowest of any state
+ third lowest of any state
-- Rankings not determined

SOURCE: U. S. Census of Population, 1900 & 1930 and Statistical Abstract of the U.S. Data for 1976 are from "Marital and Family Status of Workers State and Area," Bureau of Labor Statistics, Department of Labor, Report 545, Spring 1976, pp. 3 and 9.

TABLE 2
OCCUPATIONAL STRUCTURE OF EXPERIENCED LABOR FORCE, WEST VIRGINIA, 1960 AND 1970

OCCUPATION	Distribution of Women Workers West Virginia 1960	Distribution of Women Workers West Virginia 1970	U.S. 1970	Percentage Change by Occupation West Virginia, 1960-1970 Female Employment	Percentage Change by Occupation West Virginia, 1960-1970 Male Employment	Females as a Percentage of Total Labor Force, West Virginia 1970
				19.1%	24.5%	43.9%
Professional Technical and Kindred	17.2%	16.6%	15.4%	22.9	-3.4	18.8
Managers and Administrators	4.5	4.5	3.6	-14.8	-20.1	44.5
Sales Workers	12.0	8.3	7.4	41.9	26.6	69.7
Clerican and Kindred	25.9	30.0	34.5	123.0	5.1	3.4
Craftsman and Kindred	1.0	1.9	1.8			22.3
Opeatives, Except Transportation	12.0	11.5	14.6	22.1	-8.5	
Transportaton Operatives		0.4	0.5			2.3
Laborers, Except Farm	0.6	1.5	1.0	185.5	-27.1	7.3
Farmers and Farm Managers	0.6	0.4	0.2	-51.1	-62.8	7.9
Farm Laborers and Foreman	0.4		0.6	45.8	24.7	60.0
Service Workers	17.0	20.1	16.6	-30.3	-33.2	97.1
Private Household Workers	8.7	4.9	3.9	23.1	-7.8	31.9
TOTAL	100.0	100.0	100.0			

Source: Census of Population, U.S. Bureau of the Census, 1960 and 1970

TABLE 3

Female Labor Participation Rates*, by type of County, West Virginia, Pennsylvania, Kentucky, and Virginia, 1970

		Appalachian Portion of		
Type of County**	West Virginia	Pennsylvania	Kentucky	Virginia
Rural Coal	8.3	11.5	7.2	6.7
Rural Non-Coal	9.2	13.2	8.9	11.8
Urban Coal	12.5	12.2	9.0	NA
Urban Non-Coal	11.4	14.3	12.4	13.8

*Female Labor Participation Rates are defined as the number of women in the labor force divided by the total population times 100. Thus these figures are not comparable to other tables.

**Coal counties are counties which produced 2.4 million tons or more of coal in 1970.

Urban counties are counties in which at least 30 percent of the population lived in urban areas in 1970.

Source: *County and City Data Book,* 1970, Appachian States Data File, Division of Environmental and Urban Stystems, Virginia Tech.

NOTES

We gratefully acknowledge the research assistance of John Taylor, the computer assistance of Bruce Carveth and Dr. Tom Watts, and the typing of Jo Anne Smith and Nancy Marosy. We also think Jane Horton and Connie Mahoney for their comments at the Appalachian Studies Conference.

1. Bureau of Labor Statistics. U. S. Department of Labor, Report 572, 1979.
2. Sheila Rowbotham. *Women's Consciousness.: Man's World* (N. Y.: Penquin Books, 1973), p. 68.
3. Ibid., p. 68.
4. Ibid., p. 84.
5. Ibid., p. 89.
6. Interestingly, the deficiency in that participation rate is not accounted for by an excess in the elderly population. That portion of West Virginia in central Appalachia had 10.6 percent of its population age sixty-five or over in 1975 while Appalachian New York had 11.4 percent of its population in that category. Population 65 years of age and older, Appalachian Region and Untied States, 1970-75, *Appalachia--A Reference Book* (Washington: Appalachian Regional Commission, 1977), Table 8. p. 26.
7. See Richard M. Simon, "The Lablor Process and Uneven Development: The Appalachian Coalfields, 1880-1930," *International Journal of Urban and Regional Research* 4 (March 1980): 46-71.
8. One method of producing profit is to increase the productivity of labor. In steel, for example, productivity was increased through the organization of work and capital investment. Most of the productivity gains were appointed by the owners of the factories, but part of the productivity gains were distributed to workers in the form of increased wages. The coal operators, however, faced with intense competition and declining or unstable prices adopted policies to increase profit through the indirect and direct reduction of wages such as shortweighing and overcharges in company stores and housing. The earnings of many miners were estimated by the Bureau of Labor in the early 1920s to be inadequate to provide a minimal subsistence. For a further discussion of the role of coal in the West Virginia economy see Richard M. Simon, "The Development of Underdevelopment." Ph.D dissertation, University of Pittsburgh, 1978), especially chapter 6.
9. Simon, "Development of Underdevelopment," pp. 76 and 77.
10. Baily, "A Judicious Mixture, "West Virginia History 34 (January 1973): 141-161.
11. "Home Environment and Employment Opportunities of Women in Coal Mine Workers' Families," Bulletin of the Women's Bureau, No. 45, U. S. Department of Labor, (Washington: Government Printing Office, 1925).
12. The sons of miners often became miners. The daughters of miners, however, did not have a role to play in the coal town, other than in marrying a male miner. Therefore, unlike the sons, the daughters were forced to leave the family and the community in order to find work. In only 26 percent of the families that had daughters, were the daughters still living at home at age fifteen and over. See Ibid., pp. 39-42.
13. In fact, it is essential in a mode of production that is paying wages less than the familial subsistence wage that the family have a means of increasing its total income. Carmen Diana Deere argues that the non-capitalist mode of production within the family absorbs the cost of production and reproduction of labor power; in developing countries, this would most often take the form

of subsistence agricultural production by women. In "Rural Women's Subsistence Production in the Capitalist Periphery," *Review of Radical Political Economics* 8 (Spring 1976): 9-17.

14. "Home Environment and Employment Opportunities." It is interesting to note that West Virginia had the highest percentage of miners' wives gainfully employed; the average throughout the bituminous coal fields was 17.1 percent. The percentage of wives gainfully employed is related to the percentage of the mine related population housed in company towns. West Virginia had the highest percentage-about 80 percent.

15. Ibid., p. 37.

16. See Rowbotham, *Women's Consciousness,* pp. 103-115.

17. The very large percentage increases in the employment of women in the crafts and laborers are misleading because the large percentage are due to the very small number of women in those occupations in 1960. They do represent, however, the opening to women of jobs previously traditional to male workers, among these the employment of women in the coal mines after 1974.

18. West Virginia has never been a complete mono-economy. As early as the 1900s, glass and metal fabrication co-existed with coal in the northern West Virginia, and since World War I chemical production has coexisted with coal in the Kanawha Valley. However, these operations, primarily branch plant operations, have not materially changed the structure of the West Virginia economy.

19. See Nasser Sherafat, Angelos Pagoulatos, and Kurt R. Anschel, "The Exploitation of Coal as an Engine for Growth in Eastern Kentucky--An Input-Output Study," *Southern Journal of Agricultural Economics,* December 1978, pp. 81-86.

20. In this table, labor force participation of women had to be defined as the female labor force divided by the total population of the county, rather than the female labor force divided by the female population sixteen years of age and older. Thus, the figures are not comparable. There is some variation between counties in the participation rates due to the variation in the proportion of the total population which is female. However, this variation will not affect the comparison of the averages among the four groups of counties.

21. It is interesting to note that in West Virginia, the urban coal counties have higher female labor participation rates than do the non-coal urban counties. This is not true in Kentucky or Pennsylvania where urban coal counties, as rural coal counties, have lower female participation rates than do the urban non-coal counties. This is explained in that the West Virginia urban coal counties are also the most highly industrialized and diversified. For example, the state university is located in Monongalia County and the state capital is located in Kanawha County.

22. See *Appalachia--A Reference Book,* 2nd Edition, Appalachian Regional Commission, February 1979, p. 50.

23. As a way of comparsion, highly industrialized counties had a significantly lower percentage of women in that category. Brooke had 15.7 percent; Hancock had 14.2 percent; Ohio had 15.8 percent; Harrison had 15.8 percent and Wood had 15.3 percent. Of these, Harrison and Ohio had some production. Kanawha with the state capital had 17.1 percent and Monongalia, with the university and its hospital dominating its economy, equalled Mingo for the highest rate with 22.8 percent.

II Land in Appalachia

WHERE AMERICAN HISTORY BEGAN: APPALACHIA AND THE SMALL INDEPENDENT FAMILY FARM

John Opie

Abstract

Some historians, including F. J. Turner, believed that the independent yeoman farmer was the first uniquely American figure. A strong case can be made that this symbol first emerged in the southern Appalachian region. The small-scale independent farmer remained the most important symbol of American success from approximately 1720 to 1880, but could not cope with new agricultural conditions on the arid Great Plains. The result was a massive civilizational failure (1870-1940). That, together with endemic poverty and instability in Appalachia itself, has raised questions about the durability of one of the most powerful archetypes of American life.

This essay explores the difficult and ambiguous, but crucial and un-examined, links between the specific geography of a region, the kind of people attracted to it, the quality of life carved out a region, and the influence of a region and its people upon a national consciousness today. When we look at Appalachia and its role in the development of the American people, the geography is so commonplace and the way of life so routine that it does not attract extraordinary attention. But a landscape has human meaning, no matter how ordinary, or how inhospitable and poor. Significant features of a society are exposed by reading its landscape. The historical geographer, Peirce F. Lewis, writes:

> Our human landscape is our unwitting autobiography, reflecting our tastes, our values, our aspirations, and even our fears, in tangible, visible form. We rarely think of landscape that way, and so the cultural record we have "written" in the landscape is liable to be more truthful than most autobiographies because we are less self-conscious about how we describe ourselves. Grady Clay has said it well: "There are no secrets in the landscape." All our cultural warts and blemishes are there, and our glories too; but above all, our ordinary day-to-day qualities are exhibited for anybody who wants to find them and knows how to look for them.[1]

As farmers settled frontier regions, they themselves changed as much as the wilderness. To create a human landscape out of wilderness represented an enormous investment of skills, energy, time, and emotions. The natural features of a piece of land, the mechanics or technology of working and living on it, all suggest that a quality of life is intimately related to the geography one starts out with, and the "built landscape" one comes up with.

Since Roman and medieval times, farmers have tested the agricultural potential of an undeveloped piece of land by its natural vegetation cover. The most desirable farmland, tradition said, was covered by a thick forest.

When frontier farmers first encountered the southern Appalachians, its forest cover surpassed all expectations and may have been the greatest stand of trees and vegetation encountered since Roman time. At the bridge between the southern Great (Shenandoah) Valley of Virginia and the all-important Cumberland Gap stands the greatest and most varied deciduous forest in North America. A long history of climate and glacial movement, together with rich soil and wide range of altitude (nine hundred to six thousand feet) compressed into this region an extraordinary treasure of twenty-five hundred trees, shrubs, and other plants. No wonder the famed early American botanist William Bartram wrote in 1791 of the "sublime forest" he encountered here, and that the region attracted a special visit from the French naturalist Andre Michaux early in the nineteenth century.[2] Bartram excitedly described black oaks 30 feet in circumference, massive chestnut trees 13 feet thick at the base, and beeches and gum trees which towered to 150 feet.

This promising land stood at the base of the Great Valley and settlers poured into the top of the Valley by the 1720s. Fertile limestone soils, cheap land, and accessibility from the north but not the east drew frontier farmers. The Valley also lacked permanent Indian settlements, as would Kentucky seventy years later. Earlier native burning and hunting created a region which was fire resistant with significant, open grass covered meadows.[3] Primary agricultural needs were fully satisfied: fertile soil, water, vegetation cover, flat or rolling terrain. Limited markets, lack of capital, and labor intensive farming kept Valley farmers on a subsistence level into the 1760s, a major achievement, nevertheless, where once there had been only wilderness. Fields covered ten acres, planted in corn, wheat, or rye, yielding ten to seventeen bushels per acre. Between 1760 and 1800 the Valley shifted into a cash crop economy, changing from frontier conditions to a rural society.

Frontiersmen searching out forest land with good farming potential in the southern Appalachians had already been primed not only by the Great Valley, but also by the extraordinary agricultural successes in southeastern from its original twenty to forty acres. The family also used its cash to acquire salt, tea, coffee, iron goods, perhaps some textiles, and services when needed very rich."[4] The bounty of nature was being used as a test for good land: a temperate climate, rich soil supporting a vast forest, flat or gently rolling terrain, and an adequate water supply. But the superiority of the southern Appalachian forest to Pennsylvania and the Great Valley established a new standard for agricultural potential.

This same southern Appalachian forest would become the setting for another American standard. The historian, Frederick Jackson Turner, when he searched for a uniquely American identity, turned for his answer to the westward frontier expansion of the new nation. In most frontier epics, heroic stature belonged to the mountain man, explorer, fur trader, hunter, or backwoodsman. But when he wrote his all-important 1893 essay, "The Significance of the Frontier in American History," Turner gave his attention to "the advance of the more steady farmer."[5] This was Turner's "representative frontiersman." The sequence of waves of agrarian advance into the wilderness is constant: first, backwoods settlement, then, permanent clearings that open the forested land, and finally the extensive fields of a recognizable rural American landscape.[6] According to his 1908 essay, "The Old West," published by the State Historical Society of Wisconsin, this representative frontier farmer first appeared in the Great Valley and the colonial background: today's southern Appalachia. Turner concentrated his attention to that flow of settlement which ran through the Valley and penetrated into the Cumberland Gap. His classic statement in the 1893 essay: recalls the migration. "Stand at

Cumberland Gap and watch the procession of civilization, marching single file--the buffalo following the trail to the salt springs, the Indian, the fur trader and hunter, the cattle raiser, the pioneer farmer--and the frontier has passed by.'" Southern Appalachia was part of Turner's "Middle Region," which "was democratic and nonsectional, if not national; [it was] easy, tolerant, and contented; rooted strongly in material prosperity....the Middle region mediated between East and West as well as between North and South. Thus it became the typically American region."[8]

Aside from Turner, a strong case can be made that this small family farmer in the southern Appalachians did become the model, even ideal, by which Americans identified themselves, and which rang true to foreign observers. Westward agricultural expansion dominated the American experience in the early nineteenth century. Alternative outside influences were few: only 250,000 immigrants were added at a time when the population grew from 4,000,000 to 9,600,000. Americans turned inland and inward; in the process they arrived at a national identity.[9] The frontier family farm became a distinctively American way of life. The farmer, on his piece of land, formed the basis for major American ideological beliefs: freedom, opportunity, individualism, pragmatism, growth, and optimism. We can consider this agrarian experience, from Appalachia in 1800 to its collapse on the arid Great Plains in 1880, as the emergence and persistence of "Original America." "Original America" established, perhaps for the first time, a specifically American standard of living and quality of life.

The standards established for farm land in the southern Appalachians, together with the independent family farmer of the region, became fixtures in American history. By 1820 the magnet which pulled settlers across the Alleghenies and through Appalachia into the Midwest was the promise of land so fertile that the wheat went to straw unless you had several seasons of corn. The modern ecologist, Aldo Leopold, writing of the rich cane lands of central Kentucky, which would become the classic bluegrass country. asked,

> Would Boone and Kenton have held out? Would there have been any overflow into Ohio? Any Louisiana Purchase? Any transcontinental union of new states? Any Civil War? Any machine? Any depression? The subsequent drama of American history, here and elsewhere, hung in large degree on the reaction of particular soils to the impact of particular forces exerted by a particular kind and degree of human occupation.[10]

The transappalachian midwestern forest apparently stretched endlessly, the soil was rich and black, and most attractive of all, utterly stoneless.

Whether in the Great Valley, the vast southern Appalachian forest, or the flat, deep soils of the Midwest, basic necessities had to be adapted out of the environment with the resources the farmer could bring from civilization. Frontier settlement was like a long-term expedition into the wilderness with wife and children rather than other able-bodied, skilled men. Most adapting of raw materials depended upon muscle power, a variety of basic agricultural skills, and simple tools, the majority of which had not changed substantially since the dawn of agriculture--axe, grubbing hoe, spade, rake, sheath knife, wedge, and mallet.[11] In this regard, the ever present rifle was a new fangled device. The technological revolution and mechanical equipment would come later. Agriculture was still based on traditional, European hand tool dirt farming upon land cleared from a dense deciduous forest in a temperate climate.

In the first year, three to five acres were cleared of forest, mostly down to stumps left to rot, and fifteen more acres with trees, girdled or "deadened." The clearing was planted first in corn. By the second year, eight to ten acres were open, planted again in corn or at best half corn and vegetables, and half wheat for some cash.[12] All too often an unexpected burden for the wilderness farmer was his dismayed discovery that his livestock could not or would not survive on native American grasses for pasture. He was compelled to import English grasses with him, notably red clover and timothy, or in Kentucky, bluegrass. If any cash was available it would often be a downpayment for more land (the interest rate was twelve to twenty per cent) to enlarge the farm from its original twenty to fourty acres. The family also used its cash to acquire salt, tea, coffee, iron goods, perhaps some textiles, and services when needed of a lawyer, minister, miller, blacksmith, shoemaker, and part-time laborer. The frontier self-sustaining farm family was typically settled on eighty acres within three to five years. This settlement usually remained unchanged for about ten years before it was transformed into a post-frontier, middle America, farm community.

Contrary to the standard myths about American growth and prosperity, this small farmer had no great urge to improve his condition above a certain basic standard of living which he saw as good and which we would call subsistence.[13] But we must remember that in the long seven thousand year history of agriculture, with ninety percent of the humans of that era being farmers, this American farmer, roughly between 1750 and 1840, became one of the world's most successful agriculturalists. We must see his "subsistence" economic level in a global perspective. By modern standards, according to the naturalist Betty Flanders Thomson, life for the pioneer farmer was hard, raw, and lonesome. In the Midwest the first farms were scattered at random all over the area, most of them far from neighbors and further isolated by the widespread swampiness of the land and the impassable condition of what roads there were....there is little reason to believe that life at that time and place offered any advantages beyond independence, owning one's own land, and a hope that the future would be better.[14]

The settlement cycle was the same--clearing timber and brush, breaking the primeval soil, first corn and later wheat crops, within a ten-year span, rarely less. The attraction, likewise, remained the same: self-sufficiency and independence-at a subsistence level, to be sure, but that seemed enough. In contemporary writings, affirmations of agricultural success far out-numbered reports of disappointment and failure.[15] Reports of agricultural disillusionment and downright collapse came later, and from other places.

So little value was attached to treeless land that in the 1780s when settlers reached the first large prairie in Kentucky, the one referred to above by Aldo Leopold, they called it the "Big Barrens."[16] James Madison was convinced that Jefferson had squandered federal funds when he acquired the vast, treeless Louisiana Territory in 1803. The prairie repelled farmers; it was monotonous, empty, uninviting, and presumably barren. When they encountered the midwestern open country at roughly the Indiana-Illinois border, farmers were stymied by their tradition that open treeless country was not good farming country.[17]

Conditions were wrong on the prairie; it was not like the southern Appalachian forest model. There was no protection from wind, cold, or heat. Wood was not available for fences, buildings, and fuel. And the sod was so dense and tangled that it was unplowable with available technology: the traditional, heavy, tough, iron-sheathed wooden plow. By all rights, westward movement of the Appalachian formed small farmer should have ended at the Illinois-Indiana line. But the prairie soil was too rich to be ignored. "Sodbusting" demanded the new, thin, lightweight, highly polished steel shear plow devised by John Deere. The resulting crops exceeded all previous bounty. Unlike the East, where farms have been carved out of the forest, cultivated for some years, and then later abandoned, very little prairie country has ever lain idle. The prairie frontier farmer had a subsistence crop of corn in his first year and often a cash crop of wheat by the third to fifth year. The symbolic act on this near perfect farm land took place in 1839, when Lyman Dillon plowed a furrow a hundred miles long across the prairie to lay out the road from Dubuque through the site of Iowa City to the Missouri line.[18]

It now seemed that the small farmer in America was invincible; even the old traditions about the best land being forested land had been laid to rest in Iowa's rich black moist "gumbo." His westward advance was not only inevitable, it became the major force in America's "manifest destiny." The next challenge would be the land west of the hundredth meridian, a north-south line, lying roughly half way between Chicago and Denver today if one is traveling Interstate 80, and dividing the nation into approximately equal east-west halves. East of the line are the rich prairies just discussed. West of the line stands one of the grasslands of the world--the arid high plains country. The high plains had had a historic reputation as a dry unfarmable region since the early nineteenth century. And dry land regions, because of the limits of existing agricultural techniques, made American farmers as uncomfortable as open, treeless country had earlier until the prairie country had been opened up.

An incredible event took place in the 1870s which seemed part of the small farmer's destiny to succeed in his westward movement. For the better part of a decade, unusually heavy rains covered the arid high plains, and the "Great American Desert" became the "Great American Garden."[19] News spread rapidly that the small farmer could change the climate by plowing the land and planting trees. The famous maxim, "Rain follows the plow," carried farmers into the inhospitable region. But by the late 1880s, wagons of farmers retreated eastward carrying the bitter slogan, "In God we trusted, in Kansas we busted." The region, when its typical dryness returned, became a large-scale example of human failure. The agriculturalist's victory was brief; the farming traditions learned in the east failed dismally. A sizeable American landscape was depopulated, including massive emigration from many settled regions and the abandonment of the entire towns.[20] This failure was made worse by the stubborn persistence of the small farmer tradition in a region where its geographical usefulness was questionable. The result was agricultural failure for over seventy years, from the 1870s to the 1940s. An eastern success story, the Appalachian style small farmer became a broken myth west of the hundredth meridian. This region, whre agribusiness would get its start, was the place where the classic Jeffersonian yeoman farmer would disappear. Turner was only partly right.

Nevertheless, where the Appalachian style small farmer appeared and persisted, from the Great Valley to the midwestern prairie, one of the world's great agricultural traditions was established. Several features of this tradition were unique and gave American society its distinctive coloration.

The frontier farmer labored through his days and nights in intense isolation. His degree of separation from the civilized world was unprecedented in human history and formed the backdrop for his thoughts and actions. More often than not the farmer and his family were literally "off the map," having settled on land that had not been explored, surveyed, or mapped. The impact of backwoods isolation is suggested by the intensity of frontier religion, especially highly emotional, camp meeting revivalism.[21] Folks feared for themselves and the conditions of their souls in an alien environment which seemed filled not only with the "silence of God," but in its strangeness pointed to the absence or "death of God," or at least his disappearance. To this psychologically powerful isolation must be added the influence of the distinctive family homestead which Americans take for granted but is a pointed contrast to the rural village communities in Europe, Asia, and Africa. The American farm family lived on its piece of land, clearly separated from neighbors and usually isolated from daily contact with any established community. No wonder frontier accounts tell of the madness of wives and the violence of husbands. The strongest sense of security under these conditions may have been the farmer's psychological bond with the tract of land which he owned and worked.

By hard physical labor with hand tools, the farmer acquired a close identity with his land. Here he acquired the same solidarity with the landscape as did European, Asian, or African agriculturalists.[22] This sense of solidarity is an unexplored theme in American history. The land was part of his own personal identity; conversely, he invented the place where he lived, creating it out of wilderness placelessness. This "built landscape" signalled to him his chances for survival. One of the most crucial aspects of frontier settlement was its durability under adverse conditions. The American farmer, despite his isolation and vulnerability, believed he experienced a high degree of success and had carved out a satisfying standard of living.

Pioneer farm people were used to hard physical work under dangerous conditions. Frontier farmers lived under what behavioral psychologists today would call high risk conditions, as they wavered between failure, survival, and different levels of subsistence.[23] Their life was hazardous, because wilderness circumstances meant difficult actions happened more frequently, and tested their peak abilities constantly. There was less ability to cope with crisis when one faced it regularly and often went through defeat. Farmers on the edge of civilization more willingly accepted lower levels of performance. Desperate farmers tended to throw themselves into hopelessly optimistic projects and pollyanna solutions. Coping with an unknown, dangerous, and probably hostile environment, life for the American farmer involved more difficult work, more critical decisions, and more uncontrollable factors than in long settled regions. Hence, also, the high satisfaction with barely adequate success on a subsistence level.

Extreme physical hardship, the dangers of accidents, and the uncontrollable power of circumstances were vivid daily realities for the small frontier farmer. But essentially the farming family, when it moved into a new region, was optimistic, and with justification. Their goals were attainable; pioneer farmers did not experience the grinding hopeless labor and deep pessimism of their counterparts elsewhere in the world. The risks were worth the benefits. The danger of failure or harm seemed nominal for the high returns. If a farmer had his health, reasonable abilities, basic survival and agricultural skills (which most people had), he could expect a comfortable existence.[24]

This essay is no more than an exploratory enquiry into a neglected but hardly trivial subject. With today's "return-to-the-land" climate, it is all too easy to romanticize the historic single-family farm as an ideal way of life. But anyone who has grown up or lived on a farm hardly praises each early morning's physical chores. Yet the difficult and often desolate life of the pioneer farmer was a quantum leap beyond agrarianism elsewhere in the world, because it promised "independence, owning one's own land, and a hope that the future would be better." By the standards of today's consumer abundance, the small pioneer farm in the Great Valley, southern Appalachian mountains, and the lower midwest would only impress us by its "nothingness." But as early as 1775, the French visitor, Crevecoeur, waxed eloquently about the pioneer farmer's victory:

> The world is gradually settled...the howling swamp is converted into a pleasing meadown, the rough ridge into a fine field...hear the cheerful whistling, the rural song, where there was no sound heard before, save the yell of the savage, the screech of the owl, or the hissing of the snake.

I wish to see men cut down the first trees, erect their new buildings, till their first fields, reap their first crops, and say for the first time in their lives, "This is our own grain, raised from American soil--on it we shall feed and grow fat, and convert the rest into gold and silver." I want to see how the happy effects of their sobriety, honesty, and industry are first displayed; and who would not take a pleasure in seeing these strangers settling as new countrymen, struggling with arduous difficulties, overcoming them, and becoming happy.

> All I wish to delineate is, the progressive steps of a poor man, advancing from indigence to ease, from oppression to freedom, from obscurity and contumely to some degree of sonsequence--not by virtue of any freaks of fortune, but by the gradual operation of sobriety, honesty, and emigration.[25]

Such quasi-religious proclamations about the primitive American farmer are not surprising. Frederick Jackson Turner's perceptions of the archetypal American--the single-family farmer, owning his land and carving out a fundamentally new existence--represent a virtual profession of faith in a secular symbol derived from out own history. Turner may have done better in describing a national "myth" than in writing history. We have made a very ordinary figure into a larger-than-life ideal. This is not surprising and our task is to come to grips with our creation.

There is a great deal of truth in the myth. The verdant, forested southern Appalachian highlands did exist. The frontier farmer did enter them, and his settlement there created new levels of expectation for American agricultural expansion. The archetype that emerged out of this region and its settlement has persisted since then as a major symbol of American history. This agrarian ideal did fail miserably in the western dry grasslands, and it would fall upon extraordinarily hard days in Appalachia itself. Tillich today would call the symbol a "broken myth." And surely the single-family farmer today has difficulty matching historic expectations and standards. But one modern version of the independent farmer, the Appalachian mountaineer, also has a surprisingly strong durability even under adversity.

NOTES

NOTE: the references below are hardly exhaustive. Emphasized are works still in print or otherwise readily available. A basic environmental history of Appalachia has yet to be done.

1. Peirce F. Lewis, "Axioms for Reading the Landscape." *The Interpretation of Ordinary Landscapes: Geographical Essays,* ed. D. W. Meinig (New York: Oxford University Press, 1979), p. 12. Other important related works are DAvid Ward, ed. *Geographical Perspectives on America's Past* (New York: Oxford University Press, (1979); David Lowenthal and Martyn J. Bowden, *Geographies of the Mind: Essays in Historical Geosophy in Honor of John Kirtland Wright* (New York: Oxford University Press, 1976); and Yi-Fu Tuan, *Space and Place: The Perspective of Experience* (Minneapolis: University of Minnesota Press, 1977).

2. See Mark Van Doren, ed., *Travels of William Bartram* (New York: Dover Publications, 1955); Reuben G. Thwaites, *Travels West of the Alleghenies* (New York: Arthur H. Clark Company, 1904); Maurice Brooks, *The Appalachians* (Boston: Houghton Mifflin Company, 1965); and good popular works like May Theilgaard Watts, *Reading the Landscape of America* (New York: Macmillian Publishing Company, 1975); Eliot Porter and Edward Abbey (with Harry M. Caudill), *Appalachian Wilderness:* The Great Smoky Mountains (New York: Ballantine Books, 1973); Jerome Dolittle, *The Southern Appalchians* (New York: Time-Life Books, 1975); and Darwin Lambert, *The Earth-Man Story* (New York: Exposition Press, 1973).

3. See the excellent analysis by Robert D. Mitchell, "The Shenandoah Valley Frontier," in Ward, p. 150.

4. Still definitive is James T. Lemon, The Best Poor Man's Country: *A Geographical Study of Early Southeastern Pennsylvania* (Baltimore: Johns Hopkins University Press, 1972).

5. Turner's essay is still available; see Frederick Jackson Turner, *The Frontier in American History,* Foreword by R. A. Billington (New York: Holt, Rinehart and Winton, 1920, 1947, 1962).

6. Ray Billington, more than anyone else, has mastered the debate over Turner's significance for historical enquiry, and the relative success and failure of his frontier thesis: see especially, *America's Frontier Heritage* (New York: Holt, Rinehart and Winston, 1966); and *Frederick Jackson Turner* (New York: Oxford University Press, 1973).

7. In the 1920 anthology, p. 12; see also "The Old West," pp. 68-69.

8. "Significance of the Frontier..." in the 1920 anthology, pp. 27-28.

9. Frontier histories which give adequate attention to the farmer are still scarce; see especially, Richard A. Bartlett, *The New Country: A Social History of the American Frontier, 1776-1890* (New York: Oxford University Press, 1974): John R. Alden, *Pioneer America The History of Human Society,* ed. J. H. Plumb (New York: Alfred A. Knopf, 1966) Ralph H. Brown, *Historical Geography of the United States* (New York: Harcourt, Brace and World, 1948); and Reginald Horsman, *The Frontier in The Formative Years, 1783-1815* (New York: Holt. Rinehart and Winston, 1970).

10. Aldo Leopold, "The Conservation Ethic" (1933), reprinted in Robert Disch, ed., The Ecological Conscience (Englewood Cliffs, N. J.: Prentice-Hall, 1970), p. 46.

11. See John T. Schlebecker, *Whereby We Thrive: A History of American Farming, 1607-1972* (Ames, Iowa: The Iowa State University Press, 1975); and

the perceptive classic, Eric Sloane, *A Museum of Early American Tools* (New York: Ballantine Books, 1964).

12. The best review is still in Horsmann *The Frontier in the Formative Years,* pp. 104-120.

13. See the comments in Horsman, pp. 111, 115, 119, and 123-124; also Edward Hyams, *Soil and Civilization* (London: Thames and Hudson, 1952); and Fernand Braudel, *Capitalism and Material Life, 1400-1800* (New York: Harper and Row, 1973); as well as the important representative essays by Cratis Williams, Loyal Jones, and Harry M. Caudill in Robert J. Higgs and Ambrose N. Manning, eds., *Voices from the Hills: Selected Readings of Southern Appalachia* (New York: Frederick Ungar Publishing Company, 1975).

14. Betty Flanders Thomson, *The Shaping of America's Heartland: The Landscape of the Middle West* (Boston: Houghton Mifflin Company, 1977), p. 230; compare with Maurice Brooks, *The Appalachians* (Boston: Houghton Mifflin Company, 1965).

15. See for example the opinions of contemporaries in Clark C. Spence, ed., *The American West* (New York: Thomas Y. Crowell, 1966); Robert V. Hine and Edwin R. Bingham, eds., *The American Frontier* (Boston: Little, Brown and Company, 1972); and Martin Ridge and R. A. Billington, eds., *America's Frontier Story* (New York: Holt, Rinehart, and Winston, 1969). This is a subject which has not been adequately explored.

16. The best study on American perceptions of arid lands is still W. Eugene Hollon, *The Great American Desert* (New YHork: Oxford University Press, 1966). Seè also excellent essays by Waldo r. Wedel, John L. Allen, David M. Emmons, Martyn J. Bowden, and Leslie Hewes in Brian W. Blouet and Merlin P. Lawson, eds., *Images of the Plains: The Role of Human Nature in Settlement* (Lincoln: University of Nebraska Press, 1975).

17. The classic, and controversial study, not yet superseded, is Walter Prescott Webb, *The Great Plains* (Boston: Ginn and Company, 1931), pp. 152-159, and 319ff. See also John Opie, "Frontier History in Environmental Perspective," in Jerome O. Steffen, *The American West: New Perspectives, New Dimensions* (Norman: University of Iklahoma Press, 1979), pp. 9-34.

18. Thomson, *The Shaping of America's Heartland,* p. 239.

19. See John Opie, "America's Seventy-Year Mistake: or, How We Got Fooled by Good Weather in Difficult Country," *Proceedings of a Seminar on Natural Resource Use and Environmental Policy* (Ames Iowa: North Central Regional Center for Rural Development, 1980), pp. 27-56. An earlier version is in the *Proceedings of an AAAs-DOE Workshop on Environmental and Societal Consequences of a Possible CO-2-Induced Climate Change* (Washington, D. C.: USDOE, 1980).

20. See Gilbert C. Fite, *The Farmer's Frontier, 1965-1900* (New York: Holt, Rinehart and Winston, 1966); and Climate and Society Research Group, *The Effect on Climate Fluctuations on Human Populations* (Worcester, Mass.: Clark University, 1979).

21. See Charles A. Johnson, *The Frontier Camp Meeting: Religion's Harvest Time* (Dallas: Southern Methodist University Press, 1955).

22. See John Opie, "A Sense of Place," in *An Appalachian Sympsium,* ed, J. W. Williamson (Boone, N.C.: Appalachian State University Press, 1977).

23. See John Opie, "Environmental and Human Factors in Farming the Arid Great Plains, 1870-1940," 1980 Meeting of the Midcontinent American Studies Association, Des Moines, Iowa.

24. See Note 13.

25. Quoted in John Opie, "De Crevecoeur's Anti-Frontier Thesis: The

Cultivator's Peaceable Kingdom as a State of Mind,'' 1977 Meeting of the American Society of Church History, Dallas.

26. See John Opie, "The Merging of Space and Time, Myth and History: The Victory of the Sacred West Over Profane Modernity in the Writings of Frederick Jackson Turner," 1980 Confernce on the Hermeneutics of Myth, Athens, Ohio; and also "Frederick Jackson Turner, The Old West, and the Formation of a National Mythology," 1978 Meeting of the Organization of American Historians, New York City.

LOSING A BIT OF OURSELVES:
THE DECLINE OF SMALL FARMER

Stephen L. Fisher

Mary Harnish

Abstract

This paper surveys the literature concerned with the nationwide decline of the family farm and the concomitant rise of agribusiness. It identifies the major causes and implications of these developments, summarizes the case for the small farmer, and reviews various reform proposals. Such a survey is a necessary first step toward an understanding of how the Appalachian farm situation is similar to and different from the national scene. The paper concludes with some preliminary thoughts about a research agenda on the future of the small farmer in Appalachia.

What many Appalachians share in common is a closeness to the land, a familiarity with it and an attachment to it. Perhaps nowhere is the significance of land more clearly and poignantly illustrated than in Robert Coles' *Migrants, Sharecroppers, Mountaineers*. To mountaineers, says Coles, "the land is almost anything and everything: a neighbor, a friend, a part of the family, handed down and talked about and loved, loved dearly--loved and treasured and obeyed, it can be said, as we agree to do when we get married."[1]

Yet during the 1970s, as in the decades before, Appalachians have witnessed a constant assault on their land. We propose to examine the dimensions of one part of this assault--the displacement of hundreds of thousands of small farmers and the disintegration of the culture and communities of farming.

The decline of the small farmer is, of course, a national phenomenon. In the last thirty years the nation has lost 60 percent of its farms. Ten farmers a day leave the land, and it is estimated that two hundred to four hundred thousand farms will disappear each year for the next twenty years if present trends continue. There is an increasing amount of literature documenting and decrying this decline, but the effects of this trend on Appalachia, which has the greatest number of small farms of any region in the nation, has gone largely unreported.

The variety of farm experience in Appalachia and the absence of concerted political action on the part of small farmers explain, to some degree, the lack of any systematic treatment of the special social, political, and economic problems faced by the Appalachian family farmer. But the basic reason the small farm has been ignored is the widely held belief that it is inefficient and that the small farmer would be better off doing something else. This is clearly the perspective of the Appalachian Regional Commission (ARC) which has no overall policy and practically no programs directed toward the thousands of small farmers left in Appalachia.[2] Many radical political activists in the mountains also see no place for the family farm in Appalachia's future. While expressing sympathy for the problems the farmers face, these radicals accept the disappearance of the family farm as an inevitable consequence of capitalist development.[3]

Such beliefs can be attacked on a number of grounds. There is increasing evidence to show that large-scale farmers are not intrinsically more efficient than smaller ones. Moreover, these beliefs ignore what the disappearance of the small farm will mean for the future of our society. Societal transformation, in a sense, must begin with the land if only because the basic materials for life are acquired from the land. As Murray Bookchin explains:

> The kind of agricultural practice we adopt at once reflects and reinforces the approach we will utilize in all spheres of industrial and social life. Captalism began historically by undermining and overcoming the resistance of the traditional agrarian world to a market economy; it will never be fully transcended unless a new society is created on the land that liberates humanity in the fullest sense and restores the balance between society and nature.[4]

The paper surveys the literature concerned with the nationwide decline of the family farm and the concomitant rise of agribusiness. It identifies the major causes and implications of these developments, summarizes the case for the small farmer, and reviews various reform proposals. Such a survey is a necessary first step toward an understanding of how the Appalachian situation differs from the national scene. The paper concludes with some preliminary thoughts about a research agenda on the future of the small farmer in Appalachia.

It should be noted that efforts to focus on the family farm as a policy issue face two critical limitations. First, there is no common meaning or operational definition of a "family farm" completely satisfactory for policy purposes. The term means many things to many people, and any detailed analysis of this debate would constitute a paper in itself. For our purposes, the family farm is one operated by a farmer and his family where the farmer provides much of the labor needed for the farming operation, makes most of the management decisions, assumes most of the risk, and reaps the gains or losses from those decisions.[5] Inadequate data is the second problem faced by researchers. Aggregate farm statistics mask a wide variety of situations and needs in the American farm sector. As the United States Department of Agriculture (USDA) itself explains, "neither the existing data base nor research to date is adequate to explain the developments taking place in the farm sector, the situation of farms in various farm groups, or the individual and cumulative impacts of all the forces causing structural changes."[6]

II

In the late 1930s, there were over 6,800,000 farms in the United States, all but two or three percent of them classified as family farms. Today the number is around 2,300,000 and still dropping. In 1974, just 125,000 farms accounted for one half of all farm sales; today there are probably fewer than 100,000 such farms.[7] In the decades immediately after World War II much of the blame for this decline was placed on the "cost-price squeeze" faced by the farmer and on the USDA's rules and regulations.[8] With the publication of Victor Ray's *The Corporate Invasion of American Agriculture,* the focus shifted to a family farm versus corporate farm debate.[9] The issues in this family farm debate are complex, but it is possible to identify the major factors contributing to loss of over 4,000,000 family farms.

Financial Instability. At the heart of the farm crisis is the fact that there is little profit to be gained in farming. The high risks of failure, the cost-price squeeze, the restricted access to markets, and the problems of gaining access to capital and credit have led to a cycle of financial instability for the small farmer.

The small farmer operates in a highly competitive market and chance of failure is always present. Shirley Greene summarizes this predicament:

> The free market, especially in an elastic demand commodity like food, tends to respond to small variations in supply with wild fluctuations in price. This tendency, combined with the manuevering of traders and speculators in commodity futures markets, results in roller coaster prices which provide farmers with no reliable index of what or how much to plant or how many animals to breed. A lucky guess one year may bring windfall earnings; the next season the same farmer may lose his shirt...The typical family farmer, unlike the large corporation farmer, does not have the reserves or the diversified sources of income to withstand many bad guesses.[10]

Farmers are quite frequently caught in a cost-price squeeze where the prices they receive are not able to cover their costs. The farmers' costs are determined largely by prices charged by manufacturers, whose market conditions are much less competitive than those for farm products. The only practical way that farmers can meet increasing costs and purchase the new sophisticated and expensive machinery needed to stay competitive is to increase output. But when farmers do this simultaneously, the surplus causes a drastic drop in prices.[11] Farmers since World War II have consistently faced heavy downward pressure on prices combined with major increases in the cost of production. This is illustrated by the fact that the price farmers receive from their produce increased only six percent from 1952 to 1974, while farm operating expenses increased by 122 percent. It is little wonder that the total farm debt in the 1970s increased from $59 billion to $94 billion.[12] Since large abribusinesses, especially if they have significant non-farm sources of revenue, are better able to spread their losses over several years, it is the small farmer who is hit the hardest by the cost-price squeeze.

Inflation, of course, increases the severity of the cost-price squeeze. Because farmers have more difficulty adjusting to price changes than nonfarm businesses, inflation has an important effect on the economic health of agriculture. It affects the cost of what the farmer must buy, sooner and more seriously than the farm price of his product.[13] Consequently, inflation pressures thousands of small farmers out of business each year.

Small farmers also face special problems in the area of marketing and in gaining access to credit. Marketing trends have seen the emergence of fewer but bigger purchasers of farm goods. The small independent farmers are frequently at a severe competitive disadvantage because they do not control large enough supplies of agricultural products to give them much bargaining power with large agribusiness concerns.[14] The problem of transportation from farm to market also presents special problems for small farmers.

Farmers need ready sources of capital and credit to purchase land, to recover from a bad crop, to buy new machinery, and to cover normal operating expenses. The small farmers in general face great difficulty in obtaining credit. Many of the major lending institutions refuse to extend credit to small farmers because of the higher risks faced by these farmers, their lower equity position, and the desire of these institutions to minimize their service costs per dollar loaned.[15] The Farmers Home Administration, which is supposed to be oriented to serving the credit needs of farmers with limited resources, has tended to help affluent rather than poor farmers.[16]

In sum, it is the small farm operator who is hurt the most by the inherent instability of agricultural production and prices. He has virtually no power to affect the cost of items he must buy and little power to affect the price at which he must sell his product. In a sense, small farmers are suffering from the effects of free market competition. They constitute several million relatively small bargaining units in the marketplace at the mercy of the forces of supply and demand. It is what we say our economy is all about. Unfortunately for the small farmer, he is one of the few playing the game.[17]

Corporate Control. While the number of farmers working the land decreases each year, corporations are becoming more involved in every phase of food production and distribution. From one side, the small farmer feels the pinch from corporate "input" suppliers. Agribusiness corporations have gained enormous control over farm supplies such as machinery, feed, fertilizer, and seeds. As Jim Hightower explains:

> Before the first sprout breaks ground, American farm families are over their heads in debt to such corporate powers as Bank of America (Production loans), Upjohn Company (seeds), The Williams Companies (fertilizer), International Minerals & Chemical (pesticides), Ford Motor Company (machinery), Firestone (tires), Ralston Purina (feeder pigs), Merck & Company (poultry stock), Cargill (feed), Dow Chemical (cartons and wrappings), Eli Lilly (animal drugs), Exxon (farm fuels), and Burlington Northern (rail transportation).[18]

There is a conspicuous lack of competition in most of the farm supply industry. Economist William Sheppherd reports that four leading firms control 67 percent of petroleum products, 71 percent of tires, 74 percent of chemicals, and 80 percent of rail transport. The concentration can be even greater in specific items and local markets. For example, DeKalb AgResearch and Pioneer Hi-Bred International supply half the hybrid seeds sold, and there are many farming communities where feed must be bought from Ralston Purina or not at all.[19]

This lack of competition has had a profound effect on what farmers must pay for supplies. The Federal Trade Commission (FTC) found in 1972 that the lack of competition among farm machinery manufacturers cost farmers an extra $251,000,000.[20] Table 1 presents a sample of profit increases for some major farm suppliers in the first quarter of 1974. These large profits came at a time when the average profit increases for large corporations was 16 percent and at a time that prices paid to farmers were falling.

Farm-Supply Corporation	Farm Products and Services	First Quarter 1974 Profit Increase
Allis-Chalmers	Machinery	41%
Burlington Northern Rail	Transportation	102%
Consolidated Freightways	Trucking	75%
Federal Paper	Board Cartons	100%

Firestone	Tires, Inner tubes	19%
W. R. Grace	Chemicals	129%
International Harvester	Machinery	113%
International Harvester and Chemical	Chemicals	131%
Occidental Petroleum	Fertilizers, fuels	716%
Pfizer	Drugs	33%
Ralston Purina	Feed	32%
Rohm & Haus	Fungicides	30%
Stauffer Chemical	Chemicals	55%
Tenneco	Chemicals, machinery, fuel, packaging	57%
Upjohn	Drugs, seeds	32%
White Motor	Machinery	
White Motor	Machinery	38%

Source: *Business Week*. "Profits: Better Than Expected." May 11, 1974, p. 69.

From the other side, the farmer feels the pinch from "output" corporations --the middlemen--that process, market, and retail the farmer's product. This industry involves such familiar names as Del Monte, General Mills, Ralston Purina, Minute Maid, Kraft, Dole, and A&P. As with the farm supply industry, the food industry has become increasingly monopolistic. In 1966 the FTC revealed that the 100 largest food manufacturers--representing only .03 percent of the entire industry--accounted for 71 percent of the food industry's profits and 60 percent of its total assets.[21]

The American consumer has tended to blame the farmer for the rapid increase in food prices during the 1970s. Several different studies clearly show that it is the food industry which is at fault. As pointed out earlier, only 6 percent of the rise in food prices between 1954 and 1974 went to the farmer; the food industry accounted for 94 percent of the price increases which consumers paid for food. A USDA study revealed that the farmer in 1974 was receiving only forty-one cents out of each dollar the consumer spent on food.[22] Finally, a 1972 FTC study reported that over-pricing in 13 "monopolized" food lines cost consumers over $2 billion that year.[23]

It is not clear to what degree actual farm production is in the hands of corporate interests. Statistically, corporations account for only 5 percent of the total number of farms. However, as Walter Goldschmidt points out, this statistic is highly misleading.[24] First, some specialty crops are heavily controlled by a few large firms: 100 percent of sugar beets, 92 percent of broilers, and 47 percent of all citrus fruits.[25] Second, corporations primarily engaged in other activities and whose agricultural operations account for less than 10 percent of their gross income are not required to file separate reports on their agricultural activities with the USDA and other governmental agencies. "Thus Tenneco, the conglomerate with many enterprises, is not included in such surveys because it is not *primarily* agricultural, though it controls nearly two million acres of farmland. The same applies to Boeing, Goodyear, Purex, Penn Central, Standard Oil of California, Prudential Insurance, and Bank of America."[26]

Third, the statistic is misleading because it ignores the trend in agriculture toward vertical integration. This is achieved primarily through contract farming, which involves contractual agreements between independent farmers and non-farm corporations (i.e., suppliers, processors, retailers). Instead of a corporation directly owning a farm, it simply rents one. The arrangement has several advantages for the farmer. He is usually assured of production supplies and a market for part of his crop at a predetermined price. The contract farmer also finds it easier to obtain credit. John E. Davis explains the disadvantages:

> First, contract farming tends to eliminate competition within its sphere of influence. Where contracting prevails, other farmers often discover that to sell what they produce they must produce under contract. Second, because farmers are seldom organized to counter the market power of corporate contractors with their own collective bargaining power, contract prices are often quite low. Third, because the contractor tells the farmer what, when, and how to produce, when to harvest, and when to deliver his crop, contract farming often removes from the farmer's hands many responsibilities that have traditionally been his as an independent entrepreneur.[27]

Contract farming permits the corporation to obtain high-value commodities at low "wage" prices while controlling the essential aspects of the production process. It provides the corporation with a labor force that is self-disciplined, self-exploiting, and non-unionized. Thus, it is not surprising to learn that in the United States contract farming is at least three times as prevalent as corporate farming. The American Agricultural Marketing Association estimates that 50 percent of America's food supply will be produced under contract with corporations by 1980 (as compared to 17 percent in 1970).[28]

Government Policy. A number of governmental policies have worked to the advantage of large growers and have given impetus to the disappearance of the small farmer. The most important of these special advantages are (1) agricultural support programs; (2) tax policies; (3) agricultural labor policies; and (4) the research-orientation of the USDA and the land grant colleges.[29]

During the New Deal years, when family farms were the predominant source of food production, the government instituted agricultural support programs in order to help the farmer through the depression. The subsidy payments were directly proportional to the total productivity of the farm; so the more a person (or corporation) owned the more relief he (or it) received. In other words, income and price supports have been based on volume and acreage. As Table 2 illustrates, the wealthiest farmers with the capital necessary to expand and produce large quantities of food are now the chief beneficiaries of these government programs. The small farmer, who has the greatest need, is often unable to even qualify for support. In short, American agricultural relief policy has subsidized the corporate interest in agricultural production.[30]

TABLE 2

THE DISTRIBUTION OF FEDERAL FARM BENEFITS

	Proportion of Government Payment Received by Percentile, 1967
Top 5 percent of farmers	42.4%
Top 20 percent of farmers	69.0%
Top 40 percent of farmers	87.7%
Lower 60 percent of farmers	13.3%
Lower 40 percent of farmers	5.7%
Lower 20 percent of farmers	1.1%

Source: James T. Bonnen, "The Distribution of Benefits from Selected U. S. Farm Programs," *Rural Poverty in the United States: A Report of the President's National Advisory Commission on Rural Poverty* (Washington, D.C., 1968).

The tax laws also do not give the small farmer an even break. Family farmers find themselves at a competitive disadvantage in the face of a variety of income tax loopholes available to large corporate farm units and non-farm investors in farm land. The tax laws are complex and there is not the time or space to examine them in any detail here. Perhaps the two basic avenues by which tax regulations contribute to the corporate control of agriculture are the provisions which encourage high-income urban residents to make agricultural investments as "tax shelters" and the "accounting devices which vertically integrated corporations can use to shift their income and losses to minimize their taxable income."[31] In addition, family farmers are hurt by rising property tax rates, as expanding urban and recreational developments drive up the price of land. A recent USDA report sums up the tax situation:

> It thus appears that congressional efforts to protect the family and small sized farm through the tax system may have been somewhat self-defeating, largely because of the difficulties in limiting the benefits of special tax preferences to the intended group. The provisions are so broadly written as to invite abuse, or so narrowly defined that they provide little actual assistance.[32]

The third major corporate advantage is the exclusion of agricultural labor from the legislation governing unionization. Goldschmidt briefly summarizes how the low wages paid farm labor work to the disadvantage of the small farmer:

> The family farmer's income derives in part from his capital investment, in part from managerial skill, but in large part from the value of his labor input. Commodity prices will be affected by prevailing wages; the farmer competing with poorly paid workers thus receives less compensation for his work.[33]

A final corporate advantage is derived from farm research, much of it carried on at land grant schools with public money. Although designed as the peoples' universities with a mandate to serve the needs of a broad rural constituency, the land grant college complex has today become the sidekick and frequent servant of agribusiness. In *Hard Tomatoes, Hard Times,* an investigation of the land grant college system, Jim Hightower documents how these colleges are being called upon by big business to participate directly in the planning, research, and development stages of efforts toward the increased mechanization of agriculture.[34] These efforts have helped to develop the overly mechanized, capital intensive pattern of production which has contributed in large part to the decline of the small farm. The Extension Service, which is the land grant system's means of reaching rural people, has devoted most of its attention to achieving greater output and efficiency, thereby providing technical services to larger farmers, not to the smaller ones.

Ray Marshall and Allen Thompson, in their analysis of the status of small farmers, provide a number of examples of how the bias toward the large producer, illustrated in the four areas discussed above, is evident throughout the entire network of federal, state, and local agricultural agencies. The prevailing attitude, insist Marshall and Thompson, is that small farmers are obsolete and have no real future in the American agricultural system.[35]

Loss of Agricultural Land and Land Speculation. American agricultural land is being lost at the equivalent of 320 acres per hour or about 3 million acres a year. Over a million of these acres constitute what the government labels "prime" agricultural land.[36] Much of this land is taken over for suburban developments, shopping centers, and industrial parks. Thousands of additional acres are lost to power lines, dams, and recreational developments or are destroyed by corporations strip mining for coal. Together these developments have led to land speculation and a rapid escalation of farm land prices.

Foreign investors have recently become the most conspicuous players in the farm land sweepstakes, but the storm raised by foreign ownership has obscured the broader issue of the threat that land speculation poses to the family farm.[37] In an era where more acreage and higher-volume production is the only way a family farmer can successfully compete, he is facing increasing difficulty in buying or renting prime agricultural land. Even if the farmer can find land, he often cannot afford it because of the high price or his inability to get credit. In some areas today, an acre of farm land is worth about four times the value of what it can produce per year.[38] High land prices also cause property taxes to rise to such an extent that many farmers can no longer afford to keep their land in agricultural use. The spiralling farm land prices have made it next to impossible for new or young farmers to begin farming. If an individual is not fortunate enough to have inherited a farm, the initial investment for land and operating costs can be close to $400,000[39] Black farmers, whose problems are compounded by racial discrimination, have had particular difficulty in acquiring agricultural land.[40]

James Krohe, Jr. summarizes the effects on American agriculture if prime farm land continues to disappear at its current rate and land prices continue their precipitous rise. The effects include:

> ...more farm debt (and debt-caused foreclosures); acceleration of the trend toward fewer and bigger farms run by fewer and older farmers ...;increased concentration of production...with its attendant dangers of monopolization; neglect of the productive resources of the land by speculators interested only in its price;...and absentee corporate managements that buy their supplies and do their banking in big cities instead of small towns.[41]

III

In the spirit of Jeffersonian democracy, Americans have always paid lip service to the family farm. Yet today it is clear that the family farm is in serious trouble and that immediate and far-reaching measures are needed to save it. The question is, are family farms worth the effort?

The Social Argument. In 1946 Walter Goldschmidt, in an effort to determine the important factors in rural development, looked closely at two California communities. Each had essentially the same soil and agricultural base, but each was surrounded by farms of a different size. Goldschmidt discovered a clear and direct relationship between small farms and a high level of social and economic development in small communities. As compared to the community surrounded by large farms, the small farms community had twice as many businesses, 61 percent more retail trade and three times as many household and building supply purchases. It supported more people per dollar of agricultural production, had a better average standard of living, a much greater proportion of independent businessmen and white collar workers, more and better schools, and twice as many civic organizations, churches, and means of community decision-making.[42]

Efforts were made to suppress Goldschmidt's controversial conclusions, and large landowners, corporate interests, and the Farm Bureau were able to pressure Congress into forbidding the Bureau of Agricultural Research (the sponsor of the study) from funding any further research of a social or cultural nature.[43] As a result, little follow-up work was done, and Goldschmidt's conclusions were largely forgotten in the 1950s and 1960s. Recently, however, several studies have confirmed Goldschmidt's findings. For example, a study in South Dakota revealed that every time six family farmers left the land, one small business had to close. A 1977 California study examined 136 towns and concluded that not only were small farm towns more viable and supported more services, but that small farm regions contained more towns. This suggests that not only the quality, but the occurrence of communities depends on the structure of agriculture in the surrounding area.[44]

The Ecological Argument. Since World War II the emphasis in agriculture has shifted from the diversification of crops to a relatively new phenomenon known as monoculture.[45] The use of pesticides and synthetic fertilizers, a controlled breeding program to develop a few high-yielding, uniform crops, and the mechanization of the farm are all characteristics of monoculture farming. However, the introduction of these farming methods has upset the ecological balance. It is now questionable whether "modern" agriculture can, in the long run, maintain high yields of food production. Scientists and the Food and Drug Administration are deeply concerned about the chronic poisoning of food, and lack of plant resistance to disease, the depletion of soils, and the flood hazards related to monocultural practices. There is additional concern over the vast amount of energy resources required to power farm machinery and to produce necessary petrochemical products.[46]

Monoculture techniques require a great amount of capital. As a result, large farms are the only ones able to support the monoculture habit. The small farmer may have at one time gratefully accepted this illusory panacea. What he is now finding is that his careful handling of the land through the use of crop rotation, organic fertilizers, and solar energy offers a better, less costly alternative for the adequate provision of food and preservation of croplands for future generations.[47]

The Efficiency Argument. Many people grant that the small farm has social and ecological advantages over the corporate farm, but question whether the small farm can feed America. There exist a number of studies which establish the validity of the claim that the family farm is the most efficient unit of production. the classic summary statement on this issue, prepared by J. Patrick Madden and published by the USDA in 1967, concluded that the family farm can achieve unit costs as low as, if not lower than, giant operations.[48] This was confirmed in 1969 by Dr. Roy Van Arsdall, an agricultural economist at the University of Illinois. "The evidence suggests," wrote Arsdall, "that family farms can convert inputs into outputs in physical terms as effectively as any other form of business."[49] Another USDA study confirmed these results in 1973. As the Deputy Director of the USDA's Commodity Economics Division put it:

> We are so conditioned to equate bigness with efficiency that nearly everyone assumes that large-scale undertakings are inherently more efficient than smaller ones. In fact, the claim of efficiency is commonly used to justify bigness. But when we examine the realities we find that most of the economies associated with size in farming are achieved by the one-man fully mechanized farm.[50]

Even the Ralston Purina Company, with long experience as a corporate farmer, admits that the family farmer "can meet and many times surpass the efficiency of the large units that operate with hired management."[51] John Kenneth Galbraith, in his *Economics and the Public Purpose,* summarizes why this is so:

> Nothing regulates the hours of work of the individual entrepreneur, and nothing at all regulates the intensity of his effort. He may thus be in a position to offset the higher technical productivity of the better-equipped worker in the organized but regulated sector of the economy by working longer, harder or more intelligently than his organization counterpart. In doing so, he reduced his compensation per unit of effective and useful effort expended. He is, to put the matter differently, almost wholly free, as the organization is not, to exploit his labor force since his labor force consists of himself.[52]

Foreign experiences provide some useful insight into the efficiency of the small farm. The small farm has demonstrated remarkable viability, even in countries like the Soviet Union where it operates in a very hostile ideological environment. The experiences of Taiwan and several East European countries suggest that on the average small farms can be more efficient than larger ones in producing the same crops. The experiences in other countries also suggest that smaller farms may be more efficient in labor intensive crops requiring limited amounts of land and capital.[53]

Finally, there is, as Peter Barnes points out, the question of how much and what kind of efficiency is desirable. American agriculture is, if anything, too efficient; it is the only industry in which people are paid *not* to produce. Moreover asks Barnes, what kind of efficiency are we talking about? The mechanization of the farm has impoverished millions of rural families, sent them to overcrowded cities, and forced them onto welfare rolls. Thus, large farms are far less efficient when their total effect on the community is evaluated.[54]

The Political Argument. The family farm represents one of the few remaining areas of decentralized ownership and control in an increasingly concentrated and corporate society. Today more and more Americans are not really free to make major decisions affecting their lives. They work for large corporations or government bureaucracies or on assembly lines. They are not their own bosses, not proud of their work, and are not motivated to exercise their full rights as citizens. The family farm allows people to determine their own lifestyle and to take pride in the quality of their work; the farmer is his own employer, making his own decisions, winning or losing by his own efforts. If agriculture goes the way of the auto industry, asks Barnes, where will our independent citizens come from?[55]

There is a tendency to romanticize the democratic virtues of the small farm. Family farmers are not more virtuous nor further removed from human frailty than others in society. Not all persons now in farming should remain there and not all farms should be small or medium-sized. But we cannot have political democracy without economic democracy. A diversified system of agriculture with control dispersed among many persons is certainly more conducive to equity and justice in our society than a system where control is increasingly concentrated in the hands of a few.[56]

IV

It is clearly in our interest to make small-scale farming economically viable so that present small farmers can survive and new ones can get started. There is space here only to highlight some of the major reform proposals.

Increasing Economic Opportunities. Since it is the small farm operator who is hurt the most by the inherent instability of agricultural prices, measures must be taken to stabilize these prices. In addition to a price support system to reduce the downward movement in prices, Marshall and Thompson suggest that careful attention be given to a countercyclical purchasing program to buffer agricultural price fluctuations and increase national and international food reserves.[57] There are a wide variety of proposals designed to give small farmers access to greater marketing options. These include revival of old methods, such as farmers' markets and the promotion of growers' and consumers' cooperatives, along with newer and more far-reaching suggestions, such as using the procurement power of federal and state governments to bypass the middlemen and purchase directly from farmers and farmer cooperatives.[58] Concern over the lack of ready sources of capital and credit have led to calls for the establishment of a Rural Development Bank which could provide low-interest loans and loan guarantees to small farmers.[59]

Protection Against Conglomerates. Proposals in this area emphasize the need for a forceful antitrust policy for agriculture which would prohibit businesses with major investments in non-farm assets from engaging in agricultural production and would ban ownership of farm land by corporations. There are also demands for FTC enforcement of existing regulations against overconcentration in the food industry, for elimination of tax deductions which encourage food advertising, and for an investigation of the international grain marketing system.[60] Food processors and middlemen could be required to bargain collectively with farmers, thereby restoring some balance to the power relationship that is forcing farmers to merge into the corporate system or go out of business.[61] Government support of low-income cooperatives also wold help to strengthen the position of the working farmer and control the growth of agribusiness.[62]

Reorienting Government Policy. Current agricultural support programs, tax laws, and labor policies must be changed. No system of subsidy or price supports for agriculture should be tied to volume of production; rather it should be designed to support family farm income and to stablize prices.[63] Tax laws that provide conglomerates with unfair tax advantages should be reviewed and modified to give the competive advantage to persons earning the bulk of their income from agriculture alone. For example, tax loss farming could be minimized and special tax breaks could be given for organic farming and the use of equipment more suitable for small farmers.[64] Labor laws should guarantee to farm workers a minimum wage equal to that of other workers; this measure along with a general farm workers' bill of rights would end large landowners' ability to exploit great numbers of poor people and would allow self-employed farmers to derive more value from their own labor.[65]

The USDA must be made more responsive to the needs of the majority of farmers. Legislation that would define a farm on the basis of agricultural products "produced," not "sold," would prevent the USDA from periodically defining hundreds of thousands of small farmers out of existence. The establishment of Advisory Committees representing independent family farmers, minorities, farm workers, consumers, and environmentalists would help open up the Department to the public.[66] The USDA, land grant colleges, and the Extension Service must redirect their research, demonstration, education, and assistance programs from the current focus on large-scale and high-energy farming operations to the needs of small farmers. They must give more attention to such neglected areas as cooperative marketing, organic farming, small-scale farm machinery, appropriate technology, and the general health of the rural community.[67] Marshall and Thompson go so far as to propose that all federal programs designed to improve the conditions of small farms should be removed from the USDA and placed in a separate agency whose main interests might include the welfare of all small businesses.[68] Others, pessimistic over the possibility of breaking the grip of powerful agribusiness interests on federal agricultural policy, urge farmer and citizen activists to turn to state and local governments for help.[69]

Land Reform. There exist a number of different proposals designed to slow down the loss of farm land. The repeal of the federal capital gains privilege would be a good beginning to inhibiting land speculation.[70] Zoning rural land for specific uses, such as agriculture or new towns, would help contain suburban sprawl and ease the pressure on small farmers to sell to developers.[71] A corollary to zoning would be imposition of a real property tax based on use-value rather than market-value.[72] Some states have even passed or are considering bills that establish special agricultural districts, that place a special capital gains tax on land speculation aimed at protecting farmers, or that require owners of large land holdings to pay property taxes at a higher rate than owners of less land.[73] Land trusts should be encouraged to take the profits out of land speculation and to ensure that adequate land is available for farming at prices related to the potential returns in agriculture.[74] A federal land bank could provide low-interest loans to enable farmers to purchase property or expand farms.[75]

Other proposals call for the redistribution of land. The guiding principles behind these proposals are that land should belong to those who work and live on it and that holdings should be reasonable proportions.[76] Many of these proposals call for the enforcement of the Reclamation Act of 1902, which provides that large landholders in the West who accept federally subsidized water must agree to sel their holdings in excess of 160 acres at prewater prices within ten years.[77] Peter Barnes calls for an updating of Thaddeus Steven's old program for dividing up large plantations in the South into forty-acre parcels.[78]

The above proposals are just a few of the elements of a program that would help to save the family farm. As Jim Hightower points out, there is nothing radical or even new about them. It is not that we have lacked solution but that we have lacked the will. If we are going to make a difference in any part of our life, says Hightower, perhaps the place to start is here, with corporate power over farming,[79] For as Wendell Berry points out, to protect the small landowner, especially the small farmer, is to preserve what is human and humane in our culture. "The care of the earth," insists Berry, "is our most pleasing responsibility. To cherish what remains of it, and to foster its renewal, is our only legitimate hope."[80]

V

Appalachian farmers are among the most poverty-stricken of American farmers. Observers have labeled much of the farming area of Kentucky, Tennessee, West Virginia, North Carolina, and Virginia as an agricultural slum, "A Land of Do Without."[81] Nevertheless, little has been written on the special conditions and problems faced by Appalachian farmers. Most of the studies which have been conducted are not particularly helpful. They tend to be outdated or to share the attitude of W. B. Back and Clark Edwards.[82] The rural portion of the Tennessee Valley region, conclude Back and Edwards, provides a drag on economic development through its small farm structure and culture, antiurban and urbanization attitudes, limited ability to invest in its human resources, and physical isolation partly related to the topography and transportation facilities of the region. Agricultural development should be oriented to removing such obstacles, and a prime target from the standpoint of land tenure could be the small farm structure. This structure would serve a Jeffersonian world of free-holder subsistence farmers quite well, but not a twentieth century environment for urban expansion. The small farms are potential poverty traps according to twentieth century standards. The solution does not appear to be to increase farm production efficiency within the small farm structure--rather, it apparently resides in human resource investments to prepare people for nonfarm employment, accompanied by a tranformation of the agricultural sector into large-scale commercial operations.[83]

Appalachian farmers have much in common with small farmers elsewhere. They suffer from the same governmental neglect, financial instability, and corporate dominance that plague small farmers throughout the country. There are, however, some obvious differences. The Appalachian farmer tends to be older, less-educated, and poorer. The average farm in Appalachia is smaller, both in total land area and in cropland and harvested cropland. Moreover, the uneven topography results in the division of available cropland into such small and scattered fields that efficient use of modern machinery is at times impossible.[84] The continued destruction of farm land through strip mining, dam building, and recreation development, together with the absentee ownership of large parts of the Appalachian region, make it very difficult for hte Appalachian farmer to find new agricultural land.[85] If he can find it, he usually cannot afford it because the price of land has increased more rapidly in Appalachia than in many other parts of the United States.[86] Another key difference involves the circumstances surrounding industrial development in Appalachia. Dean Pierce maintains that the process by which the greater American community misunderstood, misused, and disrupted the Appalachian farmer's lifestyle has led to special problems for this farmer that cannot be remedied by the solutions currently proposed by the larger society.[87]

Research on the small farm in Appalachia needs to explore a number of important questions: (a) What types of farms exist and what are their characteristics? (b) What is the process by which farm units are formed? (c) To what degree and in what manner do Appalachian farmers suffer from the forces described in Part II of this paper? (d) What has been and is currently the effect of farmer displacement on culture and community life? (e) Where and under what conditions does farming hold economic promise in the mountains? (f) What must be done to ensure the viability of the small farm in Appalachia?[88]

These are difficult questions, but to ignore them is to risk a future where few will own farms and few will work on them. People will have nothing to say about how the land is used or the kind of quality of its produce. They will eat what the corporations decide for them to eat. It will be a future where, in Berry's words, "people will be detached and remote from the sources of their life, joined to them only by corporate tolerance. They will have become consumers purely--consumptive machines--which is to say, the slaves of producers."[89]

If we lose the family farm, we give up more than competitiveness and economic efficiency. We lose a bit of ourselves. We lose our grip on "the idea that individuals can make it on their own, that human enterprise is of greater value than any security that corporate systems can promise."[90] It is, as Wendell Berry reminds us, impossible to care for each other more or differently than we care for the earth.[91]

NOTES

1. Robert Coles, *Migrants, Sharecroppers, Mountaineers* (Boston: Atlantic Monthly Press-Little Brown & Co., 1973), P. 7 Vol. 2, *Children of Crisis.*

2. This is the view of Robert W. Scott, former Federal Co-chairman of the ARC. See Robert W. Scott, "The Plight of the Region's Small Farmer," *Appalachia* 11 (December 1977-January 1978) :21.

3, For an analysis of how some Marxists view the fate of the family farm in the United States, see Pat Mooney, "Class Relations and Class Structure in the Midwest," in "The Transformation of Agriculture in the United States." a manuscript prepared by a collective work group associated with the Department of Rural Sociology at the University of Wisconsin-Madison, October 1979.

4. Murray Bookchin, "Radical Agriculture," in *Radical Agriculture,* ed. Richard Merrill (New York: Harper Colophon Books, 1976), p. 13.

5. USDA, Status of the Family Farm, a report submitted to the Committee on Agriculture, Nutrition, and Forestry, United States Senate, June 18, 1979 (Washington, D.C.: USGPO, 1979), p. 2. The battle over how to define the family farm has important policy impliations. The new official USDA definition requires a place to have $1,000 minimum sales of farm products in order to be counted as a farm. This new definition, instituted in 1979, disqualifies about 302,000 farms. See also James Lewis, "Alternative Definitions of Small Farms and Low-Income Farm Families," in *Toward a Federal Small Farms Policy,* Phase I: Barriers to Increasing On-Farm Income, ed. National Rural Center (Washington, D.C., 1978), pp. 131-47.

6. USDA, *Status of the Family Farm,* p.3.

7. Donald K. Larson and James H. Lewis, "Small-Farm Profile," *in Small-Farm Issues: Proceedings of the ESCS Small-Farm Workshop, May 1978* (Washington, D.C.: USDA, 1979), pp. 10-30

8. Some of the earlier works focusing on the reasons for the decline of the small farm include Joseph Ackerman and Marshall Harris, eds., *Family Farm Policy* (Chicago: University of Chicago Press, 1947); Stanley Andrews, *The Farmer's Dilemma* (Washington, D.C.: Public Affairs Press, 1961); Lee Fryer, *The American Farmer: His Problems and Prospects* (New York: Harper & Brothers, 1947); Anna Rochester, *Why Farmers are Poor: The Agricultural Crisis in the United States* (New York: International Publishers, 1940); and Lauren Soth, *The Embarrassment of Plenty* (New York: Crowell, 1965). For additonal works, see Charles L. Smith, *A Bibliography on Land Reform in Rural America* (San Francisco: Center for Rural Studies, 1974).

9. Victor K. Ray, *The Corporate Invastion of American Agriculture* (Denver: National Farmers Union, 1968). The literature on this debate is summarized in Kevin F. Goss and Richard D. Rodefeld, *Corporate Farming in the United States: A guide to Current Literature, 1967-1977* (University Park: Department of Agricultural Economics and Rural Sociology, Pennsylvania State University, 1978).

10. Shirley E. Greene, "Struggle for Survival," *Engage/Social Action,* October 1978, p. 15.

11. Ray Marshall and Allen Thompson, *Status and Prospects of Small Farmers in the South* (Atlanta: Southern Regional Council, 1976), p. 6.

12. Joe Belden, Gibby Edwards, Cynthia Guyer, and Lee Webb, eds., *New Directions in Farm, Land and Food Policies: A Time for State and Local Action* (Washington, D.C.: Conference on Alternative State and Local Policies, 1978), p. 10.

13. Marshall and Thompson, *Status and Prospects of Small farmers,* p. 9.

14. Ibid., p. 55. See Also Center for Science in the Public Interest, *From the Ground Up: Building a Grass Roots Food Policy* (Washington, D.C., 1976); U. S. Senate, Subcommittee on Agricultural Production, Marketing and Stabilization of Prices, *Marketing Alternatives for Agriculture: Is There a Better Way?* (Washington, D.C.: USGPO, 1976); and USDA, ECSC, *Market Structure of the Food Industries,* Marketing Research Report No. 971 (Washington, D.C., 1972).

15. Marshall and Thompson, *Status and Prospects of Small Farmers,* pp. 53-54; USDA, *Status of the Family Farm,* p. 29; Center for Rural Affairs, *Where Have All the Bankers Gone?* (Walthill, NB, 1977); and Gene Swackhamer and Raymond J. Doll, *Financing Modern Agriculture: Banking's Problems and Challenges* (Kansas City: Federal Reserve Bank, 1969).

16. Marshall and Thompson, *Status and Prospects of Small Farmers,* p. 54; and George Gilbert and Nancy Smith, *The Farmers Home Administration: Its Operation and Programs* (Washington, D.C.: Congressional Research Service, Library of Congress, 1976).

17. Jim Hightower, *Eat Your Heart Out: Food Profiteering in America* (New York: Vintage Books, 1976), p. 163. For further information on the financial problems facing small farmers, see USDA, *Structure Issues of American Agriculture,* Agricultural Economic Report 438 (Washington, D.C., 1979); U.S. Senate Select Committee on Small Business and the Committee on Interior and Insular Affairs, *Will the Family Farm Survive in America?,* 4 vols., 3 parts (Washington, D. C.: USGPO, 1975-76); and U. S. House of Representatives, Sub-committee on Family Farms and Rural Development, *Obstacles in Strengthening Family Farm Systems* (Washington, D.C.: USGPO, 1977).

18. Hightower, *Eat Your Heart Out,* p. 167. The anaylsis in this section of the paper relies heavily on the Hightower study. See also Corporate Date Exchange, Inc., *CDE Stock Ownership Directory-Agribusiness: Who Owns and Controls the Nation's Food Supply* (New York, 1978); A. V. Krebs, *1976 Directory of Major U. S. Corporations Involved in Agribusiness* (San Francisco: Agribusiness Accountability Project, 1976); Interfaith Center on Corporate Responsbility, ed.) *Agribusiness Manual: Background Papers on Corporate Responsbility and Hunger Issues* (New York, 1978); Virginia Cook, *Corporate Farming and the Family Farm,* CSG Research Brief (Lexington, KY: Council of State Governments, 1076); John Shover, *First Majority-Last Minority: The Transforming of Rural Life in America* (Dekalb: Northern Illinois Univ. Press, 1976); Stanley Aronowitz, *Food, Shelter and the*

American Dream (New York: Seabury Press, 1974); Michael Perelman, *Farming for Profit in a Hungry World: Capital and the Crisis in Agriculture* (Montclair, NJ: Allan held, Osmun & Co., 1977); and National Farm Institute, ed., *Corporate Farming and the Family Farm* (Ames: Iowa State Univ. Press, 1970). For additional sources, see Goss and rodefeld, *Corporate Farming in the United States*, pp. 9-16.

19. Cited in Hightower, *Eat Your Heart Out*, p. 168.

20. Paul D. Scanlon, "TDC and Phase II: The McGovern Papers," *Antitrust Law & Economics Review* 5 (Spring 1972): Table 1, 33-36.

21. National Commission on Food Marketing, *Organization and Competition in Food Retailing*, Technical Study No. 7, Federal Trade Commission (Washington, D.C., 1966). See also Hank Frundt, "The Food Gamble," in *U.S. Capitalism in Crisis*, ed. Union for Radical Political Economics (New York, 1978), pp. 155-68.

22. Cited in "Agribusiness and the Food Crisis, *"Corporate Information Center (CIC) Brief*, November 1974, p. 3B.

23. Belden, et. al., *New Directions*, pp. 10-11. For Additional information on the food industry, see Martha Hamilton, *The Great American Grain Robbery & Other Stories* (Washington, D.C.: Agribusiness Accountability Project, 1972); William Robbins, *The American Food Scandal: Why You Can't Eat Well on What You Earn* (New York: William Morrow & Co., 1974); Catherine Lerza and Michael Jacobson, *Food for People, Not for Profit: A Sourcebook on the Food Crisis* (New York: Ballentine, 1975); and Dan Morgan, *Merchants of Grain* (New York: Viking, 1979).

24. Walter Goldschmidt, *As You Sow: Three Studies in the Social Consequences of Agribusiness* (Glencoe, Illinois: Free Press, 1947; Montclair, New Jersey: Allanheld, Osmun & Co., 1978), p. xxvi.

25. Jim Hightower, "The Case for the Family Farmer, *"Washington Monthly*, September 1973, p. 28.

26. Statement of Jim Hightower, *Role of Giant Corporations*, Hearings before the Subcommittee on Monopoly of the Select Committee on Small Business, U. S. Senate, Ninety-second Congress (November 30 and December 1, 1971; March 1 and 2, 1972), Part 3, p. 3725.

27. John E. Davis, "There's a Contract Out on the Small Farmer," *Rural America*, October 1979, p. 5. See also Marshall and Thompson, *Status and Prospects of Small Farmers*, pp. 55-56; Goldschmidt, *As You Sow*, pp. xxvi-xxvii; Hightower, *Eat Your Heart Out*, pp. 197-208; Ronald Mighell and William Hoofnagle, *Contract Production and Vertical Intergration in Farming, 1960 and 1970* (Washington, D.C.: USDA, 1972); and Shover, *First Majority-Last Minority*, pp. 175-228.

28. Belden, et al., *New Directions*, p. 10.

29. The Analysis in this section relies heavily on Goldschmidt, *As You Sow*, pp. xxxii-xxxix. For general works on U. S. agricultural policy, see Williard Cochrane and Mary Ryan, *American Farm Policy, 1948-1973* (Minneapolis: University of Minnesota, 1976); Dale Hathaway, *Government and Agriculture: Public Policy in a Democratic Society* (New York: Macmillan, 1963); and Marion Clawson, *Policy Directions for U. S. Agriculture* (Baltimore: Johns Hopkins University Press, 1968).

30. Goldschmidt, *As You Sow*, pp. xxxii-xxxiii; Don Paarlberg, *American Farm Policy*, (New York: Wiley, 1964); Reo Christenson, *The Brannan Plan: Farm Politics and Policy* Ann Arbor: University of Michigan, 1959); and USDA, *Status of the Family Farm*, pp. 30-32.

31. Goldschmidt, *As You Sow*, p. xxxiv; Isao Fujemoto and Martin Zone, *Sources of Inequities in Rural America* (Davis: Department of Applied Be-

havioral Sciences, University of California, Davis, 1976); Jeanne Dangerfield, "Sowing the Till: A Background Paper on Tax Loss Farming," *Congressional Record* 119 (May 16, 1973): 9247-55; Charles A. Sisson, *The U.S. Tax System and the Structure of Agriculture* (Washington, D.C.: National Rural Center, 1979); Thomas Carlin and W. Fred Woods, *Tax Loss Farming*, ERS-546 (Washington, D.C.: USDA, 1974); and Marshall and Thompson, *Status and Prospects of Small Farmers*, pp. 61-64.

32. USDA, *Status of the Family Farm*, p. 29.

33. Goldschmidt, *As You Sow*, p. xxxviii.

34. Jim Hightower and Susan DeMarco, *Hard Tomatoes, Hard Times: The Failure of the Land Grant College Complex* (Cambridge, Massachusetts: Schenkman, 1972). See also U. S. Senate, Committee on the Judiciary, Hearings on *Priorities in Agricultural Research of the USDA* (Washington, D.C.: USGPO, 1977); U. S. General Accounting Office, *Some Problems Impeding Economic Improvements of Small-Farm Operations* (Washington, D.C.: USGPO, 1975); William Friedland and Amy Barton, *Destalking the Wily Tomato* (Davis: College of Agricultural and Environmental Sciences, University of California, Davis, 1975); and Joe Belden with Gregg Forte, *Toward a National Food Policy* (Washington, D.C.: Exploratory Project for Economic Alternatives, 1976), pp. 103-06.

35. Marshall and Thompson, *Status and Prospects of Small Farmers*, p. 64.

36. National Agricultural Lands Study, *Where Have the Farm Lands Gone?* (Washington, D.C., 1979). See also Peter Meyer, "Land Rush: A Survey of America's Land," *Harpers,* January 1979, pp. 45-60; and Frank Browning, *The Vanishing Land: The Corporate Theft of America* (New York: Harper Colophor Books, 1975).

37. U. S. Senate, Committee on Agriculture, Nutrition and Forestry, *Foreign Investment in United States Agricultural Land* (Washington, D.C.: USGPO, 1979); U. S. General Accounting Office, *Foreign Ownership of United States Farmland-Much Concern, Little Data* (Washington, D.C.: USGPO, 1978); and Kenneth C. Crowe, *America for Sale* (Garden City NY: Doubleday, 1978).

38. James Krohe, "Farm-Land Bonanza," *The Nation,*, February 17, 1979, p. 177. See also Marvin Duncan, *Farm Real Estate Values: What's Happening and Why* (Kansas City: Federal Reserve Bank, 1979).

39. Belden, et al., *New Directions*, pp. 9-10.

40. See Leo McGee and Robert Boone, eds., *The Black Rural Landowner-Endangered Species: Social, Political and Economic Implications* (Westport, CT: Greenwood Press, 1979); James Lewis, *White and Minority Small Farm Operators in the South,* Agricultural Economic Report 353 (Washington, D.C.: USDA, 1976); and Lester Salamon, *Land and Minority Enterprises: The Crisis and the Opportunity* (Washington, D.C.: U.S. Dept. of Commerce, 1976).

41. Krohe, "Farm Land Bonanza," p. 178.

42. Goldschmidt, *As You Sow*, pp. 3-451.

43. For details of the efforts to repress Goldschmidt's study, see Goldschmidt, *As You Sow*, pp. 455-91.

44. These studies and others are summarized in Goldschmidt, *As You Sow*, pp. xxxix-xlviii; and Alabama Marketing Project, "Land Ownership Patterns and Community Development," in *A Landless People in a Rural Region: A Reader on Land Ownership and Property Taxation in Appalachia,* ed. Steve Fisher (New Market, Tennessee: Highlander Center, 1979), pp. 155-56.

45. Richard Merrill, "Toward a Self-Sustaining Agriculture," in *Radical Agriculture,* ed Richard Merrill (New York: Harper Colophon Books, 1976)

pp. 284-327; Harrison Wellford, *Sowing the Wind: Ralph Nader's Study Group Report on Food Safety and the Chemical Harvest* (New York: Grossman, 1972); and Belden, *Toward a National Food Policy*, pp. 120-50.

46. Barry Commoner, *The Poverty of Power* (New York: Bantam Book, 1977), pp. 149-64; and Michael Perelman, "Efficiency in Agriculture: The Economics of Energy," in *Radical Agriculture*, ed. Richard Merrill (New York: Harper Colophon Books, 1976), pp. 64-86.

47. A number of articles on these alternatives can be found in Richard Merrill, ed., *Radical Agriculture* (New York: Harper Colophon Books, 1976). See Also Commoner, *The Poverty of Power*, pp. 149-64; Wendall Berry, *The Unsettling of America: Culture and Agriculture* (New York: Avon Books, 1978); Garth Youngberg, "The Alternative Agricultural Movement," *Policy Studies Journal* 6 (Summer 1978): 524-30; Daniel Zwerdling, "Curbing the Chemical Fix-Organic Farming: The Secret Is It Works," *Progressive*, December 1978, pp. 16-25; and Henry Esbenshade, *Farming: Sources for a Social and Ecologically Accountable Agriculture* (Davis, California: Alternative Agricultural Resources Project, 1976).

48. J. Patrick Madden, *Economics of Size in Farming: Theory, Analytical Procedures, and a Review of Selected Studies*, Agricultural Economic Report 107 (Washington, D.C.: USDA, 1967).

49. Quoted in Hightower, *Eat Your Heart Out*, p. 157.

50. Warren R. Bailey, *The One-Man Farm*, ER S-519 (Washington, D.C.: USDA, 1973): 1. See also Gordon Ball and Earl Heady, eds., *Size, Structure and Future of Farms* (Ames: Iowa State University Press, 1972); and Philip Raup, "Corporate Farming in the United States," *Journal of Economic History* 33 (March 1973): 274-90.

51. Quoted in Hightower, *Eat Your Heart Out*, p. 158. Similarly, Tenneco admits that from the standpoint of efficiency, "there is no substitute for the small-to-medium-sized independent grower who lives on or near his farmland." See Henry J. Freundt, "Agbiz 'Insignificant' for Nation's Largest Farmer," in *Agribusiness Manual*. ed. Interfaith Center on Corporate Responsibility (New York, 1978).

52. John Kenneth Galbraith, *Economics and the Public Purpose* (Boston: Houghton Mifflin Co., 1973), p. 73.

53. These studies are summarized in Marshall and Thompson, *Status and Prospects of Small Farmers*, pp. 68-72.

54. Peter Barnes, "Land Reform in America," in *Radical Agriculture*, ed. Richard Merrill (New York: Harper Colophon books, 1976), p. 27.

55. Ibid., p. 30. See also A. Whitney Griswold, *Farming and Democracy* (New Haven: Yale University Press, 1952).

56. Greene, "Struggle for Survival," pp. 18-19.

57. Marshall and Thompson, *Status and Prospects of Small Farmers*, p. 79.

58. Belden, et al., *New Directions*, pp. 28-37, 198-213; Agricultural Marketing Project, *Marketing Report: Food Fairs* (Nashville: Center for Health Services, Vanderbilt University, 1976); William Ronco, *Food Co-ops* (Boston: Beacon Press, 1974); Deborah Bowles, *Farmers' Market Organizer Handbook* (Olympia, Washington Hunger Action Center, Evergreen College, 1976); and Hightower, *Eat Your Heart Out*, p. 304.

59. Marshall and Thompson, *Status and Prospects of Small Farmers*, p. 79; Belden, *Toward a National Food Policy*, pp. 111-14; and Belden, et al., *New Directions*, pp. 19-27.

60. Rural America, *Platform for Rural America*, revised at the Third National Conference on Rural America, December 5-7, 1977, (Washington, D.C., 1978), pp. 25-27; Hightower, *Eat Your Heart Out*, pp. 303-04; Barnes,

"Land Reform in America," pp. 30-31; and Sheldon L. Greene, "Corporate Accountability and the Family Farm," in *Radical Agriculture,* ed. Richard Merrill (New York: Harper Colophon Books, 1976), pp. 59-61.

61. Marshall and Thompson, *Status and Prospects of Small Farmers,* p. 80; *Eat Your Heart Out,* p. 304; and Greene, "Corporate Accountability and the Family Farm," p. 61.

62. Rural America, *Platform for Rural America,* p. 25; Greene, "Corporate Accountability and the Family Farm," pp. 59-60; Belden, *Toward a National Food Policy,* pp. 117-19; and Linda Kravitz, Who's *Minding the Co-op? A Report on Farmer Control of Farmer Cooperatives* (Washington, D.C.: Agribusiness Accountability Project, 1974).

63. Rural America, *Platform for Rural America,* p. 25.

64. Greene, "Corporate Accountability and the Family Farm," pp. 58-59; and Marshall and Thompson, *Status and Prospects of Small Farmers,* p. 79.

65. Barnes, "Land Reform in America," p. 31; and Greene, "Corporate Accountability and the Family Farm," p. 60.

66. Rural America, *Platform for Rural America,* pp. 24-27.

67. Hightower and DeMarco, *Hard Tomatoes, Hard Times,*. pp. 138-43; Berry, *The Unsettling of America,* pp. 221-22; Belden, et al., *New Directions,* 55-69; and Rural America, *Platform for Rural America,* p. 24.

68. Marshall and Thompson, *Status and Prospects of Small Farmers,* p. 79.

69. Belden, et al., *New Directions,* pp. 11-12. The book provides an excellent introduction to innovative state and local actions related to small farm issues.

70. Rural America, *Platform for Rural America,* p.27.

71. Belden, *Toward a National Food Policy,* pp. 114-17; Greene, "Corporate Accountability and the Family Farm," p. 61; U. S. Senate, Committee on Agriculture, Nutrition and Forestry, Hearings on the *Farmland Protection Act* (Washington, D.C.: USGPO, 1979); and Joseph H. Nash, Jr., "Farmcolony: A Development Approach to Loss of Agricultural Land," *Urban Land,* February 1976, 12-16.

72. Farm-value assessment laws are often placed in three classes: preferential assessment, deferred taxation, and restrictive agreement. Questions have been raised as to the effectiveness of these laws as land use control mechanisms. See Robert Brandon, Jonathan Rower, and Thomas Stanton, Tax Politics (New York: Pantheon, 1076), pp. 158-63; Robert J. Gloudemans, *Use-Value Farmland Assessments: Theory, Practice and Impact* (Chicago: International Association of Assessing Officers, 1974); Glen W. Atkinson, "The Effectiveness of Differential Assessment of Agricultural and Open Space Land," *American Journal of Economics and Sociology* 36 (April 1977): 197-204; Thomas F. Hady, "Differential Assessment of Farmland on the Rural-Urban Fringe," *American Journal of Agricultural Economics* 52 (February 1970): 25-32; and John Keene, *Untaxing Open Space,* prepared for the Council on Environmental Quality (Washington, D.C.: USGPO, 1976).

73. See H. E. Conklin and W. R. Bryant, "Agricultural Districts: A Compromise Approach to Agricultural Preservation," *American Journal of Aricultural Economics* 56 (August 1974): 607-13; Belden, et al., *New Directions,* pp. 97-112; and Bryon Dorgan, *The Progressive Land Tax: A Tax Incentive for the Family Farm* (Washington, D.C.: Conference on Alternative State and Local Policies, 1978).

74. International Independence Institute, *The Community Land Trust: A Guide to a New Model for Land Tenure in America* (Cambridge, Massachusetts: Center for Community Economic Development, 1972); and Belden, et al.) *New Directions,* p. 88.

75. Jerry Hardt, *The Feasibility and Design of a Central Appalachian Land Bank*, prepared for the A.R.C. (Berea, Kentucky: Human/Economic Appalachian Development Corporation, 1979); and Ann L. Strong, *Land Banking: European Reality, American Prospect* (Baltimore: John Hopkins University Press, 1979).

76. Barnes, "Land Reform in America," p. 31. See also Geoffrey Faux, "Reclaiming America," *Working Papers* 1 (Summer 1973): 31-42; Peter Barnes, *The People's Land: A Reader on Land Reform in the United States* (Emmaus, Pennsylvania: Rodale Press, 1975); and Florence Constant, *Land Reform: A Bibliography* (Cambridge, Massachusetts: Center for community Economic Development, 1972).

77. Barnes, "Land in America," pp. 31-33. See Charles Smith, *A Bibliography on the 160-Acre Anti-Monopoly Water Law* (San Francisco: Center for Rural Studies, 1974).

78. Barnes, "Land Reform in America," p. 32.

79. Hightower, *Eat Your Heart Out*, pp. 304-06.

80. Berry, *The Unsettling of America*, p. 14.

81. Ladd Haysted and Gilbert Fife, *The Agricultural Regions of the United States* (Norman: University of Oklahoma Press, 1955), p. 82.

82. See Roy E. Procter and T. Kelly White, "Agriculture: A Reassessment," in *The Southern Appalachian Region*, ed. Thomas Ford (Lexington: University of Kentucky Press, 1962), pp 87-101; *The Appalachian Region's Agriculture: Its Problems and Potentials for Development*, prepared for the President's Appalachian Regional Commission (Washington, D.C., 1963); R. I. Coltrane and E. L. Baum, *An Economic Survey of the Appalachian Region, with Special Reference to Agriculture*, Agricultural Economic Report 69 (Washington, D.C.: USDA, 1965); Anthony Pavlick, *Toward Solving the Low-Income Problems of Small Farmers in the Appalachian Area*, Bulletin 499T (Morgantown: West Virginia Agricultural Experiment Station, 1964); and USDA, *Employment, Unemployed and Low Incomes in Appalachia* (Washington, D.C.: 1965).

83. W. B. Back and Clark Edwards, "Socioeconomic Trends and Nonfarm Demands for Resources in the Tennessee Valley," in *Farmland Tenure and Farmland Use in the Tennessee Valley* (Southern Land Economic Research Committee, n. d.).

84. Proctor and White, p. 87.

85. See Steve Fisher, ed., *A Landless People in a Rural Region: A Reader on Land-ownership and Property Taxation in Appalachia* (New Market, Tennessee: Highlander Center, 1979); Judy Miller, "Where Does All of Our Farmland Go?", *Mountain Review*, January 1979, pp. 35-38; and Hal Lenke, "Land Poor: The Appalachian Farmer," *People's Appalachia* 3 (Spring 1973): 35-36.

86. USDA, *Status of the Family Farm*, p. 25.

87. Dean Pierce, "The Low-Income Farmer: A Reassessment," *Social Welfare in Appalachia* 3 (1971): 7-10. For more information on the effects of industrial development on Appalachian agriculture, see Harry Caudill, *Night Comes to the Cumberlands (Boston: Atlantic Monthly-Little, Brown, & Co., 1962).*

88. Marshall and Thompson (Status and Prospects of Small Farmers, p. 80) offer a set of specific questions which could be used in structuring a response to the problem of how to ensure the viability of the small farm in Appalachia. See also Fred Stewart, Harry Hall and Eldon Smith, "Potential for Increased Income on Small Farms in Appalachian Kentucky," *American Journal of Agricultural Economics* 61 (February 1979): 77-82; and Sammy Comer and

Roger C. Woodworth, *Improving Incomes on Limited Resource Farms in South Central Tennessee,* Bulletin 36 (Nashville: School of Agriculture and Home Economics, Tennessee State University, 1976).
  89. Berry, *The Unsettling of America,* p. 74.
  90. Hightower, *Eat Your Heart Out,* p. 188.
  91. Berry, *The Unsettling of America,* p. 123.

COMPARATIVE REGIONAL ISSUES: LAND USE AND ENVIRONMENTAL PLANNING IN THE ADIRONDACKS AND APPALACHIANS

Parker G. Marden and Alan M. Schwartz with Kealy Salomon, Gardiner Tucker, Susan Tewksbury, Timothy Jones, and Laurie Booth,
ST. LAWRENCE UNIVERSITY

Abstract

In this paper, an effort is undertaken to compare two regions--the northernmost counties in New York (commonly known as the "North Country") and the southern Appalachians. After examining the possibilities and merits of developing a comparative perspective on regional issues, a comparison is made between policies on land use and environmental planning in two areas within the larger regions: the Adirondacks and the mountains of western North Carolina. In the first case, land use and development is managed by the strictest set of controls governing private land in the United States. In the second instance, the controls are far less restrictive and administered at a local level. The notions of dependency theory are evoked to emphasize that structural arrangements are present in both instances that pass control into the hands of others.

In this report, we propose to offer a comparison of two regions--the northernmost counties of New York (commonly known as the "North Country") and the southern Appalachians. Our goals here are to suggest the value of developing a strong comparative perspective on regional issues and, by way of example, to specify some important aspects of land use and the regional character of the two areas. Such comparisons offer possibilities for understanding that are not easily revealed in each separate case. In most respects, our observations are preliminary and tentative; they are perhaps better considered as an agenda for research than as firm conclusions; and they await the enrichment (and alteration) of criticism.

These observations are the direct outgrowth of a summer program in comparative regional issues that has been offered to undergraduates at St. Lawrence University since 1978. The program was developed because, unlike Appalachia, the North Country in which the University is located has not been the object of significant and extensive attention from researchers as *a distinctive region.* Although one can draw lessons about the side effects of such attention from the experience of Appalachia, there is a knowledge base that allows that region to be better understood and appreciated. Accordingly, the program seeks to look at northern New York with perspectives gained during a trip through western North Carolina, central Tennessee, and eastern Kentucky and visits with academicians, planners, regional advocates, and residents to learn how they perceive and address the needs of their region.

Comparative Regional Issues

On the face of it, the potentialities for comparison are not easily recognizable. Despite the presence of its "Appalachian" counties, as reflected in the delineation and influence of the Appalachian Regional Commission, New York generates connotations of affluence that Appalachia does not. The sparkle and self-assuredness of New York City as a cultural and economic center for the world, despite the blight and poverty that gnaws at its core, can be blinding. But just as residents of Appalachia complain about having that region's important features blurred by media-reinforced stereotypes, the process is returned in kind and the "New Yorker" becomes a caricature and one specific to its major metropolis at that. Yet, many communities in the North Country are located as far from New York City as are some communities in western Pennsylvania or West Virginia and their cultural and social isolation may be as marked. Northern New York is not only on the periphery of the state geographically, but politically and economically as well. In a state where Westchester County, so near to New York City, is thought of as "Upstate," what chance is there for distinguishing areas that are more than 300 miles away?

The North Country reaches from Vermont on the East to Lake Ontario and the St. Lawrence River which forms the international boundary with Canada on the West and North. Its southern border is less clearly defined, although appropriately, many persons define it as the area lying North of the metropolitan centers along the old Erie Canal and now the New York Thruway (Albany-Troy-Schenectady, Utica-Rome, and Syracuse). It is a huge area geographically for at its center lies the Adirondack Park--6,000,000 acres, of which much remains as unspoiled wilderness. The North Country is set apart from the rest of the State by its poverty, high unemployment, its harsh winters, the significant out-migration of its youth, a small population (about 250,000) scattered over a large area, and an economy that is especially vulnerable to decisions made by public agencies and private corporations from outside the region and over which it has little control. Further, land use in its Adirondack core is controlled by a controversial set of strict regulations that are unique within the United States.

Many possibilities for comparison with Appalachia are obvious. Although its poverty is quite different in character, some of the nation's poorest counties are located in the Appalachians. Its economy is also based heavily on natural resources, although coal rather than timber is more commonly king. Like the Adirondacks, the natural beauty of areas in Appalachia has attracted tourists and second-home developers, thereby accentuating the struggle between development and preservation. Similarly, most economic and political decisions are made in distant cities. And as in northern New York, many young adults have had to leave the region to find rewarding employment.

A comparative approach is valuable because it can lead to a better understanding of northern New York. The focus on regional concerns that is found in Appalachia is lacking in the North Country. The arguments advanced by dependency theory, for example, can be borrowed to provide a framework for evaluating manifestations of economic and political power. The control of timber and mineral resources in the North Country can be better comprehended by learning about the history of the coal industry in Appalachia. As importantly, however, the comparative approach can sharpen the analysis of the variable being compared. For example, both northern New York and Appalachia are characterized by poverty and high unemployment. From this comparison, however, it is a short step to other dimensions of economic distress: (1) the "character" of poverty (e.g., its possible relief through subsistence farming), (2) the special costs of severe winters and a low-density population, (3) the presence of a shadow economy served by the underemployed, (4) the differential impact of welfare benefits by state, and (5) the relative proximity of extremes in wealth.

Similarly, the consequences of distinctive settlement patterns and their pace and timing can be appreciated through comparison. The Appalchians were settled quite early in the nation's history when compared to northern New York which, with the exception of its periphery along the St. Lawrence River, Lake Champlain, and central New York, was not even well-explored until the mid-1800s. Even today, much of the North Country is very sparsely populated with small hamlets and villages clinging to a limited network of roads. Some areas remain as true wilderness. Both areas can be characterized by the isolation of much of their populations, but in the Appalachians with its distinctive hollows, it is isolation imposed by geology; and in the North Country, it is the isolation of sparseness emphasized annually by winter. The implications of such settlement patterns need to be carefully examined. For example, how much do they contribute to the legacies of a rich and distinctive culture found in the Appalachians and to the lack of unique regional attributes and artifacts in the North Country? In the latter case, the history of recent and scattered settlement, especially in its Adirondack core, precludes the possibility of "trapping" a culture in time.

So the potentialities for comparative regional study are great. In looking at Appalachia and the North Country, the pattern that seems to be emerging is one of general similarities and differences in detail. The benefits rest both in moving towards better understanding of the two regions and in developing better specifications of the dimensions along which the comparisons are made. These goals can be illuminated by an examination of land use controls and environmental planning in Appalachia, here primarily the recreation areas of the North Carolina mountains, and in the Adirondack Park at the center of the North Country.

Environment and Land Use Planning

Both areas are regions of great natural beauty. Persons in the North Country talk with the same affection for the High Peaks of the Adirondacks as their counterparts speak of the Blue Ridge. The attractiveness of the regions, as known to its inhabitants, was discovered next by those of wealth and privilege and both now face the pressures of the "democratization" of leisure with an unprecedented demand for recreational opportunities, including second-home developments and other forms of intensive use. Both regions have also had to contend with the interests of large outside companies interested in timber and mineral resources. But the regions differ dramatically in the way that such challenges are being managed. While growth in western North Carolina and elsewhere along the Blue Ridge is largely the concern of local government, the Adirondack area is managed by the most stringent controls on private land use in effect in the United States. The comparisons can be most instructive.

With its 6,000,000 acres, the Adirondack Park is approximately the size of Vermont. Its population, however, is small--112,000 permanent residents and 90,000 seasonal residents--and much of the area is still wilderness. Approximately 60 percent of the land within the Park is privately owned, including the holdings of large timber companies, while the balance consists of the Adirondack Forest Preserve owned by the State. These lands are intermingled like a haphazard mosaic. All or part of 15 villages, 92 towns, and 12 counties are within the Park's boundaries or the imaginary "Blue Line."

The wilderness character of the Park has been attracting tourists and outdoor enthusiasts for more than a century. The first real threat to the character of the Adirondacks came from the timber industry in the late nineteenth century. Large tracts of land were being leased or sold to logging companies and the virgin forest was being cut. Alarmed at the rate at which state forest land was disappearing, the Legislature adopted what is now Article 14 to the State Constitution in 1895. The opening section remains unchanged to this day:

> The lands of the state, now owned or hereafter acquired, constituting the forest preserve are now fixed by law, shall be forever kept as wild forest lands. They shall not be leased, sold, or exchanged, or taken by any corporation, public or private, nor shall the timber thereon be sold, removed, or destroyed.

Despite increasing pressures, the simplicity and Constitutional character of the law have provided over eighty years of protection for the state-owned land.

The next major threat to the Adirondacks came in the middle of this century. As leisure time and incomes increased, the Aidrondacks Mountains, like many other areas of the United States, attracted an increasing number of visitors. Recreation was no longer the luxury of the rich and persons from all social backgrounds could visit the Adirondacks. Although large portions of the wilderness within the Park were publicly owned and protected by Article 14, many fragile and important ecosystems were not clearly delimited by ownership and parts were often in private hands. As long as their owners resisted development, there would be no problem. Pressures for large-scale development were increasing, however, and the State of New York could no longer be certain that the Adirondack Park would be able to escape the boom in tourism and development that was already engulfing other areas of the country.[1]

In 1968, Governor Nelson Rockefeller created the Temporary Study Commission on the Future of the Adirondacks and charged it with the responsibility of developing a long-range policy for state lands and to suggest measures that would ensure that the development of private lands would be appropriate and consistent with those long-range goals.[2] The Commission produced a report that made 181 recommendations pertaining to all aspects of the Park. The first three dealt with the creation of an Adirondack Park Agency that would be responsible for developing and implementing land use plans for both public and private lands within the Park. The Adirondack Park Agency (APA) Act was passed by both the Senate and Assembly in 1971, although it was opposed by all but one of the legislators from the region.

Immediately after its creation, the Agency produced the State Land Master Plan that was submitted to Governor Rockefeller in 1972. Legislative approval was unnecessary because the Plan dealt solely with management of the state lands. Seven land use classifications for public land and guidelines for their use were designed to maintain the Adirondack Park in as natural and unspoiled condition as possible.

The checkerboard separation of state and private lands within the Park meant that the stringent controls imposed by the APA for the state lands were really of little value if the general character of the surrounding private lands were destroyed by development. After the State Land Master Plan had been approved, the Agency set to work on the much more difficult task of developing a land use plan for the privately owned lands. The Adirondack Park Land Use and Development Plan was submitted to the Legislature in 1973. There were attempts to defeat the bill, but when strong pressure from Governor Rockefeller made passage seem certain, the representatives from the area sought a year's delay to study the Plan in depth. Rockefeller felt that delay would result in hurried and uncontrolled development of the kind that the Plan was designed to halt and he vetoed the delay bill. A few months later, the Legislature approved the Plan and, with it, the unique land use controls that apply to the Adirondack Park. Thus, the role of a politically powerful governor, committed to the preservation of the Adirondacks, made a key contribution for the passage of the Act.

The Plan called for six categories of land use. They range from "hamlets," essentially the population centers in the Park, in which there are no restrictions on land use and development, to "resource management areas" in which land use density is limited to encourage forestry and agriculture with residential development not to exceed one dwelling per forty-two acres. (53 percent of all private land falls into this category.) In the first instance, no restrictions are set in the hope that growth will be focused on such communities, so that the rest of the Park will remain relatively unspoiled while still serving visitors. Resource management areas are especially restrictive so that fragile ecosystems can be protected and the wilderness character of the Park can be maintained.

In addition to the classification of private lands, the Land Use and Development Plan also defines regional projects for which the APA has authority:

> Projects of a certain size and type and in certain locations assume regional importance. This means that they have a broader area of impact and concern that just the town in which they are proposed to be located.[3]

In hamlets, few projects are considered to be regional, while nearby all in resource management areas are regarded as such. Again, the other categories of land use range in between.

The APA also established specific regulations for the shorelines of all lakes, ponds, rivers, and streams in order to protect them from destruction and to preserve the wilderness character of the land. There are specifications of minimum width to lots and building setbacks, again varying by the classification of the land.

With the passage of the Land Use and Development Plan by the Legislature, the APA assumed control over most building and development activities within the Blue Line (the imaginary Park boundary), ranging upwards from the construction of a single family dwelling.[4] The Agency is prepared to relinquish jurisdiction of most small-scale local planning to those communities that develop a land use plan that is consistent with its goals.[5] In seven years, however, only seven towns have developed APA-approved plans, although several others are in various stages of completion and adoption. The intent is to form a partnership between the state and local governments in the Park in order to maintain its character and plan its growth. The lack of approved plans, assuming more local control over local planning, is clear evidence of the resistance of communities to this notion of partnership. At the same time, the consciousness of Park residents about the importance of planning has been raised even as the presence of the APA is opposed.[6]

Thus, land use and development in the six million acres of the Adirondack Park is regulated and controlled by a single agency, the Adirondack Park Agency, with the full force of state law behind it. Public lands (some 40 percent of the area) are managed through Article 14 of the State Constitution, and the privately owned lands (the remaining 60 percent) are controlled through the Adirondack Park Land Use and Development Plan approved by the Legislature in 1973. Both combine to insure that state lands will be maintained as "open spaces," even wilderness, and that their quality will not be marred by the development of nearby private lands.

The success of the Adirondack Park Agency is preserving the character of the Park is widely debated. In its first years of operation, it approved more than 90 percent of the applications submitted to it. Just over one percent were disapproved and another 5 percent were withdrawn before a decision was reached, presumably because the project sponsors realized that approval would not be forthcoming.[7] These figures can be misleading, however, because many projects die aborning due to the very existence of the Land Use Plan and an agency to apply its regulations. Robert Flacke, presently Commissioner of the State's Department of Environmental Conservation, says that the Adirondack Park Agency has discouraged the "fast buck" developers from considering the Adirondacks as a suitable target for easy profit.[8]

There is also evidence that the quality of applications has improved since the APA's early years. As will be discussed below, those years were especially troubled ones. The review procedures have become simpler and more efficient as generally accepted guidelines have emerged, at least in practice. Those filing applications are increasingly aware of the regulations concerning building and sewage system setbacks, wetlands, intensity to use, steep slopes, and aesthetics, and they describe more clearly how their project intends to meet the requirements. Accordingly, applications are processed more efficiently and quickly.

The high percentage of project approvals is misleading in another way. Conditions are often attached. The most common conditions involve limits on the number of buildings due to intensity restrictions, location of buildings, wetland and stream protection, and proper provision for on-site sewage disposal. It is difficult to determine how many projects are halted because of the special conditions because they prove to be too costly to the developer or home owner, but they do affirm the intentions of the Land Use and Development Plan. At the same time, the Agency has lacked an effective system of inspection and, consequently, of enforcement, so it is difficult to determine how effective the setting of special conditions is in preserving the environmental and aesthetic quality of the Adirondack Park.

Given its power to rule on matters that had heretofore been private, including the construction of a single family home, it is not surprising that the Adirondack Park Agency has been the center of controversy from its creation. Its very parentage, New York State (especially its governor and urban legislators) has never been in doubt and local residents view the Agency as an "outside" infringement of their basic liberties. In the beginning, the inefficiencies of the Agency produced several controversial cases, indeed "horror stories," that galvanized local opposition. Protest groups were active, litigation against the Agency was frequent, and legislation was introduced to curb its powers. Such activities continue, but the opposition is more sporadic and muted. The Agency's increased sensitivity and efficiency has helped in this regard. So, seven years after the Adirondack Park Land Use and Development Plan was enacted, the controls over land use and development within the Park are firmly in place.

The status of the Adirondack Park is in sharp contrast with developments in the Blue Ridge mountains. In 1974, the Legislature of North Carolina rejected the Mountain Area Management Act (MAMA) that would have provided for state regulation and controls in that state's portion of the Blue Ridge region. Those who framed the Act were reacting to the same concerns about uncontrolled growth and uncoordinated development that had been foreseen in the Adirondacks (and elsewhere). But, here planning and environmental protection was left to local agencies instead. Many are not equal to the challenge offered by organized interests.

As one result, the area around Boone and Blowing Rock has become the setting for a wide variety of fast-food restaurants, motels, amusements, and other tourist-related accouterments. Without comprehensive land use controls and zoing regulations, the growth has been uncoordinated and random. The problems escalate with new outcries for flood control and better drainage where building should have been restricted and for improved highways where the demand is generated by the newly constructed attractions.

Deeper in the mountains, large-scale developments provide a challenge of similar difficulty. Ski resorts and related second-home enterprises have been built throughout the area and others are planned. Some are carefully designed to protect their natural assets; others have taken few safeguards. The situation is further complicated by the problems that some developments have encountered in their financing. Some have been slowed or halted in mid-construction due to a lack of funds, even bankruptcy, and others have had to cut corners or ignore promises. Environmental safeguards quickly become luxuries in such situations.

The problems of growth are not just those of the physical environment, however. Even where developments follow sound advice and employ self-imposed standards on the use of land, protection of fragile ecosystems, and the management of sewage, there are difficulties that transcend specific projects. For example, accelerating commercialization of the environment in parts of western North Carolina places great pressure on residents to sell their land. Consequently, speculation is rampant. Those who would prefer to continue with the present use of land, perhaps in farming, are under increasing pressure to sell because assessments for taxes increase with land values and the best use of land becomes its sale. A more subtle difficulty which is perhaps unmanageable with even the most cautious planning concerns the "hidden injuries of class"[9] when those of economic advantage are served by those who have been figuratively or literally dispossessed. In western North Carolina, as elsewhere in the United States, the symbols become such things as roads to ski resorts that are well-maintained in winter while the schools must close because other roads are impassable, or clusters of second homes of spectacular siting and design in areas where the inadequate "first homes" of others are discreetly out of sight, but nearby.

Most of these problems are not obscure. They are very difficult ones with which to deal, however, because the tools of management--land use controls, regulations, planning--challenge the concept of property rights. *"Nobody is going to tell me what I can do with my land!"* So, efforts to set standards for new developments or to implement stricter regulations are seriously challenged. Such challenges are often encouraged by those who have the most to gain, and land developers, bankers, realtors, and politicians have vested interests in "home rule" and local determination of land use. Indeed, it is very hard to fault those who behave in accordance with their perception of their basic rights and interests.

The same arguments are heard in the Adirondacks and western North Carolina as well as any other place where the use of land is changing. But in the Adirondacks, large-scale development has virtually ceased, steep slopes and wetlands are off-limits to development, and shorelines are protected. Personal choice and local option have been supplemented in specified instances by state control of the land. One principle, environmental management, has taken priority over another--property rights. The options for development and other uses of the land have been narrowed for local residents by citizens of the entire state acting through their legislators and directly by referendum.

Regional Character

Why have these differnces occurred? Why is land use in the Adirondacks now managed by strict regulations while developments in North Carolina are governed more by the laws of gravity and the good will of the developers than by a formal set of controls?

It is not enough to say that those with deep interests in environmental quality saw that the Adirondacks required protection and it was accomplished. Not only does this interpretation commit an act of *reductio ad absurdum,* but it ignores the fact that by the same standards of natural beauty and environmental quality, and at a roughly similar point in the development of these resources, the Blue Ridge region of North Carolina needed the same foresight implied in planning and land use controls. Better explanations are needed to account for the differences in response.

Perhaps the easiest explanation can be sought in variations in regional character. By this interpretation, the people of North Carolina were more resistant to infringement on personal liberties than those in the Adirondacks. Doubtlessly, the inhabitants of the Blue Ridge and Adirondack regions differ in certain cultural and social-psychological attributes. Indeed, this is one argument for positioning the comparison of the two areas in the larger regional contexts of Appalachia and the North Country. But whatever those differences may be, it is very unlikely that passiveness to an infringement of property and other rights is among them. Adirondackers are proud and independent persons and to attribute the presence of land use controls established for the region to their indifference would be a classic case of "blaming the victim."[10]

Similarly, it is inappropriate to explain the differences as historical accidents or to attribute them to idiosyncratic factors. In doing so, one accounts for the differences simply in the votes of legislatures or particular environmental atrocities committed (or planned) in the name of development that mobilized public opinion. Such explanations imply no pattern to history or the particular relationship of a region to the larger world.

Rather, a structural interpretation seems most appropriate. In both cases, it is in the *interests of others* that the decision is made and that decision--for controls in the Adirondacks and against MAMA in North Carolina--reflects those interests. It is the politics of dependency. In the Adirondacks, those who influenced the decision were willing to have some rights surrendered, usually those of others, to protect the environment. In North Carolina, those who influenced the decision were not yet willing to surrender such options only because they had not yet obtained what they wanted. Instead, they could use the issue of such rights for their own ends. In the Adirondacks, the decision was made to protect the environment; in North Carolina, it was made to protect development. In either case, was it the politics of the people who would be most affected that mattered.

Both situations are manifestations of dependency theory and the ideas of colonialsim.[11] In the Adirondacks, we are talking about an "environmental" colony; in the Blue Ridge mountains, the colonizers are the land developers. Both areas, as part of the North Country and Appalachia respectively, are party to a long heritage of economic and political dependency in which decisions are made elsewhere.

There are two problems with evoking the ideas and imagery of dependency and colonialism in this context. First, they carry connotations that can be troubling. The implications of exploitation and the arrogance of power are not pretty. In its classic sense, dependency is an economic, political, and social mechanism, often reinforced by psychological manifestations, that allow a few to control and profit from the labors of many. It is perhaps possible to adjust dependency theory to the unique circumstances of the Adirondack Park where the relationships are the same in that the decision was made for those who are affected, but the motives for doing so were more honorable. The reasons for imposing controls were not profit-related, but ones reflecting the deep conviction that the environment needed protection. The tradeoff between property rights and control involved a calculation that the environment, including the last remaining wilderness in the Northeast, was more deserving.

In one respect, this explanation is too simplistic. It implies that the motives of all those who supported the Adirondack Park were equally honorable. For some, protection of the environment did involve a higher calling, but for others, it was a matter of protecting interests and investments. The same division, perhaps still too simple, can be made for those who opposed the Park. Nonetheless, it should be patently clear that the decision to establish strong controls in the Adirondacks was but one of a series made for local residents by others from the "outside." Here, the decision was on behalf of the environment. Conversely, the decision not to establish strong controls in the mountains of western North Carolina was also one of a series of decisions made for local residents by outsiders. Here, the decision was on behalf of development. In balance, the potential for continued exploitation both of people and the environment seems greater in the latter case. Perhaps the connotations of dependency theory, although not its logic, are misapplied when they blur such features.

This raises the second problem. The application of the dependency idea provides a structure for analysis, but leads quickly to a set of second-order questions: why and how are these interests mobilized? At this point, we come full circle to the points made at the beginning of this paper about potential for comparative study. Simultaneously, we must hide behind (under?) an agenda for further study. Essentially, we argue that whether local autonomy or "home rule" is supported or eroded, it reflects the intersts of others. In the Adirondacks, those interests were supportive of the environment; in the Blue Ridge area, the issue of "rights" supports pro-development interests. Why did the econimic and political elite in New York elect to preserve the Adirondacks? Why did their counterparts in North Carolina choose the other course? These two questions are only the beginning of a fuller exploration. Informed through comparison, it could add important specification to the nature of regional character. Attention needs to be directed to basic matters of political and economic power, control, and autonomy as well as concerns about ecological fragility and environmental protection.

NOTES

1. Fred Sullivan, "Adirondack Zoning: A National Experiment in Land Use Controls Faces Local Challenge," *Empire State Report,* December, 1975, p. 464.

2. Temporary Study Commission on the Future of the Adirondacks, *The Future of the Adirondack Part,* Albany, 1972, p.3.

3. Adirondack Park Agency, *A Citizen's Guide to Adirondack Park Agency Land Use Regulations,* January, 1979, p. 8.

4. During its first four years, 58.1 percent of the proposals reviewed by the Adirondack Park Agency involved the building of a single family dwelling or two-lot subdivisions. At the other extreme, fewer than one percent of the projects reviewed were subdivisions of greater than 50 units; cf., G. Gordon Davis and Richard A. Kiroff, "Conflict in the North Country," draft report, September, 1979, p. 18.

5. When a town is granted APA approval for a land use program, it gains (1) refinement and distribution of overall intensity guidelines, (2) local review of Class B regional projects, and (3) increased local participation in APA review of Class A projects. The Class A projects are those of "regional importance" and are generally more sensitive. The Class B projects are smaller and more localized.

6. Adirondack Park Agency, *Local Planning and Land Use Controls in the Adirondack Park,* 1975.

7. Davis and Liroff, "Conflict in the North Country, pp. iv-22.

8. Robert F. Flacks, *A Report on Implementation of the Adirondack Park Agency Act,* presented to the Eighth Annual Convention of the Environmental Planning Lobby, October 15, 1978, pp. 1-2.

9. Richard Sennett and Jonathan Cobb, *The Hidden Injuries of Class,* (New York: Vintage Books, 1973).

10. William Ryan, *Blaming the Victim* (New York: Pantheon Books, 1971).

11. See, for example, Helen M. Lewis and Edward E. Knipe, "The Colonialism Model: The Appalachian Case," in *Colonialism in Modern America: The Appalachian Case,* ed. Helen M. Lewis, Linda Johnson, and Don Askins (Boone, N.C.: Appalachian Consortium Press, 1978), pp. 9-31.

COMMUNITY DEVELOPMENT PERSPECTIVES OF OHIO APPALACHIANS: A REGIONAL STUDY

Ted L. Napier and Elizabeth G. Bryant

Abstract

Data were collected from a random sample of 1474 residents living in a five county area located within the designated Appalachian region of Ohio during the summer and fall of 1975. The focus of the study was upon the assessment of development priorities of the local populace. The study findings are employed in this paper to ascertain the validity of stereotypes commonly used to describe Appalachians and to determine the relative merits of individual deficits models for understanding unemployment. The findings are discussed in the context of alternative development strategies for rural Appalachian areas such as the study region.

INTRODUCTION

Appalachians have been characterized in the existing popular, as well as scientific, literature as being individualistic, suspicious of oursiders, localistic in terms of world perspectives, opposed to government involvement and control, opposed to socioeconomic growth and social change, anti-intellectual, poverty stricken, dependent upon reference groups for information, traditionalistic, ignorant, and numerous other stereotypes which are not complimentary to Appalachian people (Coles, 1972; Ball, 1970; Fetterman, 1970; Caudill, 1963; Harrington, 1966; Quigley, 1969; Weller, 1965; Schwarzweller, 1970; Photiadis, 1970; Mayo, 1970; Looff, 1971). Such descriptors suggest that Appalachians have internalized self-perceptions and attitudes which impede planned change programs from being implemented within the region and imply that the "culture of poverty" thesis advocated by Lewis (1966) is correct.

The culture of poverty thesis suggests that development problems can only be "attacked" via modification of the individual through changes in attitudes, knowledge bases, skills, values, beliefs, and behavior. The individual is perceived to be deficient in the sociocultural factors which are necessary to participate fully in the institutions of the society. Therefore, solutions to development problems are couched in terms of changing the person to fit the system.

Many federal and state programs designed to ameliorate socio economic problems in rural areas within the United States have tended to rely heavily upon the individual deficits model as noted by the existing literature in the field of human resources development (Schultz, 1962; Becker, 1962; Jakubauskas and Baumel, 1967; McCollum, 1967; Bloch and Smith, 1977; Niland, 1972; Stromsdorfer, 1968; Colmen, 1967; Levitan, et al, 1972; Parnes and Kohen, 1975). The long history of manpower programs in Appalachia is evidence of the commitment to the human resources development model. The logic advanced in the human resources development model is that private and public investments in developing human skills will make the recipient of such investments more functional in the existing social structure. Subsequently, it is argued that an individual who has been "developed" in terms of "improved" human resources will be absorbed into the existing social system which in turn will reduce socio economic development problems for the region. While the individual deficits model has been used extensively by governmental agencies, several researchers have raised questions about the model (Gurin, 1970; 277-

299; Grubb and Lazeson, 1975; Niland, 1972; Patten and Clark, 1968; Ballante, 1972; Koenker, 1967; 134-142; Spitze, 1970; 197-218; Blaug, 1976; Napier, et al, 1979; Napier, 1979). These writers suggest that the model has some serious limitations and some even suggest the model may be an inappropriate strategy for bringing about rural development under certain circumstances (Napier, et al, 1979; Napier, 1979).

The two objectives of this paper are to examine with empirical data the validity of the stereotypes used to describe Appalachians noted above and to evaluate the relative merits of the human resources development model for understanding unemployment within a multi-county Appalachian area of Ohio. The findings will be discussed in the context of rural development policy.

RESEARCH METHODOLOGIES

The Research Situation

The region selected for investigation is a five county area within the designated Appalachian counties of southeastern Ohio. The region is characterized by rolling hills and widely separated farmsteads and small villages. The primary occupations in the study area have traditionally been associated with the extractive industries (coal, timber and small-scale agriculture) even though the occupational structure is slowly becoming more differentiated.

An examination of the socio economic history of the region prior to the late 1970s will show a gradual reduction of socio economic viability for many years. Out-migration prior to 1975 was very common, since jobs in the local area were difficult to secure and opportunities for social mobility within the study region were quite limited. The social infrastructure of the multi-county region tended to reflect this history of decline. Services, both public and private, have been in a state of continual decline relative to other areas of the state, and unemployment rates have remained high. Other indicators of a declining area have traditionally been identified with the region.

The socio economic viability of the area looked rather bleak until several coal mines were opened in the early 1970s. The mines provided expanded employment opportunities but also created new interest in development planning among several groups to sustain the growth and, therefore, increase the probability that the recent surge of economic activity would not wane.

To aid in the planning process, a study was commissioned by the Ohio Agricultural Research and Development Center using Title V funds provided by the Rural Development Act of 1972 to ascertain the perceived development needs of the region's populace. The study findings reported here were drawn from this study.

Sampling

A systematic, random sample was drawn from the five county study area (Napier, 1971; Napier, 1975; Napier and Wright, 1976; Napier, et al, 1977; Napier, 1976; Napier and Maurer, 1978). Interviewers were instructed to conduct an interview with an adult resident from each selected occupied dwelling. The interviewers were instructed to select every fifth occupied residence, with the initial dwelling chosen at random, and to begin the selection process at different places in the sampling area each day. A structured questionnaire was developed and administered to the respondents via personal interview.

The location of each respondent's residence was noted on detailed county maps secured from the Ohio Department of Transportation which provided a means of pictorial display of the sampling distribution. Careful visual monitoring of the distribution of the sample during the data collection phase and subsequent evaluation after the data were collected revealed the sample was not clustered and approximated the population distribution by township.

The respondents drawn from villages and towns were selected using the same systematic sampling technique which was modified to be approximate to more densely populated areas (streets were selected as the starting points for the sampling and the residences were systematically chosen). The village sample was also monitored with detailed maps showing location of respondents, and evaluation of the distribution during and after the data collection revealed the village samples were not clustered.

Approximately 95 percent of the people selected to participate in the study completed an interview and the total number of respondents to the study was 1474. The characteristics of the sample are presented in Table 1.

TABLE 1: Sociodemographic Characteristics of the Study Sample (N = 1474)

Sex of Respondents	44.8% Male	55.2% Female
Mean Age of Respondents		44.3 years
Mean Length of Residence		30.6 years
Mean Number of Children Living at Home		1.25 children
Mean Number of Formal Organization Memberships		1.6 groups
Percent Home Owners		80.4%
Percent Unemployed at Sometime During Last Year (Excluding Retired)		25.9%
Percent Engaged in Full-time Farming		5.5%
Percent Engaged in Part-time Farming		11.7%
Mean Farm Size (For those Engaged in Farming)		104.0 acres
Mean Education of Head of Household		11.5 years

Occupation of Primary Income Earner	Frequency	Percent
Unclassified	61	4.1
Service Workers	116	7.9
Farmers	119	8.1
Unskilled Laborers	401	27.2
Skilled Blue Collar	375	25.4
White Collar	178	12.1
Manager-Administrator	86	5.8
Professional	138	9.4
Family Income (1974)		
$ 0 - 2,999	149	10.1
3,000 - 5,999	244	16.5
6,000 - 8,999	257	17.5
9,000 - 11,999	301	20.4
12,000 - 14,999	198	13.4
15,000 - 17,999	122	8.3
18,000 and above	118	8.0
NO response	85	5.8

The characteristics of the sample population indicate the study respondents were middle-aged people with very few children living at home. The study participants were basically working class people with moderate incomes. Most of the people were long-term residents of the region and had basically completed high school. Most of the respondents spent their early years in small towns or less densely populated areas (farm and rural nonfarm). A large majority of the respondents (80 percent) owned their homes and were not actively involved with many formal organizations.

A small minority of the respondents indicated they were farmers, and most of those who were involved indicated they were farming only on a part-time basis. This finding partially explains why the mean farm size was only 104 acres. Also, the region is quite hilly and large-scale agriculture is not common.

A relatively large number of respondents indicated that the primary income earner in the family had been unemployed at some time during the preceding year and that many remained without work for extended periods of time. Commuting to work was quite common as noted by the respondents, who revealed they commuted an average distance of eleven miles one way each day.

Instrument Construction

A questionnaire was developed from previous research instruments used by the principal author of this paper and other development studies. The questionnaire was reviewed by community development professionals in the College of Agriculture at the Ohio State University and a pretest was conducted using a similar population to the one selected for research purposes. The questionnaire was revised and the data were collected in the summer and fall of 1975.

Data were collected on the following: attitudes toward various development options, willingness to commit limited resources to development efforts, priorities for development actions, use of information sources, and perceptions of geographical areas to which the respondents identified. Data concerning unemployment were also collected and used to test the relevance of the human resources development approach. The findings for these components of the study are presented in descriptive statistical form with reference made to multivariate analysis published in journal articles and research bulletins.

FINDINGS

The findings basically support the position that the common sterotypes used to describe Appalachian people are not appropriate for the study region. the respondents were very postive toward rural industrial development and held very positive orientations toward outdoor recreation development. The respondents were willing to commit resources for collective development efforts and perceived that socio-economic growth (expansion of jobs and industrial base) was the most important development problem within the study area. Sixty-seven percent of the study respondents identified with their county of residence as opposed to multi-county districts, the State of Ohio, or the Appalachian Region. The study participants used mass media, both printed and electronic forms, as their primary information sources rather than depending upon other people within the study area. Lastly, the human resources model was shown to be an inadequate model for understanding unemployment within the study region. Data relative to each of these findings are provided below.

Attitudes Toward Rural Industrial Development

The descriptive data about attitudes toward industrial development are presented in Table 2.[1]

TABLE 2: Attitudes of Survey Respondents to Industrial Development: Presented in Frequency Counts (Percentages Within Parentheses - N⁵1474)

Question	Strongly Agree 5*	Agree 4*	Undecided 3*	Disagree 2*	Strongly Disagree 1*	Mean for Question Response
1. Industrial development in my region will benefit me or some member of my household.	720 (48.8)	489 (33.2)	76 (5.2)	126 (8.5)	63 (4.3)	4.1
2. The costs of industrial development in my region can be justified.	377 (25.6)	679 (46.1)	329 (22.3)	70 (4.7)	19 (1.3)	3.9
3. Industrial development is not needed in my region.	34 (2.3)	74 (5.0)	78 (5.3)	552 (37.4)	736 (49.9)	1.7
4. The disadvantages brought to my region by industrial development will offset the advantages.	61 (4.1)	205 (13.9)	225 (15.3)	614 (41.7)	369 (25.0)	2.3
5. Industrial development in my region will create many problems for people living here.	37 (2.5)	227 (15.4)	175 (11.0)	688 (46.7)	347 (23.5)	2.3
6. Industries should not be encouraged to locate in my region.	45 (3.1)	85 (5.8)	79 (41.4)	610 (44.4)	655	1.8
7. Industrial development of my region will provide many jobs for local people.	748 (50.7)	599 (40.6)	67 (4.5)	39 (2.6)	21 (1.4)	4.4
8. Industrial development will make my region a better place in which to live.	550 (37.3)	640 (43.4)	167 (11.3)	84 (5.7)	33 (2.2)	4.1
9. New industries employing mostly women would be harmful to family life in my region.	107 (7.3)	216 (14.7)	254 (17.2)	555 (37.7)	342 (23.2)	2.5
10. Industrial development will benefit my region.	611 (41.5)	694 (47.1)	94 (6.4)	50 (3.4)	25 (1.7)	4.2
11. New jobs are more important to me than the air or water pollution that new industries may cause.	217 (14.7)	399 (27.1)	267 (18.1)	402 (27.3)	189 (12.8)	3.0
12. Planned industrial parks are very important for industrial development.	326 (22.1)	773 (52.4)	277 (18.8)	80 (5.4)	18 (1.2)	3.9

*Weighted values given to each designated response.
Source: Napier, Pierce and Bachtel, 1977, page 13.

The findings presented in Table 2 show that the respondents were basically quite postive toward rural industrial development. The respondents believed they or members of their families would receive benefits from industrial development and believed the region as a whole would benefit. They also believed that industries should be encouraged to locate in the region.

The respondents did not believe that industrial development would destroy their community and fragment family relations. They held this view if the industries attracted to the region employed primarily women.

Multi-variate analyses of the industrial attitude data revealed that people from different socioeconomic strata held positive attitudes toward rural industrial development of the region.

The findings strongly indicate the Appalachians included in this study did not percieve socioeconomic growth and expansion negatively. general assertions that Appalachians are suspicious of outsiders does not appear to be valid either, since most people realize industries will attract people from outside the region (Summers, et al, 1976). Data collected about the possibility of outside people being attracted to the area revealed the respondents were positive toward such in-migration.

Attitudes Toward Outdoor Recreation Development

Data were collected about attitudes toward outdoor recreation as a development option. These data are presented in Table 3.[2]

TABLE 3: Attitudes of Survey Respondents to Outdoor Recreation Development: Presented in Frequency Counts (Percentages Within Parentheses-N'1474)

Question	Strongly Agree 5*	Agree 4*	Undecided 3*	Disagree 2*	Strongly Disagree 1*	Mean for Queston Response
1. Outdoor recreation development of my region will provide many jobs for local people.	312 (21.2)	809 (54.9)	197 (13.4)	134 (9.1)	22 (1.5)	3.9
2. Outdoor recreation development will make my region a better place in which to live.	366 (24.8)	872 (59.2)	141 (9.6)	79 (5.4)	16 (1.1)	4.0
3. Outdoor recreation development is not needed in my region.	(2.3)	(6.7)	(8.8)	(53.3)	(29.0)	2.0
4. Development of outdoor recreation will benefit my region.	381 (25.8)	899 (61.0)	113 (7.7)	64 (4.3)	17 (1.2)	4.1
5. The costs of outdoor recreation devlopment in my region can be justified.	226 (15.3)	705 (47.8)	422 (28.7)	97 (6.6)	24 (1.6)	3.7
6. The disadvantages brought to my region by outdoor recreation development will offset the advantages.	39 (2.6)	210 (14.2)	267 (18.1)	716 (48.6)	242 (16.4)	2.4
7. Outdoor recreation development in my region will create many problems for people living here.	17 (1.2)	124 (8.4)	200 (13.6)	845 (57.3)	288 (19.5)	2.1
8. My region will not benefit much from new outdoor recreational development.	33 (2.2)	137 (9.3)	159 (10.8)	832 (56.4)	313 (21.2)	2.1
9. Existing recreation facilities in my region are adequate for my needs.	171 (11.6)	557 (37.8)	196 (26.5)	391 (10.8)	159 (11.6)	
	(11.6)	(37.8)	(13.3)	(26.5)	(10.8)	3.1
10. Expansion of existing outdoor recreation and tourism attractions in my region will reduce my travel to other areas outside my region.	203 (13.8)	505 (34.3)	270 (18.3)	389 (26.4)	107 (7.3)	3.2
11. Outdoor recreation development is usually harmful to the environment.	13 (0.9)	67 (4.5)	136 (9.2)	848 (57.5)	410 (27.8)	1.9

*Weighted values given to each designated response.

Source: Napier, et al, 1977, page 14.

These data demonstrate that the respondendts believed that expansion of outdoor recreation facilities was a highly desirable development option even when such development efforts would attract tourists into the region. These findings can be interpreted as indicating the Ohio Appalachian respondents were neither provincial nor opposed to socioeconomic growth. Data collected about perceptions of tourists indicated the respondents perceived them in a positive manner (Napier, et al, 1977: 11), which suggests that suspicion of outsiders is not a valid descriptor of Appalachians within the study area.

The respondents believed that outdoor recreation development would benefit the region by generating jobs and stimulating economic growth. The people also believed that resources used to accomplish outdoor recreation development goals would be wise investments. Lastly, the respondents realized that the region needed such development programs.

Multi-variate analyses indicated that these feelings permeated all socioeconomic groups represented in the study. When people believed they would benefit from the efforts they tended to be more supportive.

Commitment of Resources To Development Efforts

Data were collected concerning willingness of local people to support industrial and outdoor recreation development programs. The findings demonstrated that the respondents were willing to cooperate in the accomplishment of collective community goals and that the support for cooperative problem solving permeated every segment and social class within the region (Napier and Maurer, 1978). Individuals who were most willing to commit resources for outdoor recreation and industrial development were those who perceived that the region, close family members, or they themselves would benefit from such development efforts.

The issues addressed in the commitment scale were taxation, zoning, and commitment of personal time. The first two require government involvement in the development process, which brings into question the common belief that Appalachians fear government involvement in local affairs. Also, the willingness of the respondents to pursue common goals suggests that the individualistic orientation often associated with Appalachians is probably overstated.

Priorities For Development Action

The respondents were requested to rank the top three development problems within the study area which they believed to be the most important. These data were summarized using weighted rank orders to assess the relative ranking of development problems. The findings are presented in Table 4.

TABLE 4: Weighted Rank Order of Problem Priorities in the Study Area: Survey Results (N'1474)

Problem for Region	Frequency Multiplied by Weighting Factors	Weighted Score Sample Size	Weighted Rank Order
Jobs and Industrial Expansion	2711	1.84	1
Drug Abuse	972	.66	2
Education	913	.62	3
Highway Improvements	889	.60	4
Crime, Vandalism and Trespassing	851	.58	5
New Housing	682	.46	6
Recreation Facilities	526	.36	7
Water Supply	362	.25	8
Sewage Improvements	361	.24	9
Solid Waste Pick-up	280	.19	10
Planning and Zoning	138	.09	11
Other	137	.09	12

Source: Napier, et al, 1977, page 7.

The findings presented in Table 4 show that the study populace perceived jobs and industrial development to be single most important development issue. This issue was perceived to be much more important than the other issues evaluated, the weighted value for jobs and industrial development is 1.84 which is almost 3 times greater than the weighted value for the issue ranked second. Inspection of the priorities given to the issues will show that the respondents were primarily concerned with community living and "quality of life" issues. The respondents were concerned with having secure work roles, a crime free social environment, and social amenities and public services. The respondents were apparently willing to accept the social changes and social consequences associated with economic development to achieve better life styles. Such behavioral orientations could not be defined as traditionalistic.

Sources of Information

Data were collected about the most frequently used sources of various types of information. These findings are presented in Table 5.

The findings demonstrate that mass media mechanisms for the dissemination of information were the most frequently used sources for every issue evaluated except agricultural information. The traditional mode of interpersonal interaction for the exchange of information was not frequently employed. The small number of people who do not seek information should also bring into question the idea that rural Appalachians are ignorant of contemporary issues in the community, region, nation, and world.

The findings from the Appalachian study group are quite similar to previous research undertaken by the principal author of this paper to assess information sources used in rural areas (Ross and Napier, 1978). The patterns discovered among the Appalachian group are basically the same for other rural groups evaluated in non-Appalachian areas of Ohio.

TABLE 5:
Most Important Source of Information for Survey Respondents Presented in Frequency Counts with Percentages Within Parentheses (N = 1474)*

Type of Information	Do Not Seek This Type of Information	Public Officials	Radio	County Extension Agent	Television	Newspapers	Family or Neighbors	Special Interest Magazines	Extension Bulletins	No Response
General Community Problems	72 (4.9)	318 (21.6)	239 (16.2)	39 (2.6)	67 (4.5)	485 (32.9)	245 (16.6)	2 (0.1)	3 (0.2)	4 (0.3)
Local News	2 (0.1)	1 (0.1)	623 (42.3)	3 (0.2)	197 (13.4)	530 (36.0)	115 (7.8)	0 (0.0)	1 (0.1)	2 (0.1)
Information About Your Occupation	524 (35.5)	125 (8.5)	57 (3.9)	73 (5.0)	18 (1.2)	131 (8.9)	113 (7.7)	382 (25.9)	40 (2.7)	11 (0.7)
New Development Programs	151 (10.2)	236 (16.0)	151 (10.2)	72 (4.9)	167 (11.3)	579 (39.3)	72 (4.9)	24 (1.6)	18 (1.2)	4 (0.3)
Recreation Activities	169	153	158	50	87	601	192	46	13	5
	(11.5)	(10.4)	(10.7)	(3.4)	(5.9)	(40.8)	(13.0)	(3.1)	(0.9)	(0.3)
Taxing Issues	68 (4.6)	520 (35.3)	93 (6.3)	27 (1.8)	78 (5.3)	637 (43.2)	40 (2.7)	4 (0.3)	4 (0.3)	3 (0.2)
Local School Issues	117 (7.9)	402 (27.3)	127 (8.6)	14 (0.9)	31 (2.1)	622 (42.2)	148 (10.0)	5 (0.3)	7 (0.5)	1 (0.1)
Agricultural Information	283 (19.2)	19 (1.3)	90 (6.1)	**618 (41.9)**	29 (2.0)	139 (9.4)	68 (4.6)	42 (2.8)	183 (12.4)	3 (0.2)

*The most important source of information for each issue is enclosed in boxes.

Source: Napier, Pierce and Bachtel, 1977, Page 19.

Identification With Geographical Areas

A characteristic commonly associated with Appalachians is the "Identification with place" orientation. The focus of the identification is assumed to be Appalachia, but seldom, if ever, is the place of identification specified. To address this issue, the respondents were provided maps with different geographical areas specified and asked to choose the geographical area with which they identified. The areas varied from county to the multi-state federation termed Appalachia. More than 67 percent of the respondents chose county of residence and an additonal 15 percent selected the county of residence and the counties immediately surrounding it as their area of identification. About 9.7 percent selected the multi-county study area. About 3.6 percent identified with Ohio and 2.4 selected the Appalachian region of Ohio. Only 2.3 percent of the respondents selected Appalachia as their place of identification.

These findings indicate that the concept "Appalachia" may have more literary meaning than it does as a geographical area of identification. The findings also suggest that macro-level geographical areas for addressing rural development problems are probably not appropriate.

The Human Resources Development Model

Unemployment information was collected about the primary income earner in each family represented in the study and was used to assess the merits of the human resources development model as a development strategy for attacking rural unemployment problems. The literature noted in the introductory sections of this paper was reviewed to ascertain the relevant factors to examine as predictive variables. The factors used to analyze the variance in length of unemployment of the primary income earner were: age, education, length of residence, number of children in the household, formal group memberships, and occupation. Multi-variate regression and discriminant analyses were conducted on the data set and the findings revealed that the variables selected for investigation were basically useless in predicting length of unemployment. Comparisons made between the employed and unemployed groups using the above-mentioned variables also proved fruitless (Napier, et al, 1978; Napier, 1979; Napier, Maurer, and Bryant, 1979).[3]

The study data suggest that further investment in human resources without concomitant development of the economic infrastructure of the region is probably futile. The findings strongly indicate that pursuit of the human resources development strategy within the study region will probably result in continual out-migration of the best-trained people. Even more tragic is the possibility that such an approach will produce a better-educated and trained labor force on the local level that will remain unemployed.

It was concluded from the research that human resources development approaches alone will not serve to enhance the socioeconomic viability of rural Appalachian areas, such as the study region, if the existing social infrastructure cannot absorb the newly trained people.[4] An alternative development approach focused upon expanding the local structural employment bases (private economic expansion in the production and service sectors) before enhancing human skills has been advanced from the study findings. It is argued that first priority for development action be given to the generation of permanent jobs within rural areas. It is also argued that federal and state development funds be used to facilitate location of small, privately owned and operated industrial plants in rural areas. Small firms are ususally preferable to large manufacturing firms because they have fewer adverse social and environmental impacts

(Summers, et al, 1976) but an established pattern of generating benefits for local communities (Birch, 1979). Once permanent jobs have been created on the local level and the existing pool of human resources has been depleted, more emphasis should be placed upon human resources development programs.

In sum, the unemployment component of the regional study suggests that sole reliance on the human resources development approach is probably an inappropriate development strategy for rural areas which cannot absorb newly "developed" human resources. Thus, one must conclude that the use of the individual deficits model approach for rural Appalachian development must be questioned.

CONCLUSIONS

The study findings basically demonstrated that stereotypes commonly used to describe Appalachians could not be applied to the study population. Ohio Appalachians included in the study were modernistic in their development orientations and appeared to be willing to address collective socioeconomic problems which have been adversely affecting their lives. The respondents were very much concerned about "quality of life" conditions within their communities and region. They also appeared to be willing to commit personal and collective resources to community problem solving. Comparison of preliminary statistical analyses of data collected in a non-metropolitan, multi-county region in California have shown the development orientations of the Ohio Appalachians to be very similar to the views held by rural Californians. Other studies conducted by the principal author of this paper relative to the assessment of development priorities basically have produced similar findings to those reported here.

The study findings also suggest that development programs couched entirely in individual deficits models will probably never solve rural Appalachian development problems if the goal of such efforts is to improve the life styles of rural people. If the development goal of rural Appalachians is to achieve a community which can provide secure work roles, basic public and private services, recreational facilities, opportunities for social mobility, and the many factors that constitute the "good life," then they should consider alternative strategies to the human resources development model, because such goals will probably never be accomplished by training people for jobs that do not exist on the local level.

NOTES

1. For a more detailed discussion of the industrialization findings, see Maurer and Napier (1978) and Bachtel, et al. (1979).

2. For a more detailed discussion of the outdoor recreation findings, see Pierce and Napier (1980) and Bryant and Napier (1980).

3. Recent statistical analyses of data collected in northeast central California by the principal author of this paper basically reproduced the findings generated in southeast Ohio.

4. Billings (1974) and Walls (1976) recognized the limitations of the individual deficits model for understanding poverty in Appalachia. Billings (1974) failed to suggest an alternative while Walls's (1976) dependency explanation is open to severe criticism given the expanding production capacity of Appalachia without significant reduction in regional development problems.

REFERENCES

Bachtel, E. C.; Thomas, D. W.; and Napier, T. L. "A Comparative Analysis of Recent Urban to Rural In-Migrants and Long-Term Rural Resident's Attitudes Toward Rural Industrial Development." Paper presented at the Rural Sociological Society Meeting in Burlington, Vermont, August 1979.

Ball Richard A. "The Southern Appalachian Folk Subculture As A Tension-Reducing Way of Life." In *Change In Rural Appalachia; Implications For Action Programs,* edited by John D. Photiadis and Harry K. Schwarzeller, pp. 69-79. Philadelphia: University of Pennsylvania Press, 1970.

Ballante, Donald M. "A Multivariate Analysis of a Vocational Rehabilitation Program." *Journal of Human Resources* 7 (1972): 226-241.

Becker, Gary S. "Investment In Human Capital: A Theoretical Analysis." *Journal of Political Economy* 70(1962): 9-49.

Billings, Dwight. "Culture and Poverty In Appalachia: A Theoretical Discussion and Empirical Analysis." *Social Forces* 53(1974): 315-323.

Birch, David L. "The Job Generation Process." Massachusetts Institute of Technology, Program on Neighborhood and Regional Change. Mimeographed, 1979.

Blaug, Mark. "Human Capital Theory: A Slightly Jaundiced Survey." *Journal of Economic Literature* 59 (1976): 827-855.

Bloch, Farrell E., and Smith, Sharon P. "Human Capital and Labor Market Employment." *Journal of Human Resources* 12(1977): 550-559.

Bryant, Elizabeth G., and Napier, Ted L. "The Application of Social Exchange Theory to the Study of Satisfaction with Existing Outdoor Recreation Facilities." Chapter 12 in *Outdoor Recreation Planning, Perspectives and Research.* Edited by Ted L. Napier. Dubuque, Iowa: Kendall/Hunt Publishing Company, forthcoming, fall of 1980.

Caudill, Harry. *Night Comes to the Cumberlands.* Boston: Little Brown and Company, 1963.

Coles, Robert. *Migrants, Sharecroppers, and Mountaineers.* Boston: Little, Brown and Company, 1972.

Colmen, Joseph G. "The Challenge of the Manpower Crisis." *Human Resources Development.* Edited by Edward B. Jakubauskas and C. Phillip Baumel. Ames: Iowa State University Press, 1967.

Fetterman, John. *Stinking Creek.* New York: E.P. Dutton and Company, Inc., 1970.

Ford, Thomas, ed. *The Southern Appalachian Region: A Survey.* Lexington: University of Kentucky Press, 1962.

Grubb, W. Norton, and Lazerson, Marvin. "Rally 'Round the Workplace; Continuities and Fallacies in Career Education." *Harvard Educational Review 45(1975): 451-474.*

Gurin, Gerald. "An Expectancy Approach to Job Training Programs." In *Psychological Factors In Poverty.* Edited by V. L. Allen, pp. 277-279. Chicago: Markham Publishing Company, 1970.

Hansen, Niles. *Rural Poverty and the Urban Crisis.* Bloomington: Indiana University Press, 1970.

Harrington, Michael. *The Other America.* Baltimore: Penguin Books, Inc., 1966.

Jakubauskas, Edward B., and Baumel, Phillip, eds. *Human Resources Development.* Ames: Iowa State University Press, 1967.

Koenker, William E. "Needed Directions In Human Resources Development for the College Bound." *Human Resources Development.* Edited by E. B. Jakubauskas and C. P. Baumel. Ames: Iowa State University Press, 1967.

Levitan, Sar. A.; Mangum, G. L.; and Marshall, Ray. *Human Resources and Labor Markets.* New York: Harper and Row Publishers, 1972.

Lewis, Oscar. "The Culture of Poverty." *Scientific American,* October 1966, pp. 19-25.

Loof, David. *Appalachia's Children: The Challenge of Mental Health.* Lexington: University of Kentucky Press, 1971.

Maurer, Richard C., and Napier, Ted L. "Attitudes Toward Rural Industrialization: A Test of A Social Exchange Perspective." Economic and Sociology Studies Number 566, The Ohio State University. Paper presented at the Rural Sociological Society Meetings in San Francisco, August 1978.

Mayo, Selz C. "Some Observations on Planning Effective Programs of Directed Change in Rural Appalachia." In *Change In Rural Appalachia: Implications for Action Agencies,* edited by John D. Photiadus and Harry K. Schwarzweller, pp. 221-229. Philadelphia: University of Pennsylvania Press, 1970.

McCollum, Sylvia G. "Needed Directions In Vocational Resources Development for the Noncollege Bound." *Human Resources Development.* Edited by Edward B. Jakubauskas and C. Phillip Baumel. Ames: Iowa State University Press, 1967.

Napier, Ted L. "The Impact of Water Resource Development upon Local Rural Communities: Adjustment Factors to Rapid Change." Ph.D. dissertation, Department of Sociology, The Ohio State University.

_____. "An Analysis of the Social Impact of Water Resource Development and Subsequent Forced Relocation of Populaton upon Rural Community Groups: An Attitude Study." Ohio Agricultural Research and Development Center, Research Bulletin 1080, 1975.

_____. "Structural Versus Human Resources Models for Rural Development: The Case of Unemployment." Economic and Sociology Occasional Paper Number 662. Invited paper presented at the National Association of Development Organizations Annual Meeting, Albuquerque, New mexico, 1979.

_____: Maurer, Richard C.; and Bryant, Elizabeth G. "The Revelance of a Human Resources Development Model for Understanding Unemployment Status within Southeast Ohio" (Working draft). Department of Agricultural Economics and Rural Sociology, The Ohio State University.

_____, and Maurer, Richard C. "Correlates of Commitment to Community Development Efforts." *Journal ofs the Community Development Society* 9 (1978): 12-27.

_____ ; _____; and Bryant, Elizabeth G. "Factors Affecting Unemployment Status Among Residents of a Lesser-Developed Region of Ohio." Ohio Agricultural Research and Development Center, Research Bulletin 1104, 1978.

_____; Pierce, John M.; and Bachtel, Douglas C. "A Descriptive Analysis of a Five-County Attitude Study: Outdoor Recreation and Industrialization." Ohio Agricultural Research and Development Center, Research Circular 230, 1977.

_____, and Wright, Cathy J. "A Longitudinal Analysis of the Attitudinal Response of Rural People to National Resource Development: A Case Study of the Impact of Water Resource Development." Ohio Agricultural Research and Development Center, Research Bulletin 1083, 1976.

_____, and Bryant, Elizabeth G. "Attitudes toward Outdoor Recreation Development: An Application of Social Exchange Theory." *Leisure Sciences,* forthcoming.

Niland, John R. "Prior Labor Market Experience and the Effectiveness of

Manpower Programs: Communication." *Journal of Human Resources* 7 (1972): 554-559.

Parnes, Herbert S., and Kohen, Andrew I. "Occupational Information and Labor Market Status: The Case of Young Men." *Journal of Human Resources* 10 (1975): 44-55.

Patten, Thomas H., and Clark, Gerald E., Jr. "Literacy Training and Job Placement of Hard-Core Unemployed Negros in Detroit." *Journal of Human Resources* 3 (1968); 24-26.

Photiadis, John D. "Rural Southern Appalachia and Mass Society." In *Change in Rural Appalachia: Implications for Action Programs*, Edited by John D. Photiadis and Harry K. Schwaarzweller, pp. 5-22. Philadelphia: University of University of Press, 1970.

Pierce, John M., and Napier, Ted L. "The Use of Perceptions Factors in Predicting Attitudes toward Outdoor Recreation Development." Chapter 11 in *Outdoor Recreation Planning, Perspectives and Research*. Edited by Ted L. Napier, Dubuque, Iowa: Kendall/Hunt Publishing Company, forthcoming.

Ross, Peggy J., and Napier, Ted L. "Patterns of Communication in a Rural Population." Ohio Agricultural Research and Development Center, Research Bulletin 1095.

Quigley, Michael. *April Is the Cruelest Month*. Dubuque, Iowa; Kendall/Hunt Publishing Company, 1969.

Schultz, Theordore W. "Reflections on Investments in Man." *Journal of Political Economy* 70 (1962): 1-8.

Schwarzweller, Harry K. "Social Change and the Individual in Rural Appalachia." In *Change In Rural Appalachia: Implications For Action Programs*. Edited by John D. Photiadis and Harry K. Schwarzweller, pp. 51-68. Philadelphia: University of Pennsylvania Press, 1970.

Spitze, R. G. F. "Problems of Adequacy in Rural Human Resources Development Concepts and Accomplishments." In *Benefits and Burdens of Rural Development: Some Public Policy Viewpoints*, pp. 197-218. Ames: The Iowa State University Press, 1970.

Stromsdorfer, Ernest W. "Determinants of Economic Success in Retraining the Unemployed: The West Virginia Experience." *Journal of Human Resources* 3 (1968): 139-158.

Summers, Gene F.; Evans, Sharon D.; Clemente, Frank; Beck, E. M.; and Minkoff, Jon. *Industrial Invasion of Nonmetropolitan America: A Quarter Century of Experience*. New York; Praeger Publishers, 1976.

Walls, Davis S. "Central Appalachia: A Peripheral Region Within an Advanced Capitalist Society." *Journal of Sociology and Social Welfare* 4 (1976): 232-247.

Weller, Jack. *Yesterday's People*. Lexington: University of Kentucky Press, 1965.

III: The Experience of Urban Appalachians

APPALACHIAN YOUTH IN CULTURAL TRANSITION

Clyde B. McCoy and Virginia McCoy Watkins

Abstract

Inner-city youth who have migrated from the Appalachian region are the focus of this present study. The impact of this migration and resettlement process is not clear. Little is known about Appalachian youth who now reside in urban areas. What problems of transition do they face? What behavioral and emotional patterns are evident as they confront a totally new cultural environment? This study is an attempt to begin to answer these questions.

Recent Findings Concerning Appalachian Youth

Education has received considerable attention in the literature on Appalachian youth. Much of the literature points to cultural differences which created problems for Appalachian youth in school. Language or accents of first generation youth (and some second generation youth, as well) set them apart immediately (Rhodes, 1968; Wagner, 1974, 1975). Misinterpretation of mountain dialect, idiomatic expressions, accent differences, and other cultural differences cause problems in relationships of Appalachian youth with urban peers and school personnel (McCoy and Watkins, 1979).

Appalachian culture places emphasis on individual achievement and the value of self-sufficiency--Appalachians are not "joiners" and do not relate readily to group activities. Appalachian youth are less likely to seek, or readily accept, school personnel support, such as sponsorship or encouragement by a particular teacher or counselor; they try to deal with problems on their own. They are less likely to participate in school activities (Rhodes, 1968; Wagner, 1975), and parents are less likely to participate in PTA's (Watkins, 1976). Youth do not identify with their schools, especially in junior and senior high school (Miller, 1979), since most youth are placed in an unfamiliar neighborhood for those grades. In addition, since few youth participate in school activities, few are in positions of leadership to serve as role models for others. Parents are overwhelmed by school bureaucracy, by unfamiliar extra-curricular activities, and by the eduational jargon of such groups. Class differences in terms of a mother's employment may conflict with meeting times and may preclude a work schedule to attend those meetings.

High absenteeism and truancy are related to the cultural value placed on the importance of the family, as well as to the traditional migration process. Familism requires that family situations take priority over education (and in many cases, jobs). High absenteeism (Adams, 1971; Wagner, 1974; Rhodes, 1968) is, at least in part, a result of youth being needed at home to help care for siblings and household matters. The traditional migration process, in the three to five years after initial settlement in urban areas, involves frequent relocation (Schwarzweller, 1970). A family's adjustment to an urban area can mean moving several times to find satisfactory neighborhoods, jobs, schools, doctors, and shopping areas. "Indifference" or lack of interest in education was cited by many authors as one of the prevailing features of Appalachian youth in school (Wagner, 1974, 1975; Huelsman, 1969; Henderson, 1966;

Moore, 1976). This attitude was described in various ways, as youth feeling ambivalent toward school, being shy, reticent, passive, avoiding conflict, and withdrawing. Few, however, perceived the significance of cultural conflict. Appalachian parents see more value in basic education and skills development than in extra curricular activities and abstract idea training (Miller, 1977). Parents may encourage Appalachian students into career/practical skills and vocational classes rather than college preparatory or advanced placement classes.

Parents often sacrifice personal needs in order to have their children achieve the educational level equivalent to their own (Adams). However, the low educational level of Appalachians, traditionally, complicates parents' commitment to higher education (Miller; 1977). Kunkin and Byrne found that the parents without high school degrees considered education irrelevant (Kunkin and Byrne, 1973).

Moore and Pastoor (1976) were interested in whether educational values of Appalachian youth were retained in an urban setting. They compared sixth graders in Perry County, Kentucky, and Cincinnati, Ohio, and found that both groups felt that education was moderately important to their lives. Urban youth, however, felt more positive toward education than rural youth, in that urban youth had more confidence in their teachers' abilities and urban students were more inclined to aspire toward a college education. But, based upon current evidence, urban Appalachian youth are frustrated in accomplishing such goals.

Appalachian students have also experienced difficulty in racial, class, and cultural conflicts. Wagner (1975) says, in describing the typical Appalachian student in his sample:

> If he attends a school where there are blacks, he will not understand the blacks and will tend to keep to himself or to associate only with other white students. If he is placed in a threatening situation, he normally will withdraw, not because he is afraid, but because he does not understand the more aggressive behavior of black students. If pressed too hard, he simply will take action to avoid future incidents (such as avoiding the lunchroom, the front hall, or in the extreme situation, quit attending school).

Appalachians have traditionally had little experience with urban blacks, since the black population in the Appalachian region is relatively small. Miller explains that this lack of experience continues in urban schools in elementary grades since Appalachian children attend school with other Appalachians in their own neighborhoods. However, contact increases at the junior high school level where white Appalachians often constitute a minority in the schools. Since the junior high and high schools take Appalachian youth out of their own neighborhood, away from their own "turf," they become fearful, believe rumors of reprisals, and generally feel intimidated. Class differences cause Appalachian youth to feel "looked down on" and the lack of attention given to Appalachian culture only adds to a defeated self-image. Differences in language, dress, and values are seen by other classes as deficiencies or inferiority (Miller, 1977 and 1979). These feelings of inferiority and fear were found in Cleveland to stem from the lack of skills and experiences in certain situations (Kunkin and Byrne, 1973).

The conditions affecting Appalachian youth in school have culminated in extreme dropout rates. Maloney (1974) found that all twelve of the census tracts in Cincinnati with dropout rates of 40 percent or higher were in Appalachian neighborhoods.

Several authors suggested methods of working with Appalachian youth to improve educational levels, as well as relationships with school personnel and peers. Some of these solutions have been alluded to: teacher training (Adams, 1971; Wagner, 1974; Henderson, 1966), curriculum development (Wagner, 1974) in Appalachian culture, and the use of innovative teaching methods (Wagner, 1974). Parent and community involvement in the schools (Wagner, 1974; Henderson, 1966; Watkins, 1976) was considered important in order to provide a personal approach and commitment, as well as having parents and students feel ownership in their schools.

Future roles, expectations, and aspirations of Appalachian youth are unclear. Wagner (1975) found Appalachian youths' job aspirations to be vague and unrealistic considering low school acheivement. Henderson (1966), in studying Appalachian youth, did not find any relationship between school achievement and employment aspirations. Moore and Pastoor (1976), on the other hand, observed a positive relationship between the perception of a good education and a good job among urban Appalachian youth. In addition, Ricco (1965) found a positive relationship between achievement aspirations in both Appalachian and non-Appalachian males in Whitehall, Ohio, a small urban area.

Other than school related experiences, little information exists concerning the behavior of Appalachian youth in urban environments. However, there is some evidence that the transition from the mountains to urban life presents cultural incongruities. For example, independence and freedom of movement were allowed by parents in the Appalachian mountain environment. However, when migration occurred, the spatial restrictions of the urban setting affected this lifestyle. Parental freedom, combined with alienation experienced in the school systems, and peer pressure (Huelsman, 1969) resulted in higher delinquency rates.

> Examples of cultural clashes creating adverse attitudes toward authorities among these (Appalachian) youth include domestic stress in the new environment, individualism in the face of need for legal help, and perceived prejudice in the legal system, both as to poor people and as to Appalachians in particular (McCoy, 1976).

Inner-city Appalachian youth must also deal with restricted recreational facilities. Facilities are often staffed by workers insensitive to the Appalachian value system, or are controlled by other groups.

Appalachian youth find themselves caught between the values of the urban society in which they live and the values from their heritage.

Survey Findings Concerning Appalachian Youth

This study is based on survey data collected in 1975 to assess youth behavior in four cities: Baltimore, Providence, Cincinnati, and Detroit. The National Center for Urban/Ethnic Affairs (NCUEA) developed and tested the survey instrument, and then contracted with community organizations in each city to collect the data.

NCUEA provided training and technical assistance to the community organizations during the data collection phase.

Questionnaires were administered in parochial and public schools in Detroit and Baltimore. The Providence and Cincinnati organizations were unable to obtain access to schools and utilized outreach programs to administer the questionnaire to youngsters in the community.

The out-of-school populations were selected in specific predetermined ethnic neighborhoods on the basis of a 20 percent sample of ethnic youths in each selected neighborhood. Interviewers were instructed to find and interview youths fourteen to twenty years old in the prescribed neighborhoods by locating youths where they were known to "hang out," such as recreation centers, bars, churches, neithborhood drop-in centers, and after-school programs.

Interviewers had to account for unique variations. For example, in Cincinnati an added consideration of low educational levels among out-of-school youth meant that some interviews had to be conducted in small groups; other interviews needed to be conducted with the interviewer reading the questions and filling in the answers.

Comparative Characteristics of Appalachian and Other Urban Ethnic Youth

Comparisons based on the survey data and on noting similarities and differences among the various youths should provide a certain understanding of the differences in behavioral patterns between Appalachians and other urban ethnic youths and provide some further insights into the cultural transition experienced by Appalachian youths.

The sample of 1458 youths included 445 (30.5 percent) Appalachians, 157 (10.8 percent) Blacks, 307 (21.1 percent) Polish, and 549 (37.7 percent) other ethnics. Each group contained slightly more males than females: 43.3 percent of the Appalachians were females, 44.5 percent blacks, 48.8 percent Polish, and 45.6 percent other ethnics.

The median ages of the ethnic groups in the sample are shown below. Appalachian youths were the oldest in the sample, with a median age of 17.1 years. Blacks were the youngest, 16.3 years.

	Median Age
Appalachian	17.1
Black	16.3
Polish	16.6
Other	17.1
Total Sample	16.9

Religious affiliation for Appalachians and blacks was primarily Baptist, with Roman Catholicism second in importance (see Table 1). Polish youths were overwhelmingly Roman Catholic (90 percent), as were other ethnics (53.6 percent).

Fundamentalism underlies the religious beliefs of many Appalachians and strongly influences other values. These beliefs are founded on a literal interpretation of the Bible, an expectation of reward in the next life, and a world view in which God is omnipotent and man is fallible (Jones, 1978).

TABLE 1
Religion

	Appalachians		Blacks		Polish		Other	
	N	%	N	%	N	%	N	%
Baptist	138	31.7	74	48.7	1	0.3	42	7.6
Black Muslims	8	1.8	6	3.9	0	0.0	3	0.5
Church of God	26	6.0	9	5.9	4	1.3	20	3.6
Congregational	3	0.7	1	0.7	2	0.7	3	0.5
Eastern Rite Catholic	2	0.5	0	0.0	3	1.0	10	1.8
Episcopalian	11	2.5	0	0.0	0	0.0	11	2.0
Greek Orthodox	5	1.1	0	0.0	0	0.0	12	2.2
Holiness	7	1.6	3	2.0	1	0.3	2	0.4
Islamic	0	0.0	0	0.0	0	0.0	6	1.1
Jewish	12	2.8	0	0.0	1	0.3	11	2.0
Lutheran	16	3.7	3	2.0	4	1.3	31	5.6
Methodist	27	6.2	9	3	1.0	12	2.2	
Presbyterian	10	2.3	2	1.3	2	1.3	1	0.3
Pentecostal	17	3.9	2	1.3	1	0.3	9	1.6
Roman Catholic	70	16.1	15	9.9	274	90.7	295	53.6
Other	31	7.1	9	5.9	1	0.3	18	3.3
None	53	12.2	19	12.5	6	2.0	50	9.1
Total	**436**		**152**		**302**		**550**	

Religion in the mountains (and transferred to the urban environment) was less focused on institutionalized ritual and ceremony than based on personalized beliefs in God, Christ, and the church. Specific and literal interpretations of the Bible have molded behaviors and emotions and have shaped a value system which permeates daily life routines.

Fundamentalist churches which were delineated in the questionnaire include Baptist, Church of God, Congregational, Holiness, and Pentecostal; 43.8 percent of the Appalachians and 58.6 percent of the blacks belonged to these churches.

The suprisingly large number of Appalachians (12.2 percent) who did not identify with any church may be indicative of the cultural transition Appalachian youths are experiencing. The transition from the more traditional Appalachian values to the more secular values and belief systems of urban youths could be due, in part, to influence from their peers or from obtaining a more "realistic view" of life based on their negative experiences in urban neighborhoods. The role of the church among inner-city urban youths probably reflects ambiguity as to its purpose and value for many of them. The storefront churches prevalent in manu inner-city areas represent a lack of stability that does not provide for the type of support needed by the youths in confronting various situations which occur during cultural transition.

TABLE 2
Attendance at Religious Services

	Appalachians		Blacks		Polish		Other	
	Grade School	Past Year	Grade School	Past Year	Grade School	Past Year	Grade School	Past Year
Never	19.4	35.1	11.3	15.8	2.3	8.3	14.6	29.4
Few times a year	19.6	28.7	12.0	24.3	5.0	23.4	15.7	31.1
About once a month	9.1	6.6	9.3	15.1	5.6	6.9	6.8	7.9
Few times a month	15.5	12.4	24.0	20.4	11.6	10.9	20.8	14.5
About once a month	36.4	17.2	43.3	24.3	75.5	50.5	42.0	17.1
N	439	442	150	152	302	303	547	544

Even though religion and the development of religious values are important to Appalachians, church attendance is not. More than half the Appalachians in our study either never attended, or else, only attended services a few times in the past year (Table 2). Even in grade school years, church attendance was considerably less than for the other three groups. The importance of religion to Appalachians is in shaping a belief system, not in regular church attendance.

As recent studies have revealed, Appalachian youths have substantial problems with the urban school systems. Educational attainment, measured by a median for highest grade completed, shows that Appalachians in the study had completed fewer school years than any other group, even though they were one of the oldest groups in the sample. Further, there were few Appalachians enrolled in high school academic programs or college classes (Table 3).

Median Highest Grade Completed	
Appalachians	9.9
Black	10.1
Polish	10.6
Other Ethnic	10.3
Total sample	10.2

TABLE 3
Current School Program

	Appalachians		Black		Polish		Other Ethnics	
	N	%	N	%	N	%	N	%
High School								
Academic	60	22.6	34	25.8	119	49.0	125	35.1
General	83	31.2	47	35.6	70	28.8	102	28.7
GED	20	7.5	0	0.0	2	0.8	11	3.1
Business Course	22	8.3	14	10.6	19	7.8	41	11.5
Vocational or Trade School	29	10.9	18	13.6	7	2.9	24	6.7
College	13	4.9	6	4.5	17	7.0	26	7.3
Other	39	14.7	13	9.8	9	3.7	27	7.6
Total	266	100.0	132	100.0	243	100.0	356	100.0

Since Appalachian youths' experiences with the public school systems have been negative ones, some are apparently selecting other alternatives to complete their education. Table 3 shows that Appalachians (10.9 percent) as well as Blacks (13.6 percent) were in trade or vocational schools. An additional 7.5 percent of Appalachians were enrolled in GED programs, which was a substantially higher number than for the other young people.

Debunking all the stereotypes revealed in Polish jokes, the grades reported by Polish students were substantially higher than those reported by the other groups (Table 4). In addition, Polish students had the highest proportion enrolled in high school academic programs with many enrolled in college programs (7.0 percent), as well as the highest median school years completed (10.6).

TABLE 4
Grades in School in the Previous Year

	Appalachians		Blacks		Polish		Other Ethnics	
	N	%	N	%	N	%	N	%
Fail	36	8.2	8	5.3	9	3.0	35	6.4
D-Average	52	11.9	15	9.9	16	5.3	68	12.5
C-Average	206	47.0	88	58.3	110	36.3	245	45.0
B-Average	105	24.0	34	22.5	132	43.6	162	29.7
A-Average	39	8.9	6	4.0	36	11.9	35	6.4
Total	438	100.0	151	100.0	303	100.1	545	100.0

Black youths were similar to Appalachians in the area of education, reporting the lowest grades of all groups, and low median grade completed scores. None of the Black youths were enrolled in GED programs, but some, like Appalachians, were apparently selecting alternatives to the public school system in that 13.6 percent were in trade or vocational programs.

Over one fourth of the youths in the sample were not in school, but were of school age. Appalachians comprised 49.2 percent of these, 34.2 percent were other ethnics, 11.8 percent were Polish, and 4.7 percent were blacks. In revealing their reasons for not completing school, 49.2 percent said they had dropped out. The majority of Appalachians, Polish and other ethnics had dropped out of school, while blacks evidenced a greater variety of reasons for being out of school, including almost a quarter whose education was disrupted by being in jail (Table 5).

TABLE 5
Reasons for not Completing School

	Appalachians	Black		Polish				Other Ethnics	
	N	N	%	N	%	N	%	N	%
Dropped Out		108	57.8	3	16.7	26	57.8	58	44.6
Suspended/Expelled		12	6.4	3	16.7	4	8.9	29	22.3
Hospitalized		20	10.7	2	11.1	2	4.4	5	3.8
Jail		20	10.7	4	22.2	3	6.7	14	11.5
Other		27	14.4	6	33.3	10	22.2	24	18.5
Total		187		18		45		130	
	121								

The post-high school plans of respondents (Table 6) show realistic expectations of Appalachian youths, especially in light of their current educational experiences. Only 16.2 percent planned to go to college, while nearly one fourth planned to go to work. Of the Appalachians, 20.7 percent had no plans after high school and 12.7 percent did not plan to complete high school—not an encouraging picture for further educational achievements. In light of Moore's (1976) finding that urban youths aspired more toward a college education than rural Appalachian youths, the youths in this study, who are older, have apparently reduced their expectations by the time they reach high school age. Low expectations, however, may also be a reflection of fatalism, another prominant value among many others discussed by Jones (1978).

More Black/youths and Polish youths planned to attend college than to go to work. Their higher expectations for the future are also revealed in the small number who to a future without a high school diploma.

TABLE 6
Plans After High School

	Appalachians		Black		Polish		Other Ethnics	
	N	%	N	%	N	%	N	%
Academic College	61	16.2	50	35.5	82	30.4	80	16.8
Vocational Training	30	8.0	10	7.1	20	7.4	41	8.6
Work	93	24.7	27	19.1	62	23.0	107	22.5
Go into Business	11	2.9	6	4.3	10	3.7	35	7.4
Marry/Raise Family	14	3.7	2	1.4	14	5.2	20	4.2
Join Army	24	6.4	9	6.4	19	7.0	33	6.9
Other	18	4.8	9	6.4	10	3.7	15	3.2
Dont't Know	78	20.7	24	17.0	44	16.3	107	22.5
Dont't Plan to Graduate	48	12.7	4	2.8	9	3.3	37	7.8
Total N	377		141		270		475	

Current employment data show that Polish and other ethnic youths had the highest proportions employed (Table 7). Appalachians, on the other hand, had the highest unemployment. Appalachians, traditionally, have tended not to seek jobs through state employment services or employment agencies, but have utilized the kin and friend network to find jobs (Schwarzweller and Brown, 1970). This method of finding jobs is not nearly as productive in times of high unemployment as when jobs are plentiful, and may be part of the explanation for the high number of unemployed Appalachian youths.

TABLE 7
Employment

	Appalachians		Black		Polish		Other Ethnics	
	N	%	N	%	N	%	N	%
Part-Time	78	29.0	25	50.0	88	57.1	116	38.3
Full-Time	62	23.0	6	12.0	30	19.5	93	30.7
Homemaker	18	6.7	1	2.0	4	2.6	10	3.3
Not in School-Not Employed	111	41.3	18	36.0	32	20.8	84	27.7
Total N	269	100.0	50	100.00	154	100.0	303	100.0

The conditions of inner-city Appalachian youths in this survey reveal some very discouraging patterns. The culture of Appalachian youths is undergoing change. This process of change in the urban environment has created new situations with which a changing culture must deal, but the Appalachian youths in this survey were armed with few resources for this task other than support from family and their own inner strength. In summary, the findings showed that Appalachian youths had completed fewer school grades than the comparative groups, although they were older in age. Few were enrolled in high school academic programs; however, some were selecting vocational education and GED programs as alternatives. More of the Appalachians than other groups were school dropouts, and many of those who were in school had either no plans or low expectations for their future. Some did plan to go to college and about one fourth planned to work. However, if the high unemployment of this young age group is any indication of what the future holds, their chances for employment in adult life will be less than other groups.

Implicatons for the Future of Appalachian Youths

The above research findings show consistently, that compared to other urban ethnic youths. Appalachians exhibit great symptomic behavior, indiciating severe difficulties in coping with urban environments.

Why these greater difficulties of adjustment should exist for urban Appalachian youths is not clear at the present time. Further study is needed to understand the relationship between these behaviors patterns and the differences in cultural conditions for Appalachian youths. The recency of the migrant experience of Appalachians relative to other ethnic youths is certainly one factor that needs to be considered. Empirical confirmation is needed to determine more specifically what accounts for these differences. Conflict with public institutions (in particular, the school system) is a critical factor in any attempt to understand Appalachian youths. Consistent evidence exists that Appalachian youngsters have high dropout rates, above average truancy rates, and in general, are dissatisfied with school.

Many Appalachians do not have the family and religious support systems that are needed to address medical, social, and psychological needs.

Only a proper understanding of Appalachian culture and the needs of Appalachian peoples will permit the development of appropriate community support systems. Several factors have been cited as significant to the design of support systems intended to serve urban communities containing large numbers of Appalachians. These systems should be:

1. **Family and Kinship Oriented**

   Family and kinship networks have been an important source of support for mountain families (Brown, 1970). In making the transition from mountain lifeways, there is a deterioration of these kinship support networks. The University of Kentucky Medical Center and the Bethesda North Hospital in Cincinnati found that by developing a familial orientation of health delivery, the services and responsiveness among Appalachian families improved (Watkins, 1973).

2. **Community and Neighborhood Based***

   Support systems for Appalachians should also be neighborhood based, rather than being associated with the presently structured schools or other institutions. Experience has shown that Appalachians respond best to services that are located near their homes. In Cincinnati in recent years, response by Appalachians has been favorable to programs like youth drop-in services, community organizing, and cultural heritage projects whose primary functions are based upon self and family defined needs. Human services or referrals to such agencies are provided as a secondary function. Self-involvement has served to instill ownership in the programs by Appalachians, as well as helping them to feel that they have given something in return for the services received.

3. **Culturally Sensitive***

   Cultural sensitivity is another important characteristic of a support network responsive to the needs of Appalachians. Cultural sensitivity does not necessarily mean that a program would be culturally specific. A program within the Appalachian community would need to deal with several variants of Appalachian culture, as well as other ethnic groups.

4. **Non-Bureaucratic***

   Another factor that is necessary in providing services to Appalachian youths in particular, is that support systems should be flexible, open, personal, and family oriented. A personal approach has been described by David Looff (1971) in his work with mountain children. He strongly emphasizes the Appalachian characteristics of personal support and familism as crucial to his success in working with the children. Youths tend to respond well to approaches which recognize them as people with problems, but not when labels such as "sick" or "mentally ill" or "bad" are placed on them.

5. **Comprehensive**

   A fifth factor to consider in developing supports for Appalachians is suggested by James S. Brown, a long-time scholar of Appalachian migration and migrants. He suggests that Appalachians are multiple problem families; that their arrival in the cities presents many unique problems for the family which differ for each member of the family; and that these problems are cultural inasmuch as they are economic. Urban conditions affect each member of the family in such a unique way that the support systems usually offered by kinship and family are less effective in the new environment than they were in the mountains.

Multiple, sociocultural conflicts combined with a lack of initial opportunity to gain meaningful employment create multiple problems for the family. Since the Appalachian family relied very heavily upon the support system of kinship and familism in the mountains, the conflicts and stresses confronted in the urban environment also deteriorate that support system so that it is not as effective as in the mountain tradition.

*Categories similarly named in Watkins, 1975.

CONCLUSIONS

In conclusion, an increased understanding of Appalachian culture and needs, with the provision of appropriate support systems, could improve the conditions for Appalachian youth. Although economic conditions are also part of the problem, for Appalachians, all the problems cannot be solved through economic support. Neither should these be school based at the present time due to the alienation of the youth from the schools. These supports must be rooted in the communities and neighborhoods and involve the tremendous strength that family and kinship can offer to Appalachian youths.

REFERENCES

Adams, James. "Series on Appalachians in Cincinnati: Children Face Special Problems in School." Reprinted from the *Cincinnati Post and Times-Star,* 1971.

Ball, J. C., and Bates W. M. "Nativity, Parentage and Mobility of Opiate Addicts." In J. C. Ball and C. D. Chambers *The Epidemiology of Opiate Addiction in the United States,* edited by J. C. Ball and C. D. Chambers, pp. 95-111. Springfield, Illinois: Charles C. Thomas, 1970.

Beschner, George, and Treasure, Kerry. "Female Adolescent Drug Use." In Friedmand, Alfred S. and Beschner, George, *Youth Drug Abuse:* Problems, Issues and Treatment, edited by Alfred S. Friedman and George Beschner, pp. 4-7. Lexington Books, Inc., forthcoming.

Brown, James S. "The Family Behind the Migrant." *Mountain Life and Work,* September 1968, pp. 4-7.

Chein, Isidor; Gerard, Donald L.; Lee, Robert S.; and Rosenfeld, Eva. *The Road to H: Narcotics, Delinquency and Social Policy.* New York: Basic Books, 1964.

Chitwood, Dale D.; McBride, Duane C.; and McCoy, Clyde B. "The Extent of Substance Abuse Among High School Students." Miami-Dade Metro County School System, 1976.

Cisin, I. H., and Mannheimer, D. I. "Marijuana Use Among Adults in a Large City and Suburb." *Annals of the New York Academy of Science* 191 (1971): 222-34.

Fowler, Gary L. "Residential Distribution of Appalachians in Cincinnati." In *The Invisible Minority,* edited by William Philliber and Clyde B. McCoy, pp. 79-94. University Press of Kentucky, 1980.

Henderson, George. "Poor Southern Whites: A Neglected Urban Problem." *Journal of Secondary Education* 41(1966): 111-114.

Henson, Michael. "There's Nothing Better to Do." *Mountain Life and Work,* August 1976, pp. 20-29.

Huelsman, Ben R. "Southern Mountaineers in City Juvenile Courts." *Federal Probation* 33(1969): 49-54.

Jones, Loyal. "Appalachian Values." In *Perspectives on Urban Appalachians,* edited by Steve Weiland and Phillip Obermiller. Cincinnati: Ohio Urban

Appalachian Awareness Project, 1978.

Kleinman, P. H., and Likoff, Irving. "Ethnic Differences in Factors Related to Drug Use." *Journal of Health and Social Behavior* 19(1978): 190-199.

Kunkin, Dorothy, and Byrne, Michael. *Appalachians in Cleveland.* Institute for Urban Studies, The Cleveland State University, 1973.

Loof, David H. *Appalachian Children: The Challenge of Mental Health.* Lexington: University of Kentucky Press, 1971.

Lukoff, Irving F. *Social and Ethnic Patterns of Reported Drug Use and Continguity with Drug Users.* Washington, D.C.: U.S. Department of Justice, Law Enforcement Assistance Administration, 1972.

Maloney, Michael E. The Social Areas of Cincinnati: Toward an *Analysis of Social Needs.* Cincinnati Human Relations Commission, 1974.

—————————. "The Implications of Appalachian Culture for Social Welfare Practice." *Perspectives on Urban Appalachians*, edited by Steve Weiland and Phil Obermiller. Cincinnati: Ohio Urban Appalachian Awareness Project, 1978.

McBride, Duane C. *"Social Control and Drug Use."* Ph. D. Dissertation, University of Kentucky, 1977.

McCoy, Candance. "Attitudes of Appalachian Youth Towards Legal Authority." *Focus on Law* 2(1976): 11-12.

McCoy, Clyde B., and McBride, Duane C. "Socio-Cultural Theories and Techniques in the Explanation for Social Research on Drug Abuse." Miami: Center for Social Research on Drug Abuse, 1976.

—————————. "Drug Use in Metropolitan Society." Final Report to National Institute on Drug Abuse. Miami: Center for Social Research on Drug Abuse, 1978.

—————————, and Brown, James S. "Migration Stream Systems to Midwestern Cities." In *The Invisible Minority,* edited by William Philliber and Clyde B. McCoy. University Press of Kentucky, 1980.

—————————, and Watkins, Virginia McCoy. "The Migration System Pattern of Southwest Ohio and its Relation to Southern Appalachian Migration." *Research Bulletin.* Urban Appalachian Council, 1975.

—————————. "Stereotypes of Urban Appalachians." In *the Invisible Minority*, edited by William Philliber and Clyde B. McCoy. University Press of Kentucky, 1980.

Miller, Yommie. "Education and Urban Appalachian Youth." Youth Services Training Handout. Urban Appalachian Council, 1977.

—————————. Information obtained in discussion on Appalachian youths with Virginia McCoy Watkins, 1979.

—————————. Information obtained in discussion on Appalachian youth with Virginia McCoy Watkins, 1979.

Moore, Detlef H., and Pastoor, Dirk J. "Appalachian Values: Are They Transferrable from a Rural to Urban Setting?" The Institute for Community Development. University of Louisville, 1976.

Pickard, Jerome. "Population Changes and Trends in Appalachia." In *Appalachians in Urban Areas*, edited by William Philliber and Clyde B. McCoy. University of Kentucky Press, forthcoming.

Rhodes, Charles. "Appalachian Child in Chicago Schools." *Appalachian Advance,* October 1968, pp. 6-10.

Ricco, Anthony. "Occupational Aspirations of Migrant Adolescents from the Appalachian South." *Vocational Guidance Quarterly*, Autumn, 1965, pp. 26-30.

Schwarzweller, Harry C. "Adaptation of Appalachian Migrants to the

Industrial Work Situation: A Case Study." In *Behavior in New Environments: Adaptation of Migrant Populations*, edited by Eugene B. Broey. Sage Publications, 1970.

Simpkins, O. Norman. "An Informal, Incomplete Introduction to Appalachian Culture." In Marshall Universtiy Distinguished Reading Series-2. Huntington, W. Va., 1974.

Vaillant, G.E. "Parent-Child Cultural Disparity and Drug Addiction." *Journal of Nervous and Mental Diseases.* 142-534-9. 1966.

Wagner, Thomas E. "Report of the Appalachian School Study Project." Urban Appalachian Council Working Paper No. 4. June, 1974.

_____. "Urban Appalachian School Children: The Least Understood of All." Urban Appalachian Council Working Paper No. 6. January, 1975.

Watkins, Virginia McCoy. "Consideration of Factors Relevant to the Development of Health Support Systems for Appalachian Migrants." Master's Thesis, University of Cincinnati, 1973.

_____, and West, Ray. "Relationships and Potentials Between the Urban Appalachian Family and the Neighborhood School and Neighborhood Stability." Case Study prepared for the National Center for Urban Ethnic Affairs. *Urban Appalachian Council*, 1976.

_____, and McCoy, Clyde B. *Drug Use Among Urban Ethnic Youth.* Report to the National Institute on Drug Abuse. January, 1979.

_____. *Drug Use Among Appalachian Youth.* Services Research Monograph. National Institute on Drug Abuse, 1980.

THE IMPACT OF URBAN HOUSING PROGRAMS ON APPALACHIAN NEIGHBORHOODS

Gary L. Fowler

Abstract

Traditional ports-of-entry and Appalachian neighborhoods in low-income areas of central cities have been included in target areas for a succession of urban housing and development programs. These programs have resulted in the displacement of large numbers of Appalachian families, and have contributed to the decline in the importance of the areas in the geography of urban Appalachians. The impacts of public housing programs in Chicago's Uptown community provide a case study of these changes.

This (urban population loss) is a problem--one that, yes, has to be solved or at least mitigated by both local and large, multi-state development strategies. But in the meantime, and at risk of seeming militantly cheery, the problem is also an opportunity.

In Dayton's specific case, take just one small example. The inner East Side neighborhood formerly known as Burns-Jackson and now reborn as the Oregon Historic District. It has lost population, thank goodness.

The large, old homes were crumbling a few years ago under multi-family occupancy by persons stuck short of the poverty line. Now the homes are being remodeled into classy, single-family residences.

Sorry about the implied elitism, but there can be little real question the community is better off thanks to that "population decline." Mere numbers do not always add up for the best.

> Editorial, "Population Loss--Dayton's and Others'--is an Opportunity," *Dayton Daily News,* April 17, 1977, p. 18A

INTRODUCTION

Large numbers of Appalachian people who migrated to northern cities in the 1940s and 1950s concentrated in central city ports-of-entry. These "hillbilly ghettos" were staging areas for upwardly mobile Appalachian migrants, as well as places in which newcomers with few economic resources could live. Through time, however, many of the ports-of-entry neighborhoods were included in central city poverty areas that were designated targets for a succession of urban housing and development programs. These programs have become controversial because of their impact upon the residential opportunities for low income families who are most subject to involuntary relocation.

The purpose of this paper is to discuss the impacts of urban renewal and revitalization programs upon Appalachian people in Chicago's Uptown community. The empirical data for urban renewal and code enforcement programs, and available information about revitalization programs since 1974, suggest that poor Appalachians in Uptown continue to be victimized by policies and programs that benefit the middle and upper classes.

Urban Appalachian Settlement

People from local "high" class families dominated the early migration from the Appalachian Region.[1] They went to small towns and cities near the periphery of the Region where they established roots for subsequent migrants. As the pace of migration accelerated in the 1940s and 1950s, large numbers of Appalachians who had little money and few industrial skills moved into large cities and settled in central city ports-of-entry. These neighborhoods had relatively inexpensive rental housing that was accessible to sources of employment for the newcomers. They also offered the social support of kin, friends, and familiar cultural environment that eased the adjustment to city life for people who, in many instances, considered themselves to be temporary urban residents.

The hillbilly ghettos became notorious places in the folk geography of urban America. The port-of-entry life style was, in a sense, stereotyped in the public mind (Huelsman, 1968, p. 99):

> The migrant to Dayton usually gets here in a wheezing old car full of kids with hungry bellies and maybe a guitar. In the pocket of his faded, blue work shirt is a letter from a second cousin or an uncle with an address near Fifth and Brown or Tecumseh St. in East Dayton. This is in the heart of Dayton's port of entry, a strange new style of life for the southern white mountain migrant. He brings his wife, four, five or six children and about eight years of grammar schooling because he's heard from his kinsman that "they're hirin' on at NCR" or somewhere else. The southern mountain man in the port of entry is most likely to be from one of the mountain counties of eastern Kentucky. His kinsman of Tecumseh or Brown St. has four of five young 'uns of his own, but he'll not turn down Dayton's newest migrant. They will all pile into one big flat, sleeping on couches, on the floor or in nice weather, maybe some of the kids will sleep out in the car. The family baggage is meagre...a few changes of old clothes, a toy or so, some snapshots, a few trinkets and souveniers of life back home in the hills and hollows of eastern Kentucky. The family has brought the most important baggage of all with them...the culture of the southern mountaineer, unfamiliar with city life.

Ports-of-entry were described as "natural" areas with physical and cultural characteristics that presumably suited the needs of recent migrants. They functioned as the territorial bases of an evolutionary settlement pattern in which Appalachians, just as groups of migrants who preceded them, were expected to follow an orderly progression of socioeconomic and geographical mobility in the city according to classical models of urban ecology.

The stereotype of the hillbilly ghetto has dominated the public perception of urban Appalachians for several decades. Recent research, however, points out that the port-of-entry is only one of several urban residential environments in which Appalachian people live. A large percentage, but not the majority, of Appalachians in cities such as Atlanta, Chicago, Cincinnati, and Detroit continue to live in traditional ports-of-entry and other central city neighborhoods in which they cluster by state or area of origin.[2] The housing stock in many of these neighborhoods deteriorated during the period of large-scale inmigration as the density of population increased, and various forms of disinvestment by landlords became common in areas where an increasingly large proportion of the population suffered problems of poverty, unemployment, and other disadvantages. As selective migration from these neighborhoods to other parts of the cities continued, the flow of newcomers also decreased. Many of the traditional central ports-of-entry no longer are staging areas for upwardly mobile families. The Appalachian people who remain in them are more likely to be long-term residents of the city with limited socio-economic opportunities. And the newcomers are more likely to be upper-middle-class, non-Appalachian people (Fowler, 1976).

During the late 1960s and early 1970s, many central city Appalachian neighborhoods, including traditional ports-of-entry, were incorporated within areas that were targeted for urban renewal and revitalization policies and programs. Although the roster is incomplete, Appalachian neighborhoods in Ohio cities--Cincinnati's Over-the-Rhine, Cleveland's West Side, and East Dayton, for example—were included in target areas, as well as larger communities such as Chicago's Uptown and Appalachian areas of Detroit. The impacts of these programs raise serious questions about their effect upon the quality of life of urban Appalachian people. Appalachians living in central Cincinnati, for example, were more likely to have been forced to move, or to move into a place because it was the cheapest available, than were non-Appalachian residents (Fowler, 1976). Appalachians in other cities faced similar problems of relocation because of renewal and disinvestment practices. Currently, Appalachians face the possibility that public policies and programs that are designed to promote central city revitalization will result in their involuntary dislocation by non-Appalachians, especially middle and upper-class groups.

The Uptown community in Chicago is an area of traditional Appalachian settlement that has been the site for a succession of urban public housing policies of the 1960s and 1970s. Empirical data for selected urban renewal projects suggest that Appalachian people in particular had to change their residences as a result. Furthermore, revitalization initiatives suggest that Appalachian families are more likely to be excluded, rather than included, in the process.

Appalachians in Uptown

Uptown, which is located on Chicago's north side, extends from Irving Park Road north to West Devon, and inland from the Lake Michigan shore to Ravenswood (Figure 1). It was a prosperous area during the 1920s, with a large commercial district centered on Broadway and Sheridan and a population that was predominantly German, Swedish, Irish, and Russian. Dwelling units were converted into smaller apartment units and the density of population increased dramatically during the depression. Subsequently, foreign immigration declined, and Uptown attracted large numbers of low-income migrants after 1945. These included people from Appalachia; blacks, mainly from the South; American Indians, East Indians, and Puerto Ricans. They contributed new elements to Uptown's mosaic of ethnic and cultural diversity, as well as the area's sharp distinctions in socioeconomic status.

Appalachian migrants attracted Chicago's official attention in the late 1950s. Giffin (1959) prepared a document intended for use in understanding problems of adjustment that might face the migrants; and the Cook County Department of Public Aid surveyed the public assistance use patterns of southern Appalachian families (Brooks, 1960; and Cook County Department of Public Aid, 1963). The Department of Public Aid concluded that, contrary to conventional wisdom, Appalachian families were not disproportionately represented on the public assistance roles. However, they did note, that from 1960 to 1963, the proportion of Appalachian families receiving public assistance and living in the Uptown area had increased.[3]

Subsequent decriptions of the Appalachian community in Uptown were neatly fitted into the stereotypes of a traditional central city port-of-entry. The area was described as one of several places in the city that linked urban poverty with its rural origins, and Appalachian people were depicted as having related adjustment problems that resulted from being unprepared for living in large, urban industrial areas.[4] Research on the status and welfare of Appalachians living in Uptown clearly showed that the popular portrayal of their situation was simplistic at best (e.g., Coles, 1971; Gitlin and Hollander, 1970; and Merten, 1974). The fact remained that this was the dominant perception, and that Uptown was the only area that was consistently mentioned as the urban home of Appalachian people in Chicago.

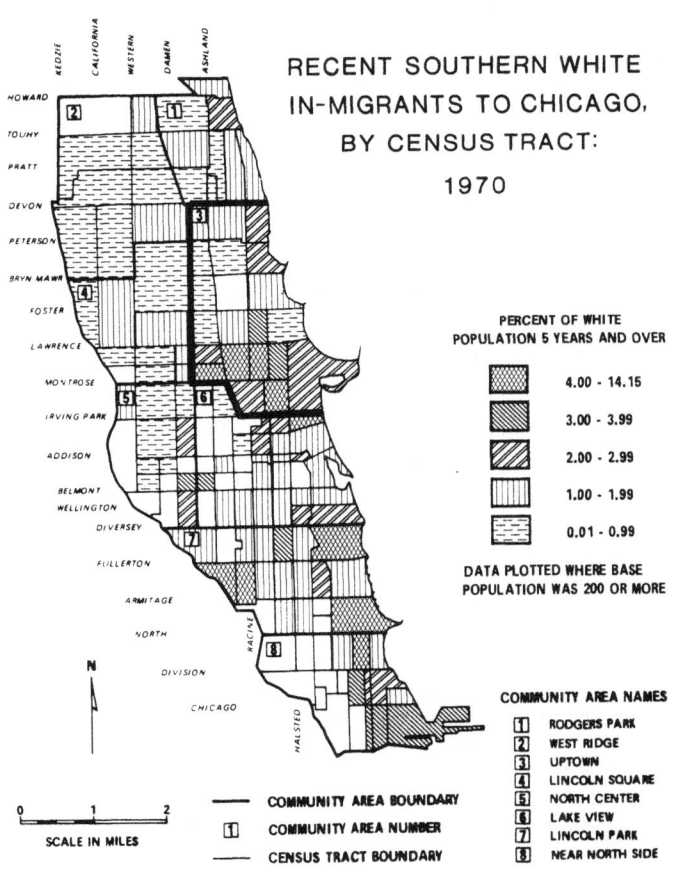

The number of Appalachians who live in Uptown and their residential distribution is unknown. However, there is general agreement that they are concentrated in a core area that focuses upon several census tracts in the southern part of the area. This is also the area with the highest rate of recent in-migration of white people from the South as well as the highest concentration of white, southern born population (Figure 1).[5] Other areas on the north side have similarly high rates of recent southern in-migration, although they are generally not identified as areas of Appalachian settlement.

Urban Renewal Programs in Uptown

The Uptown Chicago Commission was organized in 1955 to direct efforts to redevelop the Uptown area. The commission was organized by W. Clement Stone's Combined Insurance Agency and seven other business firms, including two large local banks (Uptown Federal Savings and Loan Association and Uptown National Bank of Chicago) that were committed to investment in the area. Uptown was declared an urban renewal conservation area in 1965. Subsequently, the Uptown Community Conservation Council (UCCC) and Uptown Model Cities Council were formed and assumed active roles in urban renewal planning. As their activities became more widely known, other groups representing diverse interests organized under the banner of the Uptown Area People's Planning Coalition (UAPPC) to gain influence over plans that were considered to be thinly disguised means of displacing poor people, especially Appalachians, from Uptown to the advantage of the upper-middle-class and business interests.

TABLE 1

Urban Housing Programs and Relocation in the Uptown Area, Chicago

Program	Date	Relocated Households	People
Uptown Urban Renewal Project I (DUR)	1968	783	
Truman Junior College	1970		
Interim Site*		170	545
Total Site*		785	1466
Neighborhood Service	1970-1973	253	892

*The data are from a survey of the site, as reported by Rodney and Sydney Wright, "Facts Concerning the Proposed Clifton-Racine Site for City Colleges of Chicago," June 17, 1970. The data are for total households (dwelling units) and people living within the site, rather than the number actually relocated.

Three separate activities in Uptown were included under the rubric of urban renewal legislation in the late 1960s and early 1970s (Table 1, Figure 2). The first of these, Uptown Renewal Project I, involved the acquisition and clearing of about one quarter of the nineteen block project area. Twenty-one structures were demolished, and 783 households were relocated. The construction of a city junior college on a twenty-one acre site in the heart of the Appalachian community was the second project. This threatened a total of approximately

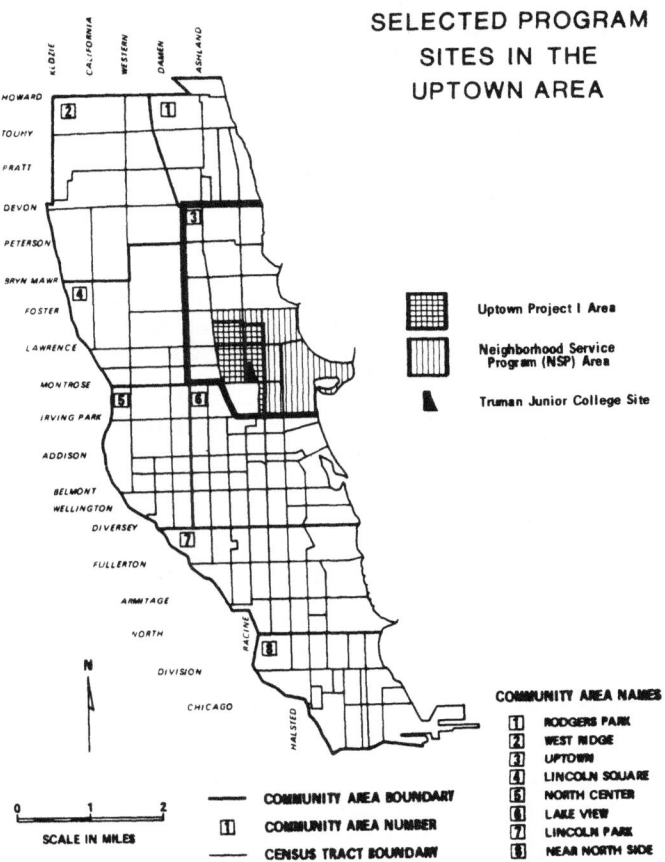

two thousand people with relocation. Third, a large area in the southern part of Uptown was designated a Model Cities area, and federal monies were used for a code enforcement program--the Neighborhood Service Program (NSP)-- designed to eliminate slum and blighted buildings. Each of these programs included the poorest areas of Uptown, and the areas that housed the largest concentration of Appalachian people, including recent immigrants.

The plans for construction of the city junior college was the catalyst of political activity over urban renewal plans for Uptown. Surveys of the site completed by UAPPC reported data that indicated that the impacts upon people living in the area was potentially quite severe.

BULLETIN

The North Side Coalition Community Organizations opposed to an Uptown Junior College Monday night announced the results of a survey taken in the 6-acre Phase One area.

In that area they found: 18 buildings (the DUR found 25); 577 people in 104 units for a family occupancy of 5.5 persons per unit; 65 percent of the families in the area contain five or more people; some families number as many as ten; 87 percent of these people have an income under $5,000.

Looking for vacancies for those to be relocated, the survey found 134 apartments on Kenmore, Winthrop, Magnolia, Beacon and Malden. Forty-four of these were one-room apartments, no children allowed. Thirty-two were 2-room apartments, no children allowed. Forty-six were 3-room apartments. Two family-sized units were found.

About 34 percent of the landlords said no children; 12 percent said only pre-school children; and 16 percent said no more than two children.

The survey also checked vacancies in the 221-D3, federally-subsidized buildings. Of nine buildings, they found 30 vacancies. But building managers reportedly told Jerry Zank, a surveyor, that they would not accept Uptown residents as tenants.

The majority (56 percent) of the 545 people in the Phase One (interim) site were from Appalachia.[6] Other whites (18.7 percent) and Spanish-speaking people (13.2 percent) were the next largest groups.

The results of a second survey for the entire twenty-two acre site counted a total of 1,466 people living in 785 dwelling units. Approximately 41 percent of them were from Appalachia, with "other whites" (25.6 percent) and black people (20.2 percent) comprising the next largest groups. The families in this area were smaller, with fewer children than in the interim site. They also had a slightly higher median income, although the majority of the households in each area received some type of welfare assistance.

The Advisory Coalition for North Side City College proposed that the City College Board seek an alternate site for the college on the north side.[7] UAPPC had assisted in preparing a plan for that site that would include a model community named Hank Williams Village, in which 80 percent of the units would be reserved for low-income families. Later renamed the Village, the model community also was to provide a variety of community services and a town hall for community organizations. Political confrontations that pitted the Village against the proposed junior college continued through 1968 and most of 1969, with the interim results that the Chicago College Board voted in early September to change to a twenty-one acre Riverview site instead. The decision was subsequently reversed, and the Clifton-Racine site was indeed cleared for construction in the summer of 1974. Truman College opened two years later. An estimated 87 percent of the enrollment came from the North Side of Chicago, with Uptown supplying 30 percent.[8] Yet a mural facing the new college reads, "I. O. U. This college must be for everyone. 1,200 families used to live here. We are watching you."

The impacts of the Neighborhood Service Program (NSP) of code enforcement were less dramatic, and affected a smaller number of people in a much larger area of Uptown. Analysis of the data on relocation, however, provides a picture of the geography of residential change that resulted. A total of 253 households were displaced from 1970-1973.[9] The majority of these were white households, although blacks, American Indians, and Spanish-speaking groups were disproportionately represented. The majority of all groups had lived at their current residence for less than two years, and they had very low mean incomes ($4,179 for whites; $4,263 for blacks).

The majority of the households that were displaced by NSP relocated in the Uptown area (Table 2). The white households remained within the southeast section of Uptown, especially around Broadway between Irving Park Road and Lawrence, and following a corridor between Sheridan Road and Broadway north to Foster and Bryn Mawr. This matched the highest concentration of low-cost residential housing units. Those who moved out of Uptown went to adjacent community areas; and seven percent left the city for various locations in the South. The white households experienced only an eight percent increase in rent after relocation (from an average of $102 to $111 per month). However, the majority remained in those parts of Uptown that had the lowest socioeconomic status.

The Revitalization of Uptown

The Housing and Community Development Act of 1974 and subsequent legislation has called for policies and programs to promote population redistribution in urban areas, specifically, to promote the spatial deconcentration of the urban poor and to attract higher income people to poor and deteriorating neighborhoods. These include federal housing subsidy programs, such as the Section 8 Lower-Income Rental Assistance Program, that are supposed to increase the spatial range of housing options for the poor. At the same time, the potential for widespread revitalization in areas such as Uptown raises serious questions about the extent to which lower-income people, including Appalachians, will be involuntarily displaced from their neighborhoods to make room for the middle and upper class. The people who are least able to control their own destinies, and who have the fewest choices in the housing market, may bear a disproportionate share of the costs of neighborhood improvement.[10]

TABLE 2
Relocation Patterns for Uptown Residents Displayed from the Neighborhood Services Program (NSP) Area, 1971-1973

	WHITE		NON-WHITE	
Uptown Community Area	107	63.3%	51	60.7%
Other North Side Community Areas				
Rogers Park	4	2.4	-	-
North Center	4	2.4	-	-
Lake View	7	4.1	2	2.4
Lincoln Park	-	-	1	1.2
Near North Side	-	-	3	3.6
Other Parts of the City of Chicago	4	2.4	9	10.7
Out of the City of Chicago	12	7.1	3	3.6
Unknown	31	18.3	15	17.9
Totals	**169**	**100%**	**84**	**100%**

Source: Based upon City of Chicago, Department of Urban Renewal data.

Uptown has become a prime target for revitalization under new urban housing and development policies. According to one developer:

> There's no question that the area's the hottest place in Chicago right now. There are sections of the neighborhood where people are buying up apartment buildings and vacant land eyeing Uptown as, potentially, a good place to live.[11]

The majority of the large-scale projects are located in the southeastern part of Uptown. Expensive new housing and rehabilitated units, including some for subsidized low and middle-income renters, are being developed with federal and state funding support. The largest of the rehabilitation projects is at 5110-12 Kenmore. It is financed by a $10.5 million loan from the Illinois Housing Development Authority; $1.6 from the City of Chicago's community development fund; and $1.3 from the developer. The project will convert an existing 399 apartment units, two thirds of which are efficiencies, into 280 units, the majority of which are one-bedroom places. Although most will be available for federally subsidized persons, the rents will be much higher than is currently the rule and the number of units available will decrease. Other projects are town houses and high-rise condominium buildings that are specifically designed for young, upper-class professionals who are considered to be pioneers in "reclaiming the city."

Controversy over the impact of revitalization programs in Uptown is focused upon alleged conflicts in the use of Community Development Block Grant Funds. The 1974 Housing and Community Development Act has a clearly stated goal:

> ...the development of viable urban communities, by providing decent housing and a suitable living environment and expanding economic opportunities principally for persons of low and moderate income.

In the absence of a comprehensive plan for redeveloping the city, the Uptown People's Community Center produced a model plan for developing the heart of Uptown as a multi-ethnic, broad economic spectrum of people living in a variety of housing units (Hafferkamp, 1979). The Center's plan was rejected out of hand in the spring of 1979. Subsequently, the Center's attorney filed an amendment to its pending 1975 class action suit in U.S. District Court. The suit, which was originally filed against William Thompson, who had proposed the Pensacola Planned Development in the southern part of Uptown, was amended to contend that HUD, as well as the City of Chicago, conspired to infringe on the civil rights of the Uptown Community by allowing private developers to displace the existing population and thus aid in the destruction of an integrated neighborhood.

The Center's attorney explained the suit in these terms:

> The 1975 suit alleged a conspiracy among the city and various developers to destroy the integrated nature of Uptown, and to create a middle- and upper-middle income, basically white neighborhood. The original suit focused on developer William Thompson because in 1975 he was the most visible enemy. Now we have added HUD because in giving money to the city, we think it has failed to live up to its mandated responsibility.
>
> I think our suit paints a very accurate history, going back 20 years

to show that as the demand for white middle-and upper-income housing has increased, there were certain neighborhoods, such as Lincoln Park and Sandburg Village, that the city and developers focused on. In one way or another the existing population was kicked out. Minorities in particular didn't get the chance to move back in when the redevelopment was completed. Prices simply went up too much. And of course when you make a strickly white neighborhood, you are making a segregated neighborhood.

In Uptown it became apparent to us that one logical step in the conspiracy was the city's refusal to put funds for rehab or construction into the Uptown community. If Federally subsidized housing were to go into selected sites in Uptown, two things would happen. One, the big developer would be discouraged. They feel that if there is subsidized housing in the area, then well-to-do whites won't want to move in. Second, the developer-encouraged destruction of the existing neighborhood would stop, and the area would begin to stabilize on its own. The city has not so far put funds for new or rehabbed housing into the heart of Uptown because the area is simply too desirable financially.

Shortly after the amendment was filed, the suit was settled as Thompson scaled down the Pensacola Place project and agreed to rehabilitate three existing buildings nearby to provide housing for lower-income people.

Epilogue

Compared with relocation under urban renewal, the impacts of urban revitalization programs upon Appalachian communities are difficult to assess. The necessary data are available only from surveys and, even then, they are subject to sharply different interpretations (Cf. Sumka, 1979; Hartman, 1979). Nevertheless, the Appalachian peoples' relationship to traditional ports-of-entry in low-income areas such as Uptown has changed. The potential for direct displacement because of reinvestment is the most obvious development. The more subtle pressure of increased housing costs may be equally significant, especially when landlords, arson, and other types of disinvestment have reduced the available housing stock. During the seventies, Appalachians have had to compete for the old and new low-income rentals with recognized minority groups. In Uptown, as in many other traditional Appalachian ports-of-entry, the number of blacks and Spanish-speaking people is increasing rapidly.

The politics of neighborhood revitalization are as controversial as the earlier politics of urban renewal. Uptown is similar to other communities in that respect (Auger, 1979). However, Appalachians have played less of a role in Uptown community politics in the late 1970s. This may reflect their diminished numbers, as well as the apparent decline in the number of new immigrants relative to other groups. In Uptown, as in other traditional central city ports-of-entry, Appalachian people no longer dominate the influx of newcomers to the neighborhood.

NOTES

1. See Fowler (1976); Petersen, Sharp, and Drury (1977); and Photiadis (1971).

2. These patterns are described by Fowler (1980). Studies of Appalachian

settlement in specific cities are by Howell (1973); McKee and Obermiller (1977); Marple, Koebernick, and Jones (1977); Petersen, Sharp, and Drury (1977); and Photiadis (1971). Also, see Maloney (1978).

3. Brooks '(1960) and Cook County Department of Public Aid (1963).

4. Cf. Backs (1968), Bruno (1974), and Montgomery (1968). Earlier studies of Appalachians in Chicago included Killian's (1970) research on southern, white laborers living in the Near West Side in the 1940's, and Harwood's (1966) description of the adaption of southern migrants in the city.

5. The census tract data are from the Fourth Count Summary Tapes, 1970 General Census of Population and Housing.

6. *Uptown News,* Tuesday, June 16, 1970, p.1. The survey data are from a report by Rodney and Sidney Wright. "Facts concerning the proposed Clifton-Racine Site for City Colleges of Chicago," June 17, 1970.

7. The advisory coalition which was composed of a number of north side groups, was formed to "assist" the City College Board in finding a suitable site for the college. The coalition recommended that the Clifton-Racine site be dropped because it would displace people and destroy residential facilities.

8. Meg O'Connor, "New Truman College Stirs Both Hope, Fear in Uptown," *Chicago Tribune,* March 20, 1977, Sec. 1, p. 37.

9. According to tabulations from relocation records in the City of Chicago, Department of Urban Renewal archives. The files, which are not complete, do not contain information that can be used to identify Appalachian people.

10. See the arguments by Sumka (1979) and Hartman (1979).

11. William P. Thompson, the late Mayor Richard J. Daley's former son-in-law; quoted in Bonita Brodt, "Rebirth of a Neighborhood Is Not Without Some Pain," *Chicago Tribune,* June 21, 1979, Sec. 6W, p.1.

12. Quoted in Hafferkamp, 1979, p. 197.

13. *Chicago Tribune,* November 25, 1979, Sec. D, p.1. The revised project will be a combined shopping center with 100,000 square feet of floor space and a high-rise tower with 252 rental units. A total of 155 apartments will be located in the rehabilitated buildings, named Scotland Yard. A $21.7 million dollar loan insured by HUD, was provided by the Government National Mortgage Association. Section 8 rental subsidies will be available for 20 percent of the units.

REFERENCES

Auger, Deborah A. "The Politics of Revitalization in Gentrifying Neighborhoods." *Journal of the American Planning Association* 45 (October 1979): 515-522.

Backes, Clarus. "Appalachia: The Source. *"Chicago Tribune Magazine,* October 6, 1978, pp. 30-33, 70.

_____. "Poor People's Power in Uptown." *Chicago Tribune Magazine,* September 29, 1968, pp. 46-56.

_____. "Uptown: The Promised Land." *Chicago Tribune Magazine,* September 22, 1968, pp. 1-6.

Brooks, Deton J., Jr., *A Study of Families from the Southern Appalachian Region Receiving Public Assistance.* Chicago: Cook County Department of Public Aid, 1960.

Bruno, Hal. "Chicago's Hillbilly Ghetto." In *Poverty in the Affluent Society,* edited by H. H. Meisner, pp. 102-107. New York: Basic Books, 1974.

Coles, Robert. *The South Goes North.* Vol. 3, *Children of Crisis.* Boston: Little, Brown and Company, 1971.

Cook County Department of Public Aid. *The Southern Appalachian Migrant on Public Aid in Cook County: A Follow-Up Study.* Chicago: Cook County Department of Public Aid, 1963.

Cross, Robert. "Uptown's Future: Are the Swingers at the Gate?" *Chicago Tribune Magazine,* September 29, 1974, pp. 20-24.

Fowler, Gary L. "The Residential Distribution or Urban Appalachians" In *The Invisible Minority: Appalachians in Urban Areas,* edited by William W. Philliber and Clyde B. McCoy, Lexington, Kentucky: The University Press of Kentucky, 1980.

_____. "Residential Mobility Among Appalachian People in Central Cincinnati." *Research Bulletin,* Urban Appalachian Council of Cincinnati, May 1976, pp. 1-3.

_____. "Up Here and Down Home: Appalachians in Cities." In *Appalachia: Social Context Past and Present,* edited by Bruce Ergood and Bruce E. Kuhre, pp. 71-82. Dubuque: Kendall/Hunt, 1976.

Griffin, Roscoe. "Newcomers from the Southern Mountains," In *Institute on Cultural Patterns of Newcomers,* pp. 15-40. Chicago: Welfare Council of Metropolitan Chicago, Migration Services Committee of the Chicago Commission on Human Relations. The Mayor's Committee on New Residents, November. 1959.

Gitlin, Todd, and Hollander, Nanci. *Uptown: Poor Whites in Chicago.* Colophon Books. New York: Harper and Row, 1970.

Goodman, John L., Jr., "Reasons for Moves Out of and Into Large Cities." *Journal of the American Planning Association* 45 (October 1979): 407-416.

Hafferkamp, Jack. "Who Owns the Neighborhoods?" *Chicago Magazine* 28 (November 1979): 192-199.

Hartman, Chester. "Comment on 'Neighborhood Revitalization and Displacement: a Review of Evidence'" *Journal of the American Planning Association* 45 (October 1979): 488-490.

Harwood, Edwin S. "Work and Community Among Newcomers: A Study of the Social and Economic Adaption of Southern Migrants in Chicago." Ph.D. dissertation, University of Chicago, 1966.

Howell, Joseph T. *Hard Living on Clay Street: Portraits of Blue Collar Families.* Anchor Books, Garden City, New York: Anchor Press/ Doubleday, 1973.

Huelsman, Ben R. "Urban Anthropology and the Southern Mountaineer." *Proceedings of the Indiana Academy of Science for 1968* 78 (1968) 97-103.

Johnson, Flora. "In Order to Save It." *Chicago Magazine* 25 (December 1976): 165-86.

Killian, Lewis M. *White Southerners,* New York: Random House, 1970.

McKee, Dan M., and Obermiller, Phillip J. *From Mountain to Metropolis: Urban Appalachains in Ohio.* Prepared for the Ohio Urban Appalachian Awareness Project. Cincinnati: Urban Appalachian Council, June 1978.

Marple, David; Koebernick, Thomas; and Jones, Richard. "Demographic and Social Characteristics of Appalachian Migrants Living in East Dayton." *Research Bulletin,* Urban Appalachian Council of Cincinnati, May 1977.

Maloney, Michael E. "Appalachian Migrants in Midwestern and Mid-Atlantic Cities. *Mountain Life and Work* 54 (January 1978): 29-32.

Merten, Don Edward. *"Up Here and Down Home:* Appalachian Migrants in Northtown." Ph.D dissertation, University of Chicago, 1974.

Montgomery, Bill. "The Uptown Story." *Mountain Life and Work* 44 (September 1968): 10-18.

Petersen, Gene B.; Sharp, Laure M.: and Drury, Thomas. *Southern New-*

comers to Northern Cities: Work and Social Adjustment in Cleveland. Praeger Special Studies in U.S. Economic, Social, and Political Issues; New York: Praeger Publishers, 1977.

Photiadis, John. *West Virginians in their Own State and in Cleveland, Ohio,* Appalachian Center Research Report 3. Morgantown: West Virginia University, Center for Appalachian Studies and Development, 1971.

Sumka, Howard J. "Neighborhood Revitalization and Displacement: A Review of the Evidence." *Journal of the American Planning Association* 45 (October 1979): 480-487.

_____. "The Ideology of Urban Analysis: A Response to Hartman." *Journal of the American Planning Association* 45 (October 1979): 491-94.

ELDERLY APPALACHIANS IN CITIES:
A CASE STUDY OF CINCINNATI

David P. Varady

Abstract

This article tests for the validity of four widely held stereotypes about elderly Applachians in cities, using the results of a survey of 862 elderly in Cincinnati, Ohio, carried out in March, 1978. As expected, the Appalachian elderly had a higher incidence of health problems and were more likely to formulate intra-metropolitan moving plans, even when other relevant background characteristics were controlled. However, in contrast to what was anticipated, the Appalachian elderly were not concentrated in older Appalachian ghettos within the city and were not less likely to utilize government social welfare and housing programs. The policy implications of these findings are discussed.

Introduction

The widely held belief that the elderly are a homogeneous group is incorrect (Raga and Davis, 1978). The elderly are in reality a diverse group in terms of income, social class, and ethnicity. Furthermore, these different subgroups "experience old age and its problems differently" (Wiseman, 1978:3).

It is important for social planners to be cognizant of the differing needs of these subgroups within the elderly population. The lack of this type of information on the characteristics and attitudes of members of these subgroups has hindered program development (see United States Department of Health, Education and Welfare, 1978a, 1978b). This information gap has been particularly serious in relation to different ethnic elderly subgroups.[1]

In order to improve existing understanding of this subject this paper focuses on differences between the Appalachian elderly and other white and other black elderly with respect to: (1) socioeconomic, health, and housing characteristics, (2) residential satisfaction and residential mobility plans, (3) spatial distribution within the metropolitan area, and (4) utilization of governmentally funded housing and social service programs. More specifically we will test for the validity of the following stereotypes: (1) that elderly Appalachians are an impoverished group, (2) that they are dissatisfied with city life and more frequently, (3) that they are concentrated in inner city Appalachian ghettos, and (4) that they tend not to utilize government funded social services and housing programs.

Methodology

This study is based on the results of interviews of 862 elderly residents (sixty and over) living in Hamilton County, Ohio (which includes, but is not limited to the City of Cincinnati) carried out during March 1978.[2] The sample was selected and interviewed using the Random Digit Dialing Technique (see Tuchfarber and Klecka, 1976). The data was collected as part of a larger study of elderly housing needs implemented by the Housing for Older Americans Coalition of Cincinnati (Better Housing League of Cincinnati, 1978). The survey included questions on moving plans (when, where, and why),[3] levels of housing and neighborhood satisfaction,[4] perceived residential problems,[5] family health and functional ability,[6] participation in government housing programs as well as background demographic and housing data.[7] Information on the socioeconomic characteristics of neighborhoods surrounding respondents, drawn from the 1970 Census, was incorporated into the data set.[8]

The householder's Appalachian background was measured by questions on the state and county of birth. We defined an Appalachian as an individual who was born in a county defined as in Appalachia by the Appalachian Regional Commission (Appalachian Regional Commission, 1971:93-99). The variable measuring Appalachian background was combined with the variable measuring race to create an index called "Appalachian status". Using this index we categorized the sample into three groups, Appalachians (15 percent of the total), "other whites" (74 percent), and "other blacks" (11 percent).[9]

Crosstabular analysis is used to compare members of these three groups with respect to socioeconomic characteristics, health and housing problems, location within the metropolitan area, residential satisfaction, moving plans, and utilization of government housing assistance programs and social services. Regression analysis is used to determine the impact of Appalachian background controlling for other background characteristics. In the first stage of the regression analysis all the theoretically relevant variables were included in the runs. In the second stage, we reran the regressions excluding those variables that did not meaningfully contribute to explaining variations in the dependent variables (i.e., housing satisfaction, neighborhood satisfaction, moving plans). We excluded those variables whose F values were statistically insignificant at the .05 level. The regression results dealing with the interrelationship between background characteristics, housing satisfaction, and moving plans are represented by a path diagram (Figure 2). The hypothesized causal relationships are represented by unidirectional arrows extending from each determining variable to each variable depending on it. Residual variables are represented by vertical unidirectional arrows leading from the residual variable to the dependent variable. Standardized regression coefficients are standardized, the two paths leading to the same variable can be compared by the order of magnitude to indicate which variable has the most powerful effect.

Discussion

1. Socioeconomic characteristics and health and housing problems.

Existing research offers contradictary evidence in terms of the degree of deprivation of urban Appalachians (elderly and non-elderly) in relation to other ethnic groups. Case studies of particular Appalachian neighborhoods (Gitlin and Hollander, 1970; Maloney, 1972; Osborne, 1970) emphasize the high rates of social pathologies and the high incidence of housing deterioration in these neighborhoods. This research implies that Appalachians are worse off than other ethnic groups in these cities. Furthermore, this research suggests that a disproportionately large number of Appalachians receive welfare and that they, therefore, constitute a fiscal drain on these cities. Fowler has challenged this viewpoint indication that "there is no compelling evidence that Appalachians are disproportionately represented among the poor or welfare recipients" (1976:78). It is not clear from Fowler's research, however, how Appalachians fare in relation to other ethnic groups, particularly blacks.

Our evidence indicates that the Appalachian elderly in Cincinnati are a deprived group in terms of socioeconomic, health, and housing indicators. They are not, however, nearly as badly off as blacks.

Table 1 shows that the mean family income of elderly Appalachians ($7416) was 15 percent lower than that of other whites ($8767). Nevertheless, the mean income level for Appalachians was still considerably higher than for other blacks ($4621).

TABLE 1
Differences between Appalchian, other white, and other black elderly with respect to socioeconomic characteristics, health, and residential problems.

Characteristic	Appalachians	Other whites	Other blacks	Sig.
Family Income (below $3000)	16% (95)	11% (404)	41% (66)	.0000
Family Income (mean)	$7416 (95)	$8767 (404)	$4621 (66)	.0000
Tenant Status (proportion owners)	63% (123)	72% (588)	44% (92)	.0000
Family Health (whether respondent or spouse unwell)	44% (126)	30% (602)	42% (93)	.002
Family functional ability (whether respondent or spouse has difficulty)	31% (125)	19% (597)	30% (90)	.002
Perceived cost problems (at least some difficulty)	37% (120)	23% (567)	54% (86)	.0000
Housing costs/income index (index relatively high)	20% (126)	14% (604)	31% (93)	.0002
Housing costs/income (mean)	15% (94)	12% (384)	17% (66)	n.s.
Perceived housing deterioration (at least some deterioration)	33% (123)	28% (599)	36% (90)	n.s.
Perceived crime problem (neighborhood not safe)	30% (123)	28% (582)	41% (90)	.04
Neighborhood socio-economic status (lowest quartile)	22% (125)	8% (594)	53%)93)	.0000
Neighborhood racial composition (25-49% black)	6% (125)	3% (1549)	8% (93)	.04

The Appalachian elderly are clearly a deprived group in terms of the existence of debilitating illnesses and functional limitations. Table 1 indicates that Appalachians closely resemble blacks in terms of both of these measures and differ sharply from other whites. Approximately two fifths of the Appalachians, as compared to one third of the whites, were in households where either the respondent or the spouse (if there was one) felt that he/she had a health problem, a disability, or a long term illness which restricted his/her ability to get around. There were similarly wide differences in terms of a more objective measure of family functional ability. In one third of the Appalachian households, as compared to one fifth of the white households, either or both of the spouses had at least some difficulty in carrying out one or more basic activities of daily living (getting around the house, walking up and down steps, getting around out of doors).

It is conceivable that these differences in health between whites and Appalachians could be due to differences these two groups in income, and the fact that health is correlated with income. The regression results refute this hypothesis. That is, there were significant negative beta coefficients between Appalachian background and both family health ($-.08$) and family functional ability ($-.11$) when other relevent background characteristics (e.g., income) were controlled.

TABLE 2

Differences between Appalachian, other white, and other black elderly in the incidence of specific health problems.[a]

Health problem	Appalachians	Other whites	Other blacks
Heart	33	29	35
Lungs	17	13	0
Limbs	17	11	0
Back	5	4	0
Arthritis	14	25	41
Stroke	7	4	9
Eyes	2	5	3
Circulation	2	4	3
Diabetes	3	5	9
	42	133	134

$x^2 = 20.7$
$df = 16$
$p > .2$

Notes:
a. This Table presents the coded first response to the questions on health problems.

We suspected that the particularly high incidence of health problems among Appalachians was due to diseases contracted in the mountains. In particular, we expected that many former miners would have contracted black lung disease and, consequently, that Appalachians would have a particularly high rate of lung illnesses. The results in Table 2 are not clearcut enough to either support or reject this hypothesis. Appalachians were more likely than other whites or other blacks to have lung illnesses, but the results are not statistically significant. In addition, it should be noted that the category "lung illnesses" in Table 2 includes illnesses unrelated to having an Appalachian background (e.g., lung cancer resulting from smoking) as well as illnesses attributable to the Appalachian experience. Additional research is needed in order to identify why elderly Appalchians suffer such high rates of debilitating illnesses.

The results dealing with the incidence of housing and neighborhood problems were more mixed. The Appalachian elderly were worse off than other whites with respect to three of seven problems. Specifically, Appalachians were far more likely than other whites to experience difficulty in affording current housing costs (or were expected to experience difficulty in affording likely future increases; 37 percent versus 23 percent). Appalachians were also more likely than other whites to be living in neighborhoods that were in the lowest quartile with respect to socio economic status (22 percent versus 8 percent). Furthermore, they were also more likely than other whites to be living in racially changing communities, as indicated by their presence in communities between 25 and 49 percent black (6 percent versus 3 percent).

It should be noted, however, that blacks were far worse off than Appalachians or whites in terms of most of the indicators of residential problems.

That Appalachians were more likely to experience a cost problem was probably attributable to their having lower incomes than other whites, rather than any aspect of their Appalachian background. This interpretation is supported by the regression results (not presented here) which indicated that the householder's Appalachian background was of no importance in predicting variations in the incidence of the cost problems when other background characteristics were taken into account.

2. Residential satisfaction and moving plans.

Existing research supports the image of Appalachian transiency. That is, Appalachians have been shown to have higher mobility rates than non-Appalachians (Coles, 1967; Fowler, 1976; Votaw, 1955). There are, however, two limitations in this research. First, there have been few attempts to compare Appalachians with specific other ethnic groups. Second, most research has relied on bivariate analyses. It is as a result unclear whether the high mobility rates are a result of demographic characteristics associated with being Appalachian (such as a high rate of renting) or are a result of some aspect of the Appalachian experience. Coles (1967) favors the second interpretation. He speculates that a dissatisfaction with city life combined with an inability to return home leads to a continual wandering within the city.

In order to determine which of these hypotheses is valid this paper tests a residential mobility model (Figure 1) developed by Speare and Associates (1974) consisting of three sets of variables: (1) personal, housing, and neighborhood characteristics (including Appalachian background), (2) housing and neighborhood satisfaction, and (3) intra-metropolitan moving plans.[10] Speare, Goldstein, and Frey's model suggests that Appalachian background, like other personal characteristics, would affect intra-metropolitan mobility plans indirectly. That is, a householder's Appalachian identity would foster housing and neighborhood dissatisfaction, which would in turn lead to intra-metropolitan moving plans.

The results (Figure 2 and Table 3) support this hypothesis.[11] Appalachian background indirectly promoted rapid intra-metropolitan moving plans through higher levels of housing dissatisfaction. This is shown by the significant path coefficient (.11) between being Appalachian and housing dissatisfaction, and by the high correlation of the latter variable with intra-metropolitan moving plans (beta = .40). Using Coles's research, we would interpret the high level of housing dissatisfaction among these elderly Appalachians as attributable to a discontent with the urban environment, generally, and an inability to return "home" to the mountains.

3. Spatial distribution

Much of the research that is available on urban Applachians is based on case

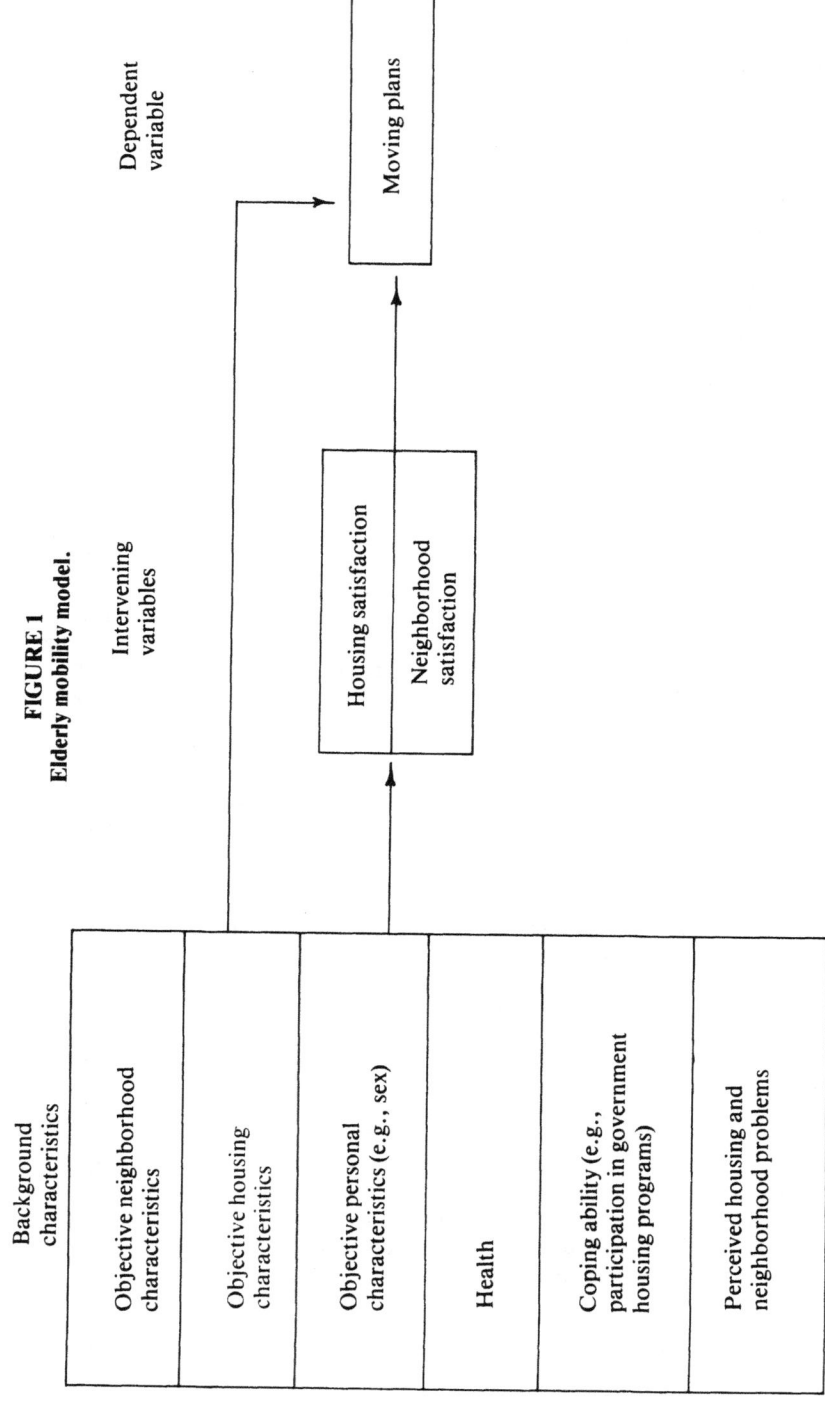

**FIGURE 1
Elderly mobility model.**

FIGURE 2

Significant Paths Influencing Housing and Neighborhood Satisfaction and Intra-Metropolitan Mobility Plans (likelihood of remaining) Among Hamilton County Elderly.

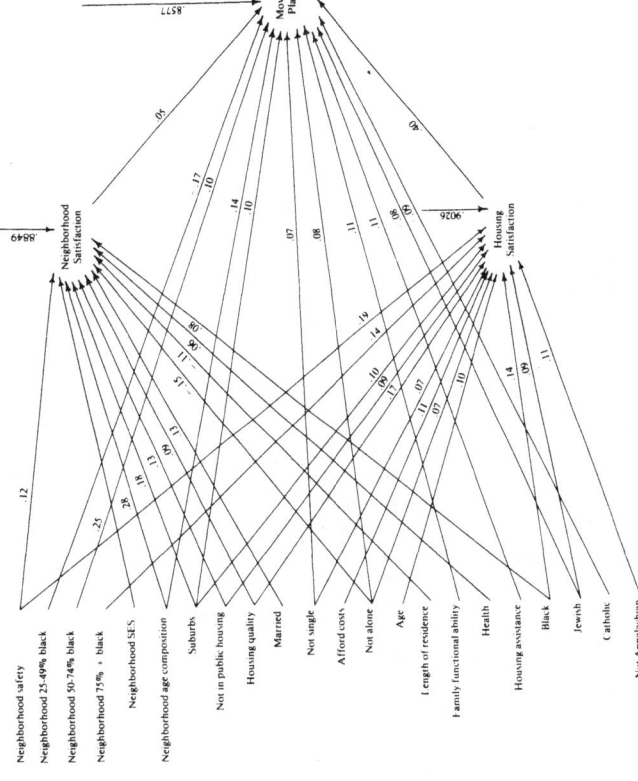

NOTE: All of the beta coefficients are statistically significant at the .05 level.

TABLE 3

Differences between Appalachian, other white, and other black elderly with respect to residential satisfaction, moving plans, and length of residence.

Characteristic	Appalachians	Other whites	Other blacks	Sig.
Housing satisfaction (proportion not very satisfied)	28% (122)	19% (590)	26% (91)	.03
Neighborhood satisfaction (proportion rating neighborhood not good)	29% (118)	27% (571)	33% (89)	n.s.
Intra-metropolitan moving plans (proportion planplanning move)	20% (113)	18% (563)	15% (80)	n.s.
Inter-metropolitan moving plans (proportion planning inter-metropolitan move)	6% (124)	5% (591)	1% (93)	n.s.
Length of residence (proportion at current address below 5 years.)	24% (126)	19% (604)	28% (93)	n.s.
Length of residence (mean no. of years)	14.9	19.3	13.0	.001

studies of port-of-entry tenement neighborhoods in the inner city like the Uptown section of Chicago (Gitlin and Hollander, 1970) and the Over-the-Rhine community in Cincinnati (Maloney, 1972). This research reinforces the stereotype of Appalachians being concentrated in this type of community. Nevertheless, this stereotype probably is inaccurate for younger Appalachian families. A recent trend is for mountain families, particularly the better off ones, to bypass the central city entirely and to settle in rural fringe communities (Fowler, 1976; Photiadis, 1970; Schwarzweller, 1970; and Stevens, 1973). The above sterotype may be applicable to the Appalachian elderly, however. Researchers have found that the white, ethnic elderly are often left behind in the inner city as younger families achieve mobility and move to the suburbs (see for example Ginsberg, 1975).

The results refute this last hypothesis. The proportion of elderly Appalachians living within the city (47 percent, 126) was identical to that for other elderly whites (47 percent, 604). Not surprisingly, the proportion of blacks living within the city (83 percent, 93) was far higher than for either of the two other groups ($X^2 = 43.0$, df = 2, p < .00001). In addition, only a small minority (15 percent, 59) of the Appalachian elderly living in the city lived in Appalachian neighborhoods (i.e. those estimated to be 50 percent or more Appalachian). Futhermore, the proportion of Appalachian elderly living in this type of community was no higher than that for other whites (17 percent, 287). A smaller proportion of blacks lived in this type of community (7 percent, 77, n.s.). The notion that the Appalachian elderly are concentrated in Appalachian ghettos is not true. Finally, as shown in Table 4 only a small

TABLE 4

Differences between Appalachian, other white, and other black elderly in neighborhood type.

Neighborhood Type[a]	Appalachians	Other whites	Other blacks
Hill newer	39%	58%	10%
Valley Established	24	29	33
Basin-Old Town	13	2	38
Transitional Dynamic	24	11	19
	(59)	(281)	(177)

$x^2 = 50.0$
$df = 2$
$p \blacktriangleright .00001$

Notes:
a. See footnote 8 for definitions of these four neighborhood types.

minority (13 percent) of the Appalachian elderly living within the city of Cincinnati reside in the "Basin-Old Town area" area. It should be noted, however, that the proportion of Appalachian elderly living in this particular area is substantially higher than for other whites.

Previous research has indicated sharp differences in income and other socioeconomic characteristics between Appalachians living in the city and the suburbs. That is, those in the suburbs tend to be more well-to-do (Photiadis, 1970). Based on this research, we expected that within an Appalachian elderly sample those in the city would be poorer, and in worse health, worse housing, and neighborhoods than those in the suburbs.

Table 5 provides no support for this assertion. As shown, the mean family incomes for the Appalachian elderly living in the city and in the suburbs are virtually identical. Furthermore, there are insignificant differences between the city and suburban Appalachian elderly with respect to the incidence of health and housing problems. The only way in which the suburban Appalachian residents are significantly more likely to be in high socioeconomic status neighborhoods and significant city-suburban differences may be due to the presence of many attractive suburban communities in the city of Cincinnati. Consequently, this fact may have led some of the relatively affluent Appalachians to move within the city rather than to the suburbs. We would expect to find wider differences between city and suburban residents in cities lacking such attractive neighborhoods.

4. Utilization of Social Services

There is consensus within the research literature that Appalachians (elderly and non-elderly) tend not to utilize existing governmental social services and housing programs. Fowler (1976) asserts that Appalachian families tend not to use public social services because of pride, because of their dependence on the kin group (which leads to an avoidance of formal public institutions generally), and because of the perception that these agencies give blacks and other groups preference. Engler (1979) found that the Appalachian elderly tended not to participate in the Independent Environments Program in Chautauqua County, New York. That is a program under which homeowners can have ramps built for wheelchairs, handrails installed for showers, and so forth. He suggests that this underutilization results from many of the Appalachian elderly having

TABLE 5

Differences between Appalachian elderly living in the city and in the suburbs

Characteristic	Cincinnati	Suburbs	Sig.
Family income (proportion below $3000)	15% (47)	17% (48)	n.s.
Family income (mean)	$4798 (47)	$4752 (48)	n.s.
Family health (whether respondent or spouse unwell)	42% (59)	46% (67)	n.s.
Family functional ability (whether respondent or spouse has difficulty)	36% (59)	27% (66)	n.s.
Perceived cost problem (at least some difficulty)	36% (56)	38% (64)	n.s.
Housing costs/income index (ratio relatively high)	22% (59)	18% (67)	n.s.
Perceived housing deterioration (at least some deterioration)	38% (56)	30% (67)	n.s.
Perceived crime problem (neighborhood not very safe)	40% (57)	21% (66)	.03
Neighborhood socioeconomic status (lowest quartile)	42% (59)	3% (66)	.0000
Neighborhood racial comp. (25-49 percent black)	12% (59)	3% (66)	.05

moved from areas where there were few federal social services or housing programs. Thus, these elderly residents did not know what help was available nor were they sure they had a right to get it.

Our results (Table 5) are in sharp contrast to previous research on the subject. There is no evidence to support the premise that the Appalachian elderly are less likely to take advantage of social services than others. As shown, there were insignificant differences between Appalachians, other whites, and other blacks in their utilization of government housing assistance programs (such as Rent Supplements) and government income supplements (such as Social Security). In addition, there were insignificant differences in the proportions preferring to move into housing for retired persons (assuming it was available), rather than to continue to live in their present home. There were significant differences in the utilization of social services delivered to the home (e.g., visiting nurses). The statistically significant difference was due, however, to the higher rate of usage of these programs by elderly blacks than either Appalachians or other whites. The greater utilization of social service programs by elderly blacks probably reflects: (1) the higher incidence of social pathologies among elderly blacks, (2) the War on Poverty which informed many blacks of their eligibility for social services, and (3) the location of many of these services (e.g., senior centers) in inner city areas that are heavily black.

Regression analysis was utilized to determine whether the lack of association between Appalachian background and social service utilization was attributable to the intercorrelation between these two variables and other background characteristics. This was not the case. The results (not presented here) indicated that Appalachian background had no impact at all on the utilization of social services or housing assistance programs when other personal characteristics were controlled. The results therefore indicate that this stereotype is not valid for the Appalachian elderly.

TABLE 6

Differences between Appalachian, other white, and other black elderly in the utilization of different social welfare and housing assistance programs

Characteristic[a]	Appalachians	Other whites	Other blacks	Sig.
Government housing assistance programs (use at least one)	30% (125)	26% (573)	26% (86)	n.s.
Government income supplements (use at least one)	81% (122)	84% (565)	87% (90)	n.s.
Social services at home (use at least one)	19% (126)	16% (600)	31% (91)	.003
Social services (mean number utilized)	.28	.23	.48	.006
Housing for elderly (proportion preferring this over home ownership)	11% (113)	11% (557)	13% (83)	n.s.

Notes:
   a. See footnote 7 for definitions of these four measures of program utilization.

Conclusions

This paper was sought to improve the understanding of differences between Appalachian, other white, and other black elderly in urban areas. Four widely held stereotypes about urban Appalachians were tested using the results of a survey of the elderly in Hamilton County (Cincinnati), Ohio.

The results supported the validity of two of the stereotypes. The Appalachian elderly were shown to be an impoverished group in relation to other white elderly. This was particularly true with respect to measures of health and functional ability. In addition, the stereotypes of Appalachian transiency was supported. An Appalachian background was shown to indirectly promote intra-urban residential mobility plans through increased housing dissatisfacation.

Two other widely held stereotypes were refuted. In contrast to what had been expected, the Appalachian elderly were not shown to be concentrated in inner city Appalachian ghettos. Not even the poor Appalachian elderly were concentrated in these areas. In addition, there was no support for the assertion made by Fowler (1976) and others that Appalachians tend not to utilize governmentally funded social services and housing programs.

Policy Implications

The results support an expansion of health care programs for the Appalachian elderly. As indicated above, the incidence of debilitating illnesses was disproportionately high among Appalachians even when other relevant background characteristics were controlled. In developing such programs, improved information is needed on the nature of the health problems affecting members of this group.

These health care programs need to be targeted to the Appalachian elderly wherever they reside. Our results show that it would be a mistake to implement them only in identifiable Appalachian communities. In Cincinnati only a small minority of the needy Appalachian elderly reside in these areas. Citywide agencies such as the Urban Appalachian Council in Cincinnati could be helpful in reaching Appalachians located throughout the metropolitan area.

Finally, attention should be given to expanding the residential choices of elderly Appalachians. The high levels of housing dissatisfaction that we discovered among elderly Appalachians probably result from a dissatisfaction with city life and and inability to return to the rural point of origin. Research needs to be directed to the obstacles preventing such return moves. With such research in hand, planners could then develop programs which would enable those Appalachian elderly wanting to return home to do so.

Notes

The author wishes to thank the Better Housing League of Cincinnati for making available the data set on which this paper is based. He is also grateful for the statistical assistance provided by Mr. Dan McKee of the Behavioral Sciences Laboratory, University of Cincinnati.

1. Among the few exceptions to this generalization are Lawton and Kleban's comparison of Jews and non-Jews in the determinants of well-being (1971) and Sterne, Phillips, and Rabushka's study of black-white variations with respect to residential satisfaction and political participation (1974).

2. Using the Random Digit Dialing technique, 11,365 telephone numbers were generated and called. Two thirds (66 percent or 7526) of these numbers were found to be not in service. Of the remaining valid numbers, one half turned out to be ineligible for the study either because there was no elderly person in the household (41 percent) or for some other reason, such as a business or institutional number, or a language barrier (13 percent). In one fifth (20 percent) of the cases, it proved impossible to reach anyone, even though three attempts were made. Three percent of the respondents refused to be interviewed. A little over one fifth (23 percent) of the valid numbers led to completed interviews with elderly householders.

The regression analysis of the determinants of moving plans reported on in this paper is based on 408 rather than 862 cases noted above. This is due to the utilization of a regression program which required complete information on all the variables included in the analysis; otherwise, the case was deleted. For this reason 416 cases were excluded. In addition 38 intended inter-metropolitan movers were deleted from the analysis.

3. In order to measure moving plans respondents were asked: "Do you plan to move from your present home in the next ten years?" There were five reponse categories: yes, considering it, no, only under unforeseen circumstances, and don't know. In the analysis the respones were recoded into three groups; those who had definite plans to move (category one), those who had plans but who were uncertain about their plans (category 2) and those who planned to remain (categories 3 and 4). Those who didn't know or who planned to move outside the Cincinnati metropolitan area were excluded from the analysis.

4. Housing satisfaction was measured by the question: "In general, how satisfied are you with your present housing?" The four response categories ranged from very satisfied to very dissatisfied. We measured neighborhood satisfaction by the question: "How would you rate your neighborhood (community) as a place for retired people to live?" The three response categories were good, fair, and bad.

5. The physical housing quality index was derived from two questions. The first asked whether there was anything about the residence that made it dangerous (e.g., a fire hazard). The second asked whether the building in which the respondent resided needed major repairs, minor repairs, or no repairs. The combined results were recoded into a three point scale: (1) most deterioration (minor or major repairs and dangerous), (2) less deterioration (either no repairs and dangerous or minor/major repairs and no danger), and (3) no deterioration (no repairs and no danger).

The housing costs index was created from two other questions. The first asked whether or not the respondent was having difficulty paying for the residence and its upkeep (including utilities). The second asked about the degree of difficulty that the individual would experience if housing costs increased by twenty-five dollars from what they were at the time of the interview. The four response categories ranged from not difficult to impossible. The combined results to these questions were recoded into a three point scale: (1) no difficulty (can afford housing costs now, and would have some or no difficulty in affording future incrases), (2) some difficulty (either experiencing difficulty in affording current costs and would have some/no difficulty in affording future increases or can afford current costs but would find it difficult or impossible to afford future increases) and (3) great difficulty (have difficulty in affording current costs and would find it very difficult/impossible to afford future increases). A second more objective measure of the housing cost problem was computed by dividing housing costs (including utilities) by monthly family income.

6. Two separate questions were used to create the family health scale. The first question asked whether the respondent had a health problem which restricted his/her mobility. The second obtained comparable information about the spouse, if there was one. The combined results were recoded into two categories: (1) families where both spouses were well or unrelated individuals who were well and (2) families where at least on of the spouses was ill or unrelated individuals who were ill.

Family functional ability was based on two separate series of items (one for the respondent and one for the spouse) dealing with the degree of difficulty each experienced in completing certain everyday activities (i.e., getting around the house, walking up and down the stairs, getting around out of doors). Respondents were asked whether they could complete each of these activities without difficulty, with difficulty but without help, or only with the help of another person. The scores for this set of items ranged between 3 and 9, with 9 representing the highest degree of functional limitation. The results for each of the two variables were separately recoded into two groups: (1) respondents or spouses who could complete all of the activities without difficulty (i.e., a score of 3) and (2) respondents/spouses who experienced at least some difficulty in completing one or more activities (i.e., scores between 4 and 9). The two separate variables were then combined and recoded into two categories: (1) families where both respondents were able to complete all the activities without difficulty or where the unrelated individual was able to complete them without difficulty and (2) families where one or both spouses (or an unrelated individual) had at least some difficulty completing one or more of these activities.

7. Homeowners were separately asked whether they received any of the following forms of governmental housing assistance: property tax reduction, utility cost assistance, and mortage interest reduction. If they didn't receive any of the three, they were then asked whether they had ever applied to the government for financial assistance to help to pay housing costs. Renters were asked a separate series of questions probing whether they received rent supplements or assistance with utility bills, and if they received neither, whether they had applied to the government to help pay housing costs. An index was created from all of these questions to distinguish between two groups of respondents: (1) those who had applied for or participated in one or more government housing assistance programs and (2) those who had not applied for or participated in any.

A second scale measured in utilization of social services for the elderly. Respondents were asked whether they had used any of the following services provided by agencies or groups over the previous three years: prepared meals or meals brought to the home, housekeeping help, assistance with minor home repairs, senior centers or clubs, transportation, visiting nurses. An ordinal level scale was created based on the number of services utilized.

A third scale measured the utilization of governmental income supplement programs. Respondents were asked whether any of the following programs provided income for them or any other other relative living in the home: social security, supplementary security income, veterans' benefits, unemployment compensation, workmen's compensation, disability insurance, food stamps, aid to dependent children/general relief. An index distinguishing between two groups of respondents was created: (1) those who were utilizing one or more of these programs and (2) those who were not utilizing any.

8. Neighborhood age composition was measured by the proportion of individuals sixty and over living in the census tract in 1970. All of the census tracts in Hamilton County were ranked on the basis of the proportion of elderly living in the tract. Each tract was assigned a value ranging from 1 to 4 depending on which quartile it fell within. A socioeconomic status index was calculated for each census tract based on the ranking of the tract with respect to the following indices: median family income, overcrowding, family composition (the presence of both spouses), occupation, and education. The tracts were then ranked from lowest SES to highest and divided into quartiles. Each tract was assigned a value (from 1 to 4) based on which quartile it was located in.

Four dummy variables were used to measure neighborhood racial composition (i.e., whether the neighborhood was under 25 percent black, 25-49 percent black, 50 to 74 percent black, 75 to 100 percent black) because there was a non-linear relationship between neighborhood racial composition and moving plans. Crosstabular analysis revealed that respondents living in neighborhoods 25 to 49 percent black were significantly more likely to formulate moving plans than those living in the three other types of neighborhoods. The first dummy variable (whether the neighborhood was under 25 percent black) was considered the reference variable and, therefore, was not included in the regression runs.

Communities within the city of Cincinnati were classified into four types using a scheme developed by the Real Estate Research Corporation (1973:1) *Hill-Newer Areas* are those "often referred to as the 'suburbs inside Cincinnati'. They are relatively new, relatively white, relatively upper-income and predominantly owner occupied as compared to the rest of the city." *Valley-Established Areas* "are older, more established and contain quite mixed types of land uses. They tend to lie along the geographical valleys of the City....Most have declining populations, moderated levels of household income and average rates of turnovers". *Basin-Old Town Areas* "are the oldest parts of the City clustered around the central business district. Their land use patterns have been significantly changed in recent years by highway or urban renewal developments; hence they lost more than one third of their population from 1960 to 1970. Their population is mainly nonwhite and have relatively low incomes." *Transition-Dynamic Areas* contain those "that do not consistently fit into the above three categories. Some are undergoing rapid transition in population characteristics whereas others are more stable".

In addition, city communities were classified as "Appalachian" or "non-Appalachian" using a scheme developed by McKee and Obermiller (1978). School survey data were used to estimate community ethnic composition. Communities were defined as Appalachian if they comprised one half or more of the population.

9. The overwhelming majority (83 percent) of the Appalachian elderly surveyed were white.

10. Our decision to focus the analyis on the determinants of intra-metropolitan moving plans rather than on moving plans, generally, was based on previous research indicating that there are different determinants of intra and inter-metropolitan mobility (Wiseman, 1978). This implied that the precision of our model could be increased if intended inter-metropolitan movers were excluded from the analysis.

It should be noted that in contrast to Spear's (1974) and Newman and Duncan's research (1978, 1979), which examined determinants of mobility behavior, ours is limited to an analysis of moving plans. Van Arsdol (1968) has indicated that there is a real distinction between moving wishes, moving plans, and moving behavior. Consequently, it is not possible to validly generalize from our results dealing with moving plans, to actual mobility behavior. Nevertheless, this study is valuable because it examines most of the components of the mobility decision and, therefore, should lead to an improved understanding of this decision.

The results of the analysis of the determinants of intra-urban mobility plans for the 1978 Cincinnati elderly sample are discussed in far greater detail in a separate paper (see Varady, forthcoming).

11. These results are in contrast to those obtained from an analysis of the determinants of moving plans and mobility behavior among a sample of elderly and non-elderly residents of the Cincinnati Model Neighborhood (Varady, 1975). Appalachian background was of no importance in explaining variations in either plans or behavior in the regression analysis. It should be noted that in contrast to the analysis in this paper, we did not then test for the indirect impact of Appalachian background through measures of housing and neighborhood satisfaction. Had such measures of satisfaction been included we might

have found that Appalachian background did have an indirect impact on mobility.

References

Appalachian Regional Commission. *1971 Annual Report.* Washington, D.C.: Appalachian Regional Commission, 1971.

Better Housing League of Greater Cincinnati. *Housing for Older Americans in Hamilton County Ohio.* Cincinnati: Better Housing League, 1978.

Coles, Robert. *The South Goes North.* Vol. 3 *Children of Crisis.* Boston: Little, Brown and Company, 1967.

Fowler, Gary L. "Up there and Down Home: Appalachians in Cities". In *Appalachia: Social Context, Past and Present,* edited by Bruce Ergood and Bruce E. Kuhre, pp. 77-81. Dubuque, Iowa: Kendall/Hunt Publishers, 1976.

Ginsberg, Yona. *Jews in a Changing Neighborhood: The Study of Mattapan.* New York: The Free Press, 1975.

Giltin, Todd, and Hollander, Nanci. *Uptown: Poor Whites in Chicago.* New York: Harper and Row Publishers, 1970.

Lawton, M. Powell, and Kleban, Morton H. "The Aged Resident of the Inner City". *The Gerontologist,* Winter 1971, Part I, pp. 277-83.

Maloney, Michael. "Appalachian Settlements: Cincinnati and Southwestern Ohio". *People's Appalachia* 2, No. 3 (July 1972).

McKee, Dan M., and Obermiller, Phillip. *From Mountain to Metropolis: Urban Appalachians in Ohio.* Cincinnati: Urban Appalachian Council, 1978.

Newman, Sandra J., and Duncan, Greg J. "Residential Problems, Dissatisfaction and Mobility." *Journal of the American Planning Association* 45 (1979): 154-166.

Newman, Sandra J., and Duncan, Greg J. "Residential Problems, Dissatisfaction and Mobility." In *Five Thousand American Families - Patterns of Economic Progress.* Vol. 6 Edited by Greg J. Duncan and James N. Norgan, pp. 297-322. Lansing, Michigan: Institute for Social Research, University of Michigan, 1978.

Osborne, Robert S. "The Migrant Spirit." *Mountain Life and Work,* July-August 1970, pp. 12-14.

Photiadis, John D. *West Virginians in Their Own State and in Cleveland, Ohio: Selected Social and Socio-phychological Characteristics.* Morgantown, West Virginia: Appalachian Center, West Virginia University, 1970.

Ragan, Pauline K., and Davis, William J. "The Diversity of Older Voters." *Society,* July-August 1978, pp. 50-53.

Real Estate Research Corporation. *Description and Partial Analyis of Cincinnati's 44 Statistical Areas.* May 1973.

Schwarzweller, Harry; Brown, James S.; and Mangalam, J.J. *Mountain Families in Transition.* University Park, Pennsylvania: The Pennsylvania State University Press, 1971.

Speare, Alden, Jr.; Goldstein, Sindey; and Frey, William H. *Residential Mobility, Migration and Metropolitan Change,* Cambridge, Mass.: Ballinger Publishing Company, 1974.

Sterne, Richard S.; Phillips, James E.; and Rabrushka, Alvin. *The Urban Elderly Poor.* Lexington, Mass.: D.C. Heath and Company, 1974.

Stevens, William K. "Appalachia's Hillbillies Trek North for Jobs." *New York Times.* March 29, 1973.

Tuchfarber, Alfred J., and Klecka, William R. *Random Digit Dialing: Lower-*

ing the Cost of Victimization Surveys. Washington, D.C.: Police Foundation, 1976.

U.S. Department of Health, Education and welfare. *Our Future Selves: Report of the Panel on Behavioral and Social Science Research.* Washington, D.C.: U.S. Government Printing Office, 1978.

U.S. Department of Health, Education and Welfare. *Our Future Selves: Summary Report.* Washington, D.C.: U.S. Government Printing Office, 1978.

Van Arsdol, Maurice D., Jr.; Sabagh, Georges; Butler, Edgar W. "Retrospective and Subsequent Metropolitan Residential Mobility." *Demography* 5 (1968): 249-67.

Varady, David P. "Determinants of Mobility in an Inner City Community." *Regional Science Perspectives* 5 (1975): 154-78.

_____."Housing Problems and Mobility Plans Among the Elderly." *Journal of the American Planning Association,* forthcoming.

Votaw, Albert N. "Hillbillies Invade Chicago." *Harper's Magazine,* February 1958, pp. 64-67.

Wiseman, Robert F. "Spatial Aspects of Aging." Resource Papers for College Geography No. 78-4. Washington, D.C.: Association of American Geographers, 1978.

IV Education in Appalachia

Innovatice Approches to Vocational-Technical Education in North Central Pennsylvania

Robert A. Rusiewski

Abstract

The focus of this paper will be on innovative approaches in vocational-technical education in the area of north central Pennsylvania. Attempts will be made to illustrate that even though the approaches discussed appear to be innovative to vocational-technical education in general, they are also fundamental to the concept of vocational-technical training in particular. The interface between and among the needs of area employers, the role of vocational-technical education to provide training to meet area employer needs, and student/adult interest in developing a skill or trade to enhance employment opportunities, will be illustrated throughout the examples provided.

Introduction

Three examples of innovative approaches to vocational-technical education in North Central Pennsylvania will be discussed in this paper. They involve the provision of training in petroleum production, powdered metals technology, and forest industry production (i.e., logging and sawmilling). A fourth example, a proposed vo-tech coal mining program, is briefly described.

Of the three training programs being highlighted, the petroleum production course is presently the most advanced. The major goal of the *Bradford Vocational-Technical Drilling-Oil Production* is the development and implementation of an on-site oil production course addressing the drilling of an oil well, the use of modern finishing techniques such as electro-logging and hydrofracturing, and the installation of a pumping unit so as to provide an avenue of training and career development for young oil field workers. The major goal of the Powdered Metals Technology Program, *Seneca Highlands Vocational-Technical School* is the development of a program to provide training, at both the secondary and adult level, in powdered metal manufacturing technology. *The North Central Pennsylvania Forest Industry Training Program at Jefferson County,* while still in the development phase, has as its goal the development of a training program for secondary and post-secondary students in the skills required for harvesting, processing, and transporting all categories of forest products to local, state, and national markets.

Subsequently, in order to depict this situation effectively, this paper is organized into four sections to describe the area of north central Pennsylvania, the vocational-technical training delivery system, the examples of innovative training, and in a final section, the summary and conclusion to be drawn from this study.

The North Central Pennsylvania Region

North central Pennsylvania consists of six contiguous counties that lie in the mountainous Allegheny plateau of northern Pennsylvania. These counties include Cameron, Clearfield, Elk, Jefferson, McKean, and Potter, and a part of a larger, sparsely populated area which is considered the only extensive "open" area remaining in the urbanized northeastern United States. The total area of the region is 5,083 square miles or 3,257,100 acres, which represents approximately 11 percent of the area of Pennsylvania.[1] Nearly 90 percent of this area is forested, with large tracts of forest land owned by the federal government (i.e., Allegheny National Forest), state government (Pennsylvania state game lands and forest lands), and private landowners.

The population of North Central Pennsylvania in 1970 was 231,490, or approximately 2 percent of the state total.[2] The latest estimates by the U.S. Department of Commerce, Bureau of the Census, compute the region's population to have grown slightly, by 6,676, to 238,166 as of July 1, 1977.[3] Population decline has been a general characteristic of the region since 1910, when the regional population was at its peak of 277,970. In general terms, population losses have been due to deteriorating economic conditions and the general rural to urban movements that have been characteristic of the United States in the past thirty years.

The region is rural, non-farm, and small town in character. There are numerous communities which have populations in excess of 1,000; however, only 36 percent of the total populaton resides in the fifteen larger (population of 2,500 or more) urban centers of the region. Bradford (12,672) and DuBois (10,112) are the only chartered cities, as well as the largest population centers. Of the 157 municipalities in the region, 146 have populations less than 5,000 persons.

Major economic activities in north central Pennsylvania include coal and clay mining, agriculture, forestry and timber production, oil and gas production, retail and personal services, and manufacturing. Decline in the extractive industries and reliance on below average growth industries have caused severe economic problems in the region, especially when the national economy is troubled.

Manufacturing is by far the single most important industry in the region. Manufacturing, in the region in 1976, employed 31,200 of the total six-county civilian labor force, or 32 percent.[4] In comparison. Pennsylvania, a highly industrialized state, employed only 28.8 percent in manufacturing in the same year.[5] Also significant is the fact that almost 75 percent of those employed in manufacturing in the region are employed in durable goods industries. This compares to only 60 percent for the state of Pennsylvania. The heaviest concentration of manufacturing is found in the counties of Elk and Cameron. Both of these counties have well over half their employment in manufacturing (54.2 percent and 57.1 percent respectively in 1976).

Mining holds an important place in the economy of the region. Coal in the southern section (Clearfield and Jefferson Counties) and oil in the northern section (McKean County) were instrumental in the region's past economic growth, and will continue to be important in the future. Mining and oil exploration have increased in the 1970s as a result of the energy shortage, but because of mechanization, especially in the case of coal, mining will never by a major employer again as in the 1940s. However, the increased mechanization has created a need for employees possessing more technical skills than in the past.

Poverty, housing shortages, high dependency ratios, low wages, low tax assessment bases, and a lack of retail outlets and personal services are all problems currently experienced in the region. These problems are not unique, but are characteristic of many areas in Appalachia.

Such problems and economic circumstances have contributed to both the need and demand for vocational training in the region in not only the traditional sense, but also for innovative curriculums with training for employment indigenous to the area. Such factors as the make-up of the local and regional economies, the desire of people - particularly young people - to remain in the area, the subsequent need and demand for vocational training, and the relevance of this training to enhancing employment opportunities and/or career development, have nurtured and fostered the present vocational-technical education delivery system in north central Pennsylvania. This system is outlined in the following section.

North Central Pennsylvania's Present Vocational-Technical Education Delivery System

The present vocational-technical education delivery system in north central Pennsylvania consists of three areawide vocational-technical schools and one comprehensive high school that has a vocational-technical department. Brief descriptions of each school are outlined.

Bradford Area High School

Bradford Area High School is a comprehensive high school including vocational-technical training. Vocational-technical training is available to students in grades 10-12, and enrollment in these grades is approximately 1,200. Enrollment in grades 10-12 is expected to remain fairly constant in the near future.

In recognition of the fact that not all jobs require college training, the vocational department offers courses in twelve vocational-technical training areas. These courses are Automotive, Carpentry, Electrical Maintenance, Machine Shop, Nursing Assistants, Distributive Education, Drafting and Design Technology, Electronics Technology and Grounds Building Maintenance, Petroleum Production, Home Economics, and Business Education.

Student selection is made on a quota basis with the selection criteria including test scores, past academic records, and attendance. Emphasis is made on the student selecting a course based on the student's interest in acquiring training in that subject area for the purpose of seeking employment or using that subject as a foundation for further training in a trade or technical school or a college.

The school is located in Bradford, McKean County, Pennsylvania.

Clearfield County Area Vocational-Technical School

The Clearfield County Area Vocational-Technical School has a maximum enrollment potential of 831 students, and at present, approximately 650 day school students and 700 evening students are enrolled. Students from five participating school districts attend the Clearfield County school, and percentage of high school students attending the school represents 15 percent of the total high school (grades 9-12) student population from the five participating districts. However, only in unusual circumstances do ninth grade students participate in vo-tech training. Thus approximately 21 percent of the total school population grades 10-12 in the five participating districts attend the Clearfield County Vo-Tech.

Sixteen major subject areas are offered and these included Auto Body Repair, Automotive Mechanics, Carpentry/Cabinet Making, Clothing Design/Sewing, Cosmetology, Beautician, Data Processing/Computer Programming, Diesel Mechanics, Distributive Education/Sales and Merchandising, Electronics, Electrical Wiring/Industrial and Residential, Food Preparation and Service, Health/Medical Assistant, Machine Shop,

Masonry/Bricklaying, and Welding.

With no vo-tech facilities in Elk and Cameron Counties (central part of the region), the Clearfield Vo-Tech has a very large service area. The $3 million facility was funded in part by a $346,500 grant from the Appalachian Regional Commission.

The school is located in Clearfield, Clearfield County, Pennsylvania.

Seneca Highlands Area Vocational-Technical School

The Seneca Highlands Area Vocational-Technical School is new and opened in February 1979. Capacity of the facility is 320 students with present capacity being approximately 300 students. The $3 million facility was funded in part by a $450,000 grant from the Appalachian Regional Commission. Five participating school districts in McKean, Potter, Cameron Counties send students to the Seneca Highlands Vo-Tech. Currently the school is in its first full year of operation.

Students in grades 10-12 are eligible for training courses. They must be at least fifteen years of age and below the age of twenty-one. Others not categorized as such can participate in the adult training sessions. Present adult enrollment is approximately 200.

Nine course offerings are available and these include: Metal Working Occupations, Heavy Equipment Construction, Automotive Mechanics, Building Construction Occupations, Building Maintenance Trades, Advanced Office Practice, Cosmetology, Health Assistant, and Powdered Metals Technology.

The school is located in Port Allegany, McKean County, Pennsylvania.

Jefferson County, DuBois Area Vocational-Technical School

The Jefferson County, Du Bois Area Vocational-Technical School has a facility capacity of 550 students with present enrollment at approximately 520 students. Both traditional academic course work and vocational-technical training are available at this school. The combined enrollment of daytime students and adult evening students is approximately 700. Four participating school districts provide the service area student population. The $4.6 million facility was funded in part by a $187,500 grant from the Appalachian Regional Commission in 1968.

Fifteen vocational-technical training courses are available and these include Auto Body, Auto Mechanics, Building Maintenance, Carpentry, Cosmetology, Electrical Construction, Food Services, Machine Shop Practice, Metal Fabrication, Graphics Arts, Distributive Education, Laboratory Technology, Data Processing, Drafting and Design Technology, and Electronic Technology.

The school is located in Reynoldsville, Jefferson County, Pennsylvania.

Regional Service Area

Upon viewing this delivery system in the six-county area, two conclusions are apparent. First, students in the northern counties of McKean and Potter have easy access to vocational training at either Bradford High School or Seneca Highland Area Vo-Tech, as do the students in the southern counties of Clearfield and Jefferson at either the Clearfield County Area Vo-Tech or the Jefferson County, DuBois Area Vo-Tech. Students in both Elk and Cameron counties have much farther to go to attend as there is no vocational-technical training offered in the central portion of the region. Second, the curriculum composition of these four schools, in terms of traditional vocational instruction, is quite similar except for the petroleum production training at Bradford High School and the powdered metals technology training at the Seneca Highlands Area Vo-Tech. It is the innovative nature of these two courses, plus two other courses in the development stage, that will be pursued in the following pages.

Examples of Innovative Approaches to Vocational-Technical Education in North Central Pennsylvania

The four examples of innovative approaches to vocational-technical education in north central Pennyslvanina are listed below with each course at a different phase of development/implementation.

Bradford Vocational-Technical Drilling-Oil Production Course

During the early to mid-1970s the petroleum industry in the Pennsylvania Grade Crude producing area of Bradford, McKean County, Pennsylvania, was experiencing a problematic series of events that projected very critical production problems in the near future. The local petroleum industry requested the vocational-technical department of Bradford High School to investigate the possibilities of developing a training program to supply the industry with training manpower.· This investigation and a survey of the local petroleum industry identified the following five specific problems. and needs of the industry:

1. The large percentage of oil field workers at the age fifty or above and the lack of younger experienced or trained workers.
2. Retirement alone will open up approximately twenty jobs per year for new employees, and the industry will need to replace 25 percent of its work force in the next fifteen years.
3. Increased drilling activity will require more workers.
4. Improved recovery techniques will require a more skilled work force.
5. Complaints by the industry that young employees have little or no knowledge of the industry and may require on-site training.

When viewed compositely, these problematic events formed an unusual dichotomy whereby, on the one hand, the petroleum industry has increased production activities to its highest level since 1960 (a peak year in the local industry); and on the other hand, the petroleum industry found itself with a trained manpower shortage at the oil field production level. The effects of this "push-pull" dichotomy on the local petroleum industry prompted representatives of the industry to request that Bradford Area High School become involved in alleviating this problem.

In 1975 Myron Crumrine, Director of Vocational Education at Bradford Area High School, requested the North Central Pennsylvania Regional Planning and Development Commission (NCPRPDC) to investigate potential sources of funding to develop and implement a petroleum production course. A project application was submitted to the Appalachian Regional Commission (ARC) and Bradford High School received $36,728 in ARC funds out of the total project cost of $45,910 to implement such a course.

However, it soon became apparent that the course needed to provide more on-site training. The school had a twenty-seven acre oil lease and both the Vo-Tech Director and the twelve man advisory committee identified a need for more equipment to provide instruction in the actual operation of drilling a producing well. An application to ARC was submitted in 1978, and a grant of $46,663 for equipment was approved.

In addition to this equipment, a drilling rig, the development and implementation of an on-site production course addressing the drilling of the well, the use of modern finishing techniques such as electro-logging and hydrofacturing, and the installation of a pumping unit all provide an avenue of training and career development for students interested in the program. In a course involving the total process in the completion of a producing well, emphasis is placed on

training in the following work activities.
1. Surveying to locate a well site
2. Securing the drilling permit
3. Preparation of an erosion and sedimentation plan
4. Construction of an access road
5. Preparation of a well site
6. Construction of pipe-line right-of-way
7. Securing the services of a drilling contractor
8. Setting up the rig
9. Provision of adequate water supply
10. Construction of pits for sand pumping
11. Drilling the well
12. Electo-logging of the well
13. Hydraulic fracturing of producing sand
14. Disassembly of rig
15. Installation of pumping equipment
16. Installation of oil run lines and gas lines
17. Erection and installation of electric lines
18. Clean-up of site
19. Grade and seed well location

The major objectives of this training program include the following:

1. To help offset a training manpower shortage in the oil industry by providing trained workers.
2. To provide students with training in the many facets of the oil industry.
3. To provide students with skill development in these multiple areas which will enable them to seek entry level employment.
4. To provide this training in an actual work setting such as the operating oil lease upon which the training is conducted.
5. To duplicate work conditions as closely as possible.
6. In addition to skill development, to make students aware of employer's needs in an employee, such as the willingness to accept responsibility, regular attendance, and willingness to work.
7. To provide area students who desire an occupation which is outdoor in nature an opportunity to find that employment through this training area.
8. To develop a formal training program in an industry over 100 years old in which none has previously existed.
9. To assist students in finding local employment which will help preserve the area's most valuable resource, its young people.
10. To develop the training program in such a way that it may be readily duplicated in another oil producing area.[8]

This course, as a mechanism for not only solving petroleum industry problems and needs but also developing skilled young employees, is unique to both vocational training and the needs of the area. The lubricating quality of Penn Grade Crude produced in this area is unsurpassed and considered a premium product worldwide. In fact, Penn Grade Crude supplies approximately 20 percent of the total lubricating sales in the nation.

In this context, it is interesting to note that McKean County is the heart of the Penn Grade Producing area, and that the Bradford Oil Field will be celebrating its 109th year of production later in 1980. This year also represents the 106th year of continuous production by the oldest producing oil well in the world, situated in Bradford. Approximately 44 percent of the total crude oil production for the state of Pennsylvania, in 1977, came from McKean

County.⁹ (This amounted to 1,198,616 barrels of the state's 2,703,763 total barrels).

At present the course has an enrollment of thirty-seven students. These students are enrolled in grades 10, 11, and 12 in a three-year vocational training program. This course is in its fourth year of operation, with twenty-seven students graduating from the program in the past three years. Of these twenty-seven graduates, fifteen are currently employed in the oil industry, eight are on active duty in the military service, and four are employed in an occupation not related to the oil industry.¹⁰ Approximate salary for these employed in the oil industry ranges from $4.50 per hour starting to $7.00 per hour.

Course activities are conducted on a twenty-seven acre operating lease where there are currently ten oil wells in production. Revenue from these wells has been approximately $4,000 during the 1979-80 school year through December 31, 1979. This represents approximately 144 barrels of crude oil, with approximately two thirds of that production the results of the ARC funding drilling project. These funds will be used to assist in making the program self-sufficient.

Both the development and operation of this program have been enhanced by the cooperation of the local petroleum industry. Donations include a complete hydrofracturing job on one new well, an electro-logging job on the same well, the donation of tools and supplies from many sources, and over 100 hours each of active participation in a curriculum writing project by the twelve-member advisory committee.

In the course's 3½ years of operation, it has become one of the most popular training offerings at the school. In addition to the training supplied to the prospective oil field workers, the lease operation has provided involvement with other vocational shop areas such as carpentry, electrical, automotive, drafting, and building maintenance.

In addition to these activities, it has provided the school and community with local and national media exposure. Two stories have been run by the national wire services, many local articles have been written, and television newscasts have covered the course activities. The program has been covered by two national magazines and was also included in the 1978 Annual Report of the Appalachian Regional Commission.

At the time of the course's initial implementation it was the only vocational-technical course of its kind in the United States. While being an innovative approach to vocational-technical training, the course fulfills the concept or fundamental philosophy of vocational education by providing a form of training relevant to the needs of both students and the employment skills required or sought by employers in the local/regional economy. In this regard it is important to highlight the response of the Appalachian Regional Commission in providing "seed money" to enable the program to be implemented. Now, the revenue obtained by selling the oil produced at the wells, plus the contributions of materials, supplies, and industry technical assistance are together enabling the program to be self-sufficient. Also, just recently the natural gas by-product from the wells was connected to the on-site classroom and is providing fuel to heat it. (A Glossary defining some of the terminology used in this course is included at the end of the paper.)

Powdered Metal Technology Program, Seneca Highlands Area Vo-Tech School

The area served by the Seneca Highlands Vocational-Technical School is one of the most important production areas in the United States for powdered metal, primary metals, and related technology products. The course was developed as a result of an initial survey conducted by the Director of the new Vo-Tech School, the desire of the powdered metal industries to remain in north central Pennsylvania, and the growth and expansion projected by the Governor's Office of State Planning and Development in 1977.

Course surveys were mailed to approximately twenty of the area powdered metal firms. Nine of the industries submitted detailed answers to the survey and these were very positive about such a course. Of the nine firms responding, the combined employment of these firms totaled 1,415 employees. These firms had a 6.8 percent turnover in employment annually, and their projected total employment for 1980 indicated a 330 employee increase, or 18.9 percent, to 1,745 workers. All of the firms indicated that they would hire properly trained graduates of the course.

Another reason for the active and viable attempt to develop a powdered metals technology course was that the industry appears to be committed to remaining and expanding existing operations in north central Pennsylvania. Some of the explanations for this commitment include:

1. The powdered metal industry is not affected to the same extent as other regional industries (especially electronics) foreign competition.
2. Large capital investments in existing physical plant and equipment have been made.
3. The powdered metal industry is growing in excess of 15 percent per year.
4. The industry, even though quite labor intensive, has a large work force to draw upon.
5. Most of the industry's various competitors have located in the area, and all are affected by quite a variety of similar factors such as labor rate, market supply and demand, and changes in product development and quality control.

Additionally, in 1977, the Governor's Office of State Planning and Development had projected significant increases in primary metal products manufacturing from the period 1980 through the year 2000. In the three local labor market areas most affected, the projections are as follows:

PRIMARY METAL PRODUCTS MANUFACTURING

Labor Market Area	Total Employment Projections		
	1980	1990	2000
Coudersport	242	439	622
St. Marys	2394	3095	3736
Emporium	524	711	884
TOTAL	**3160**	**4245**	**5242**

Together, these factors have contributed to the initial efforts of not only investigating the potential for the course, but also the aggressive pursuit of a sound, viable, and relevant approach to develop and implement the course.

The major goal of this project is the development of a program of providing training at both the secondary and adult level, in powdered metal manufacturing technology. The approach will be the development of a curriculum which will provide both basic and advanced training through a combination of classroom and shop/equipment education. The program will resolve the problem of job entry for students from this region, while meeting manpower needs for trained individuals within the powdered metals industry. It will also be designed to upgrade the skills of those people already employed.

Other objectives of the powdered metal technology course include the following:

1. To train high school students, grades "10, 11 and 12" for employment in the powdered metals industry, thus making an opportunity for employment which will encourage students to remain in the community.
2. To provide a student with entry level skills which will encompass a wide variety of actual work experiences which are essential in the powdered metals industry.
3. To meet an industry need for supplying young, able-bodied workers who have had some formalized training in the occupational areas of powdered metals manufacturing.
4. To develop a formalized course of study and training programs for the powdered metals industry, which has never attempted any organized training for production workers in this geographic location.
   a. To develop a curriculum based upon community, education and industry needs.
   b. To stimulate an industrial atmosphere in which job attitudes, performances, and expectations are stressed.
5. To provide on-site training in a skill area which meets the career needs and desires of students from a rural community, and in north central Pennsylvania.
6. To provide the image of powdered metal workers in regards to wages and working conditions by providing career guidance pertinent to the industry.
7. To establish a cooperative summer employment program for enrolled students.
8. To provide a relevant type of training in the usage of sintering equipment and modern finishing techniques such as compacting, tooling, and machining.[11]

The development of this course is in the application stage at the present time. The total cost is estimated to be $275,700. Funding for the program is projected as follows:

Pennsylvania Bureau of Vocational Education	$ 37,500
U.S. Department of Education	20,000
Appalachian Regional Commission	150,000
Jefferson County, DuBois Area Vo-Tech	42,500
Local Ineligible Contribution	25,700
TOTAL COST	$275,700

The proposed course has been ranked as a priority for state and federal funding, and if all goes as planned, the course will be ready to enroll students in the 1981-82 school year.

Clearfield County Area Vocational-Technical Coal Mining Program

This proposed course is presently in the investigatory or development phase. A craft advisory committee has been formed, with members of the committee being either producers, employees, or representatives of pro-coal organizations. A need for this course is appearing as the resurgence of the coal industry has brought about a dramatic increase in coal production in Clearfield County. In 1977 (latest figures available), Clearfield County ranked third in the state of Pennsylvania of all the counties producing bituminous coal with 9,299,741 tons mined.[12] A significant factor in this production is that 8,673,745 tons were produced via strip mining.

This course will be designed to meet the employment training needs of the bituminous coal industry in strip mining in the Clearfield County area. The Vo-Tech School has approximately fifty acres of land on which a small strip mining training operation could be initiated. The present plans are to seek funding from the Appalachian Regional Commission as "seed money" to begin the course, and the revenue obtained from selling the coal would enable the program to be self-sufficient. Optimally, the course will be ready to enroll students in the fall semester of 1982.

Summary and Conclusions

In viewing the four examples of innovative approaches to vocational-technical training in north central Pennsylvania in their various stages of either implementation or development, several important factors have been crucial not only to course development and implementation but also to the insurance of successful programs in the future. These factors focus on: (1) the interface between and among the needs of area employers and the role of vocational-technical education to provide training to meet area employer needs and student employment interests, (2) the role of the Appalachian Regional Commission in responding to such regional needs, and (3) the vehicle of vocational-technical education to provide training that is both innovative with reference to traditional forms of vo-tech education and at the same time fundamental to the needs and opportunities of the regional economy. The linkage between these factors has been of paramount importance not only in developing and implementing a meaningful training program, but also in insuring solid future for the programs based on a close relationship between the vo-tech schools and area employers. Such a situation will enable the local and regional economies to grow, reduce out-migration of the region's young people, provide employment opportunities for the young, and help renew confidence in the future of the regional extractive and manufacturing industries.

Thus, the courses described can be viewed in the following ways:

1. As examples of Appalachian Regional Commission efforts in linking vocational-technical education to private sector employment opportunities.
2. As examples of innovative vocational-technical training being offered in Appalachia.
3. As a point of departure for further investigation concerning comparisons of training opportunities linked to employment opportunities in both the Appalachian region and the nation.

Glossary

Hydro-fracturing

Hydro-fracturing involves the pumping of water under very high pressure down the well to break up the oil producing sand; then a sand solution is pumped in to keep the cracks open. The crude oil can then be freed from the producing sand and will drain into the bottom of the well much easier, thereby improving production capabilities of the individual oil well.

Electro-logging

Electro-logging is the process of taking an electronic picture of the rock strata in a newly drilled well to identify the presence of hydrocarbons in the strata. It involves lowering an instrument, similar in function to a television camera, down the well to take electronic pictures for analysis.

Surveying to locate a well site

Surveying is used primarily in conjuction with the drilling permit application procedure. The location of oil wells and new wells about to be drilled must be indicated on a topographic map to insure the location coordinates are the same as those on the permit issued to the person or firm drilling the well.

Notes

1. Commonwealth of Pennsylvania, Department of Commerce, Pennsylvania, *Industrial Census Series Release Number M-5-77,* 1978 editions. See individual booklets for each Pennsylvania County: Page 5 for Cameron, Clearfield, Elk, Jefferson, McKean, and Potter Counties.

2. U.S. Department of Commerce, Bureau of the Census, *Population Estimates and Projections,* November 1979, pp. 15,17,18,21,25,30, and 34.

3. U.S. Department of Commerce, Bureau of the Census, *Population Estimates and Projections,* November 1979, pp. 15,17,21,25,30, and 34.

4. North Central Pennsylvania Regional Planning and Development Commission, *1978 Areawide Action Program Document,* p. 49. (Material taken from the *1979 Pennsylvania Statistical Abstract.)*

5. North Central Pennsylvania Regional Planning and Development Commission, *1987 Areawide Action Program Document,* p. 49. (Material taken from the *1978 Pennsylvania Statistical Abstract.)*

6. *Bradford Vocational-Technical Drilling-Oil Production Course,* project application submitted to the Appalachian Regional Commission, May, 1978. See Attachment A. p. 1.

7. *Bradford Vocational-Technical Drilling-Oil Production Course,* project application submitted to the Appalachian Regional Commission, May, 1978, pp. 7-8 .

8. Myron A. Crumrine to Robert A. Rusiewski, January 24, 1980.

9. Pennsylvania Geological Survey, *Oil and Gas Development in Pennsylvania in 1977, Progress Report 191,* 1978, Figure 2.

10. Myron A. Crumrine to Robert A. Rusiewski, January 24, 1980.

11. *Powdered Metal Technology Program, Seneca Highlands Area Vocational Technical School,* project application submitted to Appalachian Regional Commission, April, 1979, pp. 3-4.

12. Commonwealth of Pennsylvania, Department of Environmental Resources, *1977 Annual Report on Mining, Oil and Gas, and Land Reclamation and Conservation Activities,* p. 116.

Coral Wilson Stewart
and the
"Moonlight School" Movement
James M. Gifford
Abstract

This paper traces the remarkable educational career of Cora Wilson Stewart who pioneered the "Moonlight School", a night school program for illiterate adults in her home county in eastern Kentucky. The success of her program was felt far and wide: many states adopted versions of it, the reader she devised was published for use as an aid to illiterate American soldiers in World War I, and she later served on national and international commissions on illiteracy. All told, her most satisfying accomplishment was the progress she brought to her own people of eastern Kentucky.

In 1911, Cora Wilson Stewart, an ambitious, talented, Kentucky mountaineer, began a crusade against illiteracy that dramatically improved the quality of life in Appalachian Kentucky. The "Moonlight School" Program--a night school for illiterate adults--made her a beacon of hope to the mountain people of eastern Kentucky and a legitimate hero in their eyes. "My mother thought she hung the moon," observed one Morehead State University educator, while a Kentucky legislator reportedly said that "he always told his children he wanted them to see two people, Buffalo Bill and Cora Wilson Stewart."[1] Her memorabilia are still cherished and handed down in Rowan County families today.

By the early twentieth century Appalachian Kentucky was a land of despair that desperately needed Cora Wilson Stewart's help. While many Americans worried about the Supreme Court's antitrust stance or the unfolding split in the Republican party, eastern Kentuckians "made do".[2] They had learned their survival lessons the hard way, because both geography and historical experience had separated them from the American mainstream. The Civil War had been particularly devastating.[3] The people of Appalachian Kentucky-- caught between warring armies--expressed divided sentiments. The majority supported the North, but strong Confederate ties existed, too. The resulting local conflicts divided families and destroyed friendships. When the war ended, the bitter hatreds remained and feuding continued into the twentieth century.[4]

Other horrible aftereffects of the war were less evident than the feuds but equally debilitating. When "home rule" returned to Kentucky following the Compromise of 1877, democratic, ex-Confederates again assumed control of the state government and took revenge against their wartime opponents from the mountain counties through political and economic retaliations.[5] Not surprisingly, the quality of life in Appalachian Kentucky grew worse as roads and schools suffered from discriminatory funding.

When this plight was "discovered" nationally, a great missionary intrusion to the mountains began. Thousands of teachers and preachers came "with souls afire" to lift the people of Appalachian Kentucky from their "cultural depravity".[6] In retrospect, one of the great ironies of this mountain mission was the fact that, during this same period, the Kentucky mountaineers produced their own hero in the war against illiteracy, and her efforts won national and international recognition. She was Cora Wilson Stewart and her "Moonlight School" program destroyed illiteracy in her home county and became a model for similar adult education programs throughout America and eventually the world.[7]

write and declared that he would gladly exchange twenty years of his life for the ability to read and write. Another man, a young ballad singer, sadly told Mrs. Stewart that he had forgotten many beautiful songs that had been passed down to him by his ancestors "before anybody came along to set 'em down."[16]

Against this backdrop of educational need, Cora Stewart fashioned her plan. She decided to hold classes at night, since the majority of illiterates were employed during the day. She informed Rowan County teachers of her plan, and they unanimously volunteered their assistance. On September 4, 1911, county teachers visited each home in their district and personally invited attendance at the first session that was scheduled to begin the following night. Approximately 150 were expected; 1,200 arrived. Twelve hundred persons with 1,200 sad stories about why they could not read and write came determined to improve themselves. They wanted to read their Bibles, write to their children, and sign their names rather than make "their mark." The youngest was eighteen; the oldest was a "school girl" of eighty-six. They applied themselves diligently. Many learned to sign their name the first night. Soon the county was a beehive of new writing activity, and people who had long led lives of quiet, illiterate desperation wrote their names whenever and wherever the opportunity arose. Many deposited their meager savings in banks for the first time for the pure joy of signing their names to the checks. That January, Sherman Porter, managing editor of the Lexington *Herald*, congratulated Mrs. Stewart "on behalf of the people of all Kentucky" for her devotion to her work and the special efforts she was making on behalf of "our best citizens when they are properly understood and appreciated."[17]

Encouraged by this huge response, Cora Stewart began writing a short newspaper, *The Rowan County Messenger*, as a reader for her adult students. The paper was a combination of homilies and local news and also included lessons in history, arithmetic, and some memory work from literary classics like Longfellow's "Psalm of Life." The *Messenger* inspired much good-spirited interscholastic competition which resulted in physical improvements to the buildings as well as personal progress for the students.[18]

The next year, Rowan Countians requested a continuance of the "Moonlight School" In preparation for this second session, Mrs. Stewart sponsored an "Institute" or in-service training session. Teachers attended on a voluntary, non-compensated basis and discussed both teaching and recruiting methods. It was an opportunity for them to share their progresses, their sacrifices, and their disappointments, and to renew their commitment to another arduous year of working day and night. It was also one of America's first formalized studies of adult education methodology. Cora Stewart's extensive correspondence with educators in Kentucky and throughout the nation reflected both a growing interest in her work and a recognition of the "courage and sacrifice of the teachers in Rowan County."[19]

The second year of the moonlight school was more successful than the first. Sixteen hundred students enrolled and 350 of them learned to read and write. Some individual progresses were remarkable: a lumberman doubled his salary after six weeks of schooling and two postmasters and four preachers learned to read and write. Children brought their parents and teachers brought their spouses. It was a time of progress and a rebirth of community pride. One trustee noted that the school in his district used "to drag along and nobody seemed interested." After three weeks of moonlight school, the people of his district "got together right" and made significant improvements in their schoolhouse. These revitalized schoolhouses once again became genuine community centers and the site of many civic and religious meetings. Also, during the second session, a "home department" of the moonlight school was

Cora Wilson was born to Dr. Jeremiah Wilson and Annie Eliza (Hally) Wilson in 1875 and reared in Farmers, a community in the western part of Rowan County. She attended Morehead Normal School and the National Normal University in Lebanon, Ohio, and then began a teaching career in her home county in 1895. She quickly earned a reputation as an outstanding educator, and in 1901 Rowan Countians elected her to serve as county school superintendent.‚

Success in Rowan County soon brought recognition from regional educators who often invited Mrs. Stewart to address teacher-training sessions and other groups interested in advancing public education. She was a "graceful, forceful speaker with a direct, clear message,...a rich vocabulary, and...an easy and attractive manner," observed E.C. McDougle of Eastern Kentucky State Norman School. McDougle, who heard Mrs. Stewart lecture on "That Child of Yours and His Parent" in 1908, commended her "fine presentation of some school problems that should be carefully studied by both teacher and parent" and felt that it would "do good wherever heard." ‚ Her other regional presentations were equally well received.‚ Following an address in Elliot County, the superintendent of county schools, D.F. Gray, commended, her efforts, "to urge our boys and girls into something higher and nobler in life" and pledged his support if Mrs. Stewart sought the presidency of the Kentucky Educational Association: "I think it would be real nice to have one of our home county girls at the head of educational affairs of our state, and I hope you will not hesitate to take advantage of any opportunity that may come your way." Voicing the sentiment of so many persons who heard her speak prior to 1910, Gray wrote: "We all enjoyed your lecture, but nothing you said gave me greater pleasure than your statement that the remainder of your life would be devoted to the cause of education."‚

Many others noted Mrs. Stewart's great commitment to public education. She was re-elected superintendent of Rowan County Schools in 1909, and two years later she was elected the first woman president of the Kentucky Educational Association.‚ Most state educators echoed the sentiments of J.G. Crabbe, president of Kentucky Normal School, who warmly congratulated Mrs. Stewart and pledged support of her efforts. "Count on me," he promised. "I am sure the Association will prosper under your leadership."‚

Buoyed by this statewide support, Mrs. Stewart determined, as an addition to Rowan County's overall educational program, to launch an experimental program called the "Moonlight School" that was designed to combat illiteracy among the county's adult population. Cora Wilson knew many of the 1,152 illiterate persons living in Rowan County in 1911, and, having "served as a secretary" to many of them, she knew how much they needed and wanted to learn how to read and write.‚

One older woman who lived by herself often walked seven miles to Mrs. Stewart's office in Morehead whenever she received a letter from her daughter who worked in Chicago. After a particulary long absence, the woman arrived with a letter one morning. In reply to Mrs. Stewart's offer of assistance, she reported that she could answer it for herself for she had learned to read and write. The lonely mountain woman had determined to break down "the wall" between her and her absent daughter Jane and had purchased a speller and studied "'til midnight and sometimes 'til daylight." She proudly demonstrated her success by reading the letter and penning a reply with Mrs. Stewart's advice.‚

Mrs. Stewart had many other touching personal encounters with Rowan County adults who genuinely wanted to escape the bondage of illiteracy. One middle-aged businessman cried when he confessed that he could not read or established, and teachers like Gladys Thompson taught in the homes of individuals who were too old or ill to attend night classes.[19]

The success of the first two years prompted a third-year goal of wiping "illiteracy out of the county" completely. Before the school year began, school trustees canvassed their districts and took a census of the remaining illiterates, This list was given to the teachers who in turn recruited their recently "converted" students to help them. "Each one teach one" was their motto, and, as part of a great competition that was developing between districts, they zealously sought out all remaining illiterates and taught them without mercy. Like all competitions, this one occasionally transcended the sublime and reached the absurd. One trustee for example, declared that he felt confident that illiteracy would soon be totally removed from his district, since "there's only one illiterate over there, and he's a tenant on my place; I'm going to run him over into Fleming County." Whenever a district reached its goal, a ceremony was held in the schoolhouse and the former illiterates were presented with new Bibles as a reward for their accomplishments. Remarking on this phenomenon of change, one long-time resident said, "It used to be moonshine and bullets; but now it's lemondade and Bibles."[21]

When this enormous educational crusade commenced in 1911, Rowan County had numbered 1,152 illiterates. By 1914 only 23 remained--by Mrs. Stewart's count. Of these, 6 were blind or had sight problems; 5 were bedridden invalids; 6 were defined as "imbeciles and epileptics;" 2 had only recently moved to this county and 4 "could not be induced to learn." For promotional reasons, Mrs. Stewart undoubtedly inflated the success rate by employing a very casual definition of literacy. Her qualitative results, however, remain unchallenged.

Cora Stewart did not stop to rest on her laurels. She immediately broadened her horizon and prepared to wage war against illiteracy in Kentucky.[22] In 1913, she wrote Governor James B. McCreary and proposed a state commission that would focus on the state's 208,084 illiterates and eventually place Kentucky "in a better light before the world." The governor responded positively and, in 1914, inspired by Mrs. Stewart's speech which reportedly "swept the Legislature off its feet," the General Assembly unanimously created the Kentucky Illiteracy Commission, headed by Mrs. Stewart. Other members included President J.F. Crabbe of Eastern Kentucky State Normal School, H.H. Cherry, the president of the Normal School in Western Kentucky, and Miss Ella Lewis, the superintendent of Grayson County Schools. Barksdale Hamlett, superintendent of Public Instruction, also served as an exofficio member.[24]

To promote the state effort against illiteracy and, at the same time, to reward her original Moonlight School teachers, Mrs. Stewart took her Rowan teachers on a vacation of the northern United States and Canada. A trip to Niagara Falls highlighted the tour. Financial and moral support from private organizations, like the Colonial Dames, and from many church groups and civic-minded individuals soon followed.[25] The Kentucky campaign against illiteracy quickly won national attention from both supporters and cynics.

As a teaching device, in 1915, Mrs. Stewart developed an adult reading book entitled *Country Life Reader, First Book* which encouraged reading by dealing with a wide variety of subjects, including agriculture, politics, economic development, sanitation, and thrift. The following illustrates her dual emphasis on adult content and "moral" instruction:

> I shall pay my taxes.
> I pay a tax on my home.

I pay a tax on my land.
I pay a tax on my cattle.
I pay a tax on my money.
I pay a tax on many other things.
Where does all this money go?
It goes to keep up the schools.
It goes to keep up the roads.
It goes to keep down crime.
It goes to keep down disease.
I am glad the I have a home to pay taxes on."

World War I rudely interrupted the quiet progress of Cora Stewart's educational programs. The European conflict that began in 1914 prompted America's declaration of neutrality. Soon, however, continued violations of U.S. maritime rights awakened American preparedness and military ardor. President Woodrow Wilson was re-elected in the fall of 1916, and the following April he asked Congress for a declaration of war against Germany to make the world "safe for democracy." By June, thousands of American men between the ages of twenty-one and thirty-one were registering for military service. The 700,000 illiterate national registrants included 30,000 Kentuckians."

Cora Wilson Stewart and the Kentucky Illiteracy Commission responded immediately. Realizing that the regularly scheduled fall session of the moonlight school would be too late to serve the special needs of Kentucky's soldiers, Mrs. Stewart made a special appeal to the teachers of Kentucky, and by July 23, a summer school was in session." In genuine desperation, the soon-to-be soldiers assaulted their lessons. Letters and literacy took on an urgent, new, personal meaning to many young men who had never been away from their homes and "hollers.""

As she had done with other groups of adult learners, Cora Stewart wrote a special reader for the unique needs of Kentucky's recruits. *The Soldier's First Book* was patriotic in cover, color and content. An armed soldier on the cover of the red, white, and blue text introduced lessons that dealt with war, guns, camps, flags, tent, bulletin boards, parade grounds, and the "rule of kings.""

The bewilderment and humiliation that illiterates experienced in basic training was sad, but eloquent, testimony to the continuation and extension of Cora Stewart's work. Some carried letters in their pockets for days before gathering the courage to ask someone to read the home news and pen a reply. Others were frequently transferred because their commanding officers, themselves unschooled in many respects, confused inability to read and understand orders with lack of cooperation and commitment. A few were even imprisoned for "disobeying orders" simply because they could not read and understand them. Typical of the illiterates' despair, one young soldier timidly requested that a Y.M.C.A. volunteer worker address twelve envelopes to his mother. "Are you planning to write every day?" the volunteer queried. "You must be a dutiful son."

"No, these are to last me a year," the soldier replied. "I promised my mother that I'd get some envelopes backed and that once a month I'd slip a dollar bill in one and mail it to her and by that she'd know that I was still alive.""

During the war years of 1917 and 1918, Mrs. Stewart again focused attention on the soldiers' needs by prompting the Kentucky Illiteracy Commission to hold special moonlight school sessions for the wives, mothers, sisters, and sweethearts of Kentucky's fighting men. General Joh Pershing, Commander of the American forces in Europe, had requested that American women write "long cheerful letters telling everything that happens in the old home town," because the men were "hungry for news..." Meanwhile, *The Soldier's First Book* had been revised by the Y.M.C.A. as a teaching aide for all of our country's soldiers."

When the war ended in 1918, Cora Stewart again adopted her campaign against illiteracy to the prevailing circumstances. A government agency distributed fifty thousand copies of her *Country Life Reader* to American soldiers in Europe. This new adult reader aided their educational progress while preparing them for a return to the current issues of civilian life--voting, taxation, soil conservation, transportation, and health. As the war was concluding, many former students of America's moonlight school were adapting Cora Stewart's program to European needs." Meanwhile, on the Kentucky home front, Cora Stewart and Sergeant Willie Sandlin, Kentucky's counterpart to Tennessee's Alvin York, were touring the state and promoting the work of the Kentucky Illiteracy Commission."

The success of the Moonlight School Program and the contribution it made to the state, the nation, and the war effort encouraged the state legislature to make a small post-war appropriation to support the traveling expenses of seventy-five field agents for the Illiteracy Commission. These agents continued the program that Cora Stewart had started in Rowan County and constantly sought to educate the state's adults within the context of the major social and political issues of the day. A new dimension to the crusade against illiteracy in Kentucky involved extending the program to the state penal institutions. In 1919, literacy became a condition of parole, providing additional incentive to the learning efforts of state prisoners. The Literacy Commission also expanded its efforts by taking a census of the remaining illiterates in the state, thus charting a course for future action."

Many other states launched adult education programs that were carefully patterned after Cora Wilson Stewarts Moonlight School and the Kentucky Illiteracy Commission. As the movement grew, it received support and encouragement from the National Educational Association and other national organizations. By the end of the second decade of the twentieth century, the campaign against illiteracy had blossomed into a national crusade. Ironically, after 1920 the social and political climate of Kentucky changed, and the state legislature did not refund the Kentucky Illiteracy Commission.

As Americans moved into the Roaring Twenties and embraced new ideologies and adopted new heroes, the campaign against illiteracy became a part of the American dream and Cora Stewart achieved national prominence. In 1923, she was elected to serve a one-year term on the Executive Committee of the National Educational Association. That same year, she presided over the illiteracy section of the World Conference on Education in San Francisco. She subsequently played similar roles at Edinburgh in 1925, at Toronto in 1927, at Geneva in 1929, and at Denver in 1931. From 1929 to 1933, she chaired the Executive Committee of the National Advisory Committee on Illiteracy."

This decade of national prominence also brought the story of Cora Wilson Stewart before the American public, and the "Moonlight School Lady" won awards and ever increasing recognition. In 1925, she received Pictorial Review's $5,000 achievement prize for her "contribution...to advance human welfare." She was also honored by the Kentucky Educational Association and the General Federation of Women's Clubs. A decade of honors and appointments culminated with her receipt of the Ella Flagg Young Metal for distinguished service to education in 1930."

Throughout the thirties and forties, the "Moonlight School" idea was adapted to meet the increasingly diverse needs of the national adult education movement. Meanwhile, advancing age and health problems forced Cora Stewart to accept a cameo role in this national epic-drama. She moved to Pine Bluff, Arkansas, to be near her sisters and subsequently moved to various rest homes in North Carolina. She died in South Carolina on December 9, 1958 and is buried in Tryon, North Carolina."

In retrospect, Cora Wilson Stewart emerges as a significant pioneer leader in America's burgeoning, twentieth century adult education movement. She also merits recognition as a major figure in the national crusade against illiteracy, although her methodologies have been challenged and altered by subsequent generations of educators. Her greatest achievement, however, was the human progress she fostered among the mountain people of eastern Kentucky. As a role model, a friend, and a champion of personal and regional advancement, Cora Stewart earned the love and respect of the people of Appalachian Kentucky. Their progress is an enduring tribute to her hard work, self-sacrifice, and vision for a brighter future. Their success is her greatest monument.

Notes

1. George T. Young, interview, November 19, 1979; Quoted without reference to the author in the Cora Wilson Stewart Papers, Box 1, Department of Special Collections, the University of Kentucky Libraries, Lexington, Kentucky (hereinafter cited as CWS Papers UK). The author is deeply grateful to Mrs. Grace Yoder of Morehead, Kentucky, for sharing materials that her parents, the late George and Sadie Brown, had left to her.

2. There is no definitive study of the Appalachian experience in Kentucky. For a synoptic overview, see Carol Crowe-Carraco, *The Big Sandy* (Lexington: The University Press of Kentucky, 1979). For some insight into the difficulties encountered by Appalachian miners of this period, see John W. Hevener, *Which Side Are You On? The Harlan County Coal Miners,* 1931-1939 (Urbana: University of Illinois Press, 1978), pp. 1-11, and Howard B. Lee, *Bloodletting In Appalachia: The Story of West Virginia's Four Major Mine Wars and Other Thrilling Incidents of Its Coal Fields* (Parsons, West Virginia: McClain Printing Company, 1969). See also Also Archie Green, *Only a Miner: Studies In Recorded Coal-Mining Songs* (Urbana: University of Illinois Press, 1972), chap. 7.

3. For an eloquent elaboration on the Civil War's role in the Appalachian experience, see Cratis Williams, "The Southern Mountaineer in Fact and Fiction" (Ph.D. dissertation, New York University, 1961). This monumental, three volume, sixteen-hundred-page study was abridged and edited by Martha H. Pipes and published in four successive issues of *Appalachian Journal* beginning with vol. 3, no. 1, Autumn 1975. An interesting reassessment of the theme of Appalachian isolation is Gary S. Foster, "Appalachian Isolation in Perspective," *Appalachian Heritage* 8 (Winter 1980: pp. 34-37

4. Some well-known examples of violence, emanating from the Civil War, in eastern Kentucky include the "Underwood War" in Carter County; The Hatfield-McCoy Feud which resulted in twenty-six deaths in Pike County, Kentucky, and Logan County, West Virginia; the Brammer Gap Killings in Lawrence County; the feuds of "Bloody Breathitt;" and various Guerilla conflicts that occurred after Appomattox. For more information see Harold Wilson Coates, *Stories of Kentucky Feuds* (Knoxville, Tennessee: Holmes-Darst Coal Corporation, 1942), pp. 3-46; Henry P. Scalf, *Kentucky's Last Frontier* (Pikeville, Kentucky: Pikeville College Press, 1972), p. 279. G. Elliott

Hatfield, *The Hatfields* (Stanville, Kentucky: The Big Sandy Valley Historical Society, 1974), pp. 12-14, 24; Virgil Carrington-Jones, *The Hatfields and the McCoys* (Chapel Hill, North Carolina: The University of North Carolina Press, 1948), p. 18; Mrs. A.J. Davidson, *Josie M. Davidson: Her Life and Work* (Prestonburg, Kentucky: privately printed, 1922), pp. 1-10; J. Tandy Ellis, *Report of the Adjutant General of the State of Kentucky: Confederate Kentucky Volunteers' War, 1861-1865,* Vol. 1 (Frankfort: The State of Kentucky, 1915), pp. 338-42.

5. An elaboration of this theme, as it applies to the Appalachian experience in western North Carolina, is found in James H. Horton, Theda Perdue, and James M. Gifford, *Our Mountain Heritage,* ed. Clifford R. Lovin (Franklin, North Carolina: The North Carolina Humanities Committee and the Mountain Heritage Center, Western Carolina University, 1979), pp. 70-123.

6. For an interesting historical overview, see Richard B. Drake, "The Mission School Era in Southern Appalachia, 1880-1940," *Appalachian Notes* 6 (1978): 1-8. See also F. Scott Rogers, "The Missionaries' Effect on the Appalachian Self-Image," *Appalachian Notes,* 1 (Fourth Quarter, 1973): 1-8, esp. p. 2; and Jim Wayne Miller, "Where Do You Come From, Where Do You Go? Appalacahians as Immigrants in Their Own Land," *Mountain Review* 2 (July 1976): 40-41; and Bill Best, "A Case for Appalachian Scholarship," *Mountain Life and Work* 46 (November 1970): 16-18.

7. The only adequate scholarship that focuses on Cora Wilson Stewart's life and contributions is Willie Everette Nelms, Jr., "Cora Wilson Stewart: Crusader Against Illiteracy" (M.A. thesis, University of Kentucky, 1973). The gracefully written study focuses "on her career as an educational reformer...and her contributions to adult education..." (hereinafter cited as Nelms, Crusader Agains Illiteracy"). A more specialized, synoptic, published version of this study is Willie E. Nelms, Jr., "Cora Wilson Stewart and The Crusade Agains Illiteracy In Kentucky," *The Register of The Kentucky Historical Society* 74 (January 1976): 10-29. Another helpful work is Mrs. Stewart's promotional recollections: Cora Wilson Stewart, *Moonlight Schools For the Emancipation of Adult Illiterates* (New York: E.P. Dutton and Company, 1922). This work is, in spite of biases induced by purpose and time, a valuable primary source (hereinafter cited as Stewart, *Moonlight Schools*).

8. Some basic biographical information on Cora Wilson Stewart can be found in a small brochure used to commemorate the restoration of the "Little Brushy School" on the campus of Morehead State University in 1973. Harold Rose, ed., "The Cora Wilson Stewart Moonlight Schoolhouse" (Morehead, Kentucky: Morehead State University, 1973). See also Autograph Books I-II, CWS Papers UK.

9. E.C. McDougle addressed "To Whom It May Concern," July 30, 1908, CWS Papers, Box 2, UK.

10. See, for example H.R. Dysard, lawyer in Grayson, Kentucky, to Cora WIlson Stewart, July 29, 1908; Mannie E. Fields, superintendent of Morgan County Schools, September 25, 1908; and C.C. Adams, superintendent of Schools, Grant County, Kentucky, to Coral Wilson Stewart, October 7, 1908, CWS Papers, Box 2, UK.

11. O.F. Gray, superintendent of Elliot County Schools, to Cora Wilson Stewart, August 12, 1910, CWS Papers, Box 2, UK.

12. Kentucky Educational Association, *Proceedings of the Fortieth Annual Session* (Louisville, 1911), p. 9. A brief chronology of some of Cora Wilson Stewart's achievements introduces the index to the Cora Wilson Stewart Papers. See "Biographical Information." CWS Papers, Index, UK. See also Helen Deiss Irwin, *Women in Kentucky* (Lexington: The University Press of

Kentucky, 1979), pp. 119-20.

13. Everett L. Dicks to Cora Wilson Stewart, June 30, 1911, and J.G. Crabbe, President of Kentucky Normal School, To Cora Wilson Stewart, July 6, 1911. CWS Papers, Box 2, UK. See Also J.S. Dickey, president, Bowling Green Business University, to Cora Wilson Stewart, July 30, 1911, E.C. McDougle to Cora Wilson Stewart, June 30, 1911, and W.C. Kozes, superintendent of Carter County Schools, to Cora Wilson Stewart, July 1, 1911. CWS Papers, Box 2, UK.

14. U.S. Census Bureau,*Thirteenth Census of the United States* (1910) *Population,* vol. 2, p. 749.

15. Stewart, *Moonlight Schools,* pp. 8-13.

16. Ibid.

17. Glenna Flannery Gearhart, interview, December 12, 1979; Stewart, *Moonlight Schools,* Chap. 3; Sherman Porter, Managing editor of the Lexington *Herald,* to Cora Wilson Stewart, July 29, 1912, CWS Papers, Box 2, UK; Conie Mauk Foster, interview, January 4, 1979.

18. Stewart, *Moonlight Schools,* pp. 21-31; Glenna Flannery Gearhart, interview, December 12, 1979.

19 .Stewart, *Moonlight Schools,* pp. 32-37; George T. Young, interview, November 19, 1979. Mrs. Lafon Riker, chairman of the Health Committee of the Kentucky Federation of Women's Clubs to Cora Wilson Stewart, February 9, 1914, CWS Papers, Box 2, UK.

20. Stewart, *Moonlight Schools*, pp. 38-46; Glenna Flannery Gearhart, interview, December 12, 1979; Louisville *Courier Journal,* December 29, 1912.

21. Stewart, *Moonlight Schools,* 47-56.

22. Ibid, p. 55; Louisville *Courier Journal,* February 18, 1912.

23. Stewart, *Moonlight Schools,* pp. 57-69.

24. Cora Wilson Stewart to Governor James B. McCreary, December 16, 1913, and McCreary to Stewart, February 19, 1914, quoted in Stewart, *Moonlight Schools,* pp. 56-61; Lexington *Herald,* February 12, 1914 and Frankfort *State Journal,* February 14, 1914. Kentucky Illiteracy Commission, First Biennial Report, 1914-1915 (Louisville, 1916), p. 8.

25. Glenna Flannery Gearhart, interview, December 12, 1979; Stewart, *Moonlight Schools,* pp. 62-63.

26. Cora Wilson Stewart, *Country Life Reader, First Book* (Atlantic: B.F. Johnson Publishing Company, 1915).

27. Stewart, *Moonlight Schools,* p. 82, see also pp. 145-194.

28. Cora Wilson Stewart, president, Kentucky Illiteracy Commission, "To The Teachers of Kentucky," n.d., quoted in Stewart, *Moonlight Schools,* pp. 82-85.

29. Stewart, *Moonlight Schools,* pp. 81-105.

30. Cora Wilson Stewart, *The Soldier's First Book* (New York: Association Press, 1918.

31. Stewart, *Moonlight Schools,* pp. 81-105, esp. p. 97.

32. Ibid, pp. 101-3.

33. Ibid, pp. 103-5.

34. See a poster proclaiming "public speaking tonight at the Presbyterian Church, 7:30, Mrs. Cora Wilson Stewart, eloquent Kentucky woman, and Sergeant Sandlin, famous World War speaker, on the most interesting topics of the day." CWS Papers, Box 1, UK. On September 26, 1918, Sergeant Willie Sandlin single-handedly destroyed three German machine gun nests and killed twenty-four German soldiers. See Harry M. Caudill's Boone Day Address, "Eastern Kentucky and the History of our Commonwealth," *The Register of the Kentucky Historical Society* 79 (Autumn 1979): 291.

35. Stewart, *Moonlight Schools,* pp. 112,117, and 112; Nelms, "Crusader Against Illiteracy," Chap. 3.

36. Stewart, *Moonlight Schools,* chap. 12, passim. The Cora Wilson Stewart Papers, housed in University of Kentucky libraries, contain a wealth of informantion, including letters and photographs, of the "Moonlight School" adaptation in other states.

37. For more detail, see Nelms, "Crusader Against Illiteracy," chap. 4.

38. CWS Papers UK; Nelms, "Crusader Against Illiteracy," chap. 5.

39. "Biographical File," CWS Papers UK.

40. CWS Papers, Box 1, UK; Rose, ed., "The Cora Wilson Stewart Moonlight Schoolhouse," The Cora Wilson Stewart Moonlight Schoolhouse contains several show case displays of Stewart memorabilia.

To commemorate her efforts in the state, national, and international crusade against illiteracy, Morehead State University acquired and restored the one-room school where Cora Wilson Stewart began her teaching career. The "Little Brushy School" stands on the university campus today as a museum and monument to her work and a constant reminder to the educators who continue her mission of educational services in the mountain regions of Kentucky.

UNTYING SOME KNOTS IN KNOTT COUNTY: TWO EDUCATIONAL EXPERIMENTS IN EASTERN KENTUCKY

William Terrell Cornett

Abstract

In 1902 the first rural "settlement" institution in America opened its doors at Hindman, Knott County, Kentucky. Twenty-one years later, Alice Lloyd began her junior college on nearby Caney Creek, an extension of the settlement school idea into higher education. Together these two educational facilities have long experiemented with solutions that would untie some of the persistently knotty cultural, social, educational, financial, and governmental problems which have plagued this and other eastern Kentucky counties.

Begun as a charity mission, yet with high vocational and academic standards, these Appalachian schools, having adapted to changing times and new demands, still serve as educational models.

As counties go, Knott County in eastern Kentucky was typical of much of rural Appalachia at the turn of the century: small in area and in population, rather isolated, conservative, and economically deficient. Not the kind of place suited for true innovation, most onlookers would have guessed. Yet by the time the first quarter of the new century drew to a close, the societal, occupational, and mental complexion of Knott and surrounding counties had begun to change — overtly due to the coming of large scale coal-mining operations, but just as importantly (however less noticeably) because of the success of two educational experiments in Knott County.

Conducted within eight miles of one another, established under similar circumstances and for somewhat similar reasons, these two experiments in mountain education constitute a remarkable page in Appalachian and in American history. Both were carried out by dynamic, headstrong Victorian women who faced nearly impossible odds, and whose intelligence, compassion, and single-mindedness brought the success they so desperately hoped for. These two experiments were called the Women's Christian Temperance Union (WCTU) School and the Caney Creek Community Center School. But they were more than what either name implied; they were nothing less than new ways of life for the mountains.

Today the names are changed but their sense of mission remains. The WCTU School became Hindman Settlement School (at Hindman, Kentucky), while the Caney Creek Community Center School (at Pippa Passes, Kentucky) is now better known as Alice Lloyd College.

In this study we will look at similarities and differences between these two schools, and at some of the ways (many times radically innovative, but occasionally reactionary) that each approached the common goal of untying some of the knotty social, vocational, and educational problems of Knott County and its surroundings.

Knott County, Kentucky, was created in 1884, the 119th (or next to last) county to be formed in Kentucky, and was named for the incumbent governor, James Proctor Knott. For the first decade and a half of the county's existence, life continued in its accustomed pattern. Moonshining and internecine warfare vied with the legal trades of farming, logging, and hunting as the principal occupations of the people. Isolation prevailed. Then in 1899 an eighty-year old man named Solomon Everidge set in motion a process that quietly changed that old order once and for all. That summer two wealthy young central Kentucky women, May Stone (1867?-1946) and Katherine Pettit (1869-1936) came to Hazard in neighboring Perry County and set up tents from which to operate mini-courses in practical homemaking and the three R's. Having heard of their goings-on, and possessing the stamina to walk twenty-two miles barefoot, the patriarchal "Uncle Solomon" came from Hindman to watch. The novelist Lucy Furman later created an account of how Everidge, after observing the two women all day, expressed his eagerness to have them start a school in his own area:

> "When I were just a little chunk of a shirttail boy, hoeing corn on yon hillsides, I would look up Troublesome, and down Troublesome, and wonder if anybody would come in to larn us anything. And as I got older I follered praying for somebody to come. I growed up, nobody come. My offsprings, to grands and greats growed up; still nobody come. And times a getting wusser everyday---" "Would they come?" he asked.[1]

The women did not get to Hindman at the forks of Troublesome immediately. Two other summer camps were held before the women with their "brought-on cloth houses" (the tents) fulfilled Uncle Solomon's request. The year was now 1902. Miss Stone and Miss Pettit soon marshalled much local support--not in money--but in gifts of land, building supplies, and promises of labor from Uncle Solomon's neighbors, and the WCTU School was begun in earnest.

Although both were Wellesley graduates, the two women (who were beginning to be called "the quare women" by the locals because of their unconventional, unmarried lifestyles and because of a streak of seeming impracticality) had very limited training and experience as teachers. But they approached their new work with hope and determination. They responded vigorously to what historian Arnold Toynbee referred to as the nineteenth-century doctrine of "challenge". The new school deep in the backwoods was surely a real-enough challenge, but it was also a "mission" in something of the same sense that other mountain schools, established by religious denominations, were seen to be. Not only would the WCTU provide "uplift" by means of general and, in particular, vocational education, it would also attempt to instill hatred for drinking and feuding. In those early years success with the quality of temperance came slowly. Although the feuds (such as the Jones-Wright war) had largely passed anyway, in 1915 the WCTU School renamed itself the Hindman Settlement School, in no small degree because the very obvious "temperance" part of their uplift program had generated considerable local resentment and because the other member groups of the State Federation of Women's Clubs of Kentucky were also major co-sponsors.

The most obvious need for the change in name came about fittingly, because it was realized how much like the experimental Toynbee Hall (in London) and Jane Addams' Hull House (in Chicago) the Knott County school had become. The two urban institutions were called "settlements" since the founders had settled among the working class poor, and offered classes in language, sanitation and health care, practical trades, and domesticity to all who would "improve" themselves. The school at Hindman was seen more or less as a rural counterpart of these endeavors, and thus Hindman Settlement School became the first rural "settlement" institution in America and in the world.[2] The new name was doubly appropriate since in mountain speech a "settlement" was a small town. By 1915 Hindman was certainly that, and at the school there were enough buildings to pass for a town itself.

The school begun in 1902 at Hindman was not the first one the town had known. In the 1890s "Professor" George Clarke had maintained a "subscription school" for elementary students, but this attempt had been beset with constant problems. His old classroom building became one of the new schools first structures. Apparently local residents (such as Uncle Solomon Everidge) wanted a school that had a broader-based curriculum and more signs of permanence than the Clarke school show at that time.

The new school started by "the quare women" was located on the right fork of Troublesome Creek, a few hundred yards from the main street of downtown Hindman. The situation of the school on a floodplain of the unpredictable and aptly-named creek posed many difficulties later. (Finally, after a series of both fires and floods, the school was slowly rebuilt on higher ground.) In 1902, however, all these problems were in the future. The immediate problem was that of proper staffing. Word of mouth had assured enough students, but Miss Stone and Miss Pettit had to find teachers with the same spirit of adventure that they shared. Through college friendships and letter-writing they soon had a faculty, and this informal employment procedure continued for several years. Almost all these early staff members were women. They were graduates of impressive schools: Wellesley, Vassar, Mt. Holyoke, Bryn Mawr. And they were promised little pay.

One of the first to respond to the call was Lucy Furman (1870-1958), a western Kentucky writer whose upcoming books and articles were to be thinly disguised fictions concerning events and persons in Knott County. Her writings, one of which was mentioned previously, will be discussed in more detail momentarily. Soon came Ann Cobb (1886-1960) and Elizabeth Watts (born 1890), who, along with Furman, devoted practically their entire working lives to the school. Many others came for short stints--some of them simply donating their time.

With students and teachers secured, the school entered into its life of service. An elementary program was established for the youth of the county. Plans for a high school were drafted. Thoughts were given to preparing young people for college. But the heart of the Hindman Settlement offerings was an industrial arts program which, in many ways, was the forerunner of the modern vocational-technical school. Typical courses along these lines included scientific farming, animal husbandry, blacksmithing, woodworking, use of machines and tools, practical electricity, and applied mathematics. As male students moved along in the elementary grades, they began such specialization. Girls were on a basically separate-but-equal footing. Classes for them were typically provided in general housekeeping, sewing, weaving, basketmaking, (a course also open to men), cooking, personal hygiene, and manners. Every student fit in somewhere, if not all that well in the classes, at least in the mandatory work program. All students worked, regardless of background work--sometimes as much as four hours a day, depending on the need. This work was the principal fee exacted by the school from its students. In most cases this arrangement was the only means for them to attend and pay room and board. And since the school existed by private donations alone, a steady work program assured that the Hindman Settlement School would at least have an ongoing program of maintenance.

While it is true that the school at Hindman emphasized manual training and good homemaking as its overriding educational concerns, it should not be inferred that academic subjects were neglected. As students advanced from grade school classes through high school they were met with an array of courses ranging from American history to Latin. That the humanities were stressed is made clear in the comment made by a 1920 graduate named Guy Crawford, who remarked in an interview that the teachers at Hindman made him take "a lot of Latin, English, and stuff like that--which I didn't need--and not enough math and science--which they didn't have much of."[3] Such early graduates as folklorist Josiah H. Combs, the first Kentuckian to receive a Ph.D. at the Sorbonne, attest to the concern which the humanities received in the overall Hindman program.

It has been shown how, in the early days, Hindman School set out to fight drinking and feuding. Out of this same reforming spirit came the emphasis on church attendance. Students had a choice of denominations, but they had to go to church each Sunday they remained on campus; and for many years students attended a sort of Sunday evening Bible school--also required. The Hindman Settlement was never actually a mission school like those founded in the surrounding area by Dr. E. O. Guerrant and the Rev. Harvey Murdoch, but there always was an atmosphere of mainstream Protestant Christianity.[4] Some of the more recent criticism of the school has been directed at this type of religious climate, in part because of a certain denial of the value of local fundamentalist religion by the Hindman staff. However, this aspect was not necessarily the end-product, as some revisionist historians have charged, of a colonialistic mind-set.

Nor was the cultural fabric the school found itself imbedded in all that scorned. The basketmaking, weaving, and other "fireside industries" stressed traditional mountain patterns of design. And there was a careful cultivation of folksong and folkdance material. As early as 1907 Katherine Pettit was sending off locally collected songs to Harvard's George Lyman Kittredge and to nationally prestigious folklore journals. In 1917 musicologist Cecil Sharp spent some time at Hindman uncovering there some of the oldest and most fascinating ballads on his American collecting tour. Others interested in capturing disappearing folkways--such as novelist John Fox, Jr., folk-scholar Olive Dame Campbell, and photographer Doris Ulmann--visited the Settlement in those early years.

It was this early interest in folk studies which soon motivated several faculty members to try their skills at writing. Lucy Furman was the prime example of the Hindman-inspired author. Direct from her experiences at the school came *Mothering on Perilous* (1913), *Sight to the Blind* (1914), *The Quare Women* (1923), *The Glass Window* (1925), and *The Lonesome Road* (1927). Each was published by reputable Boston or New York firms. (Miss Furman had already produced *Stories of a Sanctified Town* in 1896, but it is for her writings about the mountains that she is remembered.) Ann Cobb's *Kinfolks,* a book of dialect poetry, was published by Houghton Mifflin in 1922. Don West (born 1907) wrote many of the poems in *Crab Grass* (1931) while employed at Hindman. James Still (born 1906) spent many years at the Settlement, as librarian and teacher. From his stay there and from his forays into the surrounding countryside came *Hounds on the Mountain* (verse, 1937), *River of Earth* (novel 1940), and *On Troublesome Creek* (short stories, 1941), plus some of his subsequent writings, (Still gained a national reputation early, and he remains, of course, one of southern Appalachia's most honored living writers.) These and other members of the Hindman faculty also published much in magazines and journals (most of it presently uncollected), and assured that their school would maintain a high degree of intellectual ferment. Thus the experiment at Hindman achieved results surely unimagined at its beginning in 1902.

In that first quarter century or so the physical plant of the school greatly expanded. From log cabins and cheap board-and-batten structures rose substantial buildings of hamsome stone and solid weatherboarding. The wooden buildings were almost invariably painted a dark brown to blend in with the earth and surrounding greenery. Uncle Solomon's gray old cabin was preserved as a museum and sales office. A school farm put food in the dining hall tables. Graduates of the manual training programs found jobs with the coal companies or could confidently pursue self-employment. Schoolteachers, engineers, doctors, nurses, lawyers, bankers, writers, singers, housewives, church workers, and farm agents were set on their career paths at Hindman. Congressman Carl D. Perkins (born 1912), some members of "the Singing Family of the Cumberlands" - the Ritches (including Jean), vocational education leader Walter Prater (born 1920) and poet Albert Stewart (born 1914) all attended Hindman Settlement School. By 1930 it was apparent that the experiment was a success. The school thrived well enough as the depression gripped the country. The recently formed public school systems of Knott County and her neighbors could even begin to pick up some of the programs that the Settlement had initiated, reminding one of Elizabeth Watts's oft-repeated words that "the best social workers are those who work themselves out of a job."

The success of Hindman Settlement School prompted similar institutions to come into being. The first direct offspring of Hindman was Pine Mountain Settlement School, opened in 1913 in Harlan County, Kentucky, by Katherine Pettit. The John C. Campbell Folk School, created by Olive Dame Campbell in 1925 at Brasstown, North Carolina, bore something of the Hindman stamp, although Hindman never thought of itself as a folk school in the Danish sense, as did Brasstown. Grade schools and high schools sprang up all over the Hindman service area after the school proved itself a lasting and not a temporary experiment, and after state public school funding became more of an economic reality. Yet of all the trails of social change the Settlement helped blaze, that which opened in 1916 to one Boston-born visitor to Knott County was perhaps the most promising.

Alice Lloyd (1876-1962) and her mother, Ella Geddes (1851-1945), had come by horse and buggy to Ivis, about three miles southwest of Hindman by the summer of 1916 to an unused Presbyterian outreach mission post called Hope Cottage. From there the two women hoped to engage in social work for a time and to escape the debilitating effects of the Massachusetts winters. Both the Geddes and the Lloyd families had been fairly monied, but by the time the two women arrived at Ivis their resources had been seriously depleted, so much so that Mr. Lloyd planned to remain in Boston and pursue his career. Even from the vantage point of our time, the childless Mrs. Lloyd appears quite modern and certainly "liberated"--not only in the manner of her separation from her husband, but also due to her unusual background as editor of a female-produced newspaper called *The Cambridge Women's Chronicle,* and as a reporter for the *Boston Globe* and other New England journals. She neither came to teach nor to stay. She primarily entered eastern Kentucky to regain her health, to perform a limited amount of social service, and, since she was an amateur sociologist, to study the local mountaineers--"natives," as she called them. A bout with spinal meningitis had left her tired and her right side partially paralyzed. She came south to rest and, hearing of the availability of a rent-free house from a Boston church group, decided to come to Knott

County.

Then, in almost no time, her plans were changed and she had found an entirely new calling; and just as suddenly her personal problems took a back seat. In the fall of 1916 an illiterate but persuasive dirt farmer from nearby Caney Creek appeared at the door of Hope Cottage and began to work the same sort of spell on Mrs. Lloyd and Mrs. Geddes that Uncle Solomon Everidge had on the women with the "cloth houses" seventeen years earlier. If they would come and start a school on his creek, fifty-year-old Abisha Johnson asked, then he would let them have some of his land free, for as long as they wished it. Johnson wanted his children and his neighbors' children to get the education others were receiving in Knott County; so he had come to ask these educated "furriners" for their help. Distances were long in Knott County in 1916, and he did not want the Caney children to have to board at Hindman and elsewhere — he wanted a new school. (An apocryphal story tells of "Bysh" Johnson remarking that he wanted his children to grow up "not liken the hog, but unliken the hog," and that a 'vision' sent him to the women.)⁵ The request from this "Summonser," as Alice Lloyd later called him, was no doubt both shocking and thrilling. The answer, after some deliberation, was yes, and the spring of 1917 found Mrs. Lloyd and her mother snugly ensconced in a tiny board-and batten-shack on Johnson's land not far from the head of Caney Creek, ready to begin work.

Letters and other recorded statements from Mrs. Lloyd indicate that she held a number of views closely akin to Social Darwinism, especially in regard to genetics. She also possessed something of the sociologist's defeatism when confronted with cultural imbreeding, as well. But being the Puritan that she was, she saw a chance for success, and she drew pleasure from the rejuvenating possibilities of such a challenge. Although a Radcliffe product, she was not a licensed teacher. Nevertheless, her strong grounding in classical education and her awareness of modern pedagogical trends gleaned from reading left her not entirely unsuited for the task. Her most outstanding assets, though, were her stubbornness and her leadership ability. And leadership was what she was most interested in. As her fledgling school got underway in her home (now referred to as the "Founder's Shack") she wrote dozens of letters on her Oliver No. 9 typewriter to college friends and Boston acquaintances, for books, clothes, money, and teachers. "The leaders are here" was her constant refrain. Not only could boys and girls be trained to do manual tasks and homemaking, they could also learn to take on the work of area leadership and service promoted by stiff academics--but not all boys and girls. She was interested in helping those of obvious superiority--and those she determined herself.

The requests sent out in her letters were soon filled. Local children enrolled in the school. With land secured, dormitory and classroom buildings were erected on the narrow bottom land along the creek; pole-supported buildings climbed the hillsides. Caney Creek families donated labor, materials, and food --just as in the early days at Hindman. Since Alice Lloyd promised to stay out of the community's religion, politics, and moonshining, she got along quite well in her new surroundings--so well, in fact, that she opened a new building called the Caney Creek Community Center. From this building Mrs. Lloyd administered her elementary school, founded a high school and, in 1923, a junior college, ran a clothing exchange, oversaw manual training classes, distributed Christmas presents to needy children, established an outreach program, and engaged visitors of all kinds. (The term "community center" remained submerged as a decription for her particular brand of social improvement until the 1960s when the Federal Government's War on Poverty made it a part of the new bureaucratic jargon.) By the time her students had progressed to the point of needing the creation of the Caney Junior College in 1923, her community center was developing into the "sociological laboratory" she had envisioned.

It no doubt looked like folly to many to open a college on Caney Creek in 1923, but the good experiences with her other schools caused Alice Lloyd to remain optimistic. The need for an area college was great. Students were not that hard to get; indeed, there was soon a waiting list. Well-trained teachers, such as June Buchanan (born 1893?), who helped initiate the college program, came for short sojourns but stayed much longer. From the beginning the college curriculum took pre-emption over the older elementary and secondary schools departments and arts and crafts program. And the contrasts between the Caney way and Hindman way were considerable. Besides the usual strictures of no smoking, drinking, guns, or gambling, Mrs. Lloyd added "no unauthorized meetings with the opposite sex." This requirement was one of the best-known tenets of the school on Caney Creek, only to be relaxed at Mrs. Lloyd's death in the early 1960s. The idea of mandatory uniforms, which Hindman had only toyed with, became a reality at Caney. (This rule was also allowed to lapse shortly after Mrs. Lloyd died.) Daring young men often circumvented Mrs. Lloyd's no-dating rule by climbing a tree next to the girls' dormitory at night. This was known as "wahooing." But woe unto him who was caught wahooing! Expulsion was the general sentence. The uniform for girls consisted of the old-fashioned New England boarding school apparel of long white skirts, white middies, knee socks, and low-heeled shoes. The boys were expected to wear coats and pants of subdued colors, white shirts, and neckties-to classes and to meals. Mrs. Lloyd justified the non-romantic requirement by saying courtship interfered with studies and might lead to marital inbreeding (since many students were blood relatives). She defended her stance on uniforms by invoking the name of democracy.

At Caney Junior College humanities and social studies were emphasized. There was a great interest in drama and music--although few of the productions dealt with mountain material, as often did the faculty-written plays at Hindman's Christmas and May Day celebrations. (Later, however, the Student Crusades and Voices of Appalachia Choir stressed the Appalachian experience in their national tours.) As at Hindman, students were poor and a work program was central in defraying costs. Teacher-training was early seen as the prime duty of the college. Then followed commitment to pre-law and premedical courses of study. The school's early graduates were often sent to such schools as Harvard and Tulane, but after Mrs. Lloyd purchased the Caney Cottage in Lexington, Kentucky, for her scholarship students (generally male), most Caney associate-degree holders went to the University of Kentucky. An unwritten pledge, no longer in effect, required Caney graduates to return to the mountains.

Throughout the twenties and thirties Hindman Settlement School and Caney Junior College often stood in basically friendly competition with one another, especially in assisting the opening of other schools in the area. The heads of the two schools occasionally had personality clashes, but amicable relations were usually soon restored. As the two schools entered the forties the feelings of contention subsided as it was observed that the clientele of each diverged more and more. The 1950s as had the 1930s brought some degree of hard times to both institutions--enrollments declined, donations diminished, and the need for their particular kind of education lessened. The early 1960s forced Hindman Settlement School to phase out its boarding program, and more and more of the old responsibilities were taken over by the county school system. In later years the Settlement functioned more as a secondary school; therefore, plans for the now-completed Knott County Central High School practically sounded the death knell of the school as it was. In similar fashion Mrs. Lloyd's school had to deal with competiton from the new University of Kentucky community college system and other private and state-supported regional universities. However, the 1960s were years of seeking alternative forms to so-called assembly-line education. Because of those needs both schools survived: Hindman Settlement to become more oriented towards community arts, crafts, and recreations programs; Caney Junior College (renamed Alice Lloyd College at the founder's death) to move towards an emphasis on Appalachian Studies and developing four-year status. Although greatly changed, both schools still make their contributions with much of the old tone of purpose.

It would be hard to imagine eastern Kentucky today without the impact of the two schools. Those who believe in the vacuum theory of social groups would say others would have come into the area and done much as Miss Stone, Miss Pettit, and Mrs. Lloyd. Perhaps so, but any substitutes would have been, of necessity, clearly different. Would others have stayed as long? Would there have been another woman with the iron will of Alice Lloyd, or another Ella Geddes, starting her life over at 65? Maybe such speculation is idle, but why did so many of the denominational schools in the area fail when these two succeeded? Why did the nearby Carr Creek Center School, sponsored as an experiment by the Daughters of the American Revolution, have to close relatively soon after opening? Why did so few writers come from the faculties of the other schools?

Alice Lloyd College lays claim, among others, to folklorist Marie Campbell (born 1900), poet William Howard Cohen (born 1927), Homespun Winter Verna Mae Slone (born 1914), and the *Appalachian Heritage* Magazine, edited by poet Albert Stewart (born 1914). Why were so few well-known alumni (such as Congressman Carl D. Perkins, who attended both Hindman and Alice Lloyd) produced by the denominational schools? If, in reference to the definition of the Southern Regional Education Board, a settlement insititution in the Southern Appalachians is "a private, nonprofit, rural organization designed to promote and provide programs, services, and development with the immediate community or nearby surrounding area in which it is located," then, perhaps, the other schools did not promote and provide what was really wanted by the community or area. Perhaps it was simply survival of the fittest. For whatever reason, though, Hindman Settlement School and Alice Lloyd College thrived.

Today the two schools still teach, as we move toward the twenty-first century. Both have young, dynamic leaders who are hopeful and pragmatic. From the Settlement go art, music, and recreation teachers to add new dimensions to local public school instruction. Alice Lloyd College belongs to an outreach program called ALCOR, (which originally stood for Alice Lloyd College Outreach), and operates the highly respected Appalachian Learning Laboratory (APPLAB)--an oral history project and photographic archives.

Some have called these schools anachronisms. But the donors would not agree, nor would the alumni. As long as these schools perform needed services, why should they close?

Today the appearance of austerity has left both schools. Both are more stable financially and both have new building progams underway. There is an easy relationship between the institutions. For example the present director of the Hindmand Settlement formerly headed by APPLAB at Alice Lloyd College, and Albert Stewart of Alice Lloyd's *Appalachian-Heritage* conducts the Appalachian Writers' Workshop at Hindman each summer. Such cooperation augurs well for the future of these two private, nonsectarian schools.

On Alice Lloyd's grave at Pippa Passes (so named by Mrs. Lloyd in celebration of a Robert Browning poem) can be seen the quote: "All service ranks the same with God." Perhaps that sentence would be the fitting epitaph for the visionary founders of both schools. Their service to the poor, but deserving, mountain students might seem outdated, their upper middle-class values grating, yet their attempts to forge bonds of friendship and service were sincere. Their achievements were incredible, considering the odds. The schools these women founded can claim the distinctions of being both firsts of a kind and continuing success stories today.

NOTES

The author wishes to thank Mr. Michael L. Mullins, Executive Director of Hindman Settlement School, Dr. Jerry C. Davis, president of Alice Lloyd College, Miss June Buchanan, Mrs. Charlotte Madden, Mr. Albert F. Stewart, and Mrs. Grey Crawford for their cooperation toward research in this paper.

1. Lucy Furman, *The Quare Women* (Boston: The Atlantic Press, 1923), p. 20.
2. Lucy Furman, Afterword to *Sight to the Blind* (New York: The Macmillan Company, 1914), p. 77.
3. Interview with Guy Crawford, Whitesburg, Kentucky, January 27, 1980. Crawford is a retired civil engineer.
4. Guerrant established several Presbyterian high schools and academies, and Murdoch founded Buckhorn School and Witherspoon College.
5. Interview with June Buchanan, Pippa Passes, Kentucky, December 12, 1979.

V: Values and Culture in Appalachia

POETRY AT THE PERIPHERY:
The Possibility of People's Culture in Appalachia*

by P. J. Laska

Abstract

> The paper addresses the rise of regionalism and cultural pluralism as the major feature of American cultural life of the past decade. Poetry is seen as the bellwether of these tendencies in the arts. The evidence of a review of the seventies shows a major break with the past, so much so that an anthology like Donald Hall's **Contemporary American Poetry** (1972) would appear today changed beyond recognition. Poetry developments in Appalachia have been at the forefront of these changes in the American literary scene.
>
> The paper examines some of the reasons that lie behind this "decade of dispersal." This discussion is followed by a conceptualization of the present that sees regionalism offering new possibilities for the renewal of the genuine peoples culture of Appalachia.

* Although an editorial decision was made not to publish papers that had appeared in earlier publications, "Poetry at the Periphery" was accepted for publication in this volume prior to its publication in another journal. The Editor thanks the *West Virginia Art New* and *Hyperion* for granting permission to reprint this article.

Introduction

There are those for whom Appalachian culture is no more than "a region of the heart." The metaphor here is one of emotion and feeling, rather than one of perception of reality. The suggestion is that Appalachian culture is more past than present and more desire than fulfillment, and that therefore, it is accessible only as folk culture. In this paper I suggest a different approach to Appalachian culture, one that links the folk and heritage concepts to the idea of a living people's culture. What I mean by "people's culture" is something significantly different from mass culture and something clearly distant from the elitist culture of modernism. In Appalachia it includes the surviving part of that native folk culture that once gave a degree of identity and unity to life in these mountains. I don't want to get into a debate over the extent to which what is living about the culture exists as remenant of a way of life that has been broken up by the twin forces of industrialization and modernization.[1] The important question for my purposes is whether these remnants and the tremendous enthusiasm for them will develop a living value in the present, and whether "the mountain experience" and the "things Appalachian" will encompass reality as well as history. At this juncture I think it is the poets of the region who are pressing this question upon us, and what follows is my attempt to explain the significance of their work.

I

Side by side with the pursuit of heritage and regional self-consiousness, which has been largely a scholarly, intellectual effort, there has been a virtual explosion of activity on the part of writers and poets of the region. One critic has written recently that, "Poems are pouring out of the region as if a sensitive nerve had been touched."[2] He wonders whether all this activity will ultimately be classified as a famous literary movement. My own view is that something more basic, more revolutionary than a mere interest in literature is behind this upsurge. The outpouring of poetry in Appalachia in the past decade is part of a larger development which we have begun to see in the cultural life of the country. I would argue that in the past decade Appalachian poets have been at the forefront of a significant change emerging in American cultural life--a change that constitutes a major break with the past and with the cultural hegemony of urban modernism.

To substantiate this rather large assertion I offer the following brief survey, which will probably not convince anyone but may enable me to get a foot in the door. An urban cultural hierarchy has been in place in this country since at least the early fifties, probably since the War period. Politically, it has been decidedly right-wing, or very conservative, as has been the dominant politics of the nation. In the early fifties what survived of a left-wing cultural opposition was driven into hiding by a right-wing hysteria that came damn close to elevating another Hitler (some say he later came to power only to be dethroned by newspaper reporters). This cultural opposition has been slow in its return to public life. The "Beat Movement," which began in the fifties was not left-wing. It was hardly political at all. It was, however, opposed to the formalism and careerism of the established poets clustered around American universities. This urban cultural hierarchy had at the time enough power to reduce any cultural movement that rejected its standards of taste to the status of a *peripheral* phenomenon. And this is what happened, in spite of the media interest in the Beats. The net effect of non-recognition and ridicule was a status of cultural pariah for a whole group of writers whose literature and life-style flouted the dominant cultural values. Donald Hall's influential anthology of American poets, originally published in 1962, contained no Beats, no blacks and few women. The upheavals of the sixties brought a change to this picture of the contemporary poetry scene. In the second edition of his *Contemporary American Poetry* (1972),[3] Hall added more poets, including Allen Ginsberg, whom he admits having misjudged. More importantly, though, he included two black poets and was turned down by a third (Amiri Baraka, then Leroi Jones).

This little background survey illustrates what is an obvious truth to many, that social forces are the strength of cultural forces. It is also a truth that is born out by developments of the seventies. The seventies have seen a continuation of social upheaval in America centered around the family and racial and ethnic identity. I think it is fair to say that if Hall were to attempt a new edition of his anthology for the seventies it would have to include some of the poetry from these movements, more from the black and women's movements and also perhaps from the American Indian movement, each of which has generated several anthologies of poetry. Toward the latter part of the seventies there has also appeared a lot of poetry to which the Canadian poet Tom Wayman has given the label, "New Realism." Wayman has anthologized some of this work in two collections of Canadian poetry [4] and is now putting together a third anthology of "new realism" poetry in the U.S. He uses the rather narrow rule of selecting poetry by poets who have worked at the jobs they write about. In the U.S. there are an increasing number of the little poetry magazines that feature what we could call "new realism" poetry in a broader sense than Wayman's. Some of the ones I have seen are *Quindaro* (Kansas City), *Cultural Corespondence* (Providence, R.I.), *Working Cultures* (Washington, D.C.),

West End and *Nostoc* (Boston), *Main Trend* (New York), and *The Unrealist*. Also, established literary journals lke *Minnesota Review, Praxis* and *Left Curve* all feature poetry which embodies social and historical perspectives and which recognizes that we are social beings shaped by the labor and technology of our metabolism with nature.

An anthology of the seventies would also have to take account of the rise of regionalism in American culture. The poetry upsurge in Appalachia is contemporary with a revival of poetry in other regions of the country. Regional markets for poetry are evident all across the country, and these markets are in fact part of the mainstay of the small press publishing business. As a result certain poets have a large following in the area in which they live and publish but are virtually unknown or attract little interest outside that area. This is the case, for example, with Charles Bukowski in southern California, Ann Darr in Washington, D.C., and Tom McGrath in Minnesota, although the latter also has a reputation as a political poet going back to the fifties. I include the large urban centers as regions in the sense that there is a localized poetry audience listening to poets in their midst. The "region" can be entirely ersatz in this sense. Away from the urban centers we find poets taking localism more seriously than as a literary game, some to the point of becoming consciously regionalist. It is difficult to imagine the work of Vincent Ferrini apart from the Gloucester's fisherman and the Cape Ann area of Massachusetts. In his latest book, *Know Fish*,[5] Ferrini returns to the Italian-English dialect of his immigrant parents and writes some of his best poems. David Budbill, a regional poet in northern New England, is another example of a poet who uses dialect. In his book, *The Chain-Saw Dance*,[6] he writes of the people of the northern Appalachian mountains and reproduces some of their speech.

This sort of thing is going on outside the national literary network. But network money, in the form of subsidies from the National Endowment for the Arts, has in the past couple of years made possible a number of anthologies based on some sort of geographical definition. California, New Jersey, New York, Washington, D.C. and its suburbs, even Hawaii, have all seen anthologies of their poets. In some cases they have more than one. So far, it has been in the heavily populated urban areas of the country that the money has tended to concentrate. The South, however, is represented by *White Trash*, an anthology whose catchy title belies its academic content. Although Appalachia has as lively a poetry scene as any of these other places we don't yet rate an anthology in the eyes of NEA. I've tried proposals without success, and so have others. There is much irony in the fact that Appalachia, whose poets probably have a stronger sense of regional identity than any other section of the country, cannot get support for a representative anthology.

There are reasons for this, of course. I suspect you are aware of them. Certain prejudices exist about the periphery and about the possibility of poetry or any other art this far from the "center." And perhaps there's something more. It comes out when you compare the tone and content of Appalachian poetry with that of other sections of the country, particularly with that of the national network and with that of various urban scenes. Take a production like *Mucked*, for example.[7] It is a small homemade anthology whose occasion was the disastrous flood of the Tug Fork River that nearly wiped out the town of Williamson. The dozen or so poets represented there are a good cross section although their best work may not be included. What is there, taken as a whole, is significant. Literary critics reading this poetry will notice that nostalgia and anger are the predominant tones and that politically and morally sensitive subjects are the main content. But unless these critics have some grounding in the region's history of struggle against exploitation, which has in one way or another affected the lives of everyone who has lived here, unless they have that, they will miss the importance of what is happening in this work. It is a form of art that, consciously or not, aspires to contribute to a form of life that is significantly different from what is accepted as everyday reality in the urban centers of power. These Appalachian poets, and others not represented here, are not involved in a mere literary game of getting into print, although what they are doing obviously has an important literary aspect. They are engaged in something more fundamental--a struggle to have a culture at all, a real culture that has a base in the life of the people and in which poetry becomes a folk form rather than an aspect of literary consciousness.

In the work of Appalachian poets with roots here the very conception of art seems different, not just because it is more political or more critical or more didactic, but because it seeks to break down the wall that separates literature from life.[8] It is art that seeks to be involved in the life of the people, and tries to do this at a time when there is very little poetry being written which commits itself to the world of people, and their history, their struggles and their work.[9] Our poets are therefore out of tune with most of what goes on in the national poetry network, and are by choice I think, closer to a regional, folk conception of art. When I look at the decaying modernist alternative, it seems to me a difference well worth encouraging.

II

We can look at what is happening in the country culturally from the side of the old, which is breaking up, or from the side of the new which is just beginning to appear. What is breaking up is the cultural hegemony of the metropolis. By this I mean specifically the rule of big city cultural life, its ability by controlling the production of art to define the standards of perception and taste, as well as the modes of enjoyment, in American society. What has appeared on the horizon to replace it is the regional focus of populist cultural developments that threaten to break down the traditional hierarchy in the arts and perhaps create new hierarchies in its place. The bureaucratic scaffolding for such regional hierarchies is already in place in many states. One's reaction to this cultural dialectic is likely determined by whether one's politics are populist or elitist. Those who lament the passing of the old order talk about the seventies as "a decade of dispersal," and argue, for example, that Robert Lowell is the last of the great American poets because of the scattering of cultural focus and the fracturing of the national audience. Daniel Bell, the sociologist who pronounced the end of ideology in the fifties, argues in a recent book that American society is experiencing a crisis of values and that the most pressing problem is the loss of the center.[10] He and others are concerned to re-establish the central clearing-house concept of culture even if it takes a new idealogy to do it. But the reaction of elitists to the breakup of the cultural core cannot be better illustrated than in the recent flap which saw NEA (National Endowment for the Arts) move to withdraw its block funding from CCLM (Coordinating Council of Literary Magazines) when the latter, dominated by small magazine editors, voted to disperse their monies in equal amounts to all applicants. With action equal to their conviction, the CCLM Board refused to sit in judgment of the relative merit of the various, diverse literary magazines around the country and thus refused to play the role of Pro-Tem Cultural God that had been alloted to them. For this betrayal of elitist trust and bureaucratic authority, the Board of CCLM was roundly criticized, castigated, and ridiculed. Now CCLM continues to dispense its monies under a different board that is willing to behave more like Guardians of the Poetic

Gate, but NEA moved to set up its own awards to applications from literary magazines, thus extending the control of its own panel of successful careerists in literature.

So the fight is on. The arts are no longer divorced from politics. And although Congress continues to appropriate large funds for the arts without much debate, the day of floor fights may not be far off. In an article last year entitled, "Post Post-Art Where Do We Go from Here?" Douglas Davis described our cultural situation as a problem of perception.[11] We are "tumbling into infinitely complex sub-sets...older, tighter structures are decentralizing, spreading...[and] we do not clearly perceive the premise behind the action." Davis sees elitist culture as posed at the end of modernism without being able to define what is "post-modern." This is a humbling experience for Davis, who concludes that, "Small has to be beautiful now." What I find interesting is that Davis takes for granted that the end of modernism means the end of progress. *Apres moi, le deluge.* "Each of the great Modernist states," he says, "is breaking into component parts, the reverse of the Global Village metaphor." As though he had looked into an abyss, Davis is engaged in the desperate search for a new metaphor to stem the tide of decentralization "Before we're engulfed." Those whose politics are of a populist bent are likely to view what is happening as a positive development which opens up new possibilities. The thought that never seems to occur in these decline-of-the-West discussions is that decentralization brings with it the possibility of genuine people's culture.

The unity of art and life that occurs in folk culture is utopian to modernists (with their conception of art as commodity and museum pieces) and they are unable to take it seriously. Yet from the Appalachian vantage point, in which the remnants of real folk culture are still immediate, it can be taken seriously. And those who do take it seriously will have a very different attitude to what is happening to modernist culture. My own attitude is summed up in the statement by John Berger that: Imperialism "can no longer accomodate reality."[12]

Berger was referring to the national wars of liberation in underdeveloped countries. But the point seems equally applicable to cultural imperialism inside the U.S. In a wide sense culture is the shared beliefs which inform our work and its shaping physical existence. Cultural pluralism allows many shapes and elaborations as real. The cultural imperialism of mass culture resulting in a bureaucratically controlled consumption, cannot permit any real pluralism because it would mean the end of the mass market in many areas of life. This imperialism has taken its toll on the psyche of the population. The results are evident in the alienation and unreality that people experience and in the proliferating psychological and religious attempts to counter the meaninglessness of everyday life.

The cultural life of a people cannot be successfully controlled or managed unless the power to shape life, *poesis* as the Greeks called it, is taken away from the people. *Poesis,* lies at the basis of culture. It is the origin of all art, literature, drama, and even of language and thought itself. Originally, folk artist only embodied and articulated what was the common creation of the whole people, *their style of life.* The people created the form of life, the artist recorded it through *mimesis.* It was an understanding of this that led Vico to say, for example, that "the Greek peoples were themselves Homer,"[13] by which he meant I take it that Homer was the recorder of the language and thought and actions of the early Greek peoples and that his poetry came from the people and was not, as the modern way of thinking makes us believe, from his personal invention.

For the purposes of power what matters is that *poesis* come under the control of an elite. This is an old story. In ancient times, the priestly caste maintained control of cultural life by guarding the secrets of the hieratic script. Written language for the few and the illteracy of masses over the centuries gave us a hieratic ideology which says that the power of *poesis* is the special gift of the few. In modern culture it is known as the gift of genius. Creative activity devolves upon certain exceptional individuals who become hierophantic figures. What is creative in the culture is supposed to exist in their work. The living culture of the folk, with its union of art and life, is broken up into an elite producing the "high art" of novel experiment on the one hand, and a mass culture entertainment industry on the other. Both are virtually empty of any real content.

The elitist "high art" defends itself against the charge of emptiness and irrelevance by the argument of art for art's sake, which says that the value of the work lies in how well it deals with its own challenge, and not in any articulation of human meaning and truth.[¹⁴] The argument uses the autonomy of art as an ideological defense. It says that the absence of the human dimension is not a permissible criticism. So long as there is something novel in the work to serve as evidence of genius, any reference of human reality is inessential. It sees no struggle between form and content or between reality and unreality because everything takes place on the side of the individual's imagination. The old dualism returns. What appears in the imagination somehow escapes "the withness of the body," to use Whitehead's phrase for our material condition.

But the dues have to be paid somewhere, and they are paid through loss of meaning. Obscure, meaningless, and trivial works of art come to predominate and art is alienated from the people. The proliferation of novelty in a void is a necessary consequence of the theory and its practice. And since the only judgment of any importance about the merit of these works concerns their intrinsic qualities, we naturally have to have a captian-critic to tell us whether a new work is metal or dross.[¹⁵]

It turns out that the problem with modern culture is the *cult*, that is, the hieratic clique. Historically, the tendency has been for the cult to dislodge the spontaneous genius of the people and install its own rules, which had something secret and mysterious about them. Now the opposite appears to be taking place. People's ignorance about the power of *poesis* withing themselves, and the cultural heritage of fear and self-deprecation that comes with ignorance, is giving way everywhere to interest in the arts. Also, in Appalachia the emergence of oral history, folklore, and heritage studies has begun to reclaim some public space and funds for what was once a flourishing people's culture. The decentralization toward regionalism is a positive development, full of possibility for bringing together art and life in the region. To paraphrase the words of the French poet, Tristan Tzara: Poetry being everywhere, it is necessary to give it back to the people, to all individuals.[¹⁶]

III

Folk culture and people's culture are not identical in concept, but I think they are closely interrelated. They are on a continuous line and I think it can be shown that what survives of the folk is part of people's culture. Both are populist conceptions of culture that reverse the elitist form. They are not derived from theory or ideology but arise in response to real needs. They develop around the interchange of artists and craftsman with the people. If Appalachian poetry is seen as inclusive of mountain folk, blues, gospel, and grass songs, as well as the songs of work and protest, then I think we can document this contiuous line. It's not something that I could attempt here, but it is something that should be attempted.

There is a tendency in modern poetry and modern criticism to pooh-pooh the song, to downgrade its aesthetic value as poetry. Modern poetry anthologies don't usually include songs that had popularity over the period covered by the anthology. I think this highlights the antilyrical, antipopulist bent of modern poetry. In the days of the oral tradition, prior to the book revolution, song was the main form for the poem to take. I'm not suggesting that the new Appalachian poets should all start writing songs. The song is only one form of poetry, and the limits of the musical form resulting from use of rime and fixed beat make it inappropriate for certain purposes. My point is that *thematically* the early Appalachian poetry, whose form is the song, is closely linked to the new poetry coming out of the hills. The folk themes and the political themes are inseparable because our people's lives have been and are now filled with struggle. When we get our representative anthology, I hope it will show this.

In the past the Appalachian poetry of song was an organic part of a genuine folk culture. The modernist break has been felt as the break *from* the lyric form.[17] This break was progressive in that it opened up new forms for poetic work, but the price was paid in terms of alienation because its avant garde experimentalism tended to downgrade the folk as passé and to set modern poetry apart from people's culture. It remains to be seen whether Appalachian poetry, which is now consciously finding itself, will become an integral part of that collectivity that the folk represents in a way that modern poetry could not. To become part of the life of the people it will have to be a poetry in which the poem responds not merely to the challenge to itself but responds to the felt but perhaps unarticulated needs of the people. What makes poetry valuable to the people is not the novel linguistic inventions but the experience of the people that is articulated. In this sense Tristan Tzara was right when he wrote: "All poetic work is valuable only to the extent that it is lived."[18]

The *poesis* at the basis of popular culture is both real and repressed. We can think of the removal of this repression as the liberation of poetic power on the part of the people and as the fulfillment of the idea of art. It is an idea that traces its beginnings in the old work songs, whose practical function in one way or another assisted the laborer or assuaged his pain. Think of the prudential advice offered in the "The Miner's Lifeguard,"[19]

> Union miners stand together
> Heed no operators tale
> Keèp your hand upon the dollar
> and your eye upon the scale.

Or the humor appropriate to the asurdities of mining low coal as in Turner's "Lignite Blues,"

> Bumps all along to skin your back
> You lay your wire and hang your track.

Or of the surreal quality of the dream in which freedom is symbolized by a seagull in "Coal Loadin' Blues,"

> Thought I heard a sea-gull
> Way down in the ground;
> Must've been those miners
> A-turnin' that coal around.

Real freedom, free time and free mind, is the fulfillment of the idea of art. It is a revolutionary break to get poetry away from the cult and back into the life and consciousness of the people. In his last work the German philosopher Herbert Marcuse wrote that, "truth of art lies in its power to break the monopoly of established reality...to *define* what is *real*."[19] What he seems not to have seen is that art only has this power when it is in the hands of the people.

Appalachian people's culture is a real possibility for our generation. We have now the opportunity to nuture the growth of that organic relation between past and present, between poetry and people, as existed in the old folk world, and still exists in many countries where economic and social control is maintained through legalized terror and a genuine people's culture survives underground or at the periphery of public life. I want to conclude this paper by examining some of the obstacles that stand in our way and have to be confronted if we are to make the most of this opportunity.

First, there is the theoretical obstacle of our own perception of our situation and how we conceptualize it. David Walls's core-periphery model has done much to reshape our thinking about the region. It is less problematic to understand Appalachia as a peripheral region within the social and physical geography of "late captialism". It will be obvious how much the model is at work in this paper. But the model has an important drawback in the cultural sector, and it is well to remember in this context that it is only a model.[21] The limitation of the core-periphery model lies in the fact that in the present situation it is economically applicable but rapidly becoming culturally inapplicable. Culturally, the core is disintegrating at the same time as the Appalachian "periphery", along with other regions of the country, are experiencing a cultural renaissance. It is possible for the cultural core of American capitalism to become so weakened that there will no longer be any justification for speaking of Appalachian culture, or that of any of the other regions, as peripheral. Theoretically, then, we should remember that there is no periphery without a core.

Of course, the breakup of the "core" does not imply that a regional people's culture will emerge in its place. Other changes in the cultural superstructure are consistent with the continued functioning of American capitalism, even in its more or less dysfunctional "late", or post-Keynesian stage. One cannot say, for example, that the economics of American capitalism rules out an elitist cultural dispersal. The economic base of capitalism *is* consistent with the development of cultural pluralism under the control of regional elites.[22] The important thing for capitalism is that a bureaucratic society of controlled comsumption be preserved.[23]

Is it not understandable then, that in Appalachia the money flows in the direction of cultural heritage programs and not in the direction of contemporary programs which nourish a living people's culture, and that would, in the words of the French philosopher Lefebvre, "create a culture that is not an institution but a style of life"?[24] The practical obstacles to people's culture have to do with where the money goes and where it doesn't go. State and private investments have been lavished, even squandered, on the collection and preservation of the remnants of folk culture in museums, libraries, and heritage centers. Little or nothing has gone for festivals of the arts, artists, and writers fellowships and residencies, or for contemporary people's theater; and there has been no money for our poetry anthology, a pittance, really, in comparison to what has been spent. Heritage is a safe investment so long as it does not materially affect the present. A contemporary people's culture, on the other hand, is risky. Just how risky is stated with the exhortation of a mountain preacher in a recent paper by Cratis Williams, when he says that Appalachians are a people,

who have risen from our long fast in the
mountains, the agony of our neglect and
abuse, and the sharp thorns of perfidy
that have been our anguish, and are now shaking
our hides and flexing our muscles as we reach
for the control box that determines our destiny."

To the extent that this assessment is true, the "periphery" will turn out to be more like the front lines. Its truth value makes it dangerous to the established order because it identifies the fate of a culture with the *action* of the people. This is an important and far-reaching perception.

Socially and politically, a division takes place when there is serious talk about reaching for the control box. We know that the box is ultimately outside Appalachia, but a good many in the region who support the folksy heritage concept of culture are tied in with those whose hands are on the controls. The controllers will permit a plurality of ethnic identities; their agents will give grants to assist in their development. What they will ridicule and condemn is the possibility that these identities should have *a living value in the present,* one that possesses real social power such that the people of the region gain control over their destiny.

Our self-consciousness has brought us to a crucial juncture. Now is the time to invest in contemporary work in an unparalled manner. Heritage and "roots" are not enough for a *living* identity. We need to take another look at folk culture and recognize that the folk are the people of the present, in need of a living culture. Folk culture must extend into the present as people's culture. If it doesn't, we will lose it all.

Notes

1. The remnant character of Appalachian culture is seen best perhaps in our architecture. The architecture of building and design is the external form of culture, and in Appalachia these forms, the hill farm houses and barns, the coal camps, company stores and stables, even the distinctiveness of the small towns are fast disappearing, and the new forms of urban and suburban modernism, the shopping malls along the interstates, are springing up with characteristic uniformity.

2. Frank Steele, "Two Kinds of Commitments: Some Directions in Current Appalachian Poetry," *Appalachian Journal* 6 (Spring 1979): pp. 228.

3. Donald Hall, ed., *Contemporary American Poetry*, 2nd ed. (Baltimore: Penquin Books, 1972).

4. Tom Wayman, ed., *Beaton Abbott's Got the Contract* (Edmonton: Newest Press. 1974), and *A Government Job At Last* (Vancouver: MacLeod Books, 1977).

5. Vincent Ferrini, *Know Fish* (Storrs, Connecticut: The University of Connecticut Library, 1979). See also Ferrini's *Selected Poems* (same publisher, 1976).

6. David Budbill, *The Chain Saw Dance* (Johnson, VT.: The Crow's Mark Press, 1976).

7. Bob Baber and Jim Webb, *Mucked* (Richwood, W.Va.: The Southern Appalachian Writers Co-op, 1978).

8. The movement of proletarian literature which developed in the thirties had this as a conscious theoretical aim: "[A] synthesizing third factor is added to the Aristotelian pity and terror - and that is militancy, combativeness. The proletarian *katharsis* is a release through the action - something dismetrically

opposed to the philosophical resignation of the older idea. Audaciously breaking through the wall that separates literature and life, it impels the reader to a course of action...." In Philip Rahv's *Essays on Literature and Politics, 1932-73,* eds. Porter and Dvosin (Boston: Houghton Mifflin, 1978), p. 281.

9. Cf., Eric Homberger, *The Art of the Real: Poetry in England and America Since 1939* (Rowan, 1977), pp. 175-215.

10. Daniel Bell, *The Cultural Contradictions of Capitalism* (New York: Basic Books, 1976).

11. *The Village Voice,* June 25, 1979, ppp. 37-41.

12. John Berger, *Art and Revolution* (New York: Pantheon Books, 1969), p. 157.

13. *The New Science of Giambattista Vico,* trans. Bergin and Fisch (Ithaca, N.Y.: Cornell University Press, 1970), p. 270, Para. 875.

14. In mass culture the question of the meaning and intergrity of art does not arise since the values of art are secondary to moneymaking.

15. Aristotle raises the question, at the beginning of the *Poetics,* of "how the fables must be put together if the poetry is to be well-formed." Hieratic criticism has made much of the criteria of form. What it has usually meant is the "interposition of technical imperatives between the poet and 'reality'." (Homberger, *The Art of the Real,* pp. 86-87). The modernist movement in poetry and art began with a progressive challenge to receive techniques and campaigned for the poet's right to invent. The weakness of modernism has been in not returning to the criteria of 'reality'.

16. "The Dialectics of Poetry." in *Surrealism and the Postwar Period,* excerpted and translated by Peter Boffey in *Invisible City,* Numbers 21-22, November, 1977, p. 10.

17. The modernist direction in poetry beginning with imagism was strongly influenced by the new experiment in the art of painting.

18. Petter Boffey, trans., "The Dialectics of Poetry."

19. The complete songs from which these verses are taken are found in George Korson's *Coal Dust on the Fiddle* (Philadelphia, University of Pennsylvania Press, 1943).

20. Herbert Marcuse, *The Aesthetic Dimension: Toward a Critique of Marxist Aesthetics* (Boston: Beacon Press, 1978), p. 9.

21. A model is a conceptual tool with which to grasp and structure the facts. It will grasp some facts and not others. We should expect this, especially in the present period of transition involving what may turn out to be the cultural disintegration of the core.

22. An altered superstructure could even include the breakup of the cental TV networks as we know them into various forms of regional networks, or cable networks, with an expanded market based on local variations for products stamped out in the studios of Hollywood and New York. And even the latter coul conceivably disperse into various regional locations.

23. Cf., Henri Lefebvre, *Everyday Life in the Modern World* (New York: Harper & Row, 1971), chapter 2.

24. Ibid., p. 203.

25. Cratis Williams, "The Appalachian Experience," *Appalachian Heritage,* 7 Spring 1979, p. 11.

ALTHER AND DILLARD: THE APPALACHIAN UNIVERSE

Frederick G. Waage

Abstract

This paper explores the views of two writers, Lisa Alther and Annie Dillard, on contemporary Appalachian nature and culture. While the two authors focus on quite different realms of Appalachia, they are both concerned with returning to native peoples and places. Each author demonstrates in her own way that this return can only be genuine if it takes into account the incomplete, mysterious, and contradictory environment of present day life.

Lisa Alther and Annie Dillard are two women in their mid-thirties, whose very different prose works, *Kinflicks* and *Pilgrim at Tinker Creek*, express contemporary Appalachian nature and culture in remarkably similar ways. The primary setting of Alther's novel is Hullsport (read Kingsport) Tennessee; its structure of increasingly recent flashbacks chronicles the heroine's escape from Appalachia as she grows from adolescence into mid-womanhood; whereas its narrative present describes the return *to* Hullsport of the autobiographical protagonist, Ginny, and her vigil over her dying mother. In her return she penetrates deeper (topographically and emotionally) into the essence of Hullsport while her mother slowly dies; she sets up house in the cabin where she was born, which was built by her grandfather, the founder of Hullsport, as an escape from the town he created.

Dillard's lyrical, Waldenian narrative is centered on her house by Tinker Creek and Tinker Mountain, on the Roanoke Valley edge of the Appalachians near Salem, Virginia. It moves through time from winter and early spring to winter solstice again, and through a pattern of escapes and returns between the immediate, tiny, local observations of Tinker Creek's nature, the world's nature in its diversity, and the metaphysics of the cosmos. The movement through the year towards winter ("...Tinker Creek makes a sharp loop, so that the creek is both in back of the house, south of me, and also on the other side of the road, north of me. I like to go north."-p.4) is also, paradoxically, a movement towards a deeper, or warmer, understanding of paradoxes in existence.[1]

Both Alther and Dillard are "pilgrims" in literal and figurative senses. Their literary *personae* move through literal space and time, of course. Alther moves first through the different social milieux of Hullsport, then to a fashionable women's college near Boston, and finally, before her return, to Stark's Bog, Vermont, the rural antitype of Hullsport. Dillard moves to different spaces and places around Tinker Creek and Tinker Mountain, always returning to her house, which is much less physically real to the reader than the external moments and places she describes.

Dillard is, in her literary *persona*, a solitary pilgrim; Alther's journey is to a great extent defined by the human culture, the different social environments, that encompass Ginny, her heroine. Only in her chapter "Nightwatch" does Dillard extensively evoke the presence, problems of human settlements in "untamed" nature. In this chapter she visits the Lucas place, a "secluded magic garden" (p. 216)--a formerly cultivated, now overgrowing, property, whose centerpiece is a deserted mountainside cottage, "mostly porch" (p. 218).

Here she spends the night. This cottage is the contrary of her own house, where she can examine things under a civilized microscope by artificial light. It is a habitation, but scarcely: very open and deserted, its "five windows framed five films of the light and living world" (p. 219). All human structurers have retreated, so that in this almost-cottage Dillard can both inhabit her own natural environment and be a non-alien presence in that of non-human creation. Here she approaches a condition of total awareness, "firmness"--the goal of her pilgrimage--both in her human consciousness and in the pure otherness of pre-thought creation: "A kind of northing is what I wish to accomplish, a single-minded trek toward that place where any shutter left open to the zenith at night will record the wheeling of all the sky's stars as a pattern of perfect, concentric circles" (p. 257).

There is a remarkably similar cottage at the polar center of Alther's novel-- the one built by Ginny's grandfather, Mr. Zed, founder of Hullsport, as his "primitive" retreat from the civilized corruption he created. Here Ginny was born, and here she lives on her return to Hullsport, while she waits out her mother's slow dying. She too finds this cabin abandoned, and must, like a first pioneer, clear it of kudzu vines, (originally planted by her grandfather to overgrow the city he repudiated). Her main enterprise in this cabin is her attemped mothering of baby chimney swifts, "unnaturally" abandoned by their parents after their nest falls down the cabin's chimney. Her attempt to transcend her human condition and become the birds' mother (an enterprise of taming that half of herself rebels against), ironically unsuccessful, parallels the attempt of her mother's body to transcend the powers of human medical expertise by dying. In this, her mother is ironically successful. No coagulants can stop the progressive rupture of her capillaries; blood runs symbolically throughout this novel, as, at the end, Ginny is unable to commit suicide and spill her own blood. Here, literally torn between the needs of her human mother and her non-human bird-chicken--an irreconcilable mingled attachment to, and rejection of, two worlds and two identities--she is in the same metaphysical position as Dillard is in her cottage, but Ginny as a pilgrim cannot unmesh herself from the world. She cannot achieve a fixed, firm identity as a woman or as a human.

Ginny's search is different from Dillard's, in that her desires move inward toward knowing the One (herself) rather than outward toward a circumpolar All. It is similar in that both writers' personae experience the "Way" to true knowing as through intimacy with geographically, biologically minute concrete and particular things. For Dillard, ...the microscope at my forehead is a kind of phylactery, a constant reminder of the facts of creation that I would just as soon forget" (p. 123). Above other "intricate" particularities that are also totalities, is the sight, through the microscope, of indefatigable red blood cells in the tail of her goldfish: "...lying in bed at night, imagining that if I concentrate enough, I might be able to feel in my fingers' capillaries the small knockings and flow of those circular dots, like a string of beads drawn through my hand" (p. 127). Alther's Ginny finds truths higher than the cosmic philosophies her college mother-figure, Miss Head, worships (Spinoza's, Schopenhauer's, Descartes's works), when she experiences *death* by scraping cells from her cheek and watching them die under her microscope: "The paragraphs in the book of life and death were multicelled organisms. Cells were dying continuously in this same fashion in Aida's body, in my body, in Miss Head's body" (p. 205). She also experiences elemental *birth* on the microscope slide:

> "Professor Aitken!" I shrieked. He came rush-rushing over, his

> white coat flying behind him. "Something strange is going on with my protozoa!"
>
> He peered through my microscope. "Oh yes," he said...They're exchanging genetic material."
>
> "What does that mean?"
>
> "It's equivalent to what happens in human conception.... (p. 208)

Ginny's microscopic insights become ultimately personal for Ginny in the battle to keep the cells inside her mother's body; her death seems to have a life of its own.

Both pilgrims seek to reconcile this sort of contradictoriness in elemental things by experiencing life in its most closely knit manifestations, where the fewest abstract formulations apply:

> Just think: in all the clean beautiful reaches of the solar system, our planet alone is a blot. Our planet alone has death...The faster death goes, the faster evolution goes. If an aphid lays a million eggs, several might survive. Now, my right hand, in all its human cunning, could not make one aphid in a thousand years. But these aphid eggs--which run less than a dime a dozen, which run absolutely free--can make aphids as effortlessly as the sea makes waves. Wonderful things, wasted. It's a wretched system. (Dillard, p. 178)

Their perception of, and desire to reconcile, contradictions seem to me bound with two determinants in their natures as writers--their femaleness and their Appalachian environment.

Alther's heroine, and Dillard's literary "self," are dissatisfied with the formulary security imposed on phenomena by male consciousness. Women are privileged (or "cursed") to experience physically, pre-ideologically, within themselves, the human extremes of birthing and dying, and the sinuous experience which allies the human and the non-human. Both women acknowledge and accept a "passivity" (versus male activity) as inherent in their sexuality. For Ginny, the passivity sometimes becomes a caricatural social willingness to be seduced by male ideologies. For Dillard it is realized as a mystical "innocence," "...the spirit's unself-conscious state at any moment of pure devotion to an object" (p. 83). Self-consciousness "does hinder the experience of the present"--but in traditional male, scientific terms, self-consciousness, "the curse of the city and all that sophistication implies" (p. 82), is necessary to the objective apprehension of the experiential present. Dillard is quietly and only implicitly, opposed to a "male" objective distancing which makes false simplicities out of true complexities. She likens it to her youthful belief that English was the only language (pp. 106-7); beginning French, "I realized that I was going to have to learn speech all over again." She never explicitly associates sexuality with false or true perception, but in some telling scenes, the categorical and manipulative are clearly male. Once, where she is camping, children are playiang with newts.:

> One boy was mistreating the newts spectacularly: he squeezed them by their tails and threw them at a shoreline stone, one by one. I tried to reason with him, but nothing worked. Finally he asked me, "Is this one a male?" and in a fit of inspiration I said, "No, it's a baby." He cried "Oh, isn't he cute!" and cradled the newt carefully back into the water. (p. 112)

Dealing with males, the male-ing boy is destructive; but his identity is yet unfixed enough for him to be an "innocent" mother when confronted with a "baby."

All the males in Ginny's life--beginning with her authoritarian industrialist father, the Major--tend to err destructively or self-destructively by imposing their simple formulas on irreducible social reality. Ironically they often are winners, while she is a loser, because their obstinacy in constructing the world in their own image is so inflexible. Only older men--her grandfather, Mr. Zed, or the retired family doctor, Dr. Tyler--have gone beyond virility and dogma to become as anarchistically innocent as she is. Her first love, Joe Bob Sparks, is inflexibly ideal as a local football hero who becomes the local football coach, and is re-encountered by Ginny living in self-conscious plastic suburban splendor with a plastic wife, who has plastic breasts. Her second lover, Clem Cloyd, seemingly Joe Bob's motorcyclesque opposite, is actually his brother as an absolutist. Because of his self-consciously humiliating, crippled leg, he becomes absolute for degeneracy and self-indulgence, then for Death (whom he defies as he takes Ginny on manic motorcycle rides), and finally, on Ginny's return to Hullsport, for his own primitivistic evangelistic sect, of which he is the priest. Clem, reformed, still taunts death; his flock's immunity to copperhead bites at the snaketaming ritual Ginny attends is an ironically false transcendence of the barrier between human and non-human which Ginny cannot overcome with her swifts. Ginny's female lover, Eddie, with male role as well as name in their relationship, destroys herself in seeking total control and possession of her. Ira, her Vermont husband, fails her by seeking to mold her to the repetitious domestic, commercial, and sexual rituals that structure his public and private identity. Hawk, her final lover before her return to Tennessee, has found in her the ideal partner for a pseudo-Eastern, erotic-mystical ritual of transcendence, built up to by weeks of self-denying discipline. Ironically, its preparations so exhaust him that he falls asleep, as irrational physicality reasserts itself, at the point of fulfillment. Dr. Vogel (bird in German, earthbound opposite of Ginny's swifts), her mother's doctor, lives only through his medical jargon and ritualized experimentation. Like Hawk's sleep, her mother's death has a cause beyond the ken of the most elaborate male structures of apprehension: "Even on the perfectly ordinary and clearly visible level, creation carries on with an intricacy unfathomable and apparently uncalled for" (Dillard p. 134).

Every man, or male-defined person, Ginny encounters eventually becomes, in assurance of knowledge, insufficient to Ginny's awareness of circumstances that contradict their truths (although she often interprets their rejections as her *own* inadequacy in fulfilling their needs). It is hard to believe the author doesn't feel this male inadequacy of apprehension to be biologically inherent, rather than culturally induced. For example, here Ginny is resisting the propaganda of her family and Ira's urging that she have a second child:

> "...Well, we can't have just *one* child." Ira said.
> "Why not?"
> "But people don't *have* just one child. Jesum Crow, Ginny. Besides, you want a son, don't you?" (p. 403)

The trouble is that women are emotionally incomplete without men, and must be pilgrims until they unite with men who will inevitably either recreate them or demoralize them. Sexuality, in Dillard's book, "Fecundity," implies psychological warfare--symbolized by the battle between the organic feminist commune of "Soybean People" Ginny and her friends form in Vermont and the snowmobiling native men, led by Ira, who try to drive them out. When Ginny's jealous lover Eddie intentionally (?) kills herself on a captured snowmobile at the height of the war, Ginny capitulates emotionally to Ira, the male general, and by this victorious union of enemies (sort of akin to Ginny's protozoan vision) the Amazonian commune collapses inward and eventually dies. The women understand that the war is symbolic. The men "innocently" experience it only as the literal recapture of their sporting ground.

Compounding the irreconcilable destructiveness of sexuality is the difference between male identity as experienced by men themselves, and as experienced by women. The formulaic absolutism of men is perceptual, not real. They know, in Dillard's terms, only English, whereas women know several languages. Women can see in male behavior inconsistency, paradox, doubleness, while men see themselves through this same behavior as creatures of order. Dr. Vogel can never experience himself as other than a serious scientist, but Ginny sees his fanaticism for science as similar to her own obsessive wandering. In one of the novel's most studiedly funny scenes, Ira, following step by step his guidebook to exotic sexual techniques, trying to arouse an orgasm in Ginny, arranges a gymnastic feat involving their hanging handcuffed from a beam in his ancestral house. Ginny drops the key to the handcuffs. Throughout their surrealistic attempts to free themselves, Ira faults her for botching a very reasonably structured experience. He cannot see that in this adventure he "is" in total contradiction to his self-perceived identity as a lucid, pious, all-American businessman. Dillard also believes that male limitations are more in perception of behavior than in behavior itself. Through the ajar door of the Ichthyology Department in a famous university she sees

> ...two white-coated men seated opposite each other on high lab stools at a hard-surfaced table. They bent over identical white enamel trays. On one side, one man, with a lancet, was just cutting into an enormous preserved fish he'd taken from a jar. On the other side, the other man, with a silver spoon, was eating a grapefruit. I laughed all the way back to Virginia. (pp. 84-85)

Neither man could perceive the total incongruity of their mutual behavior; the woman, cursed by ignorance and exclusion, can.

Contemporary Appalachia is self-contradictory. For Alther and Dillard it becomes a place uniquely qualified to embody their vision of the irreconcilable and their search to reconcile. For Dillard, the self-contradiction is in western Virginia's biological and topographical diversity--it contains the world:

> It's a good place to live; there's a lot to think about. The creeks, Tinker's and Calvin's--are an active mystery, fresh every minute. Theirs is the mystery of the continuous creation and all that providence implies: the uncertainty of vision, the horror of the fixed, the dissolution of the present, the intricacy of beauty, the pressure of fecundity, the elusiveness of the free, and the flawed nature of perfection. The mountains--Tinker and Brushy, McAfee's Knob and Dead Man--are a passive mystery, the oldest of all. Theirs is the one simple mystery of creation from nothing, of matter itself, anything at all, the given. (p. 3)

For Alther, it is in the social contradictions of a human culture in the process of acute change, whose loss of assurance, traditional moorings, creates and mirrors collectively the heroine's own. Since the Hullsport setting of Alther's novel has been controversial, it is profitable to focus on how the novel actually uses this setting.

Generically, *Kinflicks* is self-consciously a *picaresque* novel, starring a wandering female Quixote of the lineage of Moll Flanders. Like a great many picaresque novels, it is set in a time of turmoil, unsettled life, violence done to basic truths; in this case the time is the late 1960s and early 1970s in the United States, dominated by social rebellion and the Vietnam war. As in real-life Kingsport, the Hullsport plastics factory run by Ginny's father--which violates nature with pollution and traditional rural culture by creating a blue-collar, urban proletariat in the mountains--is converted into a munitions factory for the Vietnam war. The Vietnam war, similarly, is defoliating nature and ravaging an agrarian people.

Hullsport is the war brought home. Ginny is Virginia, the comically virginal, innocent wanderer. Her main adventures occur in three stylized locales. Hullsport is seen in two aspects. It is experienced *generally* in the flashback chapters which cover her younger years. Here *real* southern aristicracy and aristocratic traditions mingle in a melting pot with nouveau riche aristocracy (like Ginny's father) and its prefabricated traditions; with earthy, unrepentant, and ultimately "lawless" hillbilly culture, represented in her grandfather's family from Sow Gap, Virginia; with mercantile and working-class culture, created and drawn to Hullsport by her father's factory, in various stages of rise to the bourgeois splendor of development or subdivision living. In the narrative present scenes of Ginny's return to Hullsport, the main focus is on two places *in* but not *of* Hullsport--the sterile, self-contained Community Hospital where Ginny's mother dies, and the fecund, self-contained cabin land which her grandfather established, and where she lives.

Hullsport's caricatural dissonance, inward and with its natural environment, is microcosmically that of mid-century America as well as of its failed Model Virgin, Ginny, who is inwardly divided: in her memories she's an "I," but in the present scenes she's a self-alienated "Ginny." Hullsport, the Model City planned concentrically like Washington D.C. in the symbolic year 1919, has been degenerated and corrupted from its male maker's abstract plan by its very unplanned, fecund growth (like a paradoxical cell under Ginny's microscope). Her grandfather did not foresee

> ...that six times as many people as he had planned for would one day want to leave the farms and mines and crowd into Hullsport, and that clumps of houses for them would ring the hexagon in chaotic, eczema-like patches. (p. 15)

Ginny is torn between her need to nurture life as a woman, and her rejection of her mother's role as a traditional, passive wife and mother; the Appalachians are torn between the static purity of the traditional farming and mining life and the destructive progress of their cities' growing industrial economy. Ginny, as adventuress, returns to Hullsport not only because her mother (and symbolically her mother's way of life) is dying, but also by her need for truth. The dissonance of this changing world, so easy for her to parody, is also more authentic, because unsettled, than where she has been. It is a growth-and-dying in simultaneity, more true to her complex vision of life than are the more beautiful, harmonious, self-contained places farther north and east. "There is not a guarantee in the world...Oh, your *needs* are guaranteed...But you must read the fine print. 'Not as the world giveth, give I unto you.'"(Dillard, p. 277)

The other two dominant places in *Kinflicks* are "guaranteed," as masculine formulae are, illusorily impregnable. Worthley, modelled on Alther's college, Wellesley, is expressed in and through Miss Head, the philosophy teacher, whose Okie youth was analogous to Ginny's except that her parents fought, rather than compelling, her intellectual advancement. Miss Head experiences the world purely intellectually, with her "Head", and through the world-systems of the philosophers she teaches. Like Ginny's mother, her one lover was a soldier who left her to fight in Europe; unlike her, she didn't marry or have babies by him: "Well, he was killed. In Belgium. But that's beside the point" (p. 194). Actually, invulnerable Worthley is totally vulnerable. In a battle of surrogate parents of Ginny's allegiance, Miss Head loses to Eddie, the radical fellow-student who first becomes her lover when they are "hidden" on the roof of their dormitory. The previous day Ginny has discovered her freshman neighbor, Bev Martin, losing consciousness from an overdose of sleeping pills in the dorm bathroom. She merely watches her while debating in her mind the ethics of suicide; Eddie saves Bev's life without reflection by instantly making her drink salt water to induce vomiting. Schopenhauer's and Miss Head's philosophy almost implies death: "'We must, without reserve, regard all presented objects, even our own bodies, merely as ideas, and call them merely ideas'" (p. 235). This evasive "male" abstraction (Miss Head's refuge from her femaleness and vulnerability) is agonizingly conflicted in Ginny's being with Eddie's immediate sensuality, which harmonizes with the direct experience of nature, the "ecological" philosophy derived from her biology class:

> I plucked a leaf off a forsythia bush and stared as it as though I had never seen a leaf before. Its atoms and subatomic particles were identical to those making up my fingers...Our earth was a burned-out hunk of mineral ash, but we--this leaf and Eddie and Bev and I--we were star stuff. Our bodies were almost entirely made up of light volatile elements. We had origins far grander than the cinder we inhabited would indicate. What affected one segment affected us all. (p. 236)

She accepts Eddie's passion and rejects a comforting "intellectual" vision, symbolized by Worthley, which denies life and paradox.

Northern Vermont, where Ginny and Eddie finally settle after leaving Worthley, is seemingly a place whose elemental, earthy life-patterns harmonize with Ginny's new belief in physical interdependence. Ironically, the farm the "Soybean People" establish, and the hostile neighboring town of Stark's Bog, are both such "perfect" cultural expressions of this belief that Ginny comes to experience them as of the same absolute nature as Miss Head's philosophy. Eddie's possessiveness becomes so total there also that it loses its nature as liberating passion. It demands of Ginny as much self-diminishment as will the heterosexual domesticity of its sequel, her marriage with Ira.

Stark's Bog (Charlotte?), Vermont, is the opposite of Hullsport. Its population is ethnically homogeneous, ingrown, secure, so impervious to unexpected change, penetration by the outside world that weather is virtually its only topic of conversation. Ginny and Eddie's Soybean People, so much like the Stark's Boggers in their ingrown self-sufficiency, are rejected as "Communists, lesbians, draft-dodgers, atheists, food-stamp recipients" (p. 301). This is a microcosm of the United States during the Woodstock years. Their first attempt to "connect" with the Stark's Boggers, by giving *blood* at the local blood-drawing (a very symbolic event) is a disaster. To Ginny, "it gave me a great feeling of kinship to know that my plastic bag would nestle in the blood bank next to theirs. We were all in this business of life together" (p. 302). (Later in time, Ginny will similarly give blood to her mother, under more fatal circumstances). This personification of life on the lab slide is contradicted by social reality when Ira thanks the women ("girls") "for helping out our boys in Vietnam" at this special wartime blood drawing; the Soybean People are stunned to have inadvertently aided the Enemy. The bloodletting in Vietnam is supported both by Hullsport and Stark's Bog.

With her marriage to Ira Bliss, after Eddie is ironically decapitated by a wire she herself has strung to destroy his snowmobilers, Ginny attempts individually to transform herself into a native of Stark's Bog. Initially she experiences herself as succeeding. When her radical friends visit and ask if she has succeeded in infiltrating the enemy and "laying the trip on them" (p. 396), she realizes that "by the time I had infiltrated to the heart of Stark's Bog, I had *become* a Stark's Bogger . . . People *became* what they did." Seeing how Ira's patriarchal ancestor, Father Bliss, "lived on through his genes" in the people around her, as well as the ancestral stone house she inhabits (antitype of her own grandfather's imitation ante-bellum mansion, of wood, which her dying mother sells), she determines to have a child of her own to possess likewise "a hostage against death" (p. 397). Her motivation in bearing her daughter, Wendy, is itself an act of separation from her adopted culture: to perpetuate her own identity in rivalry with Father Bliss. Her refusal to fulfill Ira's desire to have a second child--relinquishing her individuating relationship with Wendy--is another. Her ultimate one, the ultimate failure of her "northing," is her clandestine affair with Hawk. This affair culminates in Ira's expulsion of her, without Wendy, when he finds them attempting Hawk's Oriental love ritual in the Bliss family graveyard.

The symbolic mingling of contraries dominates Ginny's relationship with Hawk, whose aim in his "religion" is preversely like hers during her whole pilgrimage: "You are the eternal feminine principle. I am the eternal masculine principle. As we mate, we will balance opposing forces and requite our longing for wholeness" (p. 470). The wholeness Hawk seeks is one of abstractions, however; the senses become "principle." He fragments the already shaky wholeness of Ginny's union with Stark's Bog. He arrives there as a pilgrim, with a pack. He is a native Southerner (Atlanta), who fought in Vietnam, fled the army to Canada, and is passing through Stark's Bog heading south for home after covertly re-entering the country. He is, for Ginny, like a piece of Hullsport transferred north. He contains, unreconciled, the contradictions that have driven her from firmness (as fellow-Southerner and Canadian, soldier and war-resister, drug-taker and intellectual absolutist, virgin--he transcends ejaculation--and tyrannical male). His "impossible" identity is most like that of Hullsport. By getting Ginny expelled from the edenic Bliss world, he draws her back to the chaos of her own origins ("'I have to get south,' he muttered"--p. 495).

In Hawk the actual inner chaos that American male culture variously reduced to pretences of order has broken through and become a personal reality; so Hullsport will eventually break through the power of other places to captivate Ginny into their different illusory versions of wholeness. Hullsport-- and by extension the new, changing South as a whole--is a provincial place, but one more expressive of essential reality than the Big World outside. Ginny's daily trips between the edenic, primitive birth-cabin of her grandfather and the ultramodern hospital where her mother is uncontrollably dying are more "globegirdling" than her pilgrimages through America, just as Annie Dillard, in walking along Tinker Creek, explores the entire universe.

After her mother has died, and before her failed attempts at suicide which end her story, Ginny tries to phone Hawk at his parents' home in Atlanta. She finds from his father (an ex-General) that Hawk has arrived, half-dead, but is now in the VA Hospital, diagnosed as a paranoid schizophrenic:

> Hawk's father sounded faintly pleased: His son was not an army deserter, he was sick. His son was not rejecting his father's way of life--his son was crazy.
> "I see," she said weakly, "I'm very sorry."
> "Well, at least, he finally came home and faced up to his responsibilities like a *man*," his father said cheerfully. (p. 513)

Ultimate male responsibility just like ultimate insanity, here expresses all the irreconcilables of Hullsport's world which have continued to drive Ginny in different directions--from Clem's brother Floyd's illegal bar, the Bloody Bucket, which he can disguise in an instant as a fundamentalist chapel, to her initiation into sexual excitement with Joe Bob Sparks at Brother Buck's revival meeting, to her rural glory as Persimmon Plains Burly Tobacco Festival Queen while being princess of a plastics fortune, to, in the "present," her unnatural success as a mother in training her surviving young chimney swift to fly, and its irrational suicide flying into the cabin's closed window next to its open door.

Alther and Dillard both demand a disabused acknowledgement of *mystery* as a prerequisite to resolving mysteries, either those of the universe or those of individual identity. Ginny's swift, choosing death at the moment it is empowered to live freely, is responding to the Indeterminacy Principle which Dillard often evokes, "...That something is everywhere and always amiss is part of the very stuff of creation..." (Dillard, p. 184). Dillard with praise and wonder, Alther with lyrical self-satire, affirm the importance to individual survival, of living in and working through an environment which does not disguise fundamental mysteries. The "pilgrimage" *to* a place of fixity where personal and cosmic truths are revealed, is a Hessean illusion. The effectual pilgrimage must be a *return* to native origins--in time and space--to the small and primal elements of individual and collective existence, Tinker Creek or Hullsport, the cells of our own blood, of our own trees' leaves.

NOTES

1. All quotations are from Lisa Alther, *Kinflicks,* (New York: New American Library, 1977), or Annie Dillard, *Pilgrim At Tinker Creek* (New York: Bantam, 1975).

WOMEN FOLK HEALERS OF APPALACHIA

Karen Shelley and Raymond Evans

Abstract

This anthropological study looks at the role of the women as folk healers in Appalachian. Using data based on field research in Tennessee's Sequatchie Valley, the paper explores traditional and current practices of folk medicine. Beliefs in the curative powers of plants and other naturally occurring products of the environment provide the basis for both the prevention of disease and the restoration of good health. The paper sees the beliefs and practices of folk healing as part of the wider body of cultural adaptation to environmental conditions of the area. While the knowledge of medicinal plants and their application is part of the general body of folk traditions of this area, preparing and administering these remedies are largely the activities of females.

The importance of folk medicine in the lives of Appalachian people during the nineteenth and early twentieth centuries has been well documented in the historical and social science literature as well as the folklore of the area.[1] While both men and women healers traditionally contributed to the physical and emotional well-being of others, the role of women in the curing process is of special interest in the area of herbal medicine and maternal-infant care. This paper will consider some of the cultural factors within which curing behavior takes place and the nature of women's responsibilities and knowledge in these areas.

The authors' current interest in the topic grew out of a study of healing arts and experiences in eastern Tennessee which was part of a grant funded by the Tennessee Committee for the Humanities.[2] The goal of this project, congruent with the aims of the T.C.H., is to organize a series of public dialogues involving both humanists in various academic disciplines and members of the community. The curative practices of faith healers, herbal specialists, and psychics as well as those of biomedical personnel are all part of the focus of concern.[3]

In an attempt to locate persons, who had knowledge of traditional healing and folk practices, the reseachers conducted interviews with residents of the Sequatchie Valley. This rural area is located northwest of Chattanooga in the Cumberland Plateau. The cultural boundaries of the valley include approximately seventy miles of fertile lowland country along the Sequatchie River and its bordering mountainsides. The area includes land in Marion, Sequatchie, Bledsoe, and a small portion of Cumberland counties (see Map I).

Until recently, the resource of the valley provided a livelihood for its residents. At the close of the nineteenth century there was a brief economic boom when the Tennessee Coal and Iron Company established a coke oven complex and mining installation in Sequatchie County. There were also numerous other attempts at mining coal on the eastern side of the valley. The mining industry here is largely a low-profit, high-risk venture because of the irregular nature of the major coal seam.[4] Nevertheless, the numerous shaft and strip mines in the valley are evidence of the determination of the miners.

Today, five population centers dot the floor of the valley. The largest town has approximately 4,000 residents, but the others, which are more typical of

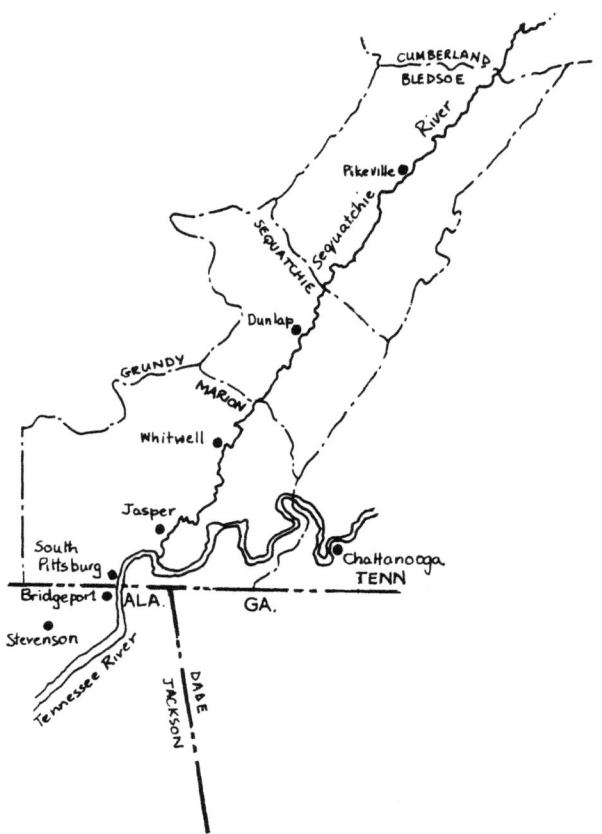

Map 1. The Sequatchie Valley. (Adapted from L. Raulston and J. Livingood, Sequatchie: A Story of the Southern Cumberlands, 1974, 149.)

the area, have no more than 2,000 residents each.⁵ Of the total 34,551 persons living in Marion, Sequatchie, and Bledsoe counties in 1970, 85 percent of the people were classified by the census as rural, non-farm dwellers. This high percentage is atypical for Tennessee as a whole, where less than one third of the population in 1970 was classified as rural, non-farm.⁶

The Sequatchie Valley residents are largely born and bred Tennesseans. Of the three-county residents, 87.6 percent live in their native state. Ninety-six percent of the people are white and many of these are descended from families who have lived in the region for five generations.⁷

Most of the wage earners are employed in small-scale businesses, manufacturing, lumbering, and mining-related jobs.⁸ While in the earlier part of this century most of the valley's people were farmers or stockbreeders or both, today the pattern has changed. Only 12 percent of the residents were classified as farmers by the 1970 Census and many of these landowners supplemented their incomes with industrial jobs. Twenty-six percent of the families had incomes below the poverty level in 1970.[9] Although there is a growing pattern for people to find work outside the valley in Chattanooga and nearby areas, Sequatchie people much prefer to maintain their homes in the valley. For the older generation, particularly, life in Chattanooga is associated with the threat of a loss of intimate family ties and the security which extended family ties provided in the past.

During the initial survey of our project, as informants were contacted, the emergence of some early patterns caused a re-evaluation of the scope of the project. References to persons who had experience and knowledge of folk healing were usually referrals to males. The typical format of the referrals can be seen in the words of one informant who said, "Yew ort'er go up thar ta Willuns Road en see Chals Nelmore's son yung Ben." Upon acting on the referral and arriving at "yung Ben's house" the researchers found Ben (now about seventy years old) and his wife Lurleen. After passing pleasantries on the porch, we were invited inside and began to ask about wild herbs which grew on the mountainsides. Repeatedly, the man would volunteer a few candidates and then turn to his wife with a questioning look. The woman would then begin enumerating plant names, descriptions, and collecting procedures. Further questions concerning medicinal plants elicited more detailed information from female informants about drying and preparation techniques. When the informants repeatedly brought samples from their pantries and refrigerators to illustrate preparation methods, the interviewers realized that they were dealing not with just an exercise in ethnohistory but with elements of an on-going set of beliefs and practices.

Although the following data are subject to further verification, some initial observations can be made on current folk medical beliefs and practices in the valley. In this area of eastern Tennessee traditional medicinal practices can be grouped into four main categories--herbal medicine, faith healing, psychic healing, and midwifery.[10] While none of these categories were or are exclusively the domains of either males or females, the roles of women as lay practitioners and as specialists consulted by kith and kin are noteworthy. The four categories are discrete systems of curing, but they are ones which are not necessarily incompatible with one another. Although herbal medicine is primarily a lay tradition, there is a small degree of specialization in the sense that some persons who are thought to have greater experience and knowledge than others, are asked to give advice on the collection or preparation of some herbal concoctions. These persons are generally elderly women. The women in this category should be distinguished from a small number of other herbal specialists, both males and females, who package or bottle their products for sale. Further interviews are planned in order to establish more clearly the extent of traditional and current beliefs associated with faith healers and psychic healers. The focus of our immediate concern, however, is the role of women as herbalists.

Before turning to consider the socialization process and female activities associated with the role of healer, we will first briefly consider the belief system of disease causation and curing operating in the Sequatchie Valley. Illness is attributed to a variety of sources and thus may be subject to several or a combination of curative procedures. Three different orientations exist. First, the germ theory of disease causation is acknowledged to be one possible reason for sickness. The most effective treatment, however, according to local tradition, does not necessarily follow a regimen prescribed by modern biomedical systems of thought. In cases of health failure, alternative treatment methods are evaluated and tried. Self-treatment, usually the first alternative, may employ herbal medicines, patent medicines, or supernatural assistance evoked through prayer. A combination of these methods is most often the course which is followed (see Figure 1). If this method fails then herbal specialists, faith healers, psychic or biomedical practitioners provide additional alternatives.

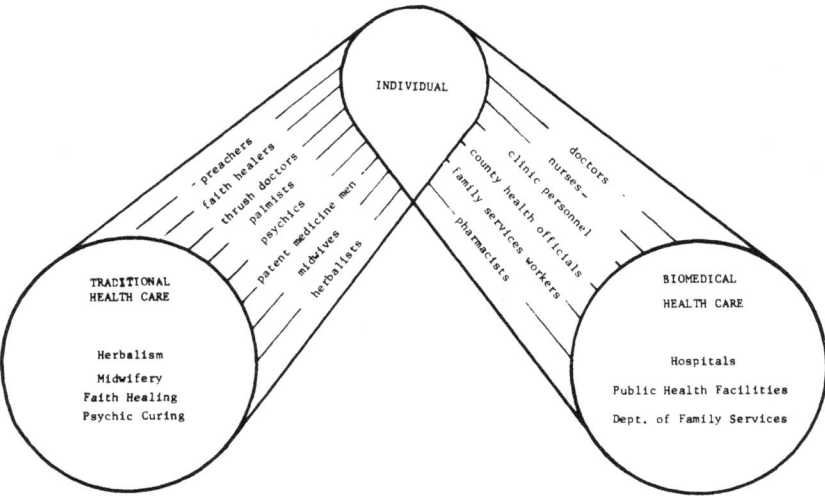

Figure 1. Alternative Curing Strategies

A second category of beliefs explaining disease causation includes those which can be described as magical or religious. Afflictions which strike children or persons usually in good states of health are often believed to be supernaturally influenced. Religious testimonials at local church services are part of the oral tradition which give clues to the health ways and belief systems of community members. Prayers which evoke assistance from the Christian God provide the primary means of cure and source of guidance in the face of sickness believed to be of magico-religious causes.

Illness is often perceived by people of the valley as a state of disequilibrium. One of the reasons for the bases of belief in the medicinal power of plants is that elements from the environment help to restore a sense of balance between the patient and his/her world. This concept of the cause of illness is similar to a traditional belief of the Cherokee Indians. According to this world view, harmony is the ideal state and results in good events. Events which are "bad" or undesirable like illness are the results of dis-harmony. Thus, sickness which arises out of states of disharmony can be cured by introducing the appropriate measures to restore harmony.[11]

The plural nature of the society in the Sequatchie Valley, like many other areas of Appalachia, is reflected in the use of multiple systems of curative strategies, as Figure 1 illustrates.[12] The strong history and commitment to self-sufficiency in the economic sphere is also evident in the dependence on lay curing practices and the patterns of self-treatment. Since women are traditionally responsible for child care and nursing in the domestic sphere, they often rely on resources from their immediate environment.

Within this context, then, we will turn to consider the traditional and current role of Sequatchie women in healing, prevention of disease, and childbirth. Traditionally, women had roles in the domestic sphere as wives, cooks, nurses, and teachers. Today, women still maintain these roles while taking on additonal ones as wage-earners. Even if a woman works outside the home, the traditional domestic responsibilities remain hers.

Beyond the lay tradition of using herbs to ease the symptoms of colds and common childhood diseases, some women are considered by their neighbors and relatives to have special knowledge and skills in herbal arts. These women do not hang out shingles to advertise their skills. Rather, their reputation as advisors and consultants and as sources for dried herbs are well-known to people of the local area.

Sequatchie women are not recruited into the herbal healing speciality because they possess any special supernatural attributes as is often believed to be the case of African and Native American healers.[13] The primary factors involved in being an herbalist are (1) a belief in the healing powers of plants, (2) knowledge and skills in identifying, gathering, and preparing medicinal plants, (3) supernatural assistance from the Christian God, and (4) some on-the-job experience. Skills and artistry associated with herbal healing are acquired through the informal socialization process of young females. Sequatchie women most often acknowledged the source of their skills as their membership in a category of elder women, including mothers, grandmothers, and mothers' sisters. These women pass on their knowledge from one generation to the next. Long leisurely walks through the woods and trips back and forth between homes of kith and kin provided opportunities for learning names, uses, and habitats of medicinal plants. No evidence of formal apprenticeships have been found among the valley's female informants. The absence of a structured apprenticeship is in contrast to the socialization process of traditional healers among some Native American groups.[14]

Although the knowledge of herbal remedies and the responsibility for transmitting such knowledge usually rested with females, males were an additonal source of knowledge in certain families.[15] One Sequatchie informant who is representative of this pattern learned many of her herbal skills from her mother who was a midwife in the valley. Her father, however, was an additional source of informaton and experience. He, like many other men of Appalachia, set out for the hills during 'sang season to dig ginseng *(Panax quinquefollum)*.[16] Men who had an interest in the commercial value of herbs were particularly well-versed in the local habitats and seasonal variations of the quality of these herbs. Although ginseng is still used locally by female herbal specialists, its commercial value is primarily as an export. While some local root diggers sell to a drugstore proprietor who acts as a middleman, others sell directly to buyers in the Midwest. One individual produced documentation of selling dried ginseng in 1979 to a midwest company for $145.00 per pound. Goldenseal, which is a prolific plant in the region under study, is the other herb which has significant commercial value.[17]

The specific kind of knowledge and the extent of knowledge about medicinal herbs has often been underestimated. Herbal curing involves knowledge in at least five areas. First, most women who are experts in the medicinal value of herbs have knowledge of identifiable plant characteristics and knowledge of the kinds of habitats in which different species are found. While some of the herbs commonly used in the area under study grow in shaded areas near streams, others thrive primarily at higher elevations, or along roadsides and pasture land. A second area of knowledge these women have is an understanding of when to collect and which part of the plant should be collected. Some herbs are believed to have their greatest potency in the spring, while others are gathered in late summer or fall. Rather than collecting the entire plant, many herbalists are conservation-minded and try to collect only the parts which are needed. A third focus of knowledge includes drying techniques to prevent molding and to retain potency. Fourth, women are particularly knowledgeable about the preparation of herbal teas, salves, poultices, and other externally applied remedies. Admixtures of several herbs together with additions of flavorings are all part of the tradition which has to be learned. Finally, and perhaps most importantly, is the body of ethnoscience which specifies which plants have curative properties appropriate for use against certain diseases or complaints.

The following table lists some of the herbs in current use in the Sequatchie.

Common Name	Scientific Name	Folk Use
Balm of Gilead	Pupulus balsamifera	Buds used to make a salve for wounds
Blackberries	Rubus villosus	Wine made for stomach disorders; diarrhea
Blackberry Roots	Rubus villosus	Tea for diarrhea
Boneset	Eupatorium perfoliatum	Teas for colds; relieves symptoms associated with rheumatism
Borage	Borago officinalis	Blood purifier
Buckvine	Mitchella repens	Tea for kidney disorders
Catnip	Nepeta cataria	Tea for newborns; tea for hives; teas used to induce drowsiness
Cherry Tree Bark	Prunus viginiana	Cough syrup
Clover Blossoms	Trifolium pratense	Tea for calming nerves
Comfrey	Symphytom officinale	Tea for calming nerves
Elderberry Roots	Sambucus canadensis	General health tonic
Ginseng	Panax quinquefollum	Tea for symptoms associated with rheumatism; tea for bolt hives; tea for "female disorders"
Goldenseal	Hydrastis canadensis	Tea for stomach disorders
Heart Leaf	Asarum canadense	Tea for colds; cough syrup
Ink Balls	Ilex verticillata	Tea for thrush
Jimsonweed	Datura stramonium	Applied to boils
Mullein or Rabbit Ears	Verbascum thapsus	Tea for colds; kidney disorders
Onions	Allium cepa	Tea for hives; poultices for pleurisy, congestion, sore throat
Pennyroyal	Hedeomia pulegioides	Tea for colds; leaves contain substance which acts as a mosquito repellant
Pine Bark	Pinus strobus	Tea for diarrhea
Polk Weed	Phytolacca americana	Roots boiled to make a bath for curing skin irritations; Berries used to make wine to relieve symptoms of rheumatism
Rat's Vein	Chimaphila umbellata	Tea for calming nerves; colds
Sage	Eupatorium perfoliatum	Tea for coughs; tonsilitis
Sassafras	Sassafras albidum	General health tonic
Sampson's Snake	Aristolochia serpentaria	Tea for measles and pleurisy
Spice Wood	Lindera binzoin	Tea made from inner bark used to calm nerves
Yellow Root	Hydrastis canadensis	Mouth ulcers; tea for stomach disorders

Yellow root is one of the most well-known locally found herbs in the Valley. Residents can also purchase the root in powdered form from drugstores in the region. Its primary value is in relieving soreness from mouth ulcers. The root is also chewed as a way of cleaning the gums and teeth.

A category of herbs used traditionally and having continuing popularity today are those which local believers cite as effective in the relief of symptoms associated with rheumatism. These concoctions are generally wines or mixtures of alcohol and herbs. Ginseng roots soaked in whiskey or wines made from polk berries or blackberries are currently in use. Tea made with the boneset plant is another remedy associated with curing arthritic discomforts.

Medicinal herbs used for curing and easing the discomforts of infants and children are well-remembered by women who is past years acted as midwives. In the case of home deliveries, catnip tea is given to infants before the mother is able to nurse. Small doses of teas made with fennel or catnip are cited as effective for infants suffering from colic. These same two herbs are prescribed for infants plagued with hives, which in years past was more common than it is today. These practices, like much of Appalachian folk medicine, were heavily influenced by Native American practices.

In most Native American cultures, the primary objective of all obstetric practices was the ease and comfort of the mother. Southeastern Indians used an infusion of the bark of poplar, wild cherry, and dogwood given to the expectant mother at regular intervals.[18] Numerous other remedies were used by Native American women during labor either to promote contractions or to relieve pain. The Alabama Koasatis used boiled roots of the cotton plant as an aid in the birt process.[19] Native American infants also received herbal teas and herbal baths. Cherokee Indian infants were bathed in golden club and water every new moon.[20]

In the Sequatchie Valley today many of the best-known and most often used herbs are intended to relieve discomforts of colds and flu. These herbs, according to local belief, act as mild diuretics and relaxants. Those most commonly mentioned are heart leaf, pennyroyal, and fever weed. Cough syrups made from cherry bark and heart leaves are also used to relieve symptoms associated with influenza.

As has been demonstrated by the above data, traditional health care concepts and folk medicine practices are still a significant part of the lives of some Appalachian peoples. To a large degree, these traditions are kept alive by women who see curing as a part of their overall role as guardians of the family. Within this context, Appalachian people usually attempt to choose between modern and traditional health care systems or sometimes both on the basis of personal and cultural factors. These cultural implications should not be overlooked by those concerned with health delivery systems involving Appalachian people. A major factor is the rising cost of biomedical health care, particularly for those who cannot afford insurance. Another basic factor relates to scheduling. Many Appalachian people, particularly those who work outside their home community, cannot consult a specialist during normal office hours. Distance presents another problem to many people. For others, their traditional religious beliefs stress a dependence on God rather than medicine for healing. A final factor is the traditional Appalachian concept of self-reliance and distrust of outsiders which creates a strong tendency to depend on family and traditional means of curing.

NOTES

1. Marion Pearsall, *Little Smokey Ridge* (Lexington, Kentucky: University of Alabama, 1959: Jesse Stuart, "New Wine in Old Bottles," *Kentucky Folklore Record* 12 (1966): 105-7; 13 (1967): 20-24; Grady M. Long, "Folk Medicine in McMinn, Polk, Bradley and Meigs Counties, Tennessee, 1910-1927," *Tennessee Folklore Society,* Bulletin 28 (1962): 1-7; Mary B. Williford, "Income and Health in Remote Rural Areas," Ph. D. Dissertation, Columbia University, 1932; John Parris, *These Storied Mountains* (Asheville, N.C.: Citizens-Times Publishing Co., 1972); Augustin Gattinger, *The Medicinal Plants of Tennessee Exhibiting Their Commercial Value* (Nashville: F. M. Paul, 1894); Arnold Krochmal, *A Guide to Medicinal Plants of Appalachia,* Forest Service Research Paper (Washington, D.C.; U. S. Forest Service, 1971). These are only a few of the noteworthy sources on folk medicine in Appalachia.

2. "The Art of Healing" was a grant funded by The Tennessee Committee for the Humanities awarded to Dr. Clive Kileff, University of Tennessee at Chattanooga. The authors acknowledge Dr. Kileff's continuing interest and cooperation.

3. Additional funding is presently being sought by the authors to conduct further household surveys on the use of traditional and biomedical curative practices in the Sequatchie Valley.

4. Earl C. Case, *The Valley of East Tennessee,* Bulletin 36, State of Tennessee Geological Survey, 1925, p. 51.

5. U.S. Bureau of the Census, Census of Population: 1970, *General Social and Economic Characteristics.* Final Report PC(1)-C44, Washington, D.C., 1971, p. 167.

6. Ibid., p. 168.

7. Ibid., pp. 325-31.

8. Leonard Raulston and James Livingood, *Sequatchie: A Story of the Southern Cumberlands* (Knoxville: University of Tennessee, 1974), pp 213-230.

9. U.S. Bureau of Census, *General Social and Economic Characteristics,* pp. 365, 369, 371.

10. Helen Bullard and Joseph Krech, *First Hundred Years* (Crossville, Tennessee: Private Publication, 1956), p. 90.

11. William H. Gilbert, *The Eastern Cherokee,* 133 (Washington, D.C.: Bureau of American Ethnology, 1943); James Mooney and Frans M. Olbrechts, Swimmer Manuscript, *Cherokee Sacred Formulas and Medicinal Prescriptions,* 99 (Washington, D.C.; Bureau of American Ethnology, 1932).

12. Marion Pearsall has written about a similar pattern for rural Kentucky. Marion Pearsall, "Healthways in a Mountain County," *Mountain Life and Work* 36 (1960): 7-13.

13. Virgil Vogel, *American Indian Medicine* (Norman: University of Oklahoma Press, 1970), p. 12.

14. David Jones, *Sanapia: Comanche Medicine Woman* (New York: Holt, Rinehart, and Winston, 1972).

15. For information on female herbalists, see Ellen J. Stekert, "Focus for Conflict, Southern Mountain Medical Beliefs in Detroit," *Journal of American Folklore* 83(1970); 126. For reference to male knowledge of herbal remedies, see the prepared comments by Marion Pearsall to E. Stekert, "Healthways," p. 150.

16. Marie B. Mellinger and Bill Stiles, "Sang Season," *Foxfire* 2(1968): 28-32, 72-77; Marie B. Mellinger, "Sang Sign," *Foxfire* 2 (1968): 47-52.

17. Nelson Coon, *Using Plants for Healing* (New York: Hearthside Press, 1963), p. 139.
18. Frank G. Speck, "An Adendum to Catawba Indian Herbal and Curative Practices," Manuscript on file with the American Philosophical Society.
19. Vogel, *American Indian Medicine,* p. 222.
20. Mooney and Olbrecht, *Cherokee Sacred Formulas,* p. 76.

RELIGIOUS LANGUAGE AND COLLECTIVE ACTION: A STUDY OF VOLUNTARISM IN A RURAL APPALACHIAN CHURCH

Michael Vaughn Carter

Abstract

> *This study is a theoretical inquiry into the nature of collective action in the local church, with application to an evangelical Protestant congregation in the southern Appalachian region. More specifically, the study examines the various interrelationships between the use of religious language in the church and the organization of the church as a voluntary association. A case study approach was utilized in which the author became a participant observer for two years while serving as pastor in a rural church in southwestern West Virginia. The study also reveals several implications in relation to a culture of poverty analysis of Appalachian culture and religion.*

Statement of the Problem

Religious language has been traditionally understood as a means of communicating the spiritual message of the church (Whiteley, 1964: 40-50). The local church, unlike other voluntary associations, relies upon its message of spirituality as the primary motivational attraction to its present and prospective members. It does not use coercion, or to any large extent selective benefits, in sustaining a viable membership. The church of the southern Appalachians articulates a message which is embodied in an idiosyncratic language system. Although the Christian-Biblical symbols used are traditional to Protestant Christianity, they sometimes differ in meaning from one local church to another due to subcultural differences and denominational interpretation. If the local church relies upon language in attaining new members and in the continued motivation of existing members, then the following two questions arise: (1) Is there an association between religious language and collective action in the local church? (2) If there is such an association, is it positive in sustaining collective action or is it negative in prohibiting collective action?

These questions acquire greater significance when applied to the local church of the Appalachians. Previous writers who have examined the Appalachian church describe it as housing "fatalistic" frontier religion which has an "individualistic" emphasis as opposed to a "social concern" (Weller, 1965, 1970, 1978; also see Brewer, 1962; Caudill, 1963; Erikson, 1976). Jack Weller (1965, 1978) one of the foremost exponents of this position concludes that the religion of the Appalachian is "personalistic," which in turn leads to a "socially passive ethic." This prevailing view originates from a "culture of poverty" paradigm (Lewis, 1966) but has also been integrated into the terminology of a variety of Appalachian theorists.[1]

In general, these descriptions of the Appalachian church result in an overall impression that the church exists only to serve the extreme individualism found within the subculture. And, no doubt, people do affiliate or attend the local church for personal reasons. This point need not be contested. But are these descriptions completely accurate? Does the religion of the Appalachian exist solely to satisfy some inherent trait of extreme individualism? Is there no collective consciousness?

It is the purpose of this paper to examine these questions in view of Olson's (1971) theory of collective action. By doing so this approach demonstrates that the local church provides an array of "generalized benefits" which can only be accrued from collective action, not extreme indivdidualism. These "generalized benefits or collective goods" must be reevaluated in lieu of the previous descriptions of Appalchian religion. Religious language is then seen as a vital link in the ability of the local church to provide these "generalized benefits."

Objective of the Study

The study's objectives are essentially threefold. First, the theoretical framework defines the purpose of organization and the implications posed by the "free rider" problem, which is inherent in collective action based on voluntarism.[2] The size or scale of the organization is also considered. Religious language is then recognized as establishing a set of common "terms and condition" which are instrumental in the organizing of the local church.

The second objective is the elaboration of a theoretical model. It is designed to examine the associational or nonassociational relationships between collective action types and the symbolic language of the church.

The third and final objective is the application of the model to a specific congregation in rural Appalachia. Thus, a brief summary is presented of a case study (Carter, 1979) of a rural parish in southern Wayne County, West Virginia, where the writer served as pastor September 1977 to September 1979.

THEORETICAL FRAMEWORK

The church, like any organization or voluntary association, exists so as to serve the common interests of its members. Mancur Olson (1971: 15) states: "The achievement of any common goal or the satisfaction of any common interest means that a public or collective good has been provided for that group."[3] In other words, the provision of "collective goods is the fundamental function of organizations generally." By collective it is meant that no one is excluded from the "benefit or satisfaction brought about by its achievement." Even those who do not pay or contribute to the collective good cannot be "kept from sharing in the consumption of the good, as they can where noncollective goods are concerned."

The local church provides an array of collective goods and services, e.g., worship, education, congregational singing, fellowship dinners. They are usually available for both the membership and the surrounding community. Therefore, if the church is a provider of collective goods it must also engage in the process of collective action; for in fact, the collective goods are the end result of a process of collective action.

The Free Rider Problem

"The free rider" problem is always present in collective action based on voluntarism. Olson (1971: 21) describes the problem as follows: "Though all of the members of the group...have a common interest in obtaining the collective benefit or good, they have no common interest in paying the cost of providing that collective good." Each member within the organization would, in fact, prefer that someone else pay the entire cost of the collective good. This phenomenon of allowing an unequal distribution of the burden of collective action to occur can be called "the free rider" problem. It may occur to some extent in both large and small voluntary associations.

The "free rider" problem consists of two stages. The first is an "assurance problem," and the second, a "commitment problem." In the "assurance problem," the participant needs to be assured that his or her action or contribution, whether it be money, energy, or time, is a shared collective event and not an individual enterprise. The ability of each individual to derive a full benefit from his or her own contribution depends upon the contribution of others. If the participant suspects that other members in the organization will not engage in a similar manner of collective action, an incentive is created for withholding one's own contribution.

The second stage is the problem of maintaining a commitment to the provision of the collective good. If the participant has been assured that fellow members will contribute, another opportunity exists for the "free rider." Once he or she is assured of the contribution of others, the "free rider" can continue to enjoy the collective good without contributing to the collective action.

This inherent problem of sustaining collective action has traditionally been confronted in one of two ways. The first is by coercion or compulsion; and the second by rewards or selective benefits (Olson, 1971: 13; see also Parsons and Smelser, 1954: 50-69).

Size or scale of the voluntary association adds a dimension which is usually overlooked when considering viable options in seeking a solution to the "free rider" problem. Human organizations, including the church, must then be analyzed according to scale (Simpkins: 1977), whether it be large, small, or intermediate in size. It is then necessary to consider the implications posed by size to the voluntary association.

The Large Organization. It would seem plausible that large organizations of an emotional or ideological element would not need to resort to a coercive or reward system in order to sustain collective action. One such example is patriotism usually draws its strength from a common ideology as well as culture or common religion. But, to support the modern state, taxes are compulsory by law. Collective action based upon voluntarism will not support most large organizations (Olson, 1971: 13). Max Weber (1947: 319-320) recognized this when he spoke of "leveraging" individuals through a selective benefit, reward, or special sanction, so that individuals might have a greater incentive to contribute.

The Small Organization. In some small organizations each of the members, or at least one of them, will discover that personal gain or interest in the collective good goes beyond the entire cost of providing some degree of the collective good. There are some members in these organizations who would be better satisfied even if they had to provide the entire collective good by themselves than to go without it. This would occur if the benefit exceeded the cost for the individual (Olson, 1971: 34). The single most important point is that a small group, association, or organization may very well be able to provide the members with a collective good simply because of the individual attraction of the good.

The Intermediate Organization. In an intermediate organization a member may or may not acquire enough of the generalized benefit to justify his or her own contribution. Groups of this size are large enough that an individual would not find it profitable to pay for the entire collective good; yet, the group would sufficiently notice the loss of only one member. If a member decides not contribute, the cost will noticeably rise for the others in the group; they too may then refuse to contribute and the collective good would cease. On the other hand, a member might realize that he or she would be worse off without the collective good even though a contribution had to be made. Therefore, the member might or might not decide to contribute for the provision of the collective good. The result is indeterminate (Olson, 1971: 43).

The local church is just one organization which falls into the intermediate classification. Although it can be found as both large and small, it is primarily an organization that belongs in the intermediate category. It is the size of this organization which renders it indeterminate as to whether it (the local church) will provide enough incentive for the provision of collective goods. Therefore, the church like other intermediate organizations may or may not be able to sustain enough collective action to supply an optimal level of collective goods. If the church is to continue the provision of collective goods, it must then overcome the inherent problems (i.e., assurance and commitment) of collective action.

Collective Action and the Local Church in Appalachia

The local church in the Appalachians stands as a curious institution when interpreted through a culture of poverty paradigm. This paradigm maintains that the subculture of the Appalachians is one of self-generating or cyclic poverty (Walls, 1976). Moreover, the organizations therein do not exist to provide Olson's concept of a "generalized benefit," but rather to meet the "personalistic" needs caused from the subculture's extreme individualism. Jack Weller contends that the Appalachian cannot engage in collective action, except it meet individualistic needs; hence, he or she must rely upon the outside, more general culture for assistance.

The puzzle within the culture of poverty analysis of collective action in Appalachia can be summed up with the following question: How does one account for the omnipresence of voluntary associations, i.e., the local church, which depends upon collective action over time? It is with this question that a culture of poverty analysis becomes somewhat anomalous. The local church, in its varied forms, is one voluntary association that can be found throughout the Appalachians. Its survival, according to a culture of poverty paradigm, has been in a subculture of (questionable) nonjoiners. In other words, the local church in Appalachia has been to overcome subcultural traits, as well as inherent problems of collective action. How then does one explain the prevalence of the local church, much less its continued provision of collective goods? In the upcoming discussion, language will be linked to culture and the local church so as to set forth a plausible answer.

Culture, Language, and Organization

A culture and the organizations contained within depend upon the existence of common languages. Human communication and human transactions cannot occur without reference to the common understanding which is inherent in a common language (Olson, 1978: 5).

Language is especially important due to its ability to affect human interaction. Whorf has emphasized that language as a system of "conceptual categories tends to shape and channelize thought processes" (Ostrom, 1977: 2).

The church must depend upon language if a common understanding is to prevail among the membership. People cannot effectively participate in the affairs of the church without first knowing what the "terms and conditions" are. Furthermore, the participation in the church, as a social organization, implies that the members are in some basic agreement about the "terms and conditions and standards of value that guide the endeavors" of the membership whether it be in individual or collective action (Ostrom, 1978: 5). If a general agreement does not prevail and the people do not perceive their interest being served, one cannot expect the membership to participate constructively in the affairs of the local church.

The church has developed a highly specialized langauge system. This langauge system for the Protestant Church is virtually uniform in content, but not in application. Cultural traits such as language patterns and modes of organization differ from one cultural setting to another. The language of the church, although basically the same as far as Christian terminology is concerned, is not always applied in like manner.

If an analysis is made of religious language, whether it be an examination of the analogy, the statement, or the parable, signs and symbols must be understood within the "subcultural ethos" (Stackhouse, 1972) of which it forms a part. Because signs and symbols have a cultural meaning many social scientists have either misquoted, misunderstood, or simply ignored their importance (Hadden, 1968).

In summary, the church stands as one social organization which provides an array of collective goods, but does not rely upon the conventional methods of motivation, such as coercion or selective benefits (to any large degree). The primary type of leverage lies in the symbolic nature of a highly specialized language system. Collective action, must in part, be motivated by this symbolic mode of communication.

THEORETICAL MODEL

The purpose of the theoretical model is to analyze the composition of religious language when it accompanies collective action events in the local church. It is designed to show the association between certain religious symbols and voluntaristic acts in the congregation. The model is based upon the working hypothesis that religious language serves as an instrument of collective action in the local church.

The highly specialized language system of the church has traditionally been viewed as a system antagonistic to the process of social organization (Whitley, 1964: 42). Contenders of this view believe the church to be a divine fellowship, not a social organization. Language may however perform two functions. The first function of religious language is to communicate the spiritual message of the church. But it also, secondly, establishes a set of common terms and conditions among people as necessary for a viable social organization.

The model (as shown in Figure 1) is composed of two complementary sections. The first half analyzes the symbolic material found within religious statements; and the second half distinguishes three criteria so as to establish collective action typologies.

Symbolic Types

Religious statements can be analyzed in terms of five symbol types: (1) God Type, (2) Commitment Type, (3) Pragmatic Type, (4) Eschatological Type, and (5) Environmental Type.

The God Type. This symbol is any symbolization which directly refers to a superior being, force, or intelligence defined as being "Godlike." In most

THEORETICAL MODEL

FIGURE 1

COLLECTIVE ACTION TYPE / SYMBOLIC TYPE	Type of Action (Contributions) of money or in-kind	Type of Leadership (Ministerial or) Lay Person	Congregational Involvement (One person to) entire congregation
God Type	Gives authoritative reason for action events	Used by both minister and Lay Person for authority	Key to greater involvement
	Represented by Trinitarian concepts of: God, Jesus Christ, Holy Spirit Similar symbols: The Savior, Lord, Heavenly Father, Good Shepherd		
Commitment Type	Necessary for commitment to a contribution of money or in kind	Key for minister or Lay Leader to communicate "commitment"	Key to greater involvement for a voluntary association in overcoming "free rider" problem

Within Evangelical Church: "Won't you give your heart to Jesus?"

	Expresses action "now" in progress	Leaders communicate it because it assures others of maintained commitment	Expresses a degree of on going involvement
Pragmatic Type	Communicates actual participation in action events: "I'm working for the Savior" or "I do the Lord's will."		
Eschatological Type	This symbol when seriously used in the rural evangelical church can stir to action. Its otherworldly connotation <u>does not</u> always mean fatalistic attitudes.	Commonly used by both minister and laity to express reason behind their action.	It can be very supportive for greater involvement if interpreted as a spiritual symbol.
	A powerful symbol, especially when accompanied by a God type: "God's Heaven," "Satan's Hell," and "Second Coming."		
Environmental Type	Acts as a supportive symbol to action events that concern the church or community.	Used by both minister and laity to express the need for action concerning a given "project."	Elicits greater involvement if buttressed by one or several of the other symbolic types.
	Two Appalachian examples are also hymn titles: "God Walks the Dark Hills," and "The Unclouded Day." Project examples could range from painting the local church to food pantries.		

instances it will be revealed through one of the three trinitarian concepts of God the Father, Jesus Christ the Son, and the Holy Spirit. Each of these have various derivations. e.g., Lord, Heavenly Father, Master, Good Shepherd.

The Commitment Type. Symbols in this category place an obligation on the individual to support a specific cause or event within the work of the church. Some "commitment" symbol usage would seem to be imperative in any voluntary association due to the constant need for volunteers. Commitment is expressed in a variety of ways within the evangelical church. It is most vividly portrayed by the "altar call" which is voiced by forms of challenge or questions such as: "Won't you give your heart to Jesus?"

The Pragmatic Type. The "pragmatic" symbol is closely related to the commitment symbol; however, the distinction lies in the difference between commitment to a future obligation and performance of that obligation. This symbol is related to actual participation in the provision of collective goods. Examples such as *"I'm working* for the Savior" or *"I do* what the Lord would have me *to do,"* emphasize performance in the present as opposed to commitment for the future.

The Eschatological Type. The "eschatological" type symbol refers to a futuristic and otherworldly event or place. "God's Heaven and Satan's Hell" are the most common examples. Others include "the Second Coming" (of Christ) and "Armageddon." Many times this symbolization will appear in phrases such as: "a land of no more tears," or "when the roll is called up yonder I'll be there." These, no doubt, convey a powerful emotional yearning within the local church.

The Environmental Type. This type provides a means of characterizing the immediate surroundings of the church. Titles of hymns and sermons often tell of the environmental setting. One case in point found in the Appalachians is that of the folk hymns "God Walks the Dark Hills" and "The Unclouded Day." These vividly portray this symbolic type within a specific cultural ethos.

Collective Action Types

The second half of the theoretical model is composed of three attributes so as to establish collective action typologies. These attributes are to distinguish (1) type of action, (2) type of leadership for initiating the action, and (3) degree of congregational involvement.

First, within the church, collective action occurs in one of two modes: contributions of money and contributions in kind. Second, it is initiated by either the pastor or a member or officer of the congregation. And third, collective action takes place with various degrees of congregational involvement, ranging from an individual to the entire congregation. These criteria are not entirely inclusive nor mutually exclusive; however, they do yield a manageable classification system when examining the evangelical church in Appalachia.

The Application

The application of the model rests upon Ostrom's (1978: 5) observation that "people cannot effectively participate in the affairs of the community without knowing what the terms and conditions are." These terms and conditions for the church rest in the symbolic meanings found within its highly specialized language system. Religious symbols establish a set of terms and conditions which then act as common instruments of collective action in the provision of collective goods in the church.

The five symbolic types and the three examining criteria for collective action provide this model with an operational set of parameters. By cataloging the symbol type and observing the three criteria of collective action, associations will or will not exist between the two respective halves of the model. The utility of the model lies in the association between langauge and the church to sustain collective action for the provision of collective goods.

SUMMARY OF CASE STUDY

This is a brief account of an in-depth case study about a rural church located in the southern half of Wayne County, West Virginia, near the town of Fort Gay (pop. 700).[4] Since its founding in the late 1860s the church has affiliated with the American Baptist Convention due to their early evangelization of West Virginia.

Organizationally, the church is congregational in polity and led by a minister employed by majority vote of the congregation. The current membership is 125, with approximately 85 active members. The difference between formal membership and active membership lies primarily in outward migration rather than lack of participation.

Doctrinally the church is conservative-fundamental, although distinguished by its heterogeneous membership in terms of social class. For instance, the Sunday School superintendent is a retired banker; the treasurer, a retired school teacher; the clerk, a housewife; and the board of deacons is composed of skilled technicians and farmers, as well as a top administrator for the State Department of Welfare.

FINDINGS OF THE CASE STUDY

Three things appear to be necessary to connect language with collective action at this Appalchian parish. *First,* the symbols must be recognized as "spiritual." If the symbols are not associated with the spirituality of the church then the congregation does not find them compelling. *Second,* the symbolic expression must contain a reference to the "God" type symbol. This symbolic type provides an authority base for undertaking collective action, one that is well recognized within, as well as outside, the church community. *Third,* the symbolic expression must contain the "pragmatic" type symbol, the use of which depends upon a general sense of commitment articulated separately through "commitment" type symbols.

The expression may or may not contain "eschatological" or "environmental" symbols. The pragmatic symbol, though it can stand alone, acquires greater weight if associated with eschatological or environmental symbols, or both. The eschatological type symbol is also helpful in establishing the spirituality of a symbolic expression.

Collective action, whether it be "contributions of money or in kind," occurs with a high frequency at this rural church. The members rise to meet a variety of challenges in the provision of collective goods. For example, if money is needed for a new fixture in the church, it is given by the congregation. If a family of the congregation needs financial assistance, it is provided. If volunteers are needed in Vacation Bible School, the members volunteer. If an individual is sick or hospitalized, assistance is made available. If a fellowship dinner is "potluck," food appears by the carload. The congregation provides these plus many more collective goods because of their deep sense of commitment to this voluntary association and the members within. If asked why, their response is voiced through one or a combination of the five symbolic types previously mentioned.

Symbolic language in this church works as an instrument for overcoming the "free rider" problem inherent in collective action. First, the language is addressed to the "assurance problem," i.e., the need for each member to be assured that others will contribute by articulating a ground of authority and jointness and establishing a shared sense of congregational participation in the provision of collective goods. The combination of "God" type and "pragmatic" type symbols, e.g., "working for the Savior," or "giving your all to Jesus," convey pragmatic terms and conditions which carry the assurance that those who believe in "the Savior" will "work."

Second, the language addresses the "commitment" problem, i.e., the need for individuals to feel committed once assured of other's contributions by providing an authoritative means of expressing a continuing commitment to the church. The occasion for expressing commitment at this rural parish is most often the altar call. By responding to the altar call, individuals manifest signs of commitment. In addition to coming forward, individuals articulate their sense of obligation through symbolic expressions both to the pastor and the congregation. To "give your heart to Jesus" is to make a basic commitment with a profound sense of personal obligation.

SUMMARY AND CONCLUSIONS

Local church congregations throughout America and especially in rural Appalachia are for the most part "intermediate" sized groups. This case study is one example. Given that collective action is indeterminate for this size of collectivity, what makes the difference at this rural parish in its ability to sustain congregational collective action on a voluntary basis? Religious language composed of meaningful symbolic expressions holds the key.

Consensus is a necessary condition for voluntary collective action to occur. Language cannot elicit collective action in the absence of consensus. Language is an essential instrument in the act of sharing consensus. The congregation's consensus in this case study rests upon common terms and conditions embodied in a language system which is composed of symbolic types representing "God," "commitment," "Pragmatic action," "eschatology," and the "environment."

Implications of the Study: Appalachia/America

This study raises several questions in relation to Appalachian culture and religion as portrayed by several previous writers, especially the proponents of a culture of poverty paradigm. The study poses an anomaly for this paradigm in at least two points.

First, in a culture of poverty analysis, Appalachian religion and culture are described as "fatalistic." The tentative conclusion reached by this research is that within the domain of the local church "spirituality" has been misinterpreted as "fatalism." Eschatological symbolism is *not* fatalistic for the congregation of this case study. To the contrary: rather than symbolizing passive acceptance and resignation, these symbols stir to action.

Second, the general effectiveness of leadership in a process of collective action in the rural Appalachian congregation may depend on using the right language. Perhaps ministers who were educated outside the Appalachian region that failed to find viable collective action used the wrong language in communicating to the congregation. It would appear that Weller and others may have disregarded the importance of conservative Christian-Biblical symbols as instruments of collective action.

Outside the Appalachian context, religious scholarship in the liberal tradition has held the principle of voluntarism in high esteem (Adams, 1976), while disparaging the use of conservative Christian-Biblical symbols. The results of this study would seem to indicate that the traditional liberal point of view is internally contradictory. Conservative symbolism may in fact be an important source of voluntarism and collective action in the local church congregation.

Notes

1. A recent exception to this prevailing view of religion in Appalachia can be found in the introduction by B.B. Maurer and the theoretical supplement by John D. Photiadis to *Religion in Appalachia* (1978). Also, an exception to the prevailing view of fatalism concerning culture can be found in O.N. Simpkins's article on "Culture" in *Mountain Heritage* (1075). Jack Weller's position does have a minor difference from the culture of poverty thesis set forth by Lewis. The distinction for Weller is that the Appalachian simply has no culture or as he states, "mountain culture is inadequate..." (1965: 154-160).

2. The phrase "collective action based on voluntarism" could be replaced by the term "voluntary associations." The longer phrase is preferred because of the distinctions between the types of collective action. Collective action does not necessarily mean that it is based upon "the voluntary principle" (Adams, 1976). It may be action that is collective, but motivated by force (coercion), cooptation, or selective benefits; each one of these cases is not voluntaristic. The distinction for this study is imperative. Collective action within the parameters of this study is meant to refer "to the joint action of individuals organized to obtain a common goal, contrasted to the separate actions of individuals" (Carter, 1979). This joint action is maintained by voluntarism, "a principle of organization based upon the *free* and *willing consent* of individuals (Carter, 1979).

3. All quotes in this paragraph come from Olson (1971:15).

4. In the space of this paper the case study cannot be fully developed; therefore, the writer will only be able to give a brief summary of the results. The full study is contained in the masters thesis of the writer (See References).

REFERENCES

Adams, James Luther. *On Being Human Religiously.* Edited by Max L. Stackhouse. Boston: Beacon Press, 1976.

Brewer, Earl. "Religion and the Churches." *The Southern Appalachian Region: A Survey.* Edited by Thomas R. Ford. Lexington: University of Kentucky Press, 1962.

Carter, Michael V. "Religious Language and Collective Action: A Study of Voluntarism in a Rural Appalachian Church." Master's thesis, Marshall University, 1979.

Caudill, Harry M. *Night Comes to the Cumberlands.* Boston: Atlantic Monthly Press Book, 1963.

_____. *The Watches of the Night.* Boston: Atlantic Monthly Press Book, 1976.

Erikson, Kai T. *Everything in its Path.* New York: Simon and Schuster, 1976.

Hadden, Jeffrey K. *The Gathering Storm in the Churches.* New York: Anchor Books, 1969.

Lewis, Oscar. *The Children of Sanchez.* New York: Random House, 1961.

_____."The Culture of Poverty." *Scientific American,* October 1966, pp. 16-25.

Mauere, B.B. Introduction to *Religion in Appalachia.* Edited by John D. Photiadis. Morgantown: West Virginia University, 1978.

Olson, Mancur. *The Logic of Collective Action: Public Goods and the Theory of Groups.* Cambridge: Harvard University Press, 1971.

Ostrom, Vincent. "Culture, Science and Politics." Paper presented at Indiana University, 1977.

_____."Language, Reason, and Discourse." Paper presented in a workshop at Indiana University, December 20, 1978.

Parsons, Talcott and Smelser, Neil. *Economy and Society.* Glencoe, Illinois: Free Press, 1954.

Photiadis, John D. Theoretical supplement to *Religion in Appalachia.* Edited by John D. Photiadis. Morgantown: West Virginia University, 1978.

Simpkins, O. Norman. "A Scale Approach to Community Development." Paper presented at Marshall University, August 1977.

_____."Culture." *Mountain Heritage.* Edited by B.B. Maurer. Morgantown: Binding and Printing Company, 1975.

Stackhouse, Max L. *Ethics and the Urban Ethos.* Boston: Beacon Press, 1972.

Walls, David S. "Central Appalachia: A Peripheral Region." *Journal of Sociology and Social Welfare.* 4(1976): 232-247.

Weber, Max. *Theory of Social and Economic Organization.* Translated by Talcott Parsons and A.M. Henderson. New York: Oxford University Press, 1947.

Weller, Jack E. *Yesterday's People.* Lexington: University Press of Kentucky, 1965.

_____."How Religion Mirrors and Meets Appalachian Culture." *Appalachia in Transition.* Edited by Max E. Glenn. St. Louis: The Bethany Press, 1970.

_____."Salvation is Not Enough." *Religion in Appalachia.* Edited by John D. Photiadis. Morgantown: West Virginia University, 1978.

Whitley, Oliver R. *Religious Behavior: Where Sociology and Religion Meet.* Englewood Cliffs: Prentice Hall, 1964.

Goals for the Collection and Use of Appalachian Oral Materials in the 1980s

Jay Robert Reese

Abstract

This paper suggests that, although the present state of Appalachian ressearch and study is healthy, new goals need to be set for the field. The sixty-year rush to record Appalachian culture has resulted in a large body of oral material that remains largely unused. The Appalachian scholar should now spend most of his energy and time on the cataloging, analysis, and use of material collected. There is a great need for an interdisciplinary method of indexing oral materials, an index of Appalachian oral resources, and a bibliography of Appalachian oral materials. Scholars must begin adapting this material to classroom use and must analyze it for answers to questions about Appalachian culture.

The present state of Appalachian research and study seems healthy indeed. Not only are the traditional perspectives of Appalachian study (e.g., English, history and folklore) still productive, but their cohabitation, if not marriage, with the newer disciplines that examine Appalachia with respect to its social and political structure, its economy, and its natural environment seems possible. Where once only Berea College was synonymous with Appalachian studies, now almost every college and university in southern Appalachia is involved either in the preservation or the teaching of Appalachian studies, now almost every college and university in southern Appalachia is involved either in the preservation or the teaching of Appalachian life and culture. Even though Appalachian study centers, workshops, and programs abound, the interest necessary to support these diverse activities is not diminishing; in fact, it is growing each year. This new popularity of Appalachian study is forcing Appalachian scholars to question whether the study of Appalachia in the next decade should be based on the theoretical principles that have guided it for the last thirty years. This question seems especially pertinent for the traditional modes of Appalachian study that, to a large extent, have brought the discipline to where it is now. In short, now that we have arrived, where do we go from here?

The specific question that must be addressed in 1980 is whether or not past justifications for Appalachian research, as well as methods of investigation resulting from these justifications, are viable for the next decade. Clearly they are not. The primary justifications for the collection of Appalachian materials since 1920 has been the imperative to record the folk ways and speech of the older Appalachians (those persons seventy years of age or more) before they and their ways of life cease to exist. This belief that the researcher's prime responsibility is to save quickly passing aspects of Appalachian culture from historical extinction engendered a method of collection that might be called, "rapid, random-recording research." For the past sixty years, the trained and the untrained, professional and the non-professional, the scholarly and the non-scholarly have flocked to the deep hollows to record the customs and speech of elderly Appalachians.

Because of this sixty-year rush to record Appalachia, the usual prerequisites of scientific and scholarly research have often been ignored. Few field projects have been preceeded by sufficient scholarship to ascertain how the material collected would fit into the broad range of Appalachian research or even if it would duplicate already existing data. Seldom has thought been given to the future use of the material nor has it been collected as an aid in the solution of particular scholarly or cultural questions. Too often in the past researchers have had no clear conception of what they wished to elicit from their informants or why the information would be valuable. Instead, they would simply appear at the cabin door, tape recorder in hand, to ask an elderly person to reminisce over old times. After an hour of such enjoyable babble, the fieldworkers would return home satisfied they had preserved some endangered species of Appalachia.

The above is not meant to disparage the research already accomplished. The result of this long rush to preserve Appalachia has produced an oral record of a culture that is undoubtedly unsurpassed anywhere in the nation. It is not unusual for the academician to be approached in his office by a person who claims to have hundreds of valuable tapes of oral interviews of "pure Appalachians" in the trunk of his car. It is also not unusual to find not only that they are there, but that they are indeed valuable. Almost every college within the Appalachian area has some type of collection of potentially valuable Appalachian material in one stage of disuse or another. The question of goals and objectives for the 1980s is not raised to criticize the past, but to evaluate directions for the future. It has been assumed that it is far better to duplicate previous studies than to chance valuable raw information being forever lost. The rush has been to record; the task of analyzing or even cataloguing has been left to someone else, to a later time.

It is now, of course, later; we are that someone else and in all truthfulness we must admit that we have either suceeded or failed in meeting the first primary goal of Appalachian research. Either that culture that was rediscovered to America in 1920 has been preserved or it is lost to history forever. It is incongruous to use the same justification in 1980 that was so urgently voiced in 1920. A full six generations of seventy and eighty year old Appalachians have died since the original subjects were found living in their 1920 mountains. Either we are now in the rather embarrassing position of admitting that the old folk ways and speech did not die out as predicted (in which case one wonders if they ever will) or that the "preservation of the culture" justification is no longer valid. Certainly if any change has taken place in the Appalachians during the past sixty years, the twentieth-century-born seventy and eighty year olds we are interviewing today are not representative of the same culture as their 1920 counterparts, who were born in pre-Civil War, frontier America.

The acceptance of the fact that we cannot still justify our research solely by a simple call to the preservation of passing folk ways and speech--because they are either passed or not passing at all--is important; for all of us still have a tendency to rush once more to the hollow. The simple observation that we may not need to spend all, or even most, of our energy collecting, that our time may now be demanded in different areas, has been obscured for several reasons, not the least of which is our love of collecting. To a true folklorist, oral historian, or dialectologist of our generation, field work is the magic of our universe. There is always a sense of loss when we finish an interview and must return to the everyday nowness of our office. If we had wished to stay in our cement cubicles and talk with our collegues we would have become "regular" teachers, not the woodscolts we are.

There are, of course, other reasons that may have hidden this simple observation from our mind's eye, such as the relative rate of cultural change.

Although Appalachian culture has altered greatly since 1920, so has the culture of the rest of the United States. As a result even though for some time we have not been preserving (i.e., recording) what was identified somewhat romantically as the southern highland culture of the 1920s, there still appeared to be sufficient superficial differences between the manners and speech of a present seventy-year-old Appalachian and that of the youth-dominated culture of the 1960s and 70s, so that the preservation theory, if not examined too closely, seemed valid. It is obvious, however, that the type of information recently received differs greatly from that of 1920. Now, time and time again, the response to a question concerning a custom or a form of speech that was commonly found in 1920 is "I don't recall that in my lifetime, but now my parents and their parents said that." It is evident that much of what we are collecting, supposedly to preserve, is now second-hand, hearsay folk speech and culture. In recent years our over-reliance on the preservation justification has constantly forced us to present the exception as the rule in Appalachian research. Since the fifties field researchers have become aware of the increasing difficulty in finding Appalachian subjects who even approximate the romantic stereotype of the pure Appalachian as identified in 1920. Occasionally one encounters subjects who sufficiently resemble the traditional mountain man or woman for us to stamp "formed in Appalachia of pure, original, old cultural ways and speech" upon them, but generally for every acceptable subject encountered, a hundred must be rejected. The areas we go to record are more and more remote and less and less representative of the present Appalachian. Even then it is not unusual to head for the farthest hollow, go up an almost impossible mountain road, walk a mile or two, sit in a non-electric cabin by the side of a pristine mountain creek and talk to an aged but talkative Appalachian only to find during the course of the interview that six other researchers have been there previously.

Perhaps because of these occurrences, one notes that a subtle but significant perceptual shift has taken place in Appalachian research. The older Appalachian is no longer viewed in the same temporal frame of reference as his non-Appalachian contemporary, rather his behavior is compared to that of the dominant culture of the 1970s, a culture sixty or seventy years his junior. This is quite different from what was seen from 1920 through the 1950s. If one reads these early accounts, it is obvious that the ways of the Appalachian were always compared to the ways and customs of persons his own age in other part of the nation. That is to say, the uniqueness of older Appalachians of 1920 did not result simply because they were old or because they differed from the younger generation, but because they differed significantly from other persons their age in other parts of the nation. Today, however, one might argue that to a large extent the Appalachian is considered unique not because he is an Appalachian, but because he is seventy years old. One wonders if most of the information we now receive from older speakers cannot be gathered from any seventy or eighty year old rural American.

In truth, of course, we are no longer doing the same type of collecting that we once did. In recent years we have begun to investigate the total range of Appalachian culture. The older person is not the only subject who is examined, recorded, and taped. More and more as we conduct mutli-generational research which gathers information on middle-aged and younger Appalachians we are increasingly focusing upon contemporary rather than past cultural characteristics. Although we seem somewhat reluctant to admit this in public, it is nonetheless true. Even though our research has changed, we have not examined where we are going as a discipline. As a result we may end up at the end of the 1980s with another generation of Appalachians stored in our personal and institutional archives, as unused and perhaps as unusable as the first.

Perhaps nothing is more indicative of the need for a new direction in our study of the Appalachian culture as the term "Appalachian studies" itself. Always before we have studied Appalachia; now we have programs of Appalachian studies, programs through which we attempt to teach others about the past and present nature of Appalachia. As we attempt to do this we find that we have collected large quantities of raw data, yet we must rely for the most part on the insights and works of those who wrote before any of that material was recorded.[1]

If it is clear that past justifications for Appalachian research and collecting are no longer valid, what are some suggestions for the decade to come? First, we must design our research projects with a great deal more care than we have in the past. Second, we must collect what is most needed and in such a way that it is most useful. The day when one could justify going up in the mountains to simply collect bits and pieces of Appalachia seems over. A researcher now should know specifically what he seeks, how that information will help the solution of a scholarly or cultural problem and whether or not similar material has been previously collected. One might even suggest that the collection of Appalachian material is no longer the prime responsibility of the Appalachian scholar. Certainly, some collecting of comparable data from younger informants needs to be undertaken, and as we find gaps in existing material they should be filled, but I would suggest that the principal need of Appalachian scholarship in the 1980s is not collection. We should spend most of our energies, our time, and our resources on the cataloguing, analysis, and use of the material already collected. One might argue that the reason the quality of cultural understanding of Appalachia reflected in most books and articles is still only slightly above moronic prejudice is not due to the lack of data, but due to our lack of analysis and explication of that data.[2] Perhaps we have played in the field too long and now we must work in our offices.

When one surveys the last twenty-year period of the collecting of oral Appalachian material, whether it be folkloric, dialectal, or historical, two points are immediately evident. The first is that in spite of the limited money available for such projects, a large and significant amount of oral materials of varied quality have been collected. The second obvious realization is that these materials, except for a few notable exceptions, remain largely unused. Stored in university library special collections or upon the shelves of the collectors, they are--for all practical purposes--useless. In many cases, because of the fragility of the tapes on which they are recorded, they will deteriorate before they are ever used.

To understand this problem one must realize a particular curse of the collector: in a year he can collect materials sufficient for lifetimes of detailed analysis. In general, the potential use of a collection is always greater than the original reasons for its collecting. Although most collectors would share their materials with other scholars and teachers, few persons know what they possess. Thus to a large extent, scholars have been forced to reduplicate the work of predecessors, often without even being aware of the reduplication. Even if a scholar is aware of other collections, because there is no standardized method of indexing such materials, there is no feasible and reliable way of learning if previously collected materials would meet his or her specific needs.

One of the primary goals of Appalachian scholars in the 1980s should be the development and use of an adequate indexing system. The development of a standardized, interdisciplinary method of indexing oral materials is essential if such materials are to be efficiently used. At present, each discipline collecting oral materials--history, folklore, and dialectology--has no systematized method of indexing; therefore, each research project indexes materials according to its own particular interests. Because of this a scholar often finds that the very information he needs to determine if a particular tape or collection is of value to his particular research project is absent from the index.

To understand this need, one must distinquish indexing from processing. The processing of oral materials might include such activites as the transcription of the tapes or the notation of musical scores. Indexing, on the other hand, provides specific information on certain technological, methodological, and contextual aspect of the materials. The information needed by a scholar of one discipline is not necessarily that needed by another. It is believed, however, that if dialectologists, oral historians, and folklorists consulted each other, a list of the basic information needed by each can be drawn up. The resultant index form might consist of two easy-to-use parts. One, which would contain more general information, would be used at the time of recording. The other, a more detailed list, would be utilized when the tapes are processed for use by the individual collectors. Both forms might be designed principally as checkforms so as to reduce the complexity of indexing; however, they should provide space for the insertion of written explanations or comments on certain predetermined aspects. The availability of such indexes, which might be compiled as the Index of Appalachian Oral Resources, would promote a greater exchange of research data among scholars and teachers.

Another major need of Appalachian studies in the 1980s is the development of a comprehensive bibliography of Appalachian oral materials. Without one there is little chance that even the best oral materials will be extensively used by teachers and scholars. Such a bibliography should be annotated so as to provide a general sense of the contents and scope of various collections. It should also tell where further information on a collection can be obtained.

Such an Index of Appalachian Oral Resources and a Bibliography of Appalachian Oral Resources should complement each other. The bibliography would serve as a means for a quick search of possible materials, while the index would provide more detailed information on the various collections, sometimes even on specific sections of a collection. After preparation, the information in bibliography and index should be collapsed and prepared for inclusion in a computerized research data bank that would be amenable to computerized bibliographical search systems.

Because of the development of Appalachian studies during the 1970s there is need of a detailed and authoritative work on the nature and range of the new multifaceted discipline. Such a work should be, of course, descriptive, but it is important that it contain a list of terms and definitions as well as an overview not only of Appalachian studies but also of the relationship of various disciplines to Appalachian studies. Without such a general guide, it is impossible for scholars who study the field from diverse perspectives to have a clear and accurate conception of the total discipline.

Even when collected materials have had a certain currency within the scholarly community, they have not reached a much wider and potentially extremely significant audience--that of the classroom teacher. The basic reason for this is that teachers are not trained in the adaption of raw research and resource materials to classroom use. That is to say, that even if teachers know that such basic materials are in a library close to them, the research will not be utilized because teachers are not trained to adapt them to their present curriculum needs. Therefore, another prime objective of Appalachian scholarship in the 1980s should be pedagogical. It should set as one of its goals the preparation of materials that will demonstrate to teachers how to adapt oral Appalachian materials to secondary and elementary classrooms situations and currently used curriculum materials. It should also develop sets of classroom materials--at least one for elementary and one for secondary use--that have been adapted from oral Appalachian collections so that teachers can actually see the potential of such materials.

There is, of course, one other aspect of Appalachian scholarship that no longer can be ignored during the 1980s. We must analyze our collections and use the data to answer questions concerning the present and past state of Appalachian culture. It is only when we address questions of significance, with our arguments supported by the raw material we have collected over these many years, that we can hope to aid the nation to see the region as it exists or to be of use as the region redefines itself in the last twenty years of this century. It is time to use the materials that we have spent much of our lives collecting to reach a more accurate understanding of the nature of the Appalachian culture.

Notes

1. See for example Maristan Chapman, "American Speech as Practiced in the Southern Highlands," *Century* 117 (March, 1929): 617-23.

2. The standard readings on Appalachia remain works such as John C. Campbell, *The Southern Highlander and His Homeland* (Russel Sage Foundation, 1921); Harry Caudill, *Night Comers to the Cumberlands* (Little Brown, 1962), Horace Kephart, *Our Southern Highlanders* (Macmillian, 1922).

3 Some insightful essays and books on the nature of Appalachian culture have appeared in recent years, such as Higgs and Manning's *Voice from the Hills* (Boone, N.C.: Appalachian Consortium Press, 1975) and recent editions of the *Appalachian Journal;* but impressionistic works such as Jack Weller's *Yesterday's People* (University of Kentucky Press, 1971) are still the rule.

VI: ABSTRACTS

MARY BRECKINRIDGE AND THE FRONTIER NURSING SERVICE: THE APPALACHIAN RURAL EXPERIENCE*

Carol Crowe-Carraco

During the early years of the twentieth century in rural Appalachia, the prenatal and postpartum treatment of mothers and babies was particularly appalling. Very often in the mountains of southeastern Kentucky, granny women, having no formal training in midwifery, "cotched" babies in their lard-greased hands; they knew nothing of prenatal, postnatal and pediatric care. In 1925 in isolated Leslie County, Kentucky, forty-four year old Mary Breckinridge, in cooperation with the area's residents, established a unique family-centered health care system, staffed by trained nurse-widwives. This organization came to be called the Frontier Nursing Service (FNS).

Using medical directives developed by an advisory body of physicians from beyond the mountains and riding on horseback, the FNS nurse-midwives provided medical services to some ten thousand people in a 375 square mile mountainous area, which had no roads or licensed doctors. Since midwifery training was unavailable in the United States, most of the FNS staff were British nurse-midwives or American nurses who had trained abroad.

By 1930 the FNS included a hospital-health center, administrative headquarters, six residential outpost nursing centers, and a referral service outside of the mountains. When WW II brought the departure of most of the British staff and the end of American overseas midwifery training, Mary Breckinridge began a graduate school of midwifery, which expanded in 1970 to include a department of family nursing, where nurse-practitioners receive training.

In its fifty plus years, the FNS has faced many problems: falls from horses, jeep wrecks, snakebites, near drownings, and the opposition of many segments of the medical profession. Yet it continues to exist, and its record is amazing. At the end of 1979, the FNS had delivered 18,535 registered maternity cases with a loss of only 11 mothers in childbirth.

Long before the principles of community involvement were enunciated, Mrs. Breckinridge recognized that in order for the FNS to be effective, the people themselves had to participate in making the decisions which affected their own welfare, and in the word of Mary Breckinridge, Appalachia's foremost nurse-midwife, "The glorious thing about it is that it works."

---

*The majority of this paper has appeared under the title "Mary Breckinridge and the Frontier Nursing Service" in *The Register of the Kentucky Historical Society* 76 (July 1978) 179-191.

THE BLUE RIDGE PARKWAY:
A UNIQUE PART OF RURAL AMERICA*

Granville B. Liles

Though the frontier is gone, there is still enough of rural America available in Appalachia to provide an opportunity to reshape public attitudes toward the land. The Blue Ridge Parkway and its adjoining lands offer Americans a starting point to better understand the land as a community to which we all belong.

Following the Blue Ridge mountains from the Shenandoah to the Great Smokies for nearly 500 miles, the Parkway must be considered an integral part of the southern Appalachians. Begun in 1935 as the first rural parkway in the world, it has served as a model in design, land-use planning, and land-use practices. Unfortunately, in recent years, changes have been occurring so rapidly that, without proper planning, the unique beauty and quality of this part of Appalachia will be lost.

We have the model and the precedent to move into a new era of cooperative land-use planning, but there is at present no cooperative force working towards this purpose. If this rural environment is to be preserved, Virginians and North Carolinians, as well as all Americans, will have to come to grips with some form of land-use control. Parkway officials have been criticized for suggesting zoning or other land-use controls as means of protecting the investment in the Parkway and the resources in that total corridor. This should not lesson recognition of the need for more aggressive action by the states, local governments, and citizens in seeking alternatives to such programs.

This paper explores some key planning concepts in cooperative land-use planning that are part of an approved Statement of Management for the Blue Ridge Parkway, identified as Management Objectives, as follows:

    Safeguarding the Scenic Corridor
    Revising the Resource Management Plan
    A Comprehensive Access Plan
    Revising the Park-wide Land Acquisition Plan
    Perpetuating the Cultural and Traditional Highlands scene

These objectives offer a challenge to the planner, politician, land owner, and the citizen to unite their efforts and develop the framework for a cooperative plan that will prevent or minimize adverse uses of this special region of America.

---

*This paper has been published as a booklet by the Appalachian Consortium Press, Boone, North Carolina, 1980.

A HERITAGE OF REGIONAL LANDSCAPES: APPALACHIAN BAPTISTRY PAINTINGS*

Jack Welch

Scattered throughout West Virginia and the Appalachian region in churches which immerse for baptism are a series of landscapes that have not previously been documented and studied, either by folklorists or art historians. These paintings are characterized by their depiction of the Appalachian landscape, usually showing a combination of mountains, water in the form of rivers, streams, or lakes, and trees. There are never any people in these paintings.

One could look at the paintings only as an artist's view of the region. Some of the paintings are primitive, such as that by Richard Liming in the Wileyville, West Virginia, Church of Christ. This painting shows a fresh stream flowing forth toward the baptistry itself, a bright yellow sky, and strong birch and oak trees surrounding the water. The colors are primary and vivid. Other paintings, such as those done by Dorothy Decker in the Emmanuel Baptist Church in Parkersburg and the Vienna Baptist Church in Vienna, West Virginia, show the subtle play of sunlight across spring mountains. In one a sycamore tree is coming into leaf, below which, in the clear water, a trout is darting. These are joyous, fresh paintings done in a very sophisticated style. Nine other paintings representing a variety of techniques are discussed in the article.

Another approach to these paintings is to consider the religious significance. In those churches which have communion only once each month, the paintings are displayed at the time of the communion, indicating a belief in the religious value of the paintings. The absence of people suggest a Reformation suspicion of images in general, but this must be investigated further. As a twentieth-century phenomenon in America, indoor baptistries created some controversy among churches which traditionally baptized only with running water. The paintings did something to assuage the anxiety about these indoor baptistries. Finally, outdoor baptisms were often aesthetically beautiful, with the congregation gathered around a deep pool in a stream singing while the candidate was immersed. The painting reproduces somewhat the aesthetic effect of that outdoor baptism. In fact, one artist indicated that he saw the painting as a kind of set before which the actual baptism would take place.

These paintings deserve much more analysis. The author is documenting other paintings now and is studying the scholarship which would help to explain their religious significance.

---

*This paper has been published in *Goldenseal* 6 (April-June 1980): 40-46.

BRINGING SISTER HOME:
THE FIGHT FOR JOB EQUITY IN APPALACHIA

Leslie Lillie

This exploration into the economic and social status of contemporary Appalachian women begins with a fictional prelude that depicts an educated Appalachian woman frustrated by how little opportunity for self-realization is available for her sister and her friends. She wonders if the change being sought for women in Appalachia today will come soon enough to make any difference in their lives.

The essay which follows this fictional statement considers the underlying reasons for this lack of advance. Primarily, the fault lies in a well-intentioned, but misguided, paternalism that has ensured that the poor of Appalachia are its women and children, that the best indices to poverty in the region are sex and marital status, and that virtually all the relative increases in poverty in Appalachia in the last ten years have been among female headed households.

The place created by women in the coal industry is not somehow a special frontier. A commitment must be made to provide women in Appalachia a full range of choices in occupations that are only nontraditional because women have been denied them. Educating women about their choices is a key factor, as well, in their struggle to achieve equal rights.

MULTICULTURALISM IN SOUTHERN APPALACHIAN SCHOOLS:
A Diagnosis and Attempted Prescription

David N. Mielke

Abstract

A general analysis of the population of southern Appalachia reveals a high degree of monoculturalism and population stability. This monoculturalism and stability is supported by the number of residents who are native born, the absence of racial diversity, and the singular religious and political orientation of the people. The pervasive nature of Appalachian monoculturalism is also supported by the fact that values, beliefs, and attitudes of southern Appalachian people are very similar throughout the region. Although the influx of outsiders and media exposure have brought a growing awareness of the multicultural world to Appalachian people, a more directed effort is necessary to promote this outlook.

Educational institutions have not done their part to foster a multicultural environment. Some prescriptive strategies are available, nevertheless, to assist the regional educational institutions in meeting multicultural needs while preserving the existing cultural traditions.

First, political pressure on behalf of education still needs to be applied in state capitols. Second, care must be taken to see that state approved textbooks are as free from ethnic bias as possible. Third, teacher education institutions must provide teachers with the multicultural experiences and survival skills not provided by earlier formal education. The teacher has the further commitment to pass on an appreciation of multiethnicity in the classroom.

American educational institutions are conservative, and the kinds of changes needed to meet the goal proposed here will be extremely difficult to obtain. Schools must respond to this need or Appalachian children will continue to occupy what has been labeled a "disadvantageous position."

APPALACHIAN YOUTHS IN THE JUVENILE JUSTICE SYSTEM:
Clues in the Search for a Distinct Culture

Phillip J. Obermiller and Dan McKee

This paper presents the main streams of Appalachian scholarship and attempts to pose the basic questions about Appalachian culture which are implicit in them. With this overview as background, the discussion turns to a report of an attempt to discover whether a grounded theory of Appalachian cultural uniqueness can be derived from empirical research.

The method chosen was a quantitative study of the juvenile court system of Hamilton County, Ohio. The county includes the city of Cincinnati and is a recognized port-of-entry for Appalachians coming to Ohio from eastern Kentucky. The response to cultural variety by the court system is observed and indications are found of a distinct cultural nuance in the court's decisions regarding white, black, and Appalchian youth. Because of this response, it is reasonable to adduce the existence of, at least, percieved culture among those affected by that institution.

The final section of the paper provides a theoretical framework based on Thorsten Sellin's concepts of conduct norms and culture conflict, which are helpful in understanding the etiology of conflicts experienced by Appalachian youth in the courts and in other institutional settings. Areas for further investigation (using Sellin's work) would be the sentencing patterns and the types of offenses for which the Appalachian juveniles were referred to court.

PROBLEMS OF URBAN APPALACHIAN YOUTH IN CINCINNATI

Larry J. Redden

This paper examines four problems for migrant Appalachian youths in Cincinnati: the schools, unemployment, drug use, and the courts. Its analysis could apply generally to youths from any ethnic or racial subgroup who are having difficulty adapting to the American mainstream.

Racial problems and school locations are the two main reasons for the high drop-out rate among Appalachian youths in Cincinnati. The incentive to complete high school may be low partly because of the lack of emphasis on formal education in the Appalachian community.

The minimal number of employment agencies in Appalachian sections of the city exacerbates the problem of finding jobs. Social service agencies suggest that Appalachian youth use the counseling provided at Cincinnati public schools, but with the high drop-out rate of Appalachians, the highest of any group in the city, many youths, never take advantage of the service.

The high number of youth involved in drugs or court cases stems from the radical disruption in lifestyle occasioned by the move to Cincinnati. Few resources for recreation exist in the new environment. Add to that the lack of success in school and in the job market, and it becomes easy to see why many youths fall into a pattern of delinquency.

STRUGGLING TO STAY TOGETHER: BLACK AND WHITE MINERS IN WEST VIRGINIA AND ALABAMA, 1880-1910

Richard Straw

Southern blacks played a major role in the development of early coal mine unionism in central Appalachia and the deep South. The study compares the contributions blacks made to the struggle to organize miners in the southern West Virginia fields with their efforts in the coal fields of the Birmingham district in Alabama during the years 1880-1910.

In both areas great tension existed between racial beliefs on the one hand and economic and class needs on the other. Most of the behavior associated with Appalachian and southern workers, especially coal miners during this period, relates to the process of class formation, since few of these workers were a part of the industrial order before coming to the coal mines. This study compares miners' participation in and reaction to the new industrial world into which they were tossed.

In both West Virginia and Alabama white working class belief and behavior cannot be squared with conventional assertions about white working class racism, since real and lasting cooperation existed between black and white coal miners during this period. The tremendous amount of evidence of blacks and whites working and striking together and continuing to do so in spite of public outrage and employer use of both white and black strikebreakers should make us rethink some of the more commonly held generalizations about working class fear and hatred of blacks as competitors in the labor market of Appalachia and the deep South.

The diversity of the labor force with its predominance of unskilled blacks might have suggested that workers would be divided in a strike and other class activity; that workers might have chosen to organize separately; that they might have chosen not to join a union at all; or that they might have accepted the companies' paternalism as benevolent. But the pre-industrial and working class experiences of southern miners during this period significantly shaped their response to industrialism--the biracial UMW was their overwhelming choice.

THE ASSIMILATION OF APPALACHIAN MIGRANTS

Frank J. Traina

Abstract

The three counties comprising the region of northern Kentucky--Campbell, Kenton, and Boone--have been a major receiving area for Appalachian migrants. This paper tries to determine to what extent Appalachian migrants in the area have acquired the economic and cultural characteristics of long-term residents, that is, become assimilated into the area population. They are compared with non-Appalachian migrants and the native born children of non-Appalachian migrants.

The data used for the present analysis come from a recent study termed The Northern Kentucky Quality of Life Survey with a total of 240 completed interviews. The general pattern uncovered is improvement in economic measures as we go from Appalachian migrants to the children of Appalchian migrants, who even though native born, are often very similar to non-Appalachian migrants.

The Appalachian migrants are the most culturally close to what have been described as Appalachian value traits. Moreover, they have the lowest education level and the highest completed marital fertility rates of the five groups. The children of Appalachian migrants have the next lowest scores indicating assimilation. But since the latter's scores are different from the long-term natives we can confidently say they are only partially assimilated. In fact, the data demonstrate that even though native born they may be no more assimilated than are non-Appalachian mirgrants.

Since the characteristics and attitudinal measures of the children on non-Appalachian migrants are frequently more mainstream than those of the long-term residents, it is suggested that some long-term residents may be third, or more, generation Appalachian. But we have no data on grandparents. It is possible that even three generations is not sufficient for assimilation to take place? This is an area for further research.

THE CULTURAL CONTEXT OF PHILOSOPHIC CRITICISM, FRANS VAN DER BOGERT*

SOME SPECIAL PROBLEMS OF TEACHING INTRODUCTORY PHILOSOPHY AND THE OCCASIONAL ESSENTIAL RELEVANCE OF APPALACHIAN STUDIES FOR TEACHING PHILOSOPHY, H. PHILLIPS HAMLIN

ACADEMIC PHILOSOPHY AND APPALACHIAN CULTURE, RICHARD A. HUMPHREY

TEACHING PHILOSOPHY IN APPALACHIA: AN EXISTENTIAL APPROACH, GARY ACQUAVIVA

The authors mentioned above presented their papers at a session of the conference entitled "Appalachian, American and Academic Philosophies." Each author shares a concern for developing pedagogical techniques in philosophy courses that take account of the questions and needs of Appalachian students. This composite abstract will attempt to distinguish each author's particular proposals for meeting this end.

Van der Bogert observes that when he first began teaching in the mountains of North Carolina, he was struck by the proverbial difference between rates of verbal exchange in northern, urban, and professional subcultures and in southern areas like the Appalachian mountains. Faced with gaps of silence in the classroom, he found himself evolving from Socratic questioner into a lecturer and, as a result, undermining his attempts to interest students in philosophical questions.

His answer to this impasse was to recognize that Appalachian people have different attitudes toward open expression of criticism than do members of the academic profession. Once aware of the problem, professors can discuss philosophic criticism with students before asking them to debate issues. If Appalachian students require a defense of criticism, then so do professional philosophers need their own defense of silence. In the interaction which occurs between teacher and students, silence serves as an integral part of the learning process, particularly as an aid in distinguishing what is essential from what is inessential.

Hamlin makes his appeal for teacher awareness of Appalachian students in terms of the goals of a liberal arts program. If the humanities are ideally supposed to develop the whole person, then an introductory philosophy course that introduces the ideas of Aristotle without relating them to the concerns of the student has defeated that purpose. Hamlin argues that the primary goal of any educator should be to know the interests of the students and to relate the course content to these interests. This goal is particularly worthy of pursuit in introductory philosophy courses where so many students have only this single exposure to the discipline. Otherwise, opportunities for gaining helpful philosophic perspectives may pass by irretrievably.

Hamlin concludes by arguing that the tendency in academic philosophy has been to look for truth in universal terms, beyond any particular or regional outlook. Perhaps this attitude could be called into question. At any rate, teaching introductory philosophy students, and in this case Appalachian students, means knowing something about them and their region.

Humphrey, in affirming this need, directly assesses the concerns of Appalachians as they relate to land, family, and religion. He states that philosophers need to have a better appreciation for the confusion Appalachians experience by living in a subculture that is in tension with mainstream America. He points to the Appalachians' identification with the land, the support of nuclear and extended families, and the heritage of the rural church as stabilizing forces in a period of rapid change.

Philosophy teachers in Appalachia can promote a search for truth in a number of ways: ethics teachers should consider questions of timber rights, zoning ordinances, and subcultural values vis-a-vis mainstream American values in their classes; philosophy of art teachers need to look beyond barn styles to consider poetry, fiction, crafts, music, and other arts of the region; philosophers need to analyze the traditional religious beliefs and practices of the region.

Acquaviva, like Hamlin, emphasizes the central place of philosophy within the liberal arts tradition. He suggests that the introductory philosophy course can address the questions of students as perhaps no other humanities course can, and that the existential philosophers provide the best material for addressing those questions.

In order to approach teaching in an existential manner, the student/teacher relationship must come into questions. The goal of the existential approach is genuine dialogue, and the use of technical dialogue or monologue disguised as dialogue on the part of the teacher interferes with his aim. The philosophy teacher should make the effort to project his interest in the points-of-view of his students' especially in the first call meeting.

Ultimately then, all four papers affirm the Socratic Quest: "Know Thyself," as it applies to the Appalachian student. To encourage that search, philosophy courses must begin with the questions at hand. A failure to do so means not just a poor reputation for philosophy departments and a decline in liberal arts enrollment, but the loss of an opportunity for Appalchian students to develop philosophic perspectives that would be useful in assimilating new experiences.

---

*Van der Bogert's article will be appearing in a forthcoming issue of *Metaphilosophy*.

FILM REVIEWS:
"THEY SHALL TAKE UP SERPENTS,"
"GANDY DANCERS," AND
"BUNA AND BERTHA"

At the conference session entitled "The Spirit of Appalachia in Faith, Toil, and Song," Thomas G. Burton and John Schrader presented three films they had made on unique aspects of traditional Appalachian life. The funding for these films was provided by the Appalachian Consortium, the Tennessee Arts Commission, and East Tennessee State University.

"They Shall Take Up Serpents" focuses on the practice of handling serpents as part of the religious service of the Holiness Church of God in Jesus Name in Carson, Tennessee. As demonstration of of their belief in the literal meaning of Mark 16: 17-18, members of the congregation filmed in the course of the service speak with "new tongues," "take up serpents," "drink...[a] deadly thing [carbon tetrachloride]," and "lay hands on the sick." Rather than exploiting the sensational possibilities of the subject, the film zeroes in on the participants' view of the event. Serpent handling and the drinking of poison serve not as the purpose or objects of faith for this congregation, but as one of several manifestations of the Holy Spirit.

"Gandy Dancers" is an energetic piece that depicts life on the railroad as it once was: track aligning songs, "knocking slack" chants, station calls, and the work of laying crossties and spiking track by hand. This way of work represents a triumph of the rhythmic, lyrical spirit of men under hard, and sometimes oppressive, conditions.

"Buna and Bertha" presents a short sketch of two mountain women in North Carolina, Buna Hicks, "going on eighty-five," and Bertha Baird, ninety-three years old. The film captures their sprightly, humorous outlook on life in an interweaving of songs, dulcimer playing, and autobiographical comment.

www.ingramcontent.com/pod-product-compliance
Lightning Source LLC
Chambersburg PA
CBHW051043160426
43193CB00010B/1052